Law and Philosophy Library

Volume 138

The Law and Philosophy Library, which has been in existence since 1985, aims to publish cutting edge works in the philosophy of law, and has a special history of publishing books that focus on legal reasoning and argumentation, including those that may involve somewhat formal methodologies. The series has published numerous important books on law and logic, law and artificial intelligence, law and language, and law and rhetoric. While continuing to stress these areas, the series has more recently expanded to include books on the intersection between law and the Continental philosophical tradition, consistent with the traditional openness of the series to books in the Continental jurisprudential tradition. The series is proud of the geographic diversity of its authors, and many have come from Latin America, Spain, Italy, the Netherlands, Germany, and Eastern Europe, as well, more obviously for an English-language series, from the United Kingdom, the United States, Australia and Canada.

More information about this series at http://www.springer.com/series/6210

Verena Klappstein • Maciej Dybowski
Editors

Theory of Legal Evidence - Evidence in Legal Theory

Springer

Editors
Verena Klappstein
University of Passau
Passau, Germany

Maciej Dybowski
Legal Theory and Philosophy
Adam Mickiewicz University
Poznań, Poland

ISSN 1572-4395 ISSN 2215-0315 (electronic)
Law and Philosophy Library
ISBN 978-3-030-83840-9 ISBN 978-3-030-83841-6 (eBook)
https://doi.org/10.1007/978-3-030-83841-6

This Springer imprint is published by the registered company Springer Nature Switzerland AG.
The registered company address is: Gewerbestrasse 11, 6330 Cham, Switzerland

Contents

Introduction to Theory of Legal Evidence - Evidence in Legal Theory

Maciej Dybowski and Verena Klappstein

1 Background of the Debate on Legal Evidence

The volume "Theory of Legal Evidence - Evidence in Legal Theory" deals with theoretical and philosophical problems of legal evidence. The concept of evidence is expected to fill a number of distinct roles in science, philosophy, but also in legal theory and law. Some of these roles are complementary, while others stand in tension or have little in common. The title of this volume suggests two types of problems.

Let us begin with the first one—that of a theory of legal evidence. Imagine a jurisprudence scholar who wants to find secure ways of navigating in the waves of evidence scholarship. Other legal theorists may overwhelm her by referring to diverse approaches to evidence and proof in legal systems of the contemporary world. Some of those differences would stem from general differences between common and civil law. E.g. parties play an active role in fact-finding in common law countries, while in civil law countries, the judge plays the main investigatory role. Describing the concept of legal evidence might therefore become something like cleaning out the Augean stables, by trying to compare the taking of evidence in the Anglo-American and continental systems, but without success. Professional lawyers are bound to deal with evidence and proof, but they are certainly not bound to theorize about it.

If our inquisitive scholar is dissuaded from comparative endeavours, he might still want to pursue an alternative project of understanding legal evidence by

M. Dybowski
Legal Theory and Philosophy Department, Adam Mickiewicz University, Poznań, Poland
e-mail: dybowski@amu.edu.pl

V. Klappstein (✉)
University of Passau, Passau, Germany
e-mail: Verena.Klappstein@uni-passau.de

V. Klappstein, M. Dybowski (eds.), *Theory of Legal Evidence - Evidence in Legal Theory*, Law and Philosophy Library 138,
https://doi.org/10.1007/978-3-030-83841-6_1

studying different theories of it. There have been countless academic attempts at a systematic analysis of the legal fact-finding. Even if they may be reduced to conceiving of legal evidence as an object of sensory evidence, as a fact, as a premise in evidentiary reasoning or as what counts as evidence in law (Ho 2008), such conceptions are susceptible to further theoretical examinations and interpretations.

A third vast area of exploration for a jurisprudence scholar who wants to get the lay of legal evidence scholarship appears to be restricted. "'Tis dangerous when the baser nature comes Between the pass and fell incensèd points Of mighty opposites."[1] *Hamlet's* warning applies here to highly specialised scholarly debates in which the concept of legal evidence is a function of adopted accounts of value or strength attached to evidence, typically admitted in trials. Such accounts may or may not be inter- or cross-disciplinary, and they may concern such fundamental issues as application of mathematical theories of probability, also by arguing against such reasoning, as e.g. in "relative plausibility" theory initiated by Allen (1986).

In brief, the problems explored within the received theories of legal evidence seem to relate the approach to such evidence to: (1) specific legal systems or types of legal systems and different fields of law; (2) different theoretical accounts of what it is for something to be legal evidence; and (3) theories concerning the ascription of value (strength, weight) to items or total body of evidence. Within each of these fields, the legal concept of evidence constantly changes, and the debate concerning the distinction between a legal concept of evidence, the ordinary concept of evidence and the concept of evidence in science is far from being settled. In short, legal theorists' interest in evidence may include such diverse objects as bloodied knives, sense data, linguistic entities or psychologically recognized beliefs. They may be accounted for in an atomistic or holistic manner, and so on.

What is more, the problem of evidence is central to both epistemology and the philosophy of science, and by extension to our academic thinking about law. This is where the second type of problems indicated in the title of this volume comes to the fore: evidence in legal theory. This is also where—often implicit—impulses from philosophers are received by legal theorists and jurisprudential analysis becomes self-centred, especially with regard to fundamental concepts and methodologies adopted in discussing the status of facts found and used in legal theory. As shown by *Haack's* commitment to bridging the gap between philosophy of science and legal theory, original and distinctive works in the theory of knowledge and philosophy of science may bear on real-life legal issues (see e.g. Haack 2014). Indeed, the point of departure for a separate range of interdisciplinary issues involving the concept of evidence and law might come from the philosophy of science or general epistemology.

Some efforts have been made recently to declutter the theoretical and philosophical debate on legal evidence. To give just a few examples in Anglo-American legal systems, next to the contribution of Haack's focus on the philosophy of science, the main ideas applied to the ordering of the field centre on various guiding principles. It

[1]The Complete Works of William Shakespeare, Vol. XIV, Boston 1881, Hamlet, Act V, p. 302.

may be moral responsibility in fact-finding and ethics in legal evidence (Ho 2008). It may also be relating the problems of evidence in law to the handling of evidence in other kinds of practical decision-making and in other disciplines, with a degree of common sense (Twining 2006). Other hybrid attempts, combining probability theory, epistemology, economic analysis and moral philosophy, involve focusing evidence law on apportioning the risk of error in conditions of uncertainty (Stein 2005). Meanwhile, European legal theory remains largely withdrawn from producing new theoretical accounts of legal evidence.

In summary, the need for theoretical investigation of evidence seems to have gathered momentum in the current state of legal scholarship devoted to problems of evidence. Not that it is scarce—on the contrary. However, when it comes to more theoretical accounts it is either at the level of layman psychology, disinterested in the use of latest trends and knowledge taken from other scholarly disciplines, or it is specialised to the degree of being detached from lawyers' perceptions. The same conclusion may apply to what the legal practitioners, especially judges, do. On the one hand, they mostly seem to rely on the 'hard science' of expert opinions, on the other, they can be satisfied with commonsensical, albeit uncritical evidence reasoning.

2 Main Ideas Guiding the Book

"Theory of Legal Evidence - Evidence in Legal Theory", being a collection of contributions from legal theorists experienced in different legal cultures, including not just Europe, but also Latin America and the United States, follows the main idea of the need for an interdisciplinary approach to the study of standards of proof and evidence-taking in law. As the opening article of *Olivier Leclerc's* suggests, the volume emphasizes the need to revive and re-assess the approach characteristic of the legal scholarship of the turn of the nineteenth and twentieth century, with its interest in social and natural sciences and openness to the transatlantic dialogue. This interdisciplinary approach, rather widespread and willingly declared in contemporary academic writing, is put to work in the present volume with regard to to two specific dimensions of integration of legal scholarship.

First, the authors of the articles differ in their theoretical profiles and methodologies, but they all share the interdisciplinary and **externally-integrating view of legal scholarship**, calling for the inclusion of social sciences and humanities in order to grasp the complex picture of *hic et nunc* law in action, and evidence functioning within it. This view, for most authors—especially those of European tradition—follows from the dissatisfaction with the **European legal scholarship's** self-imposed isolation and growing focus on the technical side of dogmatic analysis. This is true, perhaps surprisingly, of both Western and post-communist legal systems. Such an opinion about legal scholarship in Europe appears to be vague, and some exceptions to the general trend can be shown, but the intersection between social sciences and law remains, for the most part, neglected in the case of evidence scholarship. Similarly, criminology was mostly ousted from criminal law, just as logic, sociology or psychology were delegated to the periphery of legal training. Stirring the interest in an interdisciplinary study of legal evidence and external integration of legal scholarship with its scientific surroundings is, therefore, one of the most important objectives of the present book.

Second, it must be borne in mind that almost four decades ago 'the new evidence scholarship' became an official term for the common law shift in interest from rules of evidence to scientific accounts of the process of proof (see Lempert 1986). It is time to both restate the call for a change, especially in the European legal scholarship, and to rethink the strengths and weaknesses of the movement. A result of it might be the second guiding idea of the present volume, next to that of interdisciplinary integration of legal evidence scholarship: that the problem of evidence within argumentation and thinking of legislators, judges, lawyers and legal scholars requires a side by side **internal integration of legal sciences**. Most of the contributors to the present volume seem to agree that such an integration is possible and that it may be built around rethinking such fundamental legal conceptions as reasoning or facts, both of which had suffered under attacks from sceptics at the turn of the twentieth and twenty-first centuries.

3 Overview of the Book

The volume "Theory of Legal Evidence - Evidence in Legal Theory" consists of three parts. They are ordered in such a way that questions are raised starting from more general and theoretical ones (part 1), zooming in to more specific theoretical questions put in context with philosophical concepts (part 2), to end with practical questions of legal evidence as they occur during legal proceedings (part 3).

Consequently, in the opening part, two basic questions regarding legal evidence are raised: first, whether there can be a science of proof, answered from a historical point of view; second, why legal reasoning necessitates an interdisciplinary discourse, which is answered from the point of view of the theory of science.

In the second part, theory of law is put in contact with evidence issues and held against specific philosophical concepts. Here, the contributors seek to determine why lawyers are bound by evidence, what a good enough (meta) theory of evidence in law might look like, how the architecture of legal evidential justification is debated between atomistic and holistic approaches, and how coherence theories influence the idea of finding facts of a case.

At last, the third part includes articles regarding the practical questions of legal evidence during legal proceedings, concerning legal questions of expert testimonies and opinions, hearsay, the relevance of neuroscientific evidence concluding in constitutional questions of legal evidence.

Part 1: Two Big Questions Looked Upon from a Historical Point of View and the View of Contemporary Theory of Science

Olivier Leclerc's of CNRS and University of Lyon article *Can there be a science of proof? A Cross-Atlantic dialogue (1898–1947)* provides an insightful introduction to the variety of problems concerning evidence in law. *Leclerc* investigates the emergence of the science of proof at a specific historical moment, beginning at the end of the nineteenth century and lasting until the Second World War, when the project of a science of proof became a central feature of evidence scholarship, not only in the United States but also in Europe. Paying what is due to the famous contribution of John Henry Wigmore, *Leclerc* aims at giving a more complex and nuanced view of the scientific interactions between fields of knowledge interested in evidence on both sides of the Atlantic, including, among others, an Austrian criminologist Hans Gross (1847–1915) or a French evidence scholar François Gorphe (1889–1959). *Leclerc* analyses the scientific impetus that emerged at the end of the nineteenth century as regards evidence in court and focuses on the conditions of its emergence and the main reasons for its relative failure. From the late 1890s to the early 1950s, so goes the story told by *Leclerc*, the project of a science of proof was developing as an interdisciplinary field at the **junction of three closely connected domains of knowledge.** One of them was **criminology and forensic science**. Gross' or Alexandre Lacassagne's (1843–1924) books on that subject had much influence on Wigmore. The second domain was **judicial psychology** which emerged in the early twentieth century of social psychology. Its main interest was in the psychological dimensions of social interaction within a variety of domains of social life, with a specific interest in education and courts. The third element of the science of proof was the **study of logic and the theory of reasoning**. *Leclerc's* discussion of why the science of proof used to be an interdisciplinary project—in most countries—and why from the 1950s this context had largely vanished and the fields of knowledge that had once converged eventually went along separate disciplinary paths, is a great way of opening up the perspective from which to look at the problems of theorising about evidence in this volume.

Verena Klappstein's of the University of Passau article *Why does Legal Reasoning necessitate an interdisciplinary discourse and an examination from the point of the theory of science?* substantially re-opens the perspective on the **problem of evidence within argumentation and thinking of legislators, judges, lawyers and legal scholars**. *Klappstein* carefully distinguishes between different subject-matters of law and their corresponding discourses in order to guide the readers through a puzzling question: why certain reasons, e.g. economic ones, are included in the legal practice while others, e.g. philosophical ones, are critically looked upon. Those subject-matters differ, depending on whether they are connected with legislation, court proceedings or scholarship. However, as *Klappstein* convincingly argues, the difference in acceptable reasons is also due to confronting those distinct legal discourses with the background of science and/or the way science is understood. She draws a parallel between applying law and scientific procedures. Indeed, if a court decides to depart from 'canonical' reasoning, or to use legal, philosophical or economic reasons, it faces the challenge of explaining, i.e. provide special reasoning, as to why it does so. *Klappstein* argues that **the method which requires to achieve the same outcome with the same given facts is both a basic component of science**

and of the legal ideal of peace under law and justice in the form of an equal application of the law. By the way, whether jurisprudence conforms to the same ideals depends largely on the self-reference of jurisprudence as a science. The equal application of the law, *Klappstein* concludes, can only be achieved via methodological transparency and accountability which would restrain, but never fully eliminate, the inherent subjectivity of any act of recognition of both fact and law.

Part 2: Theory of Law Put in Contact with Evidence Issues and Scholarship

The second part of the volume puts the law in contact with evidence issues and different philosophical concepts. The articles raise different questions and in most cases answer them in the vein of an atomistic view, i.e. specific philosophical approaches, contending time and again in the end that as well a more holistic approach can and might prove useful.

Weronika Dzięgielewska's of Adam Mickiewicz University in Poznań article *Why Are We Bound by Evidence? On The Normative Stance of Legal Proof* seeks to determine the relationship between **two different types of normativity: epistemic and legal**. According to *Dzięgielewska*, both are needed in order to explain what it is for something to be a piece of distinctly legal evidence. She draws on a metanormative theory that accounts for any normativity in terms of discursive practice of exchanging reasons as well as on metaethics. Assuming that both the process of evidence-finding and the legal practice have a non-voluntary character, in the sense of involving relevant reasons, *Dzięgielewska* identifies two claims which challenge the interconnectivity between epistemic and legal normativity. One is associated with discerning between a robust and formal sense of normativity, the other—with separate aims of the process of forming belief and the legal practice. In the solution of those, she argues that a given domain is normative when it can be understood in terms of reasons, and even though legal reasons may not prove autonomous, the normativity of law has distinctly stronger features than mere formal ones. As to the second challenge, *Dzięgielewska* claims that different aims of the practices can be reconciled within the course of individual cases of legal proceedings. Using the metanormative account developed in metaethics by Stephen Finlay, *Dzięgielewska* distinguishes between two senses of normativity: The first, 'ontological', connected with objects having a property of some special kind, and the second, 'representative', connected with expressions or judgments about something being normative in the first, 'ontological' sense. An important contribution of *Dzięgielewska's* article is the claim that follows from the above distinction. Namely, that legal evidence is about normative ('ontological') facts and its normative character is determined in the course of the exchange of reasons during legal proceedings that also specifies its propositional content. Statements concerning evidence, on the other hand, are of normative ('representative') character and are subject to pragmatistically understood normativity within the normative practice of the exchange of reasons. With these categories applied, she is able to explain how **legal normativity can function as metanormativity for epistemic normativity**.

In his article '*A Good Enough (Meta) Theory of Evidence in Law. An Inferentialist Account*', *Maciej Dybowski of Adam Mickiewicz University in Poznań* explores meta-theoretical possibilities of a good (enough) theory of legal evidence, which needs to bridge the so far detached accounts of knowledge in general and knowledge regarding legal evidence. Theories of legal evidence and theories of law are detached. Causing factors for this detachment are allegedly the dualism of facts and norms as well as the ambiguities regarding judges' epistemological theories. The author contends nonetheless that, strictly speaking, no nonnormative realms exist, and so a normative metalanguage could be employed to specify not only what **happens** but also what is **done**. Bearing these specifications of a normative metalanguage in mind, *Dybowski* analyses the preconditions of a good-enough theory of legal evidence. Its benchmarks are to account for acquiring knowledge and to be compatible with the relevant theory of law. Comparing different concepts of knowledge and law, such as coherentism, foundationalism, internalism and reliabilism, the author suggests that one could understand these as well as benchmarks as to when it is proper to **attribute knowledge**. Robert Brandom's inferential pragmatism is used to look back at the problem of bridging the gap between the detached theories of knowledge and legal evidence. Inferential pragmatism can be understood as 'an explanatory strategy which [. . .] gives precedence to what is implicit in the practice or activity of applying concepts'. As a strategy, it enables us to recognize the practice of making material inferences, a constitutive feature for grasping the content in the first place. This is why inferential pragmatism is a plausible tool to understand human thoughts and actions, and thus a plausible tool for explaining the law as well. With the strategy of inferential pragmatism, the detached accounts of knowledge and law as seen in legal evidence can be bridged. This can be achieved by connecting the pragmatist models of human cognitive activities and the discursive legal practice. In the end, *Dybowski* puts these ideas to a litmus test with regard to the **legal syllogism**. In this vein, he understands the legal syllogism as a shortcut—holding nine implicit moves—for passage from legal reasoning to representing legal evidence. Each and every one of these nine moves consists of commitments that can serve not only as premises but as well as conclusions of inferences, which in turn can relate yet again to other commitments. Furthermore, each and every one of these nine moves is 'inferentially connected with any other one' which is why it offers means to endorse coherence.

Daniela Accatino's of the Universidad Austral de Chile (Valdivia) contribution entitled *The Architecture of Evidential Justification Between Atomism and Holism* explores the debate between atomistic and holistic approaches to legal evidential reasoning. *Accatino* evaluates the current status of this debate, assessing the **strengths and weaknesses of holistic approaches** to evidential justification. On her account, holistic approaches to judicial proof highlight the fact that disaggregated propositions' meaning as objects of proof depends on their integration into a coherent whole. According to holistic conceptions, a fact can be accepted as proven only when a case narrative is coherent with widely held knowledge or common sense. Finally, holistic approaches are important for understanding how the full set of evidentiary reasons justifies a decision about their sufficiency for considering a fact to be proven. *Accatino's* nuanced analysis leads her to argue that the architecture of evidential justification is better construed in atomistic than in holistic terms. In this, she follows the hybrid approach to legal evidential reasoning. The merit of *Accatino's* particular contribution is in **proposing a specific arrangement of atomistic and holistic elements**. She argues in favour of the following conceptions. First, an atomistic conception of the object of proof identified as the singular proposition or propositions advanced with respect to principal facts fitting the legal elements of the case. Second, an atomistic conception of the structure of evidentiary reasons for the justification of judgements concerning the items of evidence. Third, a holistic conception of the structure of legal evidentiary reasons for the justification of evaluations of the probative force of the body of evidence regarding principal facts, and the sufficiency of that evidence when compared to the applicable legal standard of proof.

Viktor Gazda's of the Charles University in Prague article *Theories of Truth in Legal Fact-Finding* claims, as a point of departure, that we naturally think about truthfulness in fact-finding and decision-making. *Gazda* then outlines two key philosophical conceptions of truth, namely correspondence and coherence theories, and two main ideological approaches to the process of finding the facts of a case as expressed in the principles of formal truth and principle of substantive (or material) truth. Further distinctions are explored within correspondence approaches, with particular attention paid to Russellian congruence and Austin's correlation with the correspondence built on a language convention. **Exploring theories of truth in the realm of judicial decision-making enables *Gazda* to formulate paradoxical observations.** Congruence correspondence theory could be used only when we observe evidence directly or when we generally think about fact-findings supposed to be objectively true, while focusing on a correlation correspondence theory forces us to admit that truth in adjudication is subjective and probabilistic. As far as coherence theory of truth is concerned, the gist of coherence rests on the judge's 'external' experience that a particular factual claim is true, typically because similar claims in similar procedural situations are usually found true. This in turn leads *Gazda* to conclude that the **legal process aiming to deliver a right and just verdict must not be confused with logical and philosophical approaches to truth**.

Part 3: Legal Evidence Put in Practice

The third part sheds light on several questions concerning legal evidence in practice, i.e. in the context of procedural law. Thus the articles in this section focus on the facts of the specific case as a fundament for the (correct) application of the legal norm according to which the specific case needs to be decided. Naturally, research regarding legal evidence is rather close to procedural law. Hence it was to be expected that most of the articles would hover around that topic. Why? Probably because lawyers approach the philosophical branch of the theory of evidence via the obvious path: The questions how the—relevant—facts enter the legal proceedings.

Adam Dyrda and *Maciej Próchnicki*, both from the *Jagiellonian University in Kraków*, focus on the important role experts have in legal proceedings in their article **'Expert's (Meta)Testimony: An Epistemological Perspective'**. Experts are appointed by the court to form an expert opinion with regard to specific facts. The authors conclude that the possibility that a judge has the power to appoint experts and do so in certain proceedings suggests the following: On the one hand, the judges perceive the experts to be—compared to themselves—epistemically superior. On the other hand, the judges perceive the experts to be their epistemic equals. Further on, they address the problem that arises when two or more experts differ substantially. Nevertheless, the judge must decide the case. Thus the authors set out to find solutions for such differing expert testimonies within the institutional structure of the judicial process. The judge is not only allowed, but must evaluate the expert testimonies by himself, may appoint a second expert or—if two experts had been heard—appoint yet another—third—expert to provide a meta-testimony. With regard to the first suggestion (experts being epistemically superior to the judges), the problem arises that a judge, who had appointed an expert, does so because the judges themselves lack certain expert knowledge. Nevertheless, they are supposed to assess the correctness of the expert testimony—in the case of two or more differing expert testimonies. However, a judge has in general no basis on which she can decide which of the expert testimonies is more plausible, let alone more rational. This problem will be tackled in the following article 'Rethinking expert opinion evidence as an argument from epistemic authority' by *Bohdan Pretkiel.* What is more: appointing another expert can be tricky. *In praxi*, experienced law firms keep lists of experts with certain "inclinations", e.g. some are more employee-friendly. But not only law firms keep such lists—so do judges. To solve this tricky problem, differing experts could conciliate with the goal to form a joint opinion. If they cannot, the authors think it to be the best solution to appoint a meta-expert who can then assess not only the disagreeing opinions' reliability, but their correctness as well. Current legal proceedings lack rules for such a method. Hence the authors suggest *de lege ferenda* to implement the institution of a meta-expert for the situation of differing expert opinions in legal proceedings.

Expert opinions are considered from a slightly different angle by *Bohdan Pretkiel of the University of Warsaw* in his article '**Rethinking expert opinion evidence as an argument from epistemic authority**'. He begins with the conundrum that judges appoint witnesses in situations they believe themselves to be epistemically inferior. The reason for this he believes to be in an overabundance of information and specialisation. The solution to the problem as accentuated in the previous article by *Adam Dyrda* and *Maciej Próchnicki* (3.1 'Expert's (Meta)Testimony: An Epistemological Perspective'), that judges need instruments to evaluate expert opinions, *Bohdan Pretkiel* suggest to be found in the base of argumentation theory. The absence of evaluative instruments is especially serious for civil law and criminal law proceedings. Whichever argumentation theory might support the judges' evaluation of expert opinions, it must consider the legal culture at hand, especially its rules and methods, traditions and underlying values. The author suggests a new tool in form of a questionnaire to gather the relevant data for the evaluation. Thus he combines *Douglas Walton's* logical argumentation, *Bayesian* probability and belief networks. In the end, a *Bayesian* theorem is applied in a calculation to assess the data gathered in the questionnaire, and the usefulness and efficiency of the suggested argumentation theory tools are reviewed. There are different degrees of usefulness and efficiency, depending not only on the quantity of the gathered data, but as well on the quantity of opportunities in which the dialectical critical testing can be performed.

The following article, '**Testimony and Hearsay**' by *Giovanni Tuzet of the Bocconi University in Milan*, tackles the problems combined by the liberal admission of hearsay in contemporary legal systems. Though in psychology not only testimony, but especially hearsay are insecure sources, testimonies are accepted as evidence in the legal context. Albeit some restrictions are made regarding everyday contexts. Testimony is in general only deemed to be of value if it derives from first-hand knowledge, thus reducing the legally valid instruments of proof (reductionist view of testimony). Hearsay can also be exceptionally admitted in legal proceedings, thus taking the beforehand reduction back (anti-reductionist view of testimony and hearsay). The different legal approaches to testimony and hearsay spelt out as reductionism and anti-reductionism are, so claims the author, satisfying in so far as they neither take social importance of testimony nor citizens' preferences for sources closer to the relevant facts into account. In this vein, a principle of maximal proximity is the most important principle to identify and assess the facts the law should in essence be applied to.

Zooming even further into expert opinions, *Marcin Romanowicz of the University of Warsaw* engages in his article '**Neuroscientific evidence in courtroom: Clash of two anthropological paradigms**' in the so-called neuroevidence. In the courtroom, forensic neuropsychologists are called upon as expert witnesses. As forensic neuropsychology, a sub-discipline of clinical neuropsychology, deals with the knowledge of the relations between the brain and behaviour, forensic neuropsychologist can be expert witnesses regarding the state of the brain, its cognitive functions and thus behaviour. In this vein, they are called upon in both civil and criminal proceedings to give their opinion on someone's 'brain-mind-behavior'. Upon that substantiated expert opinion, judges and/or members of the jury may form legal decisions. The author asserts in detail that neuropsychological and neuroscientific data is deployed increasingly in court proceedings, gradually permitting later research methods as applied in neuroscience and neuropsychology. It seems, the author purports, that neuroevidence is perceived not only by judges but as well by jurors as 'hard' evidence, since it is based upon empirical research methods and thus meeting, as he puts it, 'ideal scientific standards'. Looking back in the general history of the theory of science, that is not astonishing as natural sciences seem to yield—compared to social sciences—more robust results and more convincing methods. That holds even truer if calculations are involved. It seems to be a core belief that numbers cannot deceive. Nevertheless, judges calling upon neuropsychologists as experts witnesses are faced with the same problem as the one discussed in the first and second article of part 3 ('Expert's (Meta)Testimony: An Epistemological Perspective' and 'Rethinking expert opinion evidence as an argument from epistemic authority'). Judges or jurors must evaluate the scientifically presented evidence by the expert witness, albeit not being themselves an expert in the field. To shed some light on this problem, *Romanowicz* encourages a legal theory of neuroevidence that could resemble a refined *Daubert* standard to critically assess a given neuroevidence as submitted by the forensic neuropsychologists as experts. The author suggests an initial list of seven modulated neuroevidence Assessment Questions that should be answered to assess the given neuroevidence that to his mind is only a starting point and requires a deeper and further discourse in legal theory. In doing so, legal science may equip the practical legal discourse with tools that could help to sort the clash between neuroscientific and legal paradigms.

In the fifth article of the section, '**An Epistemic Defense of Exclusionary Rules in the Criminal Justice System**', *John R. Harris of Texas Christian University* looks into evidence in criminal cases, emphasizing the importance and—contested—relevance of exclusionary rules. These rules, based on constitutional law, prevent evidence that is collected or analyzed violating the defendant's constitutional rights from being introduced or at least used in a court of law. The author defends the value of exclusionary rules. What is more, he argues that they can be justified not merely with regard to constitutional law, but with epistemic reasons. A thought experiment can, according to the author, lead to the conclusion that jurors are not necessarily worse off, epistemically speaking, if evidence is withheld from them. Though some authors argue that exclusionary rules and their implied moral considerations outweigh the epistemic problems, *Harris* advises meeting the epistemic challenges exclusionary rules pose. The concern is that exclusionary rules make an incorrect decision more likely rather than less. Thus the pool of facts that can be validly included in the legal proceeding is—by law—artificially limited. In this vein, exclusionary rules are reasoned to be truth—thwarting as it seems plausible that more evidence might be better and that exclusionary rules to some extent rely on unproven psychological hypotheses. The author expounds on some of the exclusionary rules that serve an important epistemic function, such as excluding recanted confessions, as confessions are in some cases less reliable and thus more likely to be treated dispositive. However, this only works out if the remaining evidence sheds sufficient light on the case. On epistemic grounds, exclusionary rules seem to adhere to the principle of best practices of science that unreliably gathered evidence should either be ignored or excluded. Thus the author emphasizes that in applying exclusionary rules epistemic processes do not have to be subverted but rather ensure that judges and jurors 'arrive at the truth'. Bearing that in mind, exclusionary rules do not necessarily interfere with the truth-seeking role of the legal system.

The last article in this part focuses on '**Constitutional Evidence**'. *Margarida Lacombe Camargo of the Federal University of Rio de Janeiro* aims to provide courts, especially constitutional courts, with reliable standards to deploy the relevant factual evidence. About a decade ago, *David L. Faigman* stressed the important connection of interpreting the constitution based upon facts. According to him, the decision of whether a certain rule is constitutional or unconstitutional must adhere to evolutionary facts and consequences. *Camargo* reckons that with the evolution of humanity's knowledge on facts and the evolution of facts themselves, not only humanity will change but as well the general understanding of constitutional texts. As constitutional courts hold the power to render laws unconstitutional, hence due to their counter-majoritarian power, the constitutional judges' acceptance of evidence may amount to standards legitimizing this very task.

4 Conclusion

The articles in this volume indicate that there is more than one correct answer available regarding each and every problem discussed in the context of fact-finding, evidence and the assessment of legal proof. In this vein, the articles shed light, each for itself but also jointly, on the complex issue of legal evidence. Overall, a holistic approach to the theory of legal evidence and evidence in legal theory is chosen, though one can glimpse in every article that holism can and must be questioned. Holism's solidity as a normative guide for judicial deliberation and decision-making about proof can thus be doubted. Along these lines, some articles focus on an atomistic analysis to identify diverse arguments and counterarguments. If they do, in the end it is argued to combine both—atomistic and holistic—approaches regarding the questions asked. There are many more questions that need to be asked and answered regarding the theory of legal evidence and evidence in legal theory. As can be seen in the articles of this volume, they should be preferably approached from an interdisciplinary perspective not only by legal scholars, but also by legal philosophers and legal theorists committed to bridging the gap separating them from philosophers, especially the cognitivists. A small void could be closed with the articles of this volume. A bigger one needs to be re-assessed as the topic of fact-finding and evidence-taking in law, although important, is rather neglected.

References

Allen R (1986) A reconceptualization of civil trials. Boston Univ Law Rev 66:401–437

Haack S (2014) Evidence matters: science, proof and truth in the law. Cambridge University Press, Cambridge

Ho HL (2008) A philosophy of evidence law: justice in the search for truth. Oxford University Press, Oxford

Lempert RO (1986) The new. Evidence scholarship: analysing the process of proof. Boston Univ Law Rev 66:439–477

Stein A (2005) Foundations of evidence law. Oxford University Press

Twining WL (2006) Rethinking evidence: exploratory essays, 2nd edn. Cambridge University Press, Cambridge

Part I
Two Big Questions Looked Upon from a Historical Point of View and the View of Contemporary Theory of Science

Can There Be a Science of Proof? A Cross-Atlantic Dialogue (1898–1947)

Olivier Leclerc

Abstract Between the late nineteenth century and the 1950s, the project of establishing a science of proof was shared by a generation of criminologists, psychologists and lawyers specializing in evidence law. Their ambition was to develop theoretical and practical knowledge of the analysis and evaluation of evidence in the courts, drawing on new knowledge established in the then-emerging fields of social psychology and forensic science and technology. All this was combined with an effort to provide judges with tools capable of guiding the rigour of their reasoning with evidence. This project, which is fundamentally interdisciplinary and breaks with a dogmatic orientation in legal analysis, was made possible by an important dialogue on both side of the Atlantic. The circulation of knowledge engaged in the science of evidence was remarkable, both in Europe and between Europe and the United States, as illustrated by the figures of Wigmore and Gorphe. The conditions that allowed the development of a science of proof project to flourish disappeared after the War and this project would not be taken on by a new generation. Research in these areas continued separately in an increasingly fragmented disciplinary landscape. This article retraces this history and sheds light on the reasons for the weakening, and the recomposition, of the science of proof at the end of the Second World War.

1 Introduction

The collective memory of evidence scholars has associated the project of forging a "science of proof" in legal scholarship with the name of John Henry Wigmore (1863–1943). In his famous 1913 paper published in the *Illinois Law Review* (Wigmore 1913a)—which shortly after appeared as a chapter of his book titled *The Principles of Judicial Proof as Given by Logic, Psychology, and General*

O. Leclerc (✉)
CNRS, CTAD, University Paris Nanterre, Nanterre, France
e-mail: olivier.leclerc@cnrs.fr

V. Klappstein, M. Dybowski (eds.), *Theory of Legal Evidence - Evidence in Legal Theory*, Law and Philosophy Library 138,
https://doi.org/10.1007/978-3-030-83841-6_2

Experience and Illustrated in Judicial Trials (Wigmore 1913b)—Wigmore strongly advocated for the necessity of a science of proof: "for one thing, there is, and there must be, a probative science – the principles of proof – independent of the artificial rules of procedure. This science, to be sure, may as yet be imperfectly formulated or even incapable of formulation. But all the more need is there to begin in earnest to investigate and develop it" (Wigmore 1913a, p. 77). Wigmore did not deny the necessity of a rational description of the rules of evidence, quite the contrary. Indeed, Wigmore distinguished himself in this activity: in 1899 he was in charge of updating the first volume of the 16th edition of the then famous treatise on evidence by Simon Greenleaf (1899) and in 1904–1905 he published his own five-volume treatise (Wigmore 1905), highly praised as "perhaps the greatest modern treatise" (James 1940). Nevertheless, important as they are, the rules of procedure cannot be the sole matter that evidence scholarship investigates. Procedural rules have, indeed, changed over time and place, and above all, they are "merely a preliminary aid to the main activity, viz. the persuasion of the tribunal's mind to a correct conclusion by safe materials" (Wigmore 1913a, p. 78). Therefore, close attention must be paid to "the ratiocinative process of contentious persuasion, – mind to mind, counsel to juror, each partisan seeking to move the mind of the tribunal" (Wigmore 1913a, p. 77). This project absorbed much of Wigmore's time and energy. Between the first edition of the *Principles of Judicial Proof* in 1913 and the third edition in 1937, Wigmore refined and updated his views on the science of proof, as is illustrated in the 1937 edition now unequivocally titled *The Science of Judicial Proof as given by Logic, Psychology, and General Experience* (Wigmore 1937). Wigmore here investigated the many facets that come into play in the reasoning of judges with regard to facts. With a firm sense of eclecticism,[1] Wigmore presented and discussed many theories and experimental results in the fields of criminology, psychology, logic, etc. In so doing, Wigmore broke with the stance of his mentor (and dedicatee of his 1904 *Treatise*) at Harvard, James Bradley Thayer; Thayer did acknowledge the inputs of these disciplines but kept them well outside the scope of evidence scholarship (Thayer 1898, p. 269). Instead, Wigmore explicitly followed the path opened up by Jeremy Bentham (Wigmore 1913a, p. 78; Twining 1985), who had demonstrated a continuous interest in psychology, although with little experimental grounding. A science of proof is needed, Wigmore argued, as the process of reaching a conviction would otherwise be left unguided and prone to mistakes of reasoning. A better understanding of how to achieve a conviction, "the ultimate purpose in every judicial investigation" (Wigmore 1913a, p. 78), is desperately needed in cases where a free proof system prevails. In this situation, i.e. not only in common law systems but in continental systems as well (though more recently) the law offers no directive whatsoever to judges on how to safely reach a conclusion on facts. Therefore, the mental processes involved in fact-finding must be closely scrutinised and informed by science. In spite of the outstanding recognition Wigmore received as a major

[1]Many aspects of Wigmore's career confirm his interest in a diversity of fields, inside and outside the law, and the variety of his readings. See Twining (1985), Riles (2001), Simonin (2007).

evidence scholar in his time and despite the many institutional leverages he had at Northwestern University, where he served as dean for more than 20 years (1901–1929), and in the many professional committees on which he sat (Maguire 1963; Roalfe 1977; Porwancher 2016), his attempt to forge a science of proof has received little attention in the American law faculties and the *Principles of Judicial Proof*, though re-edited three times, has been famously depicted by Twining as no more than a "lead balloon" (Twining 1985, p. 164).

But if Wigmore retrospectively attracted most of the attention, it does not mean that he was the only one involved in the promotion and development of a science a proof. Wigmore was hardly even a forerunner in that respect. The purpose of this chapter is certainly not to reduce nor underestimate the contribution of Wigmore to the science of proof. Rather, it aims at giving a more complex and nuanced view of a historical moment, beginning at the end of the nineteenth century and lasting until the Second World War, when the project of a science of proof became a central feature of evidence scholarship, not only in the United States but also, and prominently, in Europe. In the last decade of the nineteenth century, a group of scholars began to take an interest in grounding the analysis of evidence in the courts on recent developments in the social sciences and experimental psychology. Judges—they argued—should have a thorough knowledge of the latest scientific developments in domains such as psychology, toxicology, and criminology, and base their analysis of evidence on knowledge of the latter.

During this period there were intense exchanges between European scholars—in France, Germany, Belgium, Switzerland, and Italy, the main areas where this research flourished—and between European scholars and a few academics, including Wigmore, on the other side of the Atlantic. Far from centring on only one discipline or speciality, the books and papers published at that time often referred to results and ideas taken from a wide array of scientific domains. In his *Principles of Judicial Proof*, Wigmore relied heavily on the works of European criminologists: he acknowledged Hans Gross (1847–1915), an Austrian criminologist who played an instrumental role in the foundation of criminology as a scientific domain, as a major source of inspiration for his own work. Wigmore even dedicated *The Principles of Judicial Proof* to the memory of Gross, "who did more than any other man in modern times to encourage the application of science to judicial proof".

François Gorphe (1889–1959) is another example of a vibrant voice in the scientific interactions between fields of knowledge interested in evidence on both sides of the Atlantic. After completing a doctoral dissertation at the University of Paris on the analysis of testimony (1924), Gorphe pursued a career as an investigating judge in first degree tribunals and then as a sitting judge in civil tribunals and finally as the president of a civil chamber at the Court of Appeals of Poitiers. Alongside his activity as a judge, Gorphe regularly published papers and books on the analysis of evidence. His publications reveal a remarkable familiarity with psychology and criminology. The references he analysed in his books were not only very numerous but also extraordinarily diverse as regards their origin and language (English, German, Italian, French) (See Gorphe 1924, pp. 400 sqq.). In his 1947 *L'appréciation des preuves en justice* he underlined Wigmore's major contribution to the construction of "an evidence-based technique on a positive basis, outside the formal rules", and clearly held Wigmore's *Science of Judicial Proof* as a model (Gorphe 1947, p. 22). The interaction among scholars was also facilitated by an active policy of book translation. The influential, and forerunner, treatise on evidence in criminal procedure published by Carl Mittermaier in 1834 was soon translated into French (1848), Spanish (1857), and Italian (1858). Wigmore played a significant role in promoting the translation into English of authors interested in a scientific approach to evidence. When he chaired the Modern Criminal Science Series, Wigmore managed to have Gross' main book, first published in German in 1898, translated into English as *Criminal Psychology* (Gross 1911). The decision to translate Gross' book had been taken in 1909 at the congress of the American Institute of Criminal Law and Criminology, under the presidency of Wigmore. The same series would also welcome translations of distinguished promotors of nascent criminology in Italy, France, Spain, The Netherlands, and Germany, such as Cesare Lombroso, Enrico Ferri, Raffaele Garofalo, Gabriel Tarde, Constancio Bernaldo de Quirós, Willem Adriaan Bonger, and Gustav Aschaffenburg. The circulation of ideas among European and American scholars is also noticeable in book reviews published in academic and professional journals. For instance, Gorphe's books were reviewed outside France, not only in Europe (Kleinfeller 1930; Mannheim 1955) but also and extensively in the United States (Chafee 1929; Radin 1929; Slesinger 1927; Rottschaefer 1929; Nemethy 1957).

The science of proof can be conceived of as a call to science with regards to facts, just as legal scholarship had turned to science to build systems of norms and had been striving to find in mathematics, physics and biology the models of an authentic science of law (Kargon 1986; Murphy 1997; Champeil-Desplats 2016). Indeed, Gross relied on the methods of the natural sciences not only for establishing the principles of the legal discipline and for studying "the language of dead laws", but also in the everyday activity of fact-finders: "if we are to make progress, the daily routine also must be scientifically administered. Every sentence, every investigation, every official act must satisfy the same demand as that made of the entire juristic science" (Gross 1911, p. 9).

The project of a science of proof is, as such, not specific to legal scholars interested in evidence. At the end of the nineteenth century, many social sciences shared the view that they must have a rigorous scientific basis and most often sought in the natural sciences the approaches and strategies for this project. Durkheim's *Les règles de la méthode sociologique* notoriously illustrates the attempt of the social sciences to build a solid methodological grounding (Heilbron 1995): "If this has been the case in the natural sciences, then even more so in sociology" (Durkheim 1895, p. 24). In the field of history, the French historian Charles Seignobos (1854–1942) published in 1909 *La méthode historique appliquée aux sciences sociales*. In this book, which immediately received wide attention, Seignobos argued that historians must carefully consider the many testimonies they find in archives and he designed an analytic method aimed at helping them to determine, the best they could, the trustworthiness of testimony. Both Gorphe (1924) and the Swiss psychologist and physician Jean Larguier des Bancels advocated for a scientific approach to the reliability of court testimony and explicitly referred to Seignobos as a source of inspiration. As Larguier des Bancels put it: "By studying them closely, it would be easy to convince oneself that many points of view, new to psychologists, are familiar to historians and that they have long had a solid knowledge of the processes involved in the testimony and the factors that determine it" (Larguier des Bancels 1905).

Scholars and judges interested in founding a science of proof relied heavily on empirical studies and experiments to gain knowledge of witness psychology and the logic of evidential reasoning. The German psychologist William Stern gained wide recognition by conducting a range of experiments on the psychology of witnesses. In a then famous experiment, Stern arranged a scene during his class (someone came in, talked to the teacher, picked up a book and left) and submitted his students to experiments on their perception and memories of the episode. When later interrogated on the events and on specific details, they displayed a significantly higher rate of error (25–30%) than when prompted to spontaneously recount what had happened (5–10%), thus pointing to the risk that the experimenter might, in fact, be suggesting the answers given by the witness. Other experiments also demonstrated that the rate of error was significantly higher when interrogating young children, up to 50% with 7-year-olds (Stern 1910, p. 272). Hence, Stern warned against blind trust in witnesses and suggested that examining officers should avoid suggestive questions and leave more space to spontaneous narration. Stern's experiments struck the minds of the legal scholars promoting a science of proof. Wigmore relied heavily on Stern's results when discussing the reliability of the perception of testimony in youths (Wigmore 1937, p. 328). Gorphe also mentioned Stern's experiments as an essential milestone in the construction of a scientific approach to the psychology of testimony (Gorphe 1924, p. 35; Gorphe 1947, p. 19). But the interest of legal scholars in experimental psychology was not limited to the results of professional psychologists. Some of them designed their own experimental protocols, using their professional practice as a field of investigation. Gross urged investigating judges to conduct their own experiments based on the first-hand material available to them when conducting their investigation:

> Take any occurrence in which you yourself have taken part along with others, and make these others describe it, one by one and separately; you will be stupefied to find how differently the occurrence will be reported by each, without the slightest hesitation or uncertainty on the part of any of them. To profit by such an experiment, you must at the time of observing the occurrence intend to make the experiment subsequently; and consequently must have yourself followed the course of events with scrupulous accuracy; as to be able later on to decide which of the witnesses are the better observers (Gross 1906, p. 57).

Indeed, Gorphe gave a detailed account of the experiments he conducted on the ability of witnesses to memorize pictures when he worked as an investigating judge in the French city of Libourne. Gorphe noted an accuracy in recollections of the details of an image and tried to draw conclusions from it as regards the existence of categories of mistakes and the propensity of witness error according to mental capacity: "We see that testimonial errors, despite their variety, are reduced to a few categories. It is important to look for which witnesses are particularly subject to it, which objects specifically give rise to it and, under what conditions they tend to occur" (Gorphe 1924, p. 81).

In addition to the conclusions arrived at by judges and legal scholars based on experimental protocol they designed in a scientific-like manner, they also thought their personal experience could provide many situations from which to draw conclusions on human nature. Observations taken from family life and personal anecdotes were also widely used in a much less controlled way in the hopes of providing useful conclusions (Gross 1911, pp. 133, 168; Gorphe 1924, p. 48).

This chapter aims to analyse the scientific impetus that emerged at the very end of the nineteenth century as regards evidence in court, focusing on the conditions of its emergence and the main reasons for its relative failure. From the late 1890s to the early 1950s, the project of a science of proof as an interdisciplinary field at the junction of three closely connected domains of knowledge gave rise to intense dialogue between scholars from different backgrounds. From the 1950s this context had largely vanished and the fields of knowledge that had once converged eventually went along separate disciplinary paths, challenging the project of a science of proof as a unified domain of interdisciplinary investigation and bringing its influence on legal scholarship and the training of legal practitioners to an end.

2 Criminology and Forensic Science

The project of developing a science of proof originated within the field of criminology. An essential promoter of a rationalised analysis of evidence was Hans Gross, a former investigating judge who became a professor of law at the Universities of Chernivtsi, Prague and ultimately Graz, Austria, where he established an Institute of Criminology (Wetzell 2000, p. 61; Becker and Wetzell 2006, p. 3). Gross' *Handbuch für Untersuchungsrichter, als System der Kriminalistik* was first published in 1893 and republished several times. It has been translated into eight languages, including an English edition adapted to the specific colonial context of English India (Gross 1906). This book was mainly aimed at investigating officers ("a compendious term to include all persons engaged in the investigation, official or non-official, of criminal cases": Gross 1906, p. xxvi) and explicitly took a practical stance. Gross put criminal cases as purely scientific problems that must be solved by the judge. This requires the judge to form an opinion based on the best available scientific knowledge. It does not suffice, he argued, for judges to know the procedural rules; they must also gain familiarity with scientific and technical knowledge involved in criminal investigation. Judges cannot, he asserted, only rely on experts, otherwise they will be unable to ask relevant questions of them or be sufficiently able to evaluate the expert's opinion. Interdisciplinary training is then fundamental: "An Investigating Officer requires in the execution of his duties very much more knowledge than can be given him by the Codes, supplemented by annotations and case law" (Gross 1906, p. xxiv). Therefore, Gross provided students and judges with an updated overview of the scientific knowledge available in his time, always keeping in mind the needs of investigating judges during their investigation. Gross described in a detailed fashion the main practices that he thought are part of criminal behaviour. "Criminal Phenomenology", as he termed it, is meant to provide examining judges with a basic knowledge of the ways criminals try to hide or blur the investigation; use of false names, pretending insanity or illness, use of graphic signs, codes, and secret writings. Gross also sought to provide investigating judges with a range of practical tools based on techniques such as drawing, conservation of footprints and blood traces, and provided practical advice taken from a mix of experience and scientific results.

Gross viewed Criminal Phenomenology as one branch of "the wider science of criminology"—he has often been referred to as one of its pioneers (Grassberger 1956)—together with criminal anthropology and criminal sociology. Criminal Phenomenology has two main domains: knowledge of crimes and their investigation and subjective criminal psychology. Gross developed the latter in greater length in his 1897 *Kriminal Psychologie*, later translated into English at Wigmore's instigation (Gross 1911). Criminal Psychology relates not only to the psychopathy of criminals, already a subject of study for criminology, but "all states of mind that might possibly be involved in the determination and judgement of crime". Therefore, criminal psychology focuses on the psychological dimensions that come into play when it comes to the determination of facts, i.e. in the processes of finding and evaluating evidence. This obviously includes the psychology of criminals and its influence on the motives for the commission of crime, but this aspect is far from being the only one that must be considered. Indeed, the judges themselves, like any other man or woman with a specialized knowledge, are inclined to make mistakes because of psychological bias in their reasoning. When they interact with others—the suspect, witnesses, other judges or practising lawyers—judges need to be aware of their own psychological bias in order to have an accurate view of the situation.

One part of Gross' analysis was grounded on psychological studies. He cited psychologists from his times, especially those interested in the mental ability of examinees (whether they are children or carry mental deficiencies). Nevertheless, despite the title of the volume, Gross did not exclusively base his analyses on psychological studies and he did not claim to be contributing to the field of judicial psychology, but rather to the field of criminology.[2] His eclecticism is noticeable: the reliability of his sources varies heavily from one to another and reflect the main currents of thought. For instance, Gross ascribed to Herbert Spencer's evolutionist view that "people whose ancestors have worked with their hands possess heavy hands" and consequently advised investigating officers to always examine the hand of "those who claim to be hard workers but who really try to live without work, i.e. thieves, gamblers, etc." (Gross 1911, p. 104). He also called attention to

[2]The same holds true of G. F. Arnold's *Psychology applied to legal evidence* (1906) which built on psychology to come to conclusions and advice as regards evidence in court: "This work does not claim to be an original treatise on either Psychology or Law. The author has merely aimed at applying the conclusions of the former to legal evidence and other doctrines and constructions of legal writers" (vii).

Lavater's physiognomy and Gall's phrenology, though with some reservation (p. 84). A large part of Gross' assertions rested on common knowledge and maxims [for instance, when it comes to the examination of a female witness (Gross 1911, p. 307)] or in the personal experience of the judges ("I learned from an especially significant case..." Gross 1911, p. 195). Gross's *Criminal Psychology* finally devoted limited space to psychology and mostly provided advice taken from the experience of examining officers as regards the behaviour and character of witnesses and suspects. Judges must, Gross argued, gain wide knowledge of the human mind and nature and his book aimed at providing a sum of useful knowledge taken from a variety of sources that will help investigating officers not be fooled by suspects or witnesses and not to make mistakes. The ambition of *Criminal Psychology* was then to provide judges with everything that an experienced, thoughtful, and observant judge ought to know. Judges need to learn about human character and adapt the way they conduct investigations accordingly. As Gross put it bluntly: "Speaking generally, the significant rule is this: *Egoism, laziness and conceit are the only human motives on which one may unconditionally depend.* Love, loyalty, religion and patriotism, though firm as rock, may lapse and fall" (Gross 1911, p. 27). Judges also have to learn to identify when people lie; they need to know how people behave when they are the custodians of a secret. For, as Gross asserted, concurring with Helmholtz, "every mental event must have its corresponding physical event in some form, and is therefore capable of being sensed, or known to be indicated by some trace" (Gross 1911, p. 42). Sense-perception is therefore essential and judges must be capable of observing and identifying the signs that will give them information about whether their interlocutor is dependable, trustworthy, and intelligent. Gross urged judges to pay attention and correctly interpret body language when examining a witness (tone of voice, gesticulation, blushing, closing of the eyes, sudden closing of the mouth, position of the toes, gestures of resolution, astonishment, scorn, folded arms, raising shoulders, resignation...) as much as the attitude and dress (e.g. the way a man wears a hat—perpendicular, tipped slightly, deeply tipped—was thought to be revealing of character). Gross also devoted long passages to sense perceptions (of sight, hearing, taste, smell, touch) and underlined how easily perceptual mistakes can be made, even by dependable people, and how imprecise and misleading observational perception can be.

Gross' books have been immensely influential. Wigmore not only dedicated his *Principles of Judicial Proof* to the memory of Gross but included many references to Gross in his volume. Following Gross, Wigmore extensively developed knowledge of trace evidence, blood stains, and fingerprints. He struggled to offer an overview of the latest scientific developments, attempting to be as accurate and up-to-date as possible. All these contributions helped establish Wigmore as a "pioneer" of criminology and police investigation in the United States (Vollmer 1941; Millar 1955). Wigmore's methodology also owed a lot to Gross. Just like Gross, Wigmore did not claim to be making a contribution only to the field of psychology. Rather, he relied on the latest advances in judicial psychology to design how evidence should be analysed in court. His book was mainly meant for legal practitioners that, he argued, should base their analysis on the best available knowledge in psychology and other fields of knowledge, just as in the practice of experienced judges. In the *Principles of Judicial Proof*, Wigmore referred to the work of psychologists like Sully (1892), Binet (1899), Hall (1891), as well as scientists interested in criminal investigation like the chemist C. Ainsworth Mitchell (1911). But the greater part of his references were legal scholars or practising lawyers interested in improving the practice of investigating evidence based upon second-hand reading of psychologists. Authors like A. M. Burrill (1868), J. Ram (1870), G. F. Arnold (1906), A. C. Train (1906), or Charles C. Moore (1908) have received less attention than Wigmore, perhaps because they did not publish critically praised doctrinal pieces like Wigmore, but they contributed to the existence of a scientifically based literature available to legal scholars interested in a science of proof. Wigmore also relied heavily on case accounts from the press or from anthologies of *cause célèbres* from various jurisdictions, and even on crime literature like Arthur Cheney Train (1912) or Hargrave M. Adam (1908). Wigmore claimed that law students should expand their imaginations and their experience of life through the reading of crime novels, and he famously compiled long lists of novels worth reading by students and practicing lawyers (Wigmore 1913c; Simonin 2007).

In France, at the end of the nineteenth century, criminology and forensic science were promoted in Paris by Alphonse Bertillon (1853–1914) who developed a variety of anthropometric techniques for the purpose of forensic identification of suspects (Piazza and Marlet 2019). In Lyon, Alexandre Lacassagne (1843–1924) founded the *Archives de l'anthropologie criminelle* in 1886 and engaged in a critical dialogue with the Italian positivist criminal anthropologist Cesare Lombroso. At the outbreak of the First World War, in 1914, the journal stopped being published and forensic scientists devoted much of their efforts to the development of a scientific and technical police (Mucchielli 1995; Kaluszynski et al. 2005). In 1910, Lacassagne's student, and later assistant, Edmond Locard (1877–1966) founded a laboratory of scientific police investigation in Lyon. In his 1920 book *L'enquête criminelle et les méthodes scientifiques*, Locard argued that scientific methods affect all aspects of criminal investigation, from the analysis of trace evidence to the evaluation of testimony: "Thus, scientific methods tend to penetrate the entire criminal trial: whether in terms of responsibility, observations, evidence or the assessment of testimonies, technical considerations are required everywhere as necessary progress." (Locard 1920, p. 25). Here again, Gross' contribution to the creation of a scientific police was acknowledged and his books were mentioned on several occasions.

This interest in scientific methods for criminal investigation was also carried out by Gorphe. Having served as an investigating judge since 1919, Gorphe wrote a doctoral dissertation at the university of Paris on the evaluation of testimony, published shortly afterwards by Dalloz, one of the main legal publishers in France (1924), and reprinted in 1927. In this book, Gorphe endorses the project popularized by Wigmore and emphasises the need for a science of proof:

> Judicial practice will now have to choose between two possible attitudes towards testimonies: either to continue to assess them routinely, *intuitu personae*, without method, at the risk of gross errors, or to take advantage of the new data of the science of testimony being built

> up by the work of so many scholars (psychologists, doctors, psychiatrists, lawyers, etc.), to try to submit the testimonies to a methodical psycho-judicial criticism and to extract the maximum truth with the minimum error. Science has irremediably condemned gross testimony as a means of certain proof; it has no value in itself, since it can contain error as well as truth. Only a good criticism can, by purifying it of its bad elements, restore its probative value (Gorphe 1924, p. 387).

During his entire career as a judge, Gorphe investigated the various dimensions of a science of proof and demonstrated a remarkable familiarity with the developments of criminology in France and in Europe. Gorphe's doctoral dissertation on testimony was aimed at forging a general technique for the critique of testimony. The ability to critique testimony, he asserted, rests not only on logic; it requires a turn to psychology. Therefore, he examined the psychological aspects of being a witness, such as perception, memory, reliability, etc. He also discussed witness reliability at length in terms of morality, intelligence (in relation to age, gender, social categories...), affects, and mental illness. Likewise, he examined how conditions of perception (visual, auditive, recollection) affect testimony and its evaluation. A later book, published in 1947, enlarged the scope of his investigation beyond testimony and addressed all aspects of evidence, including written evidence, confessions, etc. (Gorphe 1947). Gorphe was very much aware of the need for legal scholarship and practising lawyers to engage in a science of proof and he therefore made sure to establish intellectual contacts with criminologists, whether in France, or in the United States, Belgium, Switzerland, and Italy. Gorphe made the same efforts with psychologists until the end of his life. Indeed, the articulation of legal scholarship on evidence with criminology and psychology was at the heart of the project of fostering a science of proof.

3 Judicial Psychology

Although Bentham and Gross had both stressed the importance of psychology in handling witness and suspect examination, none of them had a professional expertise in this field. At the end of the nineteenth century, professional psychologists started to be interested in the psychological dimensions of evidence. The emergence of this field of research is related to the emergence in the early years of the twentieth century of social psychology as a sub-field of psychology interested in social interaction within a variety of domains of social life, with a specific interest in education and courts of justice. The development of scientific research on the psychology of evidence also relates to the development of experimental psychology. Psychological knowledge would no longer be drawn from the personal experience of practitioners but instead be grounded on experiments involving large groups of subjects, adults and/or children. This new field of research showed a marked scientific interest in the psychological aspects of the investigation of facts in courts and evidence, with a focus on determining the credibility of witness declarations.

In France, the *Laboratoire de psychologie physiologique de la Sorbonne*, founded by Henry Beaunis, emerged as a central institution for the development of experimental psychology (Nicolas et al. 2011). Alfred Binet (1857–1911) became its deputy director in 1892 and director in 1895 after Beaunis' retirement. Binet is nowadays mostly remembered for his contributions to the design of mental tests (Binet 1903), but his contribution to the psychological analysis of testimony in court was no less influential. In 1900, Binet published *Suggestibility* (1900) where he studied the processes of suggestion in social interactions. In so doing, Binet enlarged the scope of his previous works, which relied heavily on hypnotism (Binet 1886) and had earned him a certain notoriety in the United States after his work had been translated into English (Binet 1899). Binet claimed that the possibility of suggestibility should be taken into account when confronting a witness during an investigation or during cross-examination. Otherwise, judges might unduly influence witnesses and significantly affect the reliability of testimonies:

> I have focused on the study of the suggestive influence of speech. It is through speech, most often, that moral suggestion is exercised; I have therefore wanted to find out what is the power of suggestion of the words we pronounce – the person who pronounces them remaining as much as possible the same. (…) While I was doing this, I have almost constantly adopted the point of view of the investigating judge; and I have sought to find where the judicial interrogation process may contain possibilities for suggestions and of errors (Binet 1900, p. 245).

The French sociologist Guillaume-Léonce Duprat was another figure in this research, though of lesser notoriety and influence. Duprat held a background in medicine and had been the director of the laboratory of experimental psychology in Aix-en-Provence (his chair at the university was later occupied by the psychologist Jean Piaget). He wrote a book on lying (1903) with a strong emphasis on its psychological aspects as well as a monograph on social psychology (1920) were he described psycho-sociology as a synthesis between the sociology based on the psychological rule of imitation promoted by Gabriel Tarde and the objectification of social facts in Durkheim's sociology. Duprat's position was very much in line with the eclectic sociology of René Worms with whom he actively collaborated at the *International Institute for Sociology* founded by the latter in 1894 (Clark 1973, p. 225; Mucchielli 1998, p. 144): "the concrete being is studied neither by psychology nor by sociology, which have as their object two abstractions or entities (the psyche, society); one can only approach reality, as much as science allows, by observing the psyche in society and collective life through the individual psyche" (Duprat 1920, p. 2).

At the end of the nineteenth century, academic journals were created in this new field of applied psychology. In France, Binet founded *L'Année psychologique* in 1894 (Nicolas et al. 2000). This journal was intended for the publication of experimental results in social psychology. Many contributions related to the psychology of evidence were published in *L'Année psychologique* and the journal continuously published book reviews and information about the legal analysis of evidence. Shortly after the publication of *La suggestibilité*, Binet published a paper in *L'Année psychologique* where he called the attention of French psychologists to judicial applications of psychology and argued for the need of a "science of testimony" (1904). Based on the results he obtained in previous experiments on children, Binet asserted:

> I realized that two main processes can be used, and that these two processes are of unequal value: the first is interrogation; the second is spontaneous narrative. The latter is excellent, while interrogation is dangerous as a double-edged sword. By questioning with an urgent accent, we probably succeed in breaking the silence, loosening the languages, drawing the witness's attention to points that they often would not have the idea of talking about. If you want abundant testimonies, ask! But if you want faithful testimony, beware of interrogation! (...) There are questions that, just by their form, are formidable suggestion machines. They dictate the answer, without giving the impression that they do. (Binet 1900, p. 129).

This paper was also the occasion for Binet to reaffirm his role as a forerunner in this matter; a claim that had been acknowledged by some (Dupré 1910) and contested by others, as Gross had already called attention to the psychology of testimony in his 1898 *Kriminal Psychologie* (Wolffram 2018, p. 79). In a footnote of his book *La suggestibilité*, Binet had incidentally mentioned that it would be useful to create a "practical science of testimony" (footnote 1, 285). This claim, he asserted, had not received an echo among his fellow colleagues: "You are never a prophet in your country, that's for sure. This part of my book on suggestibility had no echo in France. (...) It was in Germany that the grain germinated" (Binet 1904, p. 130). Indeed, although the direct influence of Binet remains in doubt, there had been a converging effort of research in Europe in the early twentieth century on the psychology of testimony. In 1902, the German psychologist William Stern published a paper on the psychology of witnesses (Stern 1902a), and an extended version as a book the very same year (Stern 1902b). Shortly afterwards, he created a journal dedicated to the study of testimony (*Beiträge zur Psychologie der Aussage*). In its short existence (1903–1906), the journal succeeded in bridging the investigations of psychologists and legal scholars on testimony (Wolffram 2018, p. 71). The Institute for Applied Psychology founded by Stern in 1906 in Berlin, together with the psychologist Otto Lipmann, hosted studies on the psychology of testimony and suggestibility (e.g. Lipmann 1908). In Switzerland, meanwhile, Edouard Claparède (1905), a psychologist and physician at the University of Geneva, and Jean Larguier des Bancels (1905), a psychologist and physiologist at the University of Lausanne, conducted experimental works on the psychology of witnesses. Jean Larguier des Bancels soon published a synthetic overview of the field in *L'Année psychologique* (1905).

The psychology of testimony and the reliability of the testimony of children was one of the main areas of focus of this research. This was illustrated by the influential experimental study conducted by the Belgian psychologist and pedagogue Julien Varendonck (1914) in which the capacity of children to recollect events was analysed in various situations as well as the reliability of their testimony [Varendonck was called to testify in court as an expert on the reliability of the testimony of children (Varendonck 1911)] and G. Stanley Hall's studies on the psychology of children in the United States (1891). Legal scholars and practitioners interested in the science of proof were remarkably familiar with the research in judicial psychology and built upon it to provide operational advice for judges and investigating officers, fulfilling William Stern's wish that "the jurist himself should be a psychological expert; for this reason it is before all else desirable that jurists should be thoroughly trained in applied psychology and its methods and results" (Stern 1910, p. 275). Wigmore's *Science of Proof* built extensively on psychological research. He mentioned a variety of works in this domain, including the above-mentioned Stern, as well as Sully, Binet, Duprat, and Hall. Wigmore also relied on the already renowned William James' *Principles of Psychology* (1890) which would have a lasting impact on social sciences at large including on psychology and pragmatist sociology. James had also been referenced by Gross, either explicitly (Gross 1911, pp. 187, 467), or implicitly, in Jamesian concepts such as stream of consciousness[3] (James 1890, p. 239). Wigmore also referred to the work of the American psychologist Guy Montrose Whipple, who designed psychological tests of human intelligence (Whipple 1910) and contributed to the introduction in the United States of the debates raging around the psychology of testimony (Whipple 1909).

When it comes to the evaluation of the credibility of a testimony, judges must, Wigmore argued, be informed of the latest developments of experimental psychology. Wigmore gave a detailed account of psychological experiments that suggested the capacity for witness recollection varied under certain conditions (such as mental capacity, experience, age, gender, character, etc.). In his *Principles of Judicial Proof*, later *The Science of Judicial Proof* (1937), Wigmore extensively developed the influence of "generic human traits" over testimonial evidence, with a special emphasis on character, the psychology of the liar, and on "mental derangement". "Perception" and "recollection" were two other domains where Wigmore relied heavily on psychological studies (among many other sources, including famous cases, personal experience and literary accounts). This led Wigmore to discuss the more recent insights of psychological research. In 1937, his *Science of Judicial Proof* included a new section on the latest developments in psychometry, a new field of psychological research that developed in the first two decades of the twentieth century with the objective of providing a quantified measure of intelligence and emotions. Tests and experiments were then designed with the aim of recording physical changes related to emotional states and mental processes. Wigmore revealed a certain hesitancy about accepting these new methods; he believed the methods can provide interesting information but must not be over-evaluated. His attitude is well illustrated by the very cautious reception he gave to blood-pressure measurement and word-association methods. The first device, known later as the lie-detector, had been refined by the physiologist and policeman John Augustus Larson and used by the Berkeley police in 1921 to solve the case of a thief (Adler 2007). This episode captured of lot of attention in the United States. Wigmore did not see how

[3] As Gross states, "the study of the human soul as psychology, has for its subject the whole stream of conscious life and for its aim the discovery of the occurrence and relation of the laws of human thought" (1911, p. 105).

blood-pressure measurement methods could possibly provide dependable evidence. Nevertheless, they could, he admitted, call attention to certain elements of the case and therefore offer new avenues for investigating police officers. They might also lead to a voluntarily confession (Wigmore 1937, p. 769). Wigmore was even more reluctant about the use of word-association methods during trial. The latter had been crafted by the German psychologist Wilhelm Maximilian Wundt (who also founded the first academic journal in psychology, *Philosophische Studien*, in 1881). In a paper published in 1904 in the *Archiv für Kriminal-Anthropologie und Kriminalistik* (a journal founded by Gross in 1898), M. Wertheimer and J. Klein supported the idea that this method could be used in courts (Gorphe 1947, p. 87). In the United States the strongest promoter of word-association methods in the analysis of evidence was the psychologist Hugo Münsterberg (1908), a strong and somewhat clumsy advocate of applied psychology in the courts (Hale Jr 1980, pp. 111 sqq.). The basic idea of these methods was to draw conclusions from the unconscious association of terms by a person under interrogation. Wigmore was nevertheless reluctant about this method, based on experiments he himself conducted and of which he provided a detailed account (Wigmore 1937, p. 781). He even engaged in a vivid controversy with Münsterberg and claimed that the former had proved far too optimistic as regards the utility of this method in assisting the judge in fact-finding (Wigmore 1909). Word association methods, he concluded, could be helpful in revealing consciousness of guilt but certainly could not, at least thus far, provide help with regards to the evaluation of testimony.

The same familiarity with psychological literature can be found in Gorphe's work. His doctoral dissertation rested extensively on the work of psychologists, notably Binet (Gorphe 1924) and he had been personally acquainted with psychologists from the very beginning of his career. These contacts, although not as developed as those he had with criminologists, lasted until the end of his life. In 1929, he attended the International Congress of Applied Psychology and published, in the journal *La Psychologie et la Vie: Revue de psychologie appliquée*,[4] a paper on the "educability of testimony" (Gorphe 1929). In 1957, he again encouraged (in the *Bulletin de psychologie*) young psychologists to consider orienting their professional career towards the practice of judicial psychology (Gorphe 1957). His last book, published in 1952 (but partly written earlier and published as articles as early as 1931), under the title *Les Décisions de justice: Etude psychologique et judiciaire* (Gorphe 1952), explicitly stated the ambition to investigate the psychological processes involved in the act of judging and to discuss the mix of intuition and reasoning involved in the judges' mental processes. Reciprocally, Gorphe's work interested psychologists, as illustrated in the reviews of his books in journals of psychology. In *L'Année psychologique*, Henri Piéron (Binet's successor at the head of the journal and of the *Laboratoire de Psychologie de la Sorbonne* after the untimely death of the latter) praised the considerable work of Gorphe on the psychology of testimony and

[4]This journal was edited from 1927 to 1939 by the Institut Pelman, which contributed in the 1920s to the elaboration of methods for the individual training of mental capacities.

underlined his accurate knowledge of the psychological literature in this domain (Piéron 1924). When he later edited a series on applied psychology, Piéron turned to Gorphe to write a substantial chapter on Psychology Applied to Courts of Justice, his last publication as he died the very same year (Gorphe 1959).

4 The Logic of Evidential Reasoning

Although the logical rigour of reasoning is certainly part of an appropriate assessment of evidence, the authors involved in the development of a science of proof dedicated substantially less attention to logic and to the theory of reasoning. A notable exception, here again, is Gross. In *Criminal Psychology*, he developed the notion of inference, coherence and even statistics in legal reasoning (Gross 1911, pp. 105 sqq.). Indeed, Gross acknowledged that the evaluation of facts requires inferences that are consistent and logically free of errors. It falls therefore to judges to evaluate how inferences have been made (by the parties, by the trier of fact) and to determine to what extent these inferences are sound and robust enough to sustain the judgement. It is all the more important when a jury, i.e. lay persons, are endowed with the task of determining the facts during a trial, as it might be feared that untrained reasoning might be mistaken if left unguided.

The formal observance of legal procedures hardly suffices, therefore, in ensuring the reliability of the fact-finding process, Gross argued. It cannot be ignored that the mental states of the person who draws an inference from a fact has a tantamount influence on the outcome of the process of reasoning on evidence. Therefore, means of proof must first be scrutinized for psychological consistency. Indeed, the reasons why a statement (say a confession) is uttered counts as much as the contents of the confession, as it can draw attention to bias in reasoning or suspicious motives which undermine the credibility of the confession. In addition to the psychology of the accused and of the witness, Gross also turned to logic. He identified the problem of causation as being central to jurists: the criminalist "must indeed study not only whether and how crimes and criminals are causally related, but also how their individual elements are bound to each other and to the criminal; and finally, what causation in the criminal, considered with regard to his individual characteristics, inevitably led to the commission of the crime" (Gross 1911, p. 117). In his *Criminal Psychology*, Gross mostly discussed the conceptions of causality in laypersons and underlined the need to rely on a much more informed view of causality taken from other fields of knowledge interested in the notion, especially philosophy (Hume, Mill, Schopenhauer), provided that they are adapted to the needs of justice.[5] Based on Hume, Gross insisted on the influence of personal experience, on what we know and infer in everyday activity. And yet, he noticed, experience offers a slippery

[5] "Though it is not the lawyer's problem to take an attitude with regard to philosophical skepticism, his work becomes essentially easier through the study of Hume's doctrines" (p. 129).

grounding for decision-making as it lacks logical foundation. As lawyers also base their evaluation of evidence on their own experience, they need to remember that it is necessarily limited and that therefore no such thing as an indubitable rule is available to them in the evaluation of evidence. Limited as their experience necessarily is and dangerous as analogy can be, criminologists must nonetheless engage, Gross argued, in establishing empirical laws on crime based on the experience drawn from criminal trials (e.g. the role of superstition in crime; the slyest person generally perpetrates some gross stupidity after committing a serious crime; gamblers show some significant resemblances, etc. [pp. 136–137]). But, if the determination of facts based on our experience might be difficult, drawing correct inferences from these premises is a matter of logical connexion and is not open to uncertainty.

Gross' originality does not stem from the claim that there exists a causal relation from the criminal to a crime, an idea widely shared among criminologists, it is to insist on the need for a causal analysis of all the elements involved in the case. The omission of one single inference, above all when the case involves a "long series of inferences", or the neglect of a supposedly self-evident inference, can mislead the investigating officers. Despite the fact that the evaluation of facts by investigating officers is often granted strong authority, they must not grow overconfident and lose sight of the weaknesses that affect their knowledge. Investigating officers must be particularly aware of the suggestibility they may exert on witnesses, and therefore they must not give too much weight to their testimony: "I am certain that every one of us has made the frightful observation that by the end of the examination the witness has simply taken the point of view of the examiner, and the worst thing about this is that the witness still thinks that he is thinking in his own way" (p. 163). But suggestibility is hardly the only bias that might affect perception and create inferential leaps, and finally mislay conviction. For instance, one fact might be unduly inferred from another because of unconscious associations (e.g. a witness asserts he or she saw a clock when in fact they heard the ticking of a clock) or of perceptive bias (e.g. a witnesses does not perceive a situation they wrongly think is impossible to have occurred—"hence the rule that a witness's assertion that a thing is impossible must never be trusted" (p. 171)); we have a tendency not to trust round numbers but rather irregular figures, while both should be examined with equivalent attention; written documents tend to be considered particularly convincing as compared to oral statements; we tend to over-value statistics of morality (for instance statistical distribution of criminals depending on age and we lose sight of the particularities of the case at hand). Gross finally offered a classification of errors affecting inferences: (1) aprioristic mistakes; (2) mistakes in observation; (3) mistakes in generalization; (4) mistakes of confusion; (5) illogical fallacies (p. 177). Original as his analyses were when published at the very end of the nineteenth century, Gross' ideas on inferences and logic did not have a solid theoretical or empirical basis and were to a large extent based on intuition. It would be one of Wigmore's contributions to bring these ideas to an operational stage and to design a practical scheme that could guide the judge's inferences.

Wigmore's *Principles of Judicial Proof* developed an analysis of inferences in evidential reasoning, an analysis that was substantially refined in the third edition of the book (Wigmore 1937, pp. 18–48). In some respects, Wigmore's views were close to Gross' intuitions: he similarly focused on situations where inferences form a chain ("catenate inferences") and he strived to offer guidance in order to avoid fallacious inferences. However, Wigmore's views appear to be much more articulated than Gross' and offer a more rigorous analysis of a variety of situations.

Building on William Stanley Jevons and Alexander M. Burrill (again, an eclectic set of references), Wigmore emphasised that according to psychology, the human mind cannot handle a large mass of mixed evidence. Faced with a large amount of evidence judges might not be able to reason correctly and, therefore, give appropriate factual grounding to their decisions. So Wigmore proposed a highly sophisticated chart method designed to guiding judges' reasoning. This method offered a symbolic representation of inferences in evidential reasoning and would thus help to detect mistakes in reasoning (Wigmore 1913b, pp. 744 sq).

The chart proposed by Wigmore represents the strength of available evidence and the soundness of the inferences which may be drawn from the evidence. The purpose of the chart is to allow judges to isolate the reasoning they have followed, and to ensure that the inferences they have made are well founded. The chart does not answer the question of whether the disputed fact has been established; rather it offers an analytical view of the reasoning engaged in by the judge. Wigmore emphasized this point:

> (...) it must be understood that the desired scheme is not expected to tell us what *ought* logically to be our belief, — either as to individual subordinate data or as to the final net fact in issue. What it *does* purport to achieve is to *show us explicitly* in a single compass how we do *reason and believe* for those individual facts and from them to the final fact. To achieve this much would be a substantial gain, in the direction of correctness of belief (Wigmore 1913b, p. 750).

Due to its complexity and considering the reluctance of legal practitioners with regard to formal reasoning, Wigmore's chart method received almost no interest among legal scholarship in the United States, nor abroad. Not even Gorphe, an acknowledged admirer of Wigmore, devoted more than a mere allusion to Wigmore's method (Gorphe 1947, p. 21); he did not refer to the details of the chart method nor did he suggest it might be of interest to judges.

5 Conclusion

In the first half of the twentieth century, there was a convergence of criminologists, psychologists and evidence scholars willing to put their knowledge at the service of the development of a rationalised analysis of evidence. Nevertheless, despite the significant progress it had made in the analysis of evidence, the interdisciplinary project of a science of proof did not succeeded in establishing itself permanently on the intellectual landscape. The applied psychologists, criminologists and legal scholars interested in a science of proof were dead or retired by the middle of the twentieth century (Stern passed away in 1938, Wigmore in 1943, Gorphe in 1957,

Piéron in 1964) and no new generation endorsed the project of their mentors. In the United States, Wigmore's *Science of Judicial Proof* received considerably less attention than his *Treatise on Evidence*, and his chart method did not eventually find its way to the universities and to the training offered to judges (Twining 1985, p. 164). In France, Gorphe was very isolated in his defence of a science of proof. Despite all his efforts to enrol psychologists and criminologists and in spite of the attention he received from a few scholars interested in criminal procedure and criminology, Gorphe's work had a limited influence on legal scholarship (Leclerc 2021). A notable exception is Henri Donnedieu de Vabres, a professor at the University of Paris who wrote the preface to Gorphe's two last published books (1947 and 1952). Donnedieu de Vabres specialized in international criminal law and was a judge at the Nuremberg Tribunal after the Second World War, a function that prompted his interest in the evaluation of testimony (Donnedieu de Vabres explicitly related his interest in Gorphe with his position at the Nuremberg Tribunal). The limited interest that Gorphe's work has received in the academic world illustrates the limited interaction that exists in France between legal doctrine, practising judges, and lawyers. While it is readily accepted that judicial practice matters to doctrinal analysis, judges have never acquired a sufficient legitimacy to have a real influence on the scientific interests of legal doctrine. As a practising judge, not even sitting at the *Cour de cassation* (he finished his career at the Court of Appeals in the city of Poitiers), Gorphe could not find a successor who would give a wider audience and posterity to his work.

The project of fostering a science of proof certainly benefited from an intellectual context where, in the last decade of the nineteenth century and until the outbreak of the Second World War, part of French legal scholarship had developed an interest and connection to the emerging social sciences (Audren and Halperin 2013). By the 1950s, the situation had changed dramatically and French legal scholarship adopted a much more isolated stance, centred on the technicalities of doctrinal analysis and paid limited attention to other disciplines within or outside the social sciences.

While the science of proof was explicitly an interdisciplinary project, in most countries, disciplinary logic ultimately took over. In most European countries, criminology developed in relative isolation from the law faculties. In France, criminology is not even part of the law curriculum and it forged its own disciplinary institutions apart from the law schools (Mucchielli 1995; Colson 2013). In the same way, the development of social psychology, and especially judicial psychology, has had virtually no impact on the law curriculum and on the vocational training of judges. Unsurprisingly, the more the culture of law faculties has centred on doctrinal analysis, the less the interest the science of proof has elicited (Gorphe 1959, p. 1586). In its vast majority, legal scholarship has devoted time to the law of evidence and has hardly paid any attention to the psychological and logical dimensions of evidential reasoning. The time for an interdisciplinary study of a science of proof based on the latest developments of a vast range of scientific fields was over. The development of a science of judicial proof had been possible in a time when the social sciences were emerging as an all-encompassing project and when the frontiers of the disciplines in social sciences were not firmly established. By the Second World War, the situation was radically different and the fluidity that once existed between law, criminology, psychology, sociology and philosophy had retreated and vanished (Mucchielli 1995; Heilbron 2003; Audren and Barbou des Places 2018).

It was not until the 1970s that the project of a science of proof finally found renewed interest, under the heading of "new evidence scholarship". But this resurgence of the science of proof has brought profound changes in its scientific orientation: although "new evidence scholarship" had the ambition of encompassing all aspects of evidence and fact-finding, including psychology and criminology (Twining 1990), it mainly contributed to the analysis of evidential reasoning. In the early 1990s, Twining and Anderson sought to popularize Wigmore's chart method among students and judges, with admittedly limited success (Anderson and Twining 1991). The main development of this research came a few years later when Wigmore's chart method was confronted with probabilistic theories of legal reasoning, first developed in the United States and mostly grounded in the field of decision theory (Schum 1994). While Wigmore's method was intended for practising lawyers and judges (Wigmore 1913b) and while Gross held that probability, though useful in modern criminal procedure, could never decide a case (Gross 1911, p. 148), the new probabilistic approach—mainly the Bayesian approach to probabilities—developed as an even more formalised field, with a high level of mathematical complexity. In spite of their sophistication, Bayesian approaches to evidence didn't succeed in making their way to the courtroom as a practical tool for routinely guiding the reasoning of judges on evidence.

In the main fields of knowledge discussed in this paper, criminology, judicial psychology and evidential reasoning, all three have experienced remarkable developments since the Second World War. But these developments have occurred increasingly in isolation, and the project of a science of proof has not found voice like it had in the first half of the twentieth century. There has not been a science of proof as a unified and interdisciplinary project but rather burgeoning investigations on specific facets of proof in largely isolated subfields. The science of proof ceased to be an all-encompassing project and no new generation has been able to cross the boundary of disciplinary realms.

References

Adam Hargrave L (1908) The story of crime. T. Werner Laurie, London

Adler K (2007) The lie detectors. The history of an American obsession. Free Press, New York

Anderson T, Twining W (1991) Analysis of evidence. How to do things with facts based on Wigmore's science of judicial proof. Northwestern University Press, Evanston

Arnold GF (1906) Psychology applied to legal evidence and other constructions of law. Thacker, Spink and Co., Calcutta

Audren F, Barbou des Places S (eds) (2018) Qu'est-ce qu'une discipline juridique? Fondation et recomposition des disciplines dans les facultés de droit. LGDJ, Paris

Audren F, Halperin J-L (2013) La culture juridique française. Entre mythes et réalités. XIXe-XXe siècles. CNRS éditions, Paris

Becker P, Wetzell RF (2006) Criminals and their scientists: the history of criminology in international perspective. Cambridge University Press, Cambridge
Binet A (1886) La psychologie du raisonnement. Recherches expérimentales par l'hypnotisme. Félix Alcan, Paris
Binet A (1899) The psychology of reasoning, based on experimental research in hypnotism. The Open Court Publ. Co., Chicago
Binet A (1900) La suggestibilité. Schleicher Frères, Paris
Binet A (1903) L'étude expérimentale de l'intelligence. Schleicher Frères, Paris
Binet A (1904) La science du témoignage. L'Année psychologique 11:128–136
Burrill AM (1868) A treatise on the nature, principles and rules of circumstantial evidence. Baker, Voorhis & Co., New York
Chafee Z (1929) Review of F. Gorphe, La critique du témoignage. Harv Law Rev 42(6):839–843
Champeil-Desplats V (2016) Méthodologies du droit et des sciences du droit. Dalloz, Paris
Claparède E (1905) La psychologie judiciaire. L'Année psychologique 12:275–302
Clark TN (1973) Prophets and Patrons: The French University and the emergence of the social sciences. Harvard University Press, Cambridge
Colson R (2013) Criminology à la française. Br J Criminol 53(4):552–567
Duprat GL (1903) Le mensonge: étude de psychologie pathologique et normale. Félix Alcan, Paris
Duprat GL (1920) La psychologie sociale. Sa nature et ses principales lois. Octave Doin, Paris
Dupré E (1910) Le témoignage: étude psychologique et médico-légale. Revue des Deux Mondes 55:343–370
Durkheim E (1895) Les règles de la méthode sociologique. Félix Alcan, Paris
Gorphe F (1924) La critique du témoignage. Dalloz, Paris
Gorphe F (1929) L'éducabilité du Témoignage. La Psychologie et la Vie: Revue de psychologie appliquée 3:53–55
Gorphe F (1947) L'appréciation des preuves en justice. Essai d'une méthode technique. Sirey, Paris
Gorphe F (1952) Les décisions de justice. Etude psychologique et judiciaire. Sirey, Paris
Gorphe F (1957) Le rôle des psychologues dans les examens en justice. Bulletin de psychologie 11 (12):149
Gorphe F (1959) La psychologie appliquée en justice. In: Piéron H et al (eds) Traité de psychologie appliquée, Livre VII: Les grands domaines d'application. Puf, Paris, pp 1395–1790
Grassberger R (1956) Pioneers in criminology. XIII Hans Gross (1847–1915). J Crim Law Criminol Police Sci 47(4):397–405
Greenleaf S (1899) A treatise on the law of evidence, 16th edn. Revised, Enlarged and Annotated by J. H. Wigmore. Little, Brown & Co., Boston
Gross H (1906) Criminal investigation. A practical handbook for magistrates, police officers, and lawyers (trans: Adam J, Adam JC). A. Krishnamachari, Madras
Gross H (1911) Criminal psychology. A manual for judges, practitioners, and students (trans: Kallen HM). Little, Brown & Co, Boston
Hale M Jr (1980) Human science and social order. Hugo Münsterberg and the origin of applied psychology. Temple University Press, Philadelphia
Hall GS (1891) Children's lies. Pedagogical Seminary 1(2):211–218
Heilbron J (1995) The rise of social theory. University of Minnesota Press, Minneapolis
Heilbron J (2003) A regime of disciplines. Towards a historical sociology of disciplinary knowledge. In: Camic C, Joas H (eds) The dialogical turn: new roles for sociology in the postdisciplinary age. Rowman & Littlefield, Lanham
James W (1890) The principles of psychology, 2 vol. Henry Holt & Co., New York
James GF (1940) The contribution of Wigmore to the law of evidence. Univ Chic Law Rev 8 (1):78–87
Kaluszynski M et al (2005) Histoire de la criminologie. Criminocorpus. https://journals.openedition.org. Accessed 15 Sept 2019
Kargon R (1986) Expert testimony in historical perspective. Law Hum Behav 10(1-2):15–27

Kleinfeller G (1930) Review of F. Gorphe, La critique du témoignage. Archiv für die civilistische Praxis 3:370–372
Larguier des Bancels J (1905) La psychologie judiciaire. L'Année psychologique 12:157–232
Leclerc O (2021) A critical method for the evaluation of evidence. François Gorphe's (1889–1959) contribution to a science of Proof à la française. Quaestio Facti. Int J Evidential Leg Reason 2:29–52
Lipmann O (1908) Die Wirkung von Suggestivfragen. Barth, Leipzig
Locard E (1920) L'enquête criminelle et les méthodes scientifiques. Flammarion, Paris
Maguire JM (1963) Wigmore – two centuries. Nw Univ Law Rev 58:456–460
Mannheim H (1955) Review of F. Gorphe, Les Décisions de justice: Etude psychologique et judiciaire. Br J Delinquency 5(2):163
Millar RW (1955) Pioneers in criminology. VI. John Henry Wigmore (1863–1943). J Crim Law Criminol Police Sci 46(1):4–10
Mitchell CA (1911) Science and the criminal. Brown, Little & Co, Boston
Mittermaier CJA (1834) Die Lehre vom Beweise im deutschen Strafprozesse nach der Fortbildung durch Gerichtsgebrauch und deutsche Gesetzbücher in Vergleichung mit den Ansichten des englischen und französischen Strafverfahrens. J W Heyer, Darmstadt
Moore C C (1908) A treatise on facts or the weight and value of evidence. Edward Thompson Company, Northport
Mucchielli L (1995) Histoire de la criminologie française. L'Harmattan, Paris
Mucchielli L (1998) La découverte du social. Naissance de la sociologie en France. La Découverte, Paris
Münsterberg H (1908) On the witness stand. Essays on psychology and crime. The McClure Company, New York
Murphy T (1997) The oldest social science? Configurations of law and modernity. Oxford University Press, Oxford
Nemethy I (1957) Review of F. Gorphe, Les Décisions de justice: Etude psychologique et judiciaire. Am J Comp Law 1:146–147
Nicolas S, Segui J, Lefrand L (2000) Les premières revues de psychologie: la place de L'Année Psychologique. L'Année psychologique 100(1):71–110
Nicolas S, Gras D, Segui J (2011) Alfred Binet et le laboratoire de Psychologie de la Sorbonne. L'Année psychologique 111(2):291–325
Piazza P, Marlet R (2019) La science à la poursuite du crime. D'Alphonse Bertillon aux experts d'aujourd'hui. Editions de La Martinière, Paris
Piéron H (1924) Recension F. Gorphe, La critique du témoignage, 1924. L'Année sociologique 1:579
Porwancher A (2016) John Henry Wigmore and the rules of evidence: the hidden origins of modern law. University of Missouri Press, Columbia
Radin M (1929) Review of F. Gorphe, La critique du témoignage. Calif Law Rev 1:95–96
Ram J (1870) A treatise on facts as subjects of inquiry by a jury, first American edition by J. Townshend. Baker, Voorhis & Co, New York
Riles A (2001) Encountering amateurism: John Henry Wigmore and the uses of American formalism. In: Riles A (ed) Rethinking the masters of comparative law. Hart, Oxford, pp 94–126
Roalfe WR (1977) John Henry Wigmore. Scholar and reformer. Northwestern University Press, Evanston
Rottschaefer H (1929) Review of F. Gorphe, Le principe de la bonne foi. Michigan Law Rev 27:601–604
Schum D (1994) The evidential foundations of probabilistic reasoning. Northwestern University Press, Evanston
Simonin A (2007) Éloge de l'éclectisme. Penser le champ 'Droit et Littérature' à partir des listes de *Legal Novels* (1900–1987). Textyles 31:12–27
Slesinger D (1927) Review of F. Gorphe, La critique du témoignage. Yale Law J 37(3):399–403

Stern W (1902a) Zur Psychologie der Aussage. Zeitschrift für die gesamte Strafrechtswissenschaft 22(2-3):362–418
Stern W (1902b) Zur Psychologie der Aussage. Experimentelle Untersuchungen über Erinnerungstreue. Guttentag, Berlin
Stern W (1910) Abstracts of lectures on the psychology of testimony and on the study of individuality. Am J Psychol 21(2):270–282
Sully J (1892) The human mind. A text-book in psychology. D. Appleton & Co, New York
Thayer JB (1898) A preliminary treatise on evidence at the common law. Little, Brown & Co, Boston
Train AC (1906) The prisoner at the bar. Charles Scribner's Sons, New York
Train AC (1912) Why do men kill? Collier's Weekly, 27 January 1912
Twining W (1985) Theories of evidence: Bentham and Wigmore. Weidenfeld & Nicolson, London
Twining W (1990) Rethinking evidence. Exploratory essays. Northwestern University Press, Evanston
Varendonck J (1911) Les témoignages d'enfants dans un procès retentissant. Archives de Psychologie 7:129–171
Varendonck J (1914) La psychologie du témoignage. Maison d'éditions & d'impression, Gand
Vollmer A (1941) John H. Wigmore and the modern police. J Crim Law Criminol 32(3):293–296
Wetzell R (2000) Inventing the criminal. A history of German criminology, 1880–1945. The University of North Carolina Press, Chapel Hill
Whipple GM (1909) The observer as reporter: a survey of the 'Psychology of Testimony'. Psychol Bull 6(5):153–170
Whipple GM (1910) Manual of mental and physical tests. A book of directions compiled with special reference to the experimental study of school children. Warwick and York, Baltimore
Wigmore JH (1905) Treatise on the system of evidence in trials at common law, including the statutes and judicial decisions of all jurisdictions of the United States. Little, Brown & Co, Boston
Wigmore JH (1909) Professor Muensterberg and the psychology of testimony. Illinois Law Rev 3:399
Wigmore JH (1913a) The problem of proof. Illinois Law Rev 8(2):77–103
Wigmore JH (1913b) The principles of judicial proof as given by logic, psychology, and general experience and illustrated in judicial trials. Little, Brown & Co, Boston
Wigmore JH (1913c) Introduction. In: Gest JM (eds) The lawyer in literature. The Boston Book Company, Boston, pp vii–x
Wigmore JH (1937) The science of judicial proof, 3rd edn. Little, Brown & Co, Boston
Wolffram H (2018) Forensic psychology in Germany: witnessing crime, 1880–1939. Palgrave Macmillan, London

Why Does Legal Reasoning Necessitate an Interdisciplinary Discourse and an Examination from the Point of Theory of Science?

Verena Klappstein

Abstract Lawyers in a wider sense, such as judges, legislators, lawyers and legal scholars, look for certain reasons regarding Legal Reasoning, however, it is not at all clear, why certain reasons are included, such as an economic analysis of the law, but others are critically looked upon, such as philosophical Reasons.

Legal Reasoning is a method of argumentation and thought as utilized by legal scholars, lawyers and judges while applying legal rules to specific interactions among persons. Legal Reasoning follows a certain path: first, the *issue*, of what is debated, secondly the *legal rule*, which governs the issue, thirdly the *facts*, which are relevant for the rule, fourthly, an *application of the rule to the facts* and fifthly, the *conclusion* of the application of the rules to the facts, which is the outcome. That said, during the process of Legal Reasoning, different methods are applied, and different reasons are given.

To understand the different stages of Legal Reasoning, first Law's subject matter will be looked upon and three different matters identified with discourses while legislating, discourses at court and the scholarly discourses on texts, oral words and non-verbal resources. The thus concretized subject matters will secondly be set in context with the requirement of jurisprudence as such to be—and/or attempt to be—a science. Thirdly the narrative of law, its history and development over time, will be

This article is based on the findings of the interdisciplinary research group "Generative Hermeneutik" and its legal section, in which Prof. Dr. Sebastian Martens (University of Passau), Prof. Dr. Olaf Muthorst (Free University of Berlin), Dr. Thomas Heiß (University of Passau) and Dr. Verena Klappstein, M.A., LL.M. participate. Theological participants are: Prof. Dr. Bernd Harbeck-Pingel and Dr. Britta Müller-Schauenburg, philosophical participants are: Prof. Dr. Mathias Gutmann and Dr. Benjamin Rathgeber. This article is the extended version of a speech "Why do lawyers, legal scholars, judges and legislators need reasons for Legal Reasoning and how can those Reasons be recognized?" given at the XXIXth World Congress of IVR—Dignity, Democracy, Diversity, in Lucerne, 7th–13th July 2019 during the Special Workshop "Theory of Legal Evidence, Evidence and Recognition in Law and Legal Theory".

V. Klappstein (✉)
Passau University, Passau, Germany
e-mail: verena.klappstein@uni-passau.de

V. Klappstein, M. Dybowski (eds.), *Theory of Legal Evidence - Evidence in Legal Theory*, Law and Philosophy Library 138,
https://doi.org/10.1007/978-3-030-83841-6_3

looked upon. In the final and fourth step the purposes of law, identified in peace under law and justice in the form of an equal application of the law, will be determined.

Throughout these four steps it will be assessed, which reasons are generally given to create and identify the subject matter, the requirement of jurisprudence to be a science, law's history as well as its purposes, and which reasons could and should be given in each of these four steps. Within different subject matters, such as in legal or scientific discourses, different reasons are commonly included or excluded than in discourses at court or during discourses while legislating. However, it is not at all broadly reflected or theoretically/scientifically asked, why different reasons are considered to be sufficient or insufficient.

This paper stands with the *Caveat*—that it will not develop a safe new method of reasons to be recognized as such, but will advocate the necessity of an interdisciplinary discourse as well as an examination from the point of theory of science. Thus subjectivity prevails. As lawyers, judges, legal scholars and theoretical scientists are human beings, they are bound as hermeneutical subjects and can not entirely free themselves of their own preferences, prejudices and preconceptions. However, they can reflect on them and be thus self aware to critically assess these.

1 Introduction

1.1 What Is Legal Reasoning?

Legal Reasoning is a method of argumentation and thought. It is utilized by legal scholars, lawyers and judges while applying legal rules to specific interactions among persons. Legal Reasoning follows roughly spoken five steps: It must address first the *matter of the facts*—the *issue*. This regards the question, what exactly is debated. Secondly the "*legal rule*" must be found, which governs the aforementioned issue. It may consist of different rules. In a manner one can think of the legal rule as being a case rule (*Fallnorm*).[1] Thirdly the *facts*, which are relevant for the extracted "legal rule", must be prepared. The preparation must take place in a way, that fourthly the "*legal rule*" can be *applied* to the found facts in at least a legal syllogism.[2] This leads fifthly to the *conclusion* of the application of the rules to the

[1]Esser (1972), pp. 56 et seq.; Fikentscher (1975–1977), vol. 4, pp. 202 et seq. and 382; similarly concerning the judicial premiss: Kuchinke (1964), p. 77; Müller and Christensen (2013), pp. 42 and 241 et seq.; Schünemann (1993), p. 313; Scheuerle (1958/1959), pp. 38 et seq., 49 et seq. and 76.

[2]Regarding the contested construct of a legal syllogism: Alexy (2003), pp. 433 et seq.; Engisch (1963), pp. 8 et seq.; Riehm (2006), pp. 4 et seq.; Rödig (1973), pp. 163 et seq.; von Schlieffen (2011a), pp. 111 et seq. See as well below regarding the ἐνθύμημα (Greek: *enthymeme*, *enthumēma*) at Sect. 2.1.2.4, p. 49 and in fn. 56.

facts, which is, in other words, the outcome answering the first, the raised question or issue.

1.2 *The Course of Investigation*

During the five stepped procedure not only different methods are applied but also different reasons are accepted. During this article it will be assessed, which reasons are generally given, and which reasons could be given. For this purpose, four topics will be looked into that somewhat correlate with the five stepped procedure: First law's subject matter must be looked into (Sect. 2.1).[3] This will regard the legal discourses—understood as a discussion and weighing of arguments on a certain issue to be solved in a legal context—that take place while legislating (Sect. 2.1.1),[4] as well as the discourses at court (Sect. 2.1.2)[5] and those on different texts in a scientific legal discourse (Sect. 2.1.3).[6] Law's matter mainly relates to the issue and the legal rule. Thus there can be some issues that are in want for answers, however, if no legal rule can be found that governs the very issue at stake, no legal rules at all might be found or the answer to the question risen in the issue is to be negated.

To understand which reasons can be included and which not, law's form must be looked into (Sect. 2.2).[7] The form it takes leads to the issue of law as a science. This is relevant for all the five steps, regarding how to actually find the *issue* at hand, find the *relevant facts* and *legal rule*, how to *prepare the rule* and *conclude*.

Thirdly law's origin or history have to be looked at (Sect. 2.3),[8] which includes the relevance of legal history (Sect. 2.3.1)[9] as well as the varied interrelationships of the real authorities (Sect. 2.3.2).[10] This shows how the five steps are approached *in praxi* and the consistency over time in doing so.

Fourthly and lastly, whatever method is applied for the five different steps, it must be suitable for the purpose the step serves and in accordance of the law's purpose in itself (Sect. 2.4).[11] Only if it can measure up to fulfill these purposes, the methods applied can be useful.

---

[3] See Sect. 2.1, pp. 40 et seq.

[4] See Sect. 2.1.1, pp. 41 et seq.

[5] See Sect. 2.1.2, pp. 44 et seq.

[6] See Sect. 2.1.3, pp. 50 et seq.

[7] See Sect. 2.2, pp. 54 et seq.

[8] See Sect. 2.3, pp. 57 et seq.

[9] See Sect. 2.3.1, pp. 57 et seq.

[10] See Sect. 2.3.2, pp. 58.

[11] See Sect. 2.4, pp. 61 et seq.

2 Four Topics: Many Reasons

Within the four topics to be tackled in this article, law's subject-matter,[12] law's form,[13] law's development over time[14] and law's purposes[15] one can see, that different reasons are deemed to be valid for the discourse. The validity does not only depend on the knowledge of the people participating in the discourse but as well on the preconception (*Vorverständnis*) they have regarding the theory of science, its different theories and of course jurisprudence. The same holds true for any article, including this one.

2.1 Law's Subject Matter: Or Law and Facts Intertwined

Law's subject matter is first of all—law. For the purpose of this article law can be understood as a set of rules to regulate human behavior with intersubjective binding force. What exactly law is, and thus which questions must be asked and answered, is not at all clear, but depends on the further legal concept one has of the law. However, no matter which concept one accepts—taking a naturalistic or positivistic approach in the widest sense as the two different concepts—insofar as law is a subject-matter one can enter a discourse and research about, it *must* verbalized, which can either take place in writing or entirely orally.

This process of verbalization has its origin in human beings, who can either decide to initially legislate the law and from there to decide cases in a different body, at court, like in the civil system, or to decide *ad hoc* the presenting cases at court, like in a case law system. Both the discourses are the basis of a certain practice of the law (*Rechtspraxis*), which is relevant to real cases taking place in real life. These verbalization acts are accompanied by a third one, a scholarly and thus theoretical one that not actually leads to a systematization of the law—while it is developed—but as well suggests other options in the present and changes for the future, as it is done by legal scholars. Another resource for legal discourses are spoken words, such as an oral contract, judicial hearing or the rendition of judgment. In which manner these are legally relevant, is again defined by legal rules, judicial decisions and other jurisprudential texts.

Hence for the process of law's verbalization three different discourses can be detected. First of all legal discourses can be found while legislating (Sect. 2.1.1). Furthermore, discourses will take place while executing the law, for which the discourses at court will be looked at *pars pro toto* (Sect. 2.1.2). This discourse is the stress test for the legal system and Legal Reasoning in itself, because only if it is

---

[12] See Sect. 2.1, pp. 40 et seq.

[13] See Sect. 2.2, pp. 54 et seq.

[14] See Sect. 2.3, pp. 57 et seq.

[15] See Sect. 2.4, pp. 61 et seq.

conducted in a manner before the court, that the parties understand and accept the judgment which falls within the purpose of the law, to ensure peace under the law, Legal Reasoning served its purpose.[16] Thirdly the scholarly discourse to accompany and further, comment on the other two discourses in a scientific way (Sect. 2.1.3).

For each of the three discourses, the questions of its material, form—regarding as well the reasons that might be introduced in the discourse and which not—the origin and purpose will be assessed.

2.1.1 Discourses While Legislating

The law is not only concerned with the trial at court, in which the law applicable to a particular case needs to be found. It holds as well procedures which—in an open manner—leads to enact norms.

2.1.1.1 The Legislative Subject-Matter

The legislative subject-matter can be traced back to the facts leading to a conflict of interest in the widest sense in the real world.

2.1.1.2 The Form and the Procedure

Law needs to have a certain form that it can be recognized as such. It needs to describe the factual situation and determine a consequence—a legal one, both in abstract terms.

2.1.1.2.1 The Legislative Procedure

The discourse while legislating includes the procedures for legislation and the adoption of statutes and regulations. They are in their procedural aspects governed by simple law. The material competence for the remission is always derivative. That is, it comes from a higher-ranking source of the hierarchy of norms.[17] Thus, for example, the adoption of simple-law rules is derived from Constitutional Law. Leading in essence to the necessity of an *Archimedean* point to find the reason for legitimation. The outcome of the legislative process leads to different texts, that are further systematized in a hierarchy of norms.[18] This serves the purpose to decide which of a possibly contradicting text might prevail.

---

[16] See below: Sect. 2.4, pp. 61 et seq.

[17] See above in fn. 46.

[18] Heckmann (1997), pp. 145 et seq. and 163; Katz and Sander (2019), 18th edition 2010, § 1 III., paras 8 et seq.; Kloepfer and Bröcker (2001), pp. 9 et seq.; Sodan (1999), pp. 864 et seq.

To typify and describe—the mere hypothetical and perceived as only a possibility—case plays a central role in the process of developing the law for the abstract cases, e.g. via expert opinions. At the same time, good legislation involves a deep dialogue with other sciences,[19] including those concerned with the respective realm of life, which can assess the actual effects of the scheme, such as economics, philosophy, politics, psychology or social sciences.

In this respect, a "marginal discourse" (*Grenzdiskurs*) with other sciences takes place.[20] "Good" legal regulation must be taken into account when preparing the relevant objects.[21] Otherwise, the controlling devices, the connections to extralegal grammars and languages, cannot succeed. While this bid is self-evident, its methodological tools are largely lacking for its proper implementation, particularly for enabling expertise and thus interdisciplinary understanding.[22] A further tool is, however, also the instrument for dealing with the legal process, which is in the true sense of the word—and in the fashionable nowadays diction: a political process regarding their evaluation and purposes.[23]

It is not so much a matter of *whether* there are substantive guidelines for this political process—apart from the consideration of higher-ranking law, such as fundamental or human rights—regarding its contents, for example, represented by natural law. Rationality should rather be sought by elaborating the vocabulary used, employing the legislative process, the recourse to extrajudicial valuations[24] could be systematically disclosed. This could allow the philosophical background and implications of the political discourse to be included—and not excluded[25]—in the legislative and scientific discourse.[26]

2.1.1.2.2 The Standards of Administrative Legislation

The administration legislates as well or sets certain standard rules. While adopting administrative acts, the legislator's purposes to regulate are put into action. The authorities are bound both in procedural terms as well as in terms of content to legal rules—or by case law, but sometimes also indirectly via guidelines of other authorities or self-imposed ones.

---

[19] See: Baldwin et al. (2010), pp. 620 et seq.; Baldwin et al. (2012), pp. 1 et seq. and 26 et seq.

[20] Baldwin et al. (2010), pp. 620 et seq.; Baldwin et al. (2012), pp. 1 et seq.

[21] See, for example, the relevant questions as asked by Baldwin et al. (2012), p. 27: "Is the action or regime supported by legislative authority? Is there an appropriate scheme of accountability? Are procedures fair, accessible, and open? Is the regulator acting with sufficient expertise? Is the action or regime efficient?".

[22] Baldwin et al. (2012), pp. 29 et seq.

[23] Baldwin et al. (2012), p. 30.

[24] Carrier (2017), pp. 161 et seq.

[25] Kelsen (1960), pp. 73 et seq.

[26] See below: Sect. 2.1.3, pp. 50 et seq.

Again in pragmatic and legal-theoretical terms, one has to ask what exactly the subject matter is for this procedure. The administrative activity is similar to the judicial procedure, in so far as the administrative authority determines the legal framework, substantiates it (*konkretisieren*), which is yet again a regular process of subsumption. Thus it is also based on legal rules—albeit on a different basis than court procedures. Officers need to decide on the application of the law. And here again, the questions regarding the subject-matter—as addressed before courts[27]—arises with the necessary modifications once more. Thereafter typically for administrative acts an additional decision-making level is put in place. It is based on the current understanding of jurisprudence but does not occur in the judicial decision-making process on the same level. As discretionary decision it fills the margins of regulations in which the authority cannot just find the correct answer, but has to *find* the solution which seems appropriate and purposive (*zweckmäßig*).[28] However, the question is, how and with which method that very purpose is to be found as well as the solution.[29]

A particular problem, which arises in this context, is also present in the legislative process, as well as in a pure theoretical form: What exactly is the "*object*" in the previous processes to determine the regulation? Already the merely pragmatic questions, which materials, which normative and actual reference points in such processes are and should be taken into account, are hard to answer.[30]

For the administrative procedure, there are—in the field of discretionary theory[31]—elaborate statutory provisions, which restrict the legal reasoning. Looking back at the legislative process a comparable system is largely lacking. Even the large field of legisprudence[32] cannot give fully satisfying answers. Thus the urgent task to develop a canon of rational "rules" and guidelines does still exist.

It is particularly striking that this task has in its core the same problem, jurisprudence has regarding its methods *in toto*: The determination of the conditions, which reasons and arguments may be added to the legal discourse, but which can only be answered in a dialogue with other disciplines. A margin discourse concerning both other fields of science as well as the theory of science needs to be employed.

2.1.1.3 The Overall Origin: The People and the Craftmanship

In a parliamentary and thus indirect democracy the overall origin of the legislature, and thus as well the legislation, can be traced back to the people, which passed on the

[27] See above: Sect. 2.1.2, pp. 44 et seq.

[28] Neupert (2011), pp. 14 et seq.

[29] See: Kaffenberger (2017), pp. 53 et seq.; Neupert (2011), pp. 4 et seq.; Wendel (2019), pp. 3 et seq.

[30] See above: Sect. 2.1.1, pp. 41 et seq.

[31] See those mentioned in fn. 29.

[32] See those mentioned in fn. 19 and 85.

competence to the parliament, which itself might utilize different panels and experts to prepare the legislation. To give law a certain structure and form, e.g. legal criteria and legal consequences, a certain craftmanship is necessary, which again is aided by juris- or legisprudence.

2.1.1.4 The Solution to the Conflict of Interests as Purpose

The subject-matter and overall origin of the legislation leads as well to its overall purpose: to find a binding solution to the concrete conflict of interests in a binding way. Hence the purpose of the discourse while legislating must be to find such a solution.

2.1.2 Discourses at Court

Necessary for any legal system and the stress test for it is the legal discourse at court as it takes place in the existing lawsuits. Without these judges and courts could not decide.

The discourse at court is an institutionalized procedure that leads to a judgment with a specific—legally given—procedure of perception (*Erkenntnisverfahren*). On no account can this procedure of perception be hold against the standard of a theory of cognition, as e.g. procedural law itself minimizes[33] possible tools of recognition to procure the facts to five formalized types of evidence: documents, expert witnesses, appearance, witnesses and party attendance, according to sections 371 et seq.; 373 et seq.; 402 et seq., 415 et seq.; 445 et seq. German *ZPO*; sections 48 et seq.; 72 et seq.; 86 et seq.; 157 et seq.; 249 et seq. German *StPO*. In civil procedure two further means of non-formalized types of evidence are available: the insurance *affidavit* (*eidesstattliche Versicherung*), according to section 294 para 1 German *ZPO*, and the official information of an authority *(amtliche Auskunft einer Behörde)*, according to sections 273 para 2 Nr. 2, 358a Sentence 2 Nr. 2 German *ZPO*. However, the latter merely substitutes the witness hearing or the expert opinion and is thus no independent instrument of proof.

The procedure after the judgment is called the enforcement procedure (*Vollstreckungsverfahren*). Thus what was perceived as an ought is put forth into reality—if needs to be according to the law with force. For this purpose a legal

[33]This minimization from the point of view of theory of cognition starts with cognizing subject, who must decide in the present on a past object of cognition. From a logic point of view, if the object of cognition is material and still exists more or less unchanged due to the course of time, it can be looked at by the judge herself, e.g. appearance and documents. If the object of cognition is non-material and/or not re-producible, witnesses and party attendances may be asked. If the cognizing subject cannot decide, what exactly it cognizes with his own expertise it may call on expert witnesses.

procedure has to exist, so that law can be valid and be applied or transferred to reality—and thus sets the parameter for the legal reality itself.

2.1.2.1 The Legal Subsumptive Process Under the General Concepts of the Relevant Rules and the Subject Matter

Ultimately, it is a matter of describing the (pre-textual) individual, the concrete real actuality (*Gegebenheit*), as a particular one, which then is accessible to the—legal—subsumptive process under the general concepts of the rules relevant for the decision. Only subjects and objects described in this manner—and not the concrete case and its facts—are suitable subjects and objects of subsumption.

To understand how discourses at court take place more deeply, it must be further explained what exactly the subject matter at court is and then addressed what the factual data relevant for the legal case might be. With regard to the subject matter, civil procedural lawyers and legal scholars struggle to decide what exactly the matter of dispute for a civil case *(zivilprozessualer Streitgegenstand)* might be.[34] Depending on the answer, the pendency of proceedings (*Rechtshängigkeit*), legal force (*Rechtskraft*) or the limitation of action (*Verjährung*) are affected. Though from a point of view of the theory of cognition and science the subject matter must be prepared and one must be able to describe its parameters on a meta-level, legal scholars still fight about what parameters exactly the matter in dispute must have. Of course, the matter in dispute in itself cannot solve these disputes once and for all, but one has to decide in each context, and thus in each dispute, what the matter in dispute

[34]See: Regarding the question, how many aspects the matter of dispute has: Becker-Eberhard, in: Münchener Kommentar zur ZPO (2016), § 253 ZPO, paras 32 et seq.: The matter of dispute consists of the complaint (action for performance, affirmative action for a right or action requesting a change of a legal right or status) as can be found in the demand of relief (*Klageantrag*) and the submitted circumstantial facts to it, forming the bipartite concept of the matter of dispute (*zweigliedriger Streitgegenstandsbegriff*), whereas according to the onepartite concept of the matter of dispute (*eingliederiger Streitgegenstandsbegriff*) only the demand of relief determines the concept. According to another conception, which is a mixture of the former two in a relative way (Jauernig and Hess 2011, § 37 paras 39 et seq.; Stein et al. 2016, before § 253 paras 46 et seq.), one can apply, in line with the norm, either the onepartite concept, e.g. in the case of the pendency of the proceedings (*Rechtshängigkeit*), joinder of actions (*Klagehäufung*) or limitation of actions (*Verjährung*), however, the twopartite concept for the material legal force (*materielle Rechtskraft*)—so the latter—or must decide on the legal target of protection—so the former.

About the procedure before the constitutional court the twopartite concept of subject matter, consisting of the designation of the sovereign act that is contested and the claim to be violated by it in at least one basic right, prevails: Decision of the constitutional court, 15.06.1988, 1 BvR 1301/86, BVerfGE 78, 320 (328); Bethge, in: Maunz et al. (2019), § 90 BVerfGG, para 175g.

About criminal a major difference occurs: As the criminal procedure is not, like the civil procedure, based on the principle of party disposition (*Dispositionsmaxime*), but on the principle of *ex officio* disposition (*Offizialmaxime*, see section 155 para 2 German StPO), it merely depends on the circumstantial facts.

exactly is.[35] Regarding law's purposes[36] and form,[37] such an approach cannot lead to a guaranteed prognosis, but merely an accidental equal application of the law.

In this manner, to prepare and limit the subject matter one has to accept that legal procedure can only be in a very limited way governed by procedural legislation. The question of factual data influences the legal procedure by far more. Taking into account a modern civil law system's understanding of the concept of law, it might be that all the abstract rules together with the individual's action determine the action, but it is the subsumptive application of the case at hand, that leads to the judicial deliberation *(Urteilsfindung)*, and not the abstract rules on their own or in combination with a legal method.[38]

Legal interpretation and understanding is thus a practical and not only a mere theoretical action. In this manner, it is speaking with *Aristotle*, φρόνησις (*phrónesis*) and not ἐπιστήμη (*epistēmē*), because one has to decide how the case at hand should be decided according to the law.[39] The question, how to understand a rule in an abstract way is not the real question. This is even true for the scientific discourse, if it is understood as a suggestion for the discourse at court.[40] In this vein one does not look for objective truth in the law, but needs to ask a practical question as to how one should decide.[41]

2.1.2.2 The Form of the Judicial Decisions

This relationship of legal procedure and legal application leads to the conclusion that the judicial deliberation in itself must have a specific form. Whilst a judge decides a case via procedural law at court he follows a basic structure of a legal syllogism (*Justizsyllogismus*), so that it is possible to prove and assert legal assertions.[42] To serve one overall purpose of the law, legal peace,[43] any dispute that concerns the authoritative application must be solved. However, as the judges are not allowed to shrug their shoulders and claim a *non liquet*, but must decide any case brought before them, the case's concrete facts must be subsumed under the established rules at least at the end of the procedure. On account of this, the judicial deliberation itself has to

[35] Though for a relative understanding of the matter in dispute: Jauernig and Hess (2011), § 37 paras 39 et seq.; Stein et al. (2016), before § 253 paras 46 et seq.

[36] See below: Sect. 2.3, pp. 57 et seq.

[37] See below: Sect. 2.2, pp. 54 et seq.

[38] Kriele (1981), pp. 409 et seq.

[39] See as well: Nierhauve (2016), pp. 123 et seq.

[40] Kriele (1981), pp. 410 et seq.

[41] Kriele (1981), p. 410.

[42] For the legal syllogism: Dannecker (1993), pp. 377 et seq.; Gast (2015), pp. 25 et seq.; Gabriel (2019), pp. 116 et seq.; Gröschner (2013), pp. 269 et seq. and 361; Jandach (1993), pp. 103 et seq.; Möller (1997), pp. 94 et seq.; Neupert (2011), pp. 70 et seq.; Schnapp (2016), pp. 140 et seq.

[43] See below: Sect. 2.4.2, pp. 62 et seq.

be regarding its *genus* an act of determination of the concrete and individual situation of the legally relevant facts. Hence the subject matter of the proceedings must consist of all either factual or legal relevant allegations that concern the concrete and individual legal situation. Though in so far the subject matter of any legal dispute is—concerning it's *genus*—sketched, neither the legal rules nor the case's facts as the regular starting point of each and every legal procedure can be clearly detected. They are in the contradictory (civil) procedure merely points of reference for the further contradictory assertions of the parties.[44]

A further *genus* of texts which might be relevant in the judicial discourse regards the legislative materials, which is decided by each person, whether it will take these into account or not. However, in which scientifically valid manner as to which legislative material might be relevant and which not, is generally not discussed.[45]

At last, by origin non-verbal resources might have legal relevance for customary law as an *usus* or as *factum* to decide the case. Whether it really exists is determined according to a meta-rule as developed over time by legal scholars.[46]

Concerning the legal and/or scientific discourse of judicial decisions form kind of a hybrid, as the way they need to be issued is more or less stipulated by the law.[47] Thus the decision itself can be guided by the jurisprudential discourse, e.g. in Germany Art. 20 para 3 German Constitution.[48] In this manner, to apply the law is more than a mere interpretation and subsumption, but leads to a *creation of the*—relevant and interpreted—*law* for each case. Thus judicial decisions might—in a civil law system—not be a source of law, but at least a source to recognize law.[49] In this vein it is still unclear, whether case law and customary law are the same and whether or how they bind.[50] As such a source to recognize the law and taking one of the purposes of any scientific method into account,[51] to achieve predictable similar outcomes for similar cases, the interpretation of the relevant *rationes decidendi* and

---

[44] See above in fn. 34.

[45] With regard to this, see below: Sect. 2.2.3, pp. 56 et seq.

[46] This meta rule consists of the following criteria: 0. an existing gap, 1st the possibility to express the envisaged custom as an abstract rule, 2nd a *longa consuetudo*, 3rd *opinio iuris sive necessitatis*, which is a certain legal practice as it is observed and as the relevant actors consider it to be law, and 4th the congruence with higher ranking law. See instead of all for the German context: Krebs and Becker (2014), p. 97; Larenz (1991), p. 433; Säcker (1971), p. 148; regarding the comparability of the different methods to form and interpret different legal sources in the light of *Aristotle's* Theory of Four Causes: Klappstein (2017), pp. 111 et seq.; Klappstein (2016), pp. 405 et seq.

[47] Instead of all: Kriele (1981), p. 409.

[48] "The legislature shall be bound by the constitutional order, the executive and the judiciary by law and justice".

[49] So: Larenz and Canaris (2002), pp. 256 et seq. and 260; for further discussion regarding the source of law for case law: Klappstein (2009), pp. 266 et seq. with further references; Langenbucher (1996), pp. 115 et seq.

[50] For Germany regarding the category of case law: Klappstein (2009), pp. 266 et seq. with further references.

[51] See below: Sect. 2.2, pp. 54 et seq.

obiter dicta need a certain method. A method, that is guided by legal and scientific methods yet again.[52]

2.1.2.3 The Determination of the Relevant Facts with Regard to Legal Rules and the Origin of the Judicial Decision

In the end, the law determines which facts the judges need to revert to, in principle after taking evidence (*Beweisaufnahme*). But as it is a human being, that needs to decide, and not a machine, it reverts to his very own conviction as the judge deems it to be true or untrue (section 286 para 1 German *ZPO*;[53] similarly in section 261 German *StPO*;[54] section 108 German *VwGO*[55]). To this extent, the judge appears explicitly as a hermeneutical subject, in fact, as an individual.

This process of decision-making obtains additional levels of complexity via the mutual influence of factual and legal assessments (*Sachverhalts- und Rechtslageermittlung*). Their topics and the direction of the ascertainment are determined by those legal norms, which the judge assumed to be decisive in the matter in the first place. Thus the elaboration of the facts is always at the same time a process of a typifying description (*typisierende Beschreibung*).

However, which instruments may be involved in preparing and procuring the facts—the five formalized types of evidence—is yet again determined by normative texts. In doing so, the judge must not only adopt a language of foreign disciplines for expert opinions, e.g. architecture, biology, chemistry, engineering sciences medicine, psychology, etc. but as well foreign languages or foreign legal orders about their—possibly different—relevant texts. Here again a margin discourse takes place.

[52] Langenbucher (1996), pp. 63 et seq.

[53] "Evaluation of evidence at the court's discretion and conviction

(1) The court is to decide, **at its discretion and conviction**, and taking account of the entire content of the hearings and the results obtained by evidence being taken, if any, **whether an allegation as to fact is to be deemed true or untrue**. The judgment is to set out the reasons informing the conviction of the judges.

(2) The court shall be bound to statutory rules of evidence only in the cases designated in the present Code."—citations omitted.

[54] "The court shall decide on the result of the **evidence taken according to its free conviction gained from the hearing as a whole**."—citations omitted.

[55] "(1) The court shall rule in accordance with **its conviction gained from the overall outcome** of the proceedings. The judgment shall state the grounds which were decisive for the judicial conviction.

(2) The judgment may only be based on facts and results of evidence on which those concerned have been able to make a statement."—citations omitted.

2.1.2.4 The Relationship of Legal Rules and Relevant Facts Serving the Purpose of the Discourses at Court

From a point of view of the theory of cognition, of course, the judges can neither decide on the facts of the case, which had actually taken place, as it is impossible to reveal these very facts to the deciding judge. Nor can the judge merely "find" the applicable rules, but has to interpret them, and thus prepare them in a manner that they are for each subsumption concrete and thus a subsumable premiss. In so doing the precise nature of the matter of decision, the judge decides regarding both, the legal and factual terms, must be looked upon: On the one hand, the *legal* dimension of the decision-making process is only a case of application of all those problems which are associated with the legal activity that can be strictly understood as text-hermeneutics. Of course, it needs to be distinguished from other cases concerning its specific peculiarities, e.g. the legal decision's binding force. But yet, the methods needed while applying the law can be named as the derivation from the law "as the only accepted mode of justification". It necessitates subsumption and the *modus barbara*—or at least an ἐνθύμημα (Greek: *enthymeme*, *enthumēma*)[56] with a somehow inbuilt shortened—*legal*—syllogism[57] but as well the integration of normative moments, a limited canon of scientifically and practically valid methods or the binding effect of prejudices.

On the other hand, the actual (concerning the factual decisive) dimension of judicial decisions follows entirely separate rules. This factual process leads to the *praemissa minor* (factual premiss) for the subsumption. It consists essentially of the fact that the judge uses and evaluates the material submitted to him via means of the five formalized types of evidence.[58] These can be original text-like artifacts of the past's happenings. She then produces a description, which, in turn, must be guided by the selection and combination of laws, case law and jurisprudential parameters.

This description holds the cases facts and is in itself yet again a—text. The legal reasons (*Entscheidungsgründe*) given by the court for its decision must not only refer to this description of the facts, but as well conform to it. And they need to do so, to serve the purposes of the law,[59] which is the key to decide on their own purpose: To decide the legal dispute at hand within the boundaries of an equal application of the law, but as well to materialize a forecast for the people to ensure the predictability of legal decisions and thus overall legal certainty.

---

[56] Aristotle, translated by Rapp (2002), I 1355a, 1356b, 1357a and 1403a; Dörpinghaus (2002), pp. 59 et seq. and 67 et seq. Rapp (2002a, b), p. 360; on the enthymeme in jurisprudence see the different articles in von Schlieffen (2011b); see as well: Schnapp (2016), pp. 127 et seq.; Simon (2011), pp. 700 et seq.; von Schlieffen (2011a), pp. 112 et seq.

[57] See above: Sect. 2.1.2.1, pp. 45 et seq.; Dannecker (1993), pp. 377 et seq.; Gast (2015), pp. 25 et seq.; Gabriel (2019), pp. 116 et seq.; Gröschner (2013), pp. 269 et seq. and 361; Jandach (1993), pp. 103 et seq.; Möller (1997), pp. 94 et seq.; Neupert (2011), pp. 70 et seq.; Schnapp (2016), pp. 140 et seq.

[58] See above: Sect. 2.1.2, pp. 44 et seq.

[59] See below: Sect. 2.4, pp. 61 et seq.

2.1.3 Scientific Legal Discourses

2.1.3.1 The Subject-Matter of Scientific Legal Discourses

First of all the scientific legal discourses and the legal relevance are determined by words again. A wider range of jurisprudential texts, e.g. articles, commentaries, dissertations, judicial decisions, lectures, speeches during conferences etc., can provide auxiliary means for the interpretation of the rule of law itself. Regarding the subject-matter of the scientific discourse, one has first to answer the question what is essential to science (section "What Is Science at All?") and how jurisprudence can thus be a science (section "Jurisprudence as Science").

2.1.3.1.1 What Is Science at All?

According to *Aristotle* science is on the lookout for the causes of any subject matter, regarding a certain method, e.g. the four causes, to give answers.[60] *Kant's* concept of science was somewhat different: Any doctrine if they have a system, is to be a "whole" according to principles of knowledge, is called science [. . .] Actual science can only be called the one whose certainty is apodictic; knowledge, which can contain only empirical certainty, is a knowledge that is only improperly called knowledge. Exactly because that *totality of knowledge is systematic* it can be called science. Moreover, if the organization of knowledge in such a system is a chaining together of principles and consequences can it even be called rational science. But if these reasons or principles in it, as e.g. in chemistry, are at last merely empirical, and the laws from which the given facts are explained by reason, are merely laws of experience, they do not convey an awareness of their necessity (are not apodictic-certain), and deserve the whole in a strict sense, not the name of a science, and chemistry should, therefore, be called rather *systematic art*, rather than science.[61] Apart from the different approaches in the theory of sciences with the two major branches of scientific realism and non-realism, science necessitates for all those

[60] Aristotle (1975), II 194b–195a, pp. 65 et seq.; Aristotle (1995), I 71b 9–11, p. 115 and II 94a, pp. 156 et seq.; Höffe (2014), p. 116; Rapp (2012), p. 127; with regard to *Aristotle's* theory of four causes, see: Klappstein (2016), pp. 405 et seq.; Klappstein (2017), pp. 92 et seq.

[61] *"Eine jede Lehre, wenn sie ein System, d.i. ein nach Prinzipien geordnetes Ganze der Erkenntnis sein soll, heißt Wissenschaft [. . .] Eigentliche Wissenschaft kann nur diejenige genannt werden, deren Gewißheit apodiktisch ist; Erkenntnis, die bloß empirische Gewißheit enthalten kann, ist ein nur uneigentlich so genanntes Wissen. Dasjenige* ***Ganze der Erkenntnis, was systematisch ist****, kann schon darum Wissenschaft heißen, und, wenn die Verknüpfung der Erkenntnis in diesem System ein Zusammenhang von Gründen und Folgen ist, so gar rationale Wissenschaft. Wenn aber diese Gründe oder Prinzipien in ihr, wie z.B. in der Chemie, doch zuletzt bloß empirisch sind, und die Gesetze, aus denen die gegebene Facta durch die Vernunft erklärt werden, bloß Erfahrungsgesetze sind, so führen sie kein Bewußtsein ihrer Notwendigkeit bei sich (sind nicht apodiktisch-gewiß) und alsdenn verdient das Ganze in strengem Sinne nicht den Namen einer Wissenschaft, und Chymie sollte daher eher* ***systematische Kunst****, als Wissenschaft heißen."*—Kant (1786), Vorrede—citations omitted.

disciplines of human *research goals* to explore *facts* and *structures* about areas of nature as well as the spiritual, cultural, political, technical and social lifeworld in a systematically structured and *methodologically controlled* way developing theories.[62]

What all three have in common and what is hence needed for any discipline to be a science is thus to give the subject matter a systematic structure in a methodologically controlled way, so that the outcome and certainty is apodictic, hence the reasons given and taken must be of such a matter, that they could procure such a result.

2.1.3.1.2 Jurisprudence as Science

In jurisprudence, there are no clear conditions set, as to when the "giving or taking of reasons" (*Das Geben und Nehmen von Gründen*) is scientifically sufficient for any of its reasoning. Albeit, of course, there are for the subsumption (logical) rules.[63] But aside from these, for the interpretation, no "hard rules" exist. In a quantitative analysis regarding the topic of interpretation in connection with the above-mentioned three genera of subject matters (texts, oral words, and non-verbal resources), the legal literature is mostly concerned with the interpretation of legal texts and with the declarations of intentions and treaties. Both the latter are governed by—yet again to be construed—norms with sections 133, 157 German *BGB*. For the interpretation of legal rules, the German legislative decided to let legal scholarship research a method of interpretation.[64] However, even for the first, the result as to the scientific state of the art of interpretation is by far unclear, which is presented as an example.

Due to the lack of legislation, it is jurisprudence's scientific task to design and develop a method for the interpretation of legal texts. Although there are decisions by the German Federal Constitutional Court on the methodological approach to the interpretation of legal texts, these, however, merely refer to the existing *repertoire* developed by legal scholars.[65] The reasons and their requirements for the interpretation of legal rules are mainly developed within(!) the discipline of jurisprudence and there in the field of legal methodology.[66]

---

[62] See: Okasha (2016), p. 2.

[63] See above references mentioned in fn. 42 and 56.

[64] Rüthers et al. (2019), 10th edition 2015, p. 417, para 704; that can be different, e.g. in Austria the rather vague sections 6 et seq. Austrian *ABGB* or in Switzerland Art. 1 ZGB.

[65] Decision of the *BVerfG* of 23.10.1985, 1 BvR 1053/82, BVerfGE 71, 108, 115; decision of the *BVerfG* of 20.10.1992, 1 BvR 698/89, BVerfGE 87, 209, 224.

[66] Beaucamp and Treder (2019), 3rd edition 2015, pp. 33 et seq., paras 138 et seq.; Bydlinski (1991), p. 437; Gast (2015), pp. 257 et seq.; Koch and Rüßmann (1982), pp. 166 et seq.; Kramer (2019), 4th edition 2013, p. 56; Larenz and Canaris (1995), pp. 141 et seq.; Müller and Christensen (2013), pp. 328 et seq.; Muthorst (2019), pp. 104 et seq.; Rüthers et al. (2019), 10th edition 2015, pp. 416 et seq.; Zippelius (2012), pp. 35 et seq.; see as well further references at: Klappstein (2016), pp. 423 et seq. in fn. 150.

Although it overlaps with the theory of (legal) science, it persists in the discussions of legal themes and hardly leaves its legal scope. For example, there is hardly a discussion of hermeneutic philosophy to be found in modern research on legal methodology. Even the new discourse in the philosophy of science for jurisprudence (*Rechtswissenschaftstheorie*), which is to be welcomed, does not lead to any new discoveries.[67]

It is contested as to when sufficient reasons for the interpretation of legal texts are given, which arguments are more or less convincing, and which have to prevail ultimately. Rather, the judicial practice shows that rules and reasons can lead once and for all to one or even a contradictory conclusion within the same discussion. The reasons to be given have thus only a special status as mere justifications.

The reasons thus given are either already pre-structured by the legal text with its applicability prerequisites, elements of a statutory act and legal consequences (*Anwendbarkeitsvoraussetzungen, Tatbestandsmerkmalen, Rechtsfolgen*). In the unlikely case that they are absent, e.g. if an unwritten element of a statutory act is added or, in the entire absence of a regulation, when analogous application (analogy of rules [*Gesetzesanalogie*]) or development (analogy of law [*Rechtsanalogie*]), these legal justifications are linked to already verified content.[68]

Interdisciplinary marginal discourses (*interdisziplinäre Grenzdiskurse*) of juridical and general hermeneutics are described in methodological textbooks and deepened in some research groups.[69] In this manner, there exist some approaches to find general hermeneutics inductively from different disciplinary hermeneutics.[70] In such an applicatory and practical approach, each a legal, theological and literal text was interpreted with the method in each discipline.[71] It is, however, needed, if the legislator had access to the various sciences while legislating,[72] that the legal applicator enters in such an interdisciplinary marginal discourse as well. Judges and lawyers can do so via the instrument to call for an expert witness. However, a discourse concerning the theory of science cannot hardly be included in this way, though it is due to the training at university the underlying and concomitant methodology. Another aspect is that judges, lawyers and legal scholars must be aware that in their doing they shoulder as well a certain responsibility.[73]

These are, however, not made manifest in the broad masses of legal discourse, the discourse in jurisprudence and legisprudence, for example, or in judicial decisions.

---

[67] van Aaken (2008), passim; Adrian (2014), pp. 29 et seq.; Zabel (2017), p. 176.

[68] Regarding the argument of analogy: Decision of the *BGH* of 16.07.2003, VIII ZR 274/02, NJW 2003, 2601, 2603; decision of the *BGH* of 13.03.2003, I ZR 290/00, NJW 2003, 1932, 1933; Luther (2013), p. 449; Würdinger (2006), pp. 946 et seq.

[69] Bottke (1993), passim; Fuhrmann et al. (1981), passim; Thiel (1980), passim.

[70] See for example: Betti (1972), pp. 218 et seq.; Crifò (2000), pp. 365 et seq.; Dannhauser (1652); Gadamer (1990).

[71] Fuhrmann et al. (1981), pp. 9 et seq.; Herzog (1981), pp. 367 et seq.; Kriele (1981), pp. 409 et seq.

[72] See above: Sect. 2.1.1.2, pp. 41 et seq.

[73] Carrier (2017), pp. 180 et seq.

2.1.3.2 The Form of the Scientific Legal Discourses

They must themselves have a certain form and thus measure up to the state of the art, like laws and judicial decisions must measure up to the standards of legistic and judicial methodology, articles, commentaries, and dissertations must measure up to the scientific standard.[74] However, where and how such a standard is to be found seems like a *petitio principii* as at this point one cannot say, what exactly the state of the art consists of.

2.1.3.3 The Legal Scholar as Subject

The authors of the texts are legal scholars, who interpret and research the law, holding a certain expertise with certain preconcepts as trained during their studies and a set of epistemic, ethical and social values.[75] Though this is true for all the actors in the process of verbalizing the law, one looks at scholars with a different pair of glasses, hoping for some kind of objectivity and scientific standard. As human beings they may not loose their subjectivity, but they can make sure to meet a certain standard, by disclosing their set of preferences, e.g. by not merely secretly setting but as well stating the relevant premisses for the research in form of theories, openly discussing different perspectives and refraining from rhetorical instruments that do not hold a tangible argument.

In judicial decisions and scientific articles these are characterized by the fact that different authors and/or judgments are named, who likewise support the arguments, and it is even openly reasoned with mere *ἔνδοξα* (*endoxa*)—majority views or prevailing opinions—as an argument of authority.[76] This impedes an unbiased spectrum of perspectives, which takes the different values and convictions scholars import in their research into account.[77] In this manner a pluralistic approach to a more reasonable and reliable science via means of a spectrum of perspectives at the very least more complicated.[78]

2.1.3.4 The Purposes of the Scientific Discourse

There are several purposes for the scientific legal discourse: To deepen the understanding of the law including the underlying principles and purposes, to develop the

[74] See below: Sect. 2.2, pp. 54 et seq.

[75] Carrier (2017), pp. 161 et seq.

[76] For the relevance before the court already *Aristotle* in the Rhetoric, cited at Gröschner (2013), p. 275 in fn. 31.

[77] Carrier (2017), pp. 175 et seq.

[78] Brown (2001), pp. 198 et seq.; Carrier (2017), pp. 175 et seq.; Longino (2002), pp. 128 et seq.

underlying theory, to suggest changes, to discover flaws and, of course, to develop a method regarding law's form.[79]

2.1.4 Intermediate Results

The different subject matters of law and their discourses ask for reasons to be given, as to which reasons can enter the discourse and which cannot. For some, the law itself decides, whether they are relevant. For others, an interdisciplinary dialogue, including the theory of science and hermeneutics, need to be employed.[80] The philosophy of science is the basis for any further understanding: Its purpose is the understanding of the techniques applied in different disciplines, such as experimentation, observation and in the end development of theories.[81]

Absolute answers which reasons should be included and which not or an abstract method with definitive answers as to when a reason is rational enough can neither be found nor given, even from the point of view of the theory of science.[82] This leads to the second topic where one has to deal with (legal) reasons: namely law's form or law as a science.

2.2 *Law's Form and Systematization on Different Levels: What Reasons Can Be Included in the Legal Discourse?*

Regarding law's different forms and systematizations, one need to access the different reasons that can be included in the discourse regarding the different legal subject-matters. A scientific discourse on the admission of specific descriptions and reasons in the legal discourse does not take place in depth,[83] though it is needed. Why is it needed? Because otherwise random arguments might be admitted to the legal discourse.

2.2.1 The Reasoning by the Legislator: Legisprudence

The legislator nowadays is not left alone to legislate at will. Aside from the procedural and constitutional preconditions, legal scholarships offers assistance in the whole range of legisprudence to research and thus found the scientific basis for

[79] See below: Sect. 2.2, pp. 54 et seq.

[80] Concerning a legal theory of science there are different approaches: van Aaken (2008), passim; Adrian (2014), pp. 29 et seq.; Zabel (2017), p. 176.

[81] Okasha (2016), p. 2.

[82] Okasha (2016), pp. 36 et seq.

[83] See, e.g.: van Aaken (2008), pp. 79 et seq.; Adrian (2014), pp. 98 et seq.

the method to legislate. Of course, with the scholarly assistance, the legislative may form a state of the art to regulate. This can be found in the "Better Regulation Toolbox" as set by the *European Commission* with its different principles.[84] There are useful questions, e.g. for the impact assessment of the planned initiative, that should be answered, such as:

"1. What is the problem and why is it a problem?

2. Why should the EU act?

3. What should be achieved?

4. What are the various options to achieve the objectives?

5. What are their economic, social and environmental impacts and who will be affected?

6. How do the different options compare (effectiveness, efficiency and coherence)?

7. How will monitoring and subsequent retrospective evaluation be organised?"[85]

However, these questions can and will be answered differently, according to the person who asked and answered the questions. There must be valuations in answering these questions. This is why the value-relating aspect of law and its subjectivity prevail.

To develop such a (normative) theory of legislation can not, however, be produced only by lawyers with jurisprudential methods. Establishing rules always holds the attempt to put forth an object of real life into legal texts, but based on certain *evaluations* which must be subjective.[86]

2.2.2 The Reasoning at Court

Thus, for example, if a court decides not to use a type of reasoning (that is, an interpretative canon) at all, or to use legal philosophical or economic reasons primarily in its decision, it should explain and reason as to why it does not or does so in the first place. Why should it do so? Because the method—to achieve the same outcome with the same given facts—is one basic component of science. We will see that it is such a component not only due to the "equal application of the law" as one purpose of law itself,[87] but as well due to the understanding of science, forecasting results for the citizens. In this vein any lawyers own epistemic value has and leads to certain social causes and consequences.[88]

However, that kind of reasoning is—mostly—missing. One can find arguments as to, that a certain argument does not weigh as much as another. But there is no discourse, as to why a philosophical argument is not to be applied, an economic one,

[84] See: European Commission (2017).

[85] European Commission (2017), p. 17.

[86] Carrier (2017), pp. 161 et seq.

[87] See below Sect. 2.4, pp. 61 et seq.

[88] Carrier (2017), p. 181.

as it is nowadays *en vogue*, is though. On the contrary, philosophical arguments such as the theories of justice are not applied, if ever, they are only implicitly exploited, whereas for cartel law or the justification of the legislative process economic arguments which can be understood as utilitarian, are applied.

2.2.3 The Reasoning by Legal Scholars

The legal scholar, unlike the courts and authorities, which are subject to the law by virtue of a higher authority, has the freedom to regard the positive law from the outset as an expressed cognitive process in which she participates as a diagnosing subject. Her recognition and development of the legal meaning of laws and justice only directs but does *not* limit.

Contrary to the constellations described so far, there are no normative requirements to admit certain arguments in jurisprudence. Jurisprudence allows a wide range of possible perspectives and arguments: Legal scholars are free in the choice of their point of view. They can put themselves in the position of the judicial decision-maker,[89] understand the legal system as it is handled by the courts, and on this basis forecast what the courts will do in fact. Likewise, they can choose a historical scientific standpoint and reconstruct the development of the law of this and all times under this aspect. As well they can take a stand from the point of view of past law to the law of the present.

Furthermore, jurisprudence, like the courts, may ask for the correct application of laws, for the correct solution of cases, but at the same time jurisprudence can put aside the mode of work and the limitations of knowledge courts have with the constitution, especially the strict limitations of the positive law. Thus it can provide innovative impulses for the further development and improvement of the system of law as created by courts and legislators, and is by far more open for a free dialogue with neighboring sciences, such as economics, natural sciences, or philosophy.

The more fundamental underlying problem to which such an overstatement refers to is the self-reference of jurisprudence as a science: Jurisprudence should assure itself of the conditions which of its statements, on the one hand, qualify as expressions of scientific knowledge and, on the other hand, as such, on the law. Neither lawyers nor legal scholars can achieve that by merely applying legal methods. It is only scholars who are trained in both, law and the theory of science, who can further the discourse in this field. That affords as well to be aware of the own values, which are brought into research. If these values are non-epistemic they can mold the content of the scientific knowledge; if they do, the entire venture of scholarship can be jeopardized.[90]

---

[89] Kriele (1981), pp. 409 et seq.

[90] Carrier (2017), p. 184.

2.2.4 Intermediate Results

For jurisprudence to be a science scientific methods are necessary. These methods cannot be found merely within jurisprudence, but need to be tested against different sciences as well as the theory of science. For this, reasons need to be given. Why which method is applied and why which argument or reason is to be included in the discourse is not discussed. Without arguments and awareness on this frontier, jurisprudence cannot predict results and has no method worthy to procure it. A method is as well necessary to procure one of law's purposes, an equal application of the law. An awareness of these circumstances is essential, as then the inbuilt subjectivity can be sceptically taken into account.

2.3 Law and Its History: Or Law and Its Development Over Time

Regarding law and its history, the normative consequences that occur as a historic fact and its relevance *in praxi* need to be looked at (Sect. 2.3.1). That leads as well to the varied interrelationships the different authorities in a wider sense have (Sect. 2.3.2) and to the actual people, who apply the law, as hermeneutical subjects (Sect. 2.3.3).

2.3.1 The Normative Consequences Throughout History and Its Relevance *In Praxi*

2.3.1.1 The Direct and Indirect Normative Consequences Throughout History

If one asks for the normative conditions of jurisprudence, it is obvious to look at the relations of academic jurisprudence to the activity of the institutions applying the law and legislating—hence at their direct and indirect normative consequences throughout history. In these relations, jurisprudence appears as a partner in a complex dialogue and is relevant as well with regard to legal history. As rules and their application are not merely observable facts, one cannot conclude from the application's observation a valid reasoning.[91] Its role is very diverse: it can be a mere auxiliary tool for the courts and authorities which, in their practical activities, support them by systematizing and preparing their decisions, or it can be a quasi-normative instrument, at least with a critical claim (albeit without a decision-making power), with the aim of recognizing and showing which solution is the "correct one".

---

[91] Carrier (2017), p. 44.

In any case, jurisprudence seeks to obtain general statements about its subject matter, and in any case, perhaps with the exception of purely historical or sociological research, it is to be heard and received by its dialogue partners that are empowered to apply the law. But this means as well that their efforts are directed towards influencing the output of real decision-making processes in a sense which they have recognized—in the past and present—to be the "correct one".[92]

2.3.1.2 The Relevance of Legal History In Praxi

For jurisprudence as a dogmatic science, which deals with application-related individual questions, but also with the systematic questions prompted by them, legal history, researching law's practice in the past is relevant. However, also the disciplines of legal theory, which are more distant from the field of application, produce insights. In particular insights on the conditions of system formation, which indirectly affect the patterns of thought and the contents of dogmatics and, via these, on practice, are developed. The results obtained in legal history and juridical sociology have often influenced how jurisprudence looks at their legitimate objects—even if only to enable them to gain insight into the potential for optimization *de lege ferenda*.[93]

2.3.2 The Varied Interrelationships with the Processes of Institutions Exercising Authority

The varied interrelationships with the processes of real authority exercising in the social world of society are, roughly spoken, the background in which jurisprudence has to determine the normative starting conditions of its own activity. Thus before it sets the guidelines for the system of legal scientific, internal systematic discourse, as they were, the barriers to access to this discourse must be assessed. This can not, inevitably, take place with its inner vocabulary, but only in a dialogue with other disciplines, with recourse to extra-juristic, especially philosophical—preconceptions, in margin discourses. A classical source for the acquisition of such presuppositions is the examination of the conceptions of justice, to be found in the philosophy of law.

---

[92] Kriele (1981), pp. 410 et seq.

[93] Kriele (1981), pp. 410 et seq.

2.3.3 The People Who Apply the Law as Hermeneutical Subjects: As *pars pro toto*—The Judge

The people who apply the law (*Rechtsanwender*) are persons that interpret the law and/or apply it in the very case in the aforementioned five stepped manner. It may be an administrative agency granting permission or a criminal court rendering a verdict. In applying and interpreting the law, they act as hermeneutical subjects. To assess some relevant aspects the judge will be looked upon as *pars pro toto*.

The judge, as a hermeneutical subject, steps apparently in the background. She does that especially in the following cases: If the methods of interpretation approach fields for which objectivity can not be posited without further ado, especially in the case of all relapses to the teleology of norms—in the case of teleological interpretation, or analogy and teleological reduction. Here the judge asks something "which unintentionally passes through the texts". Hence considerable effort is expended to establish standards for intersubjective control, thus aiming to preserve a kind of objectivity of knowledge—which is in fact impossible to achieve.[94] What is more, since these relapses are caused by a shifting of contexts, legal science is a matter of understanding and not merely explaining of the law.[95]

One can think of the discussion, as to with which aim the historical canon is determined, i.e. the so-called subjective theory of interpretation—by the legislator's will—by the objective meaning of the law—the so-called objective theory of interpretation.[96]

The tense relation to the interpreters subjectivity emerges within the judge: The theory of methodology's aim is to grasp the operation to be performed by the judge as far as possible by the formation of corresponding rules of method and to render it controllable. This is necessitated yet again by the purpose of the law, the "equal application of the law" and the necessity to lead to peace while protecting the confidence of the forecast legal result.[97]

Thus even amid the objective-deductive model there always remains a last remnant of a vision "on the outside". One could also say: A recourse to subjective conviction, to the judge's sense of justice. The rules of methodology can push this remainder of subjectivity back into ever-smaller spaces. However, they can never eliminate them. Without any methodological approach, they would be far bigger. They might be reduced if the hermeneutic subject recognizes and acknowledges to be such, a hermeneutic subject.

---

[94] Carrier (2017), pp. 161 et seq. and 170 et seq. Whether or not social values can be (McMullin 1983, p. 23) or cannot (Kitcher 2001, pp. 65, 71 et seq. and 118 et seq.; Kitcher 2004, p. 53) be filtered from sciences, is contested.

[95] See, e.g., the forthcoming proceedings, edited by Klappstein and Heiß of the conference in May 2019: "*Fragen & Antworten – Verstehen & Erklären in den Wissenschaften*".

[96] Jandach (1993), p. 102; Larenz (1991), pp. 33 and 316; see as well: Klappstein (2016), pp. 426 et seq.; Klappstein (2017), pp. 100 et seq. each with further references.

[97] See below: Sect. 2.4.2, p. 62.

Corresponding effects appear wherever discretionary decisions are in order—setting aside the values and preferences in weighing that always exist:[98] This is almost always the case when applying law, even within the subsumption model. In this respect, the interpreter appears again as an individual, as it were, in the midst of a mechanism that has been alienated from its subjectivity: The recognition of the object ultimately takes place through the subjectivity of the interpreter. To recognize this domain as what it really is, is the precondition for the disclosure of its inherent, procedural, and substantive, rationality.

To what extent the judge's very own sense of justice and not just a different set of rules are applicable, is a question of how these norms are handled. This is a dogmatic question, charged with the problems of legal theory. A different case, which is particularly interesting for the purpose here pursued, is, on the other hand, the regulation of judicial justification, which directly refers to the conviction of the decision as a criterion (sections 286 para 1 German *ZPO*; 261 German *StPO*, 108 para 1 German *VwGO*).

Assuming that even the configuration of the case to be decided by the court in itself is a hermeneutic process offers a promising entry for the apprehension of the discerning and eminent individual's role and function within the legal—or scientific[99]—system.

2.3.4 The Purpose of Law and History

In practice law develops over time.[100] Tracing its origin and history deepens the understanding and consistency of the law, leading to a preconception of jurisprudence and the law, one would hardly have without it. Furthermore certain and longer reaching forecasts can be made in a more profound way: "The longer you can look back, the farther you can look forward".[101]

2.3.5 Intermediate Results

The reasons given over time can show the development of law and jurisprudence. It may thus give reasons. But the reasons given are only those of time and an *is*. They cannot be that of an *ought*. What can be seen is, that auxiliary means, such as the historical or philosophical sciences are and must be taken into account. The judge,

---

[98] Carrier (2017), pp. 161 et seq.

[99] Regarding the social theory of cognition and science's ethos concerning universalism, communism, institutional non-interest (independence) and organized scepticism: Carrier (2017), pp. 173 et seq.; Merton (1973).

[100] This notion can, of course, be contested from the point of view of natural law.

[101] Citing a quote of *Winston Spencer Churchill*: Wrigley (2002), p. XXIV.

like any other applicant of law (*Rechtsanwender*), is a hermeneutic subject with preconceptions.

2.4 *Law's Purposes: Peace Under and Justice in the Form of an Equal Application of the Law*

At last law's purposes will be looked at. For this first of all the private addressees of the law will be looked at (Sect. 2.4.1) and in a second step the national institutions, yet again, with the court as major relevant authority to decide a lawsuit (Sect. 2.4.2).

2.4.1 The Private Addressees of the Law

Since the law is, according to its immanent self-understanding, not only a sanctioning but as well a behavioral order not only original institutions to apply the law (judicative and executive) belong to it, but as well private subjects. To these law's primary imperatives—even if only implicitly—are directed.

The extent to which law addresses individuals as qualified to ethically decide is subject to a long controversy. Law as imperatives, the arrangement of its oughts (*Gesolltsein*), presupposes at least a will to be influenced by this content. Similar to the commandments of morality, the legal concept is based on the assumption that these rules are correctly recognized by those to whom they apply, and that they are recognized as unconditional, categorically *Oughts*. As such they must be recognized by the private addressees in their acts of will.

The conception of the legal subordinate as an autonomous subject is institutionalized in the system of private law at the legal level: This structure allows its subjects extensive freedom in the design of their lives. It empowers them to regulate their private affairs by themselves. As long as and to the extent that all the parties involved agree on the legal relationship existing between them, and thus their power to shape their lives has in law only essential, *de facto* and *in praxi* nearly no limits. Thus they are co-creators of the law, which they claim to recognize as their own.

However, the imperatives of law are without the claim or even trying to convince the private addressees of the (moral) justification of the ends pursued. Law thus only orders the *external behavior* of those subject to it. In fact, its "persuasive power" is also derived from a very different element, that of institutionalized coercion. The legal *ought* (*rechtliches Sollen*) is, if the addressee fails to comply with the primary order, followed by an obligation or a legal must (*rechtliches Müssen*), even if this is a mere possibility.

Though one can say that this legal structure speaks to the subject in their free will. It is formed of—again spoken with *Kant*—Hypothetical Imperatives.[102] They hold

[102] Klappstein (2018), pp. 79 et seq. with further references.

the conditions each individual needs to fulfill to aim for the wanted consequences and thus avoid the possibly unwelcome consequence of the sanction.

2.4.2 The National Institutions: *pars pro toto*—The Court

The legal system, as already mentioned, does not only address the private addressees but as well the national institutions, especially the courts. They are addressed not as individual actors, but primarily in their institutional function as judges. The same legal norms, which for the actors of the legal life contain rights, behavioral demands, boundaries (in private law: the citizens subject to law, in the public law: the authorities of the executive and the legislature), etc., to gain peace under the law (*Rechtsfrieden*) hold in reverse of these provisions the imperative for the judiciary to decide accordingly in the event of a dispute. Thus leading to an equal application of the law (*Rechtsanwendungsgleichheit*), via means of transparency and accountability (*Transparenz* and *Nachvollziehbarkeit*) is necessary.

The whole understanding of judicial jurisprudence as a process of the recognition of extraneous or intersubjective normative realities (*Vorgang der Erkenntnis außer- oder auch intersubjektiver normativer Gegebenheiten*) expresses the idea that law can be an object of objective cognition (*objektive Erkenntnis*). Numerous institutions of methodology, but also of dogmatics, exist, whose purpose is to construct the judicial recognition as an intersubjective control of correctness via the means of deduction from the rule of law to achieve an equal application of the law. However, no matter how far the methods are developed, the hermeneutical subjectivity can never be extinguished.[103] Even not, if an artificial intelligent machine judges, as an AI is again programmed by humans.

2.4.3 Intermediate Results

Leading peaceful lives in a bigger society via law (peace under the law, *Rechtsfrieden*) affords justice by equal application of the law. For these purposes transparency and accountability (*Transparenz* and *Nachvollziehbarkeit*) are necessary. The latter necessitates a certain methodology, interpretation, argumentation, subsumption as well as procedural law, to ensure an equal application of the law.

[103] See Sect. 2.3.3, pp. 59 et seq.

3 Theses and Conclusion

Looking at the four different topics, there are different necessities for Legal Reasoning. Stringing the relevant subject-matter and the purpose of law together, it necessitates a certain form, to achieve the purposes. The necessary form ensures not only the potential actualization of law's—and the legal rules'—purposes via means of a legal methodology, but as well guides jurisprudence to be a science in an interdisciplinary discourse not only with other sciences but as well with the theory of science.

1. The different subject matters of law[104] and their respective discourses ask for reasons to be given, as to which reasons might enter the discourse and which cannot. For some, such as procedural law, the law itself can pre-decide, whether they are relevant.[105] For others, an interdisciplinary dialogue, including the theory of science and hermeneutics, need to be employed.[106]
2. For jurisprudence to be a science scientific methods are necessary.[107] These methods cannot be found merely within jurisprudence, but need to be tested against different sciences as well as the theory of science. For this, reasons need to be given. Regarding the relevant subject matter, different reasons are given.[108] They need to be adjusted regarding the method and purpose/goals assigned to the science.[109] It was not discussed when a given reason will be sufficient.
3. The reasons given over time and history can show the development of law and jurisprudence.[110] It may thus give reasons. But the reasons given are only those of time and an is. They cannot be that of an ought but are those of an is and the praxis.[111] What can be seen as assessing an is, that auxiliary means, such as economic an political sciences are taken into account.[112]
4. Leading peaceful lives in a bigger society via law (peace under the law, *Rechtsfrieden*) is the purpose of law and justice.[113] It is to be achieved by an *equal application of the law*.[114] Such an equal application can only be achieved via transparency and accountability (*Transparenz* and *Nachvollziehbarkeit*), regarding the method.[115] These need not only subsumption and the rules of

[104] See Sect. 2.1.3, pp. 50, Sect. 2.1.2, pp. 44 et seq. and Sect. 2.1.1, pp. 41 et seq.

[105] See Sect. 2.1.2.3, p. 48.

[106] See the Sect. 2.1.1.2, "The Standards of Administrative Legislation", pp. 42 et seq.

[107] See Sect. 2.2.2, pp. 55 et seq.

[108] See Sect. 2.2.3, p. 56.

[109] See Sect. 2.2.3, p. 56.

[110] See Sect. 2.3, pp. 57 et seq.

[111] See Sect. 2.3.1.2, p. 58.

[112] See the Sect. 2.1.1.2 "The Legislative Procedure", pp. 41 et seq.

[113] See Sect. 2.4.2, p. 62.

[114] See Sect. 2.4.2, p. 62.

[115] See Sect. 2.4.2, p. 62.

logic but as well methods regarding interpretation and argumentation, ensuring transparency and accountability.
5. The methodology can push the inherent subjectivity of any act of recognition of fact or law to ever smaller spaces.[116] However, they can never eliminate them.

References

Adrian A (2014) Grundzüge einer allgemeinen Wissenschaftstheorie auch für Juristen, Konsequenzen aus Zweifeln postmoderner/zeitgenössischer Philosophie für eine allgemeine Wissenschaftstheorie sowie für jede juristische Methodenlehre, Berlin
Alexy R (2003) On balancing and subsumption, a structural comparison. Ratio Juris, pp 433–449
Aristoteles (2002) Rhetorik, translated by Christof Rapp.
Baldwin R, Cave M, Lodge L (2010) Chapter 25, Conclusion. In: Baldwin R, Cave M, Lodge M (eds) The Oxford handbook of regulation. Oxford, pp 613–625
Baldwin R, Cave M, Lodge M (2012) Understanding regulation: theory, strategy, and practice, Oxford
Barnes J (1995) Posterior analytics. In: Barnes J (ed) The complete works of Aristotle, the revised Oxford translation, vol 1. Princeton
Beaucamp G, Treder L (2019) Methoden und Technik der Rechtsanwendung. Heidelberg
Betti E (1972) Die Hermeneutik als allgemeine Methodik der Geisteswissenschaften. Tübingen
Bottke (1993) Juristische und biblische Hermeneutik. In: Die personale Struktur des gesellschaftlichen Lebens. Berlin, pp 469–488
Brown JR (2001) Who rules in science. Cambridge
Bydlinski F (1991) Juristische Methodenlehre und Rechtsbegriff. Wien
Carrier M (2017) Wissenschaftstheorie zur Einführung. Hamburg
Crifò G (2000) Emilio Betti und die juristische Hermeneutik. In: Johan H, Adriaanse HJ, Enskat R (eds) Fremdheit und Vertrautheit: Hermeneutik im europäischen Kontext. Leuben, pp 365–378
Dannecker G (1993) Das intertemporale Strafrecht. Tübingen
Dannhauser JC (1652) Idea boni interpretis et malitiosi calumniatoris. Strasbourg
Dörpinghaus A (2002) Logik der Rhetorik, Grundriss einer Theorie der argumentativen Verständigung in der Pädagogik. Würzburg
Engisch K (1963) Logische Studien zur Gesetzesanwendung. Heidelberg
Esser W (1972) Vorverständnis und Methodenwahl in der Rechtsfindung. Frankfurt/Main
European Commission (2017) Staff working document, better regulation guidelines, Brussels, 7 July 2017 SWD (2017) 350, Brussels
Fikentscher W (1975–1977) Methoden des Rechts, vol 4. Tübingen
Fuhrmann M, Jauß HR, Pannenberg W (1981) Vorwort. In: Fuhrmann M, Jauss HR, Pannenberg W (eds) Text und Applikation, Theologie, Jurisprudenz un Literaturwissenschaften im hermeneutischen Gespräch. Munich, pp 9–12
Gabriel G (2019) Präzision und Prägnanz, Logische, rhetorische, ästhetische und literarische Erkenntnisformen. Paderborn
Gadamer H-G (1990) Gesammelte Werke, vol 1, Hermeneutik I, Wahrheit und Methode. Grundzüge einer philosophischen Hermeneutik, Tübingen
Gast W (2015) Juristische Rhetorik. Heidelberg
Gohlke P (1975) In: Gohlke P (ed) Aristoteles Physikalische Vorlesung, die Lehrschriften. Paderborn
Gröschner R (2013) Dialogik des Rechts, Grundlagenarbeiten 1992–2012. Tübingen

[116] See Sect. 2.3.3, pp. 59 et seq.

Heckmann D (1997) Geltungskraft und Geltungsverlust von Rechtsnormen. Tübingen
Herzog R (1981) Vergleichende Bemerkungen zur theologischen und jurisitschen Applikation (am Beispiel zweier Auslegungen von 2. Sam. 11). In: Fuhrmann M, Jauss HR, Pannenberg W (eds) Text und Applikation, Theologie, Jurisprudenz un Literaturwissenschaften im hermeneutischen Gespräch. Munich, pp 367–394
Höffe O (2014) Aristoteles. Munich
Jandach T (1993) Juristische Expertensysteme, Methodische Grundlagen ihrer Entwicklung. Berlin
Jauernig O, Hess B (2011) Zivilprozessrecht. München
Kaffenberger K (2017) Das intendierte Verwaltungsermessen. München
Kant I (1786) Metaphysische Anfangsgründe der Naturwissenschaft. Riga
Katz A, Sander GG (2019) Staatsrecht, Grundlagen, Staatsorganisation, Grundrechte. Heidelberg
Kelsen H (1960) Reine Rechtslehre. Wien
Kitcher P (2001) Science, truth, democracy. Oxford
Kitcher P (2004) On the autonomy of the sciences. Philosophy Today 28, pp 51–57
Klappstein V (2009) Die Rechtsprechungsänderung mit Wirkung für die Zukunft, eine rechtsmethodische und rechtsvergleichende Untersuchung im Zivilrecht. Berlin
Klappstein V (2016) How much of Aristotle's Four Causes can be Found in the German Legal Method to Interpret Laws? ARSP, 405–444
Klappstein V (2017) Warum ist Aristoteles Vierursachenlehre das wissenschaftstheoretische Fundament juristischer Auslegung und warum eignet sie sich als Matrix für eine Generalhermeneutik? In: Klappstein V, Heiß T (eds) als bis wir sein Warum erfasst haben, Die Vierursachenlehre des Aristoteles in Rechtswissenschaft, Philosophie und Theologie. Stuttgart, pp 87–117
Klappstein V (2018) The concept of purpose in Kant's metaphysical elements of justice. In: Klappstein V, Dybowski M (eds) Ratio Legis, philosophical and theoretical perspectives. Cham, pp 77–117
Kloepfer M, Bröcker T (2001) Das Gebot der widerspruchsfreien Normgebung als Schranke der Ausübung einer Steuergesetzgebungskompetenz 1 nach Art. 105 GG. DÖV, 1–12
Koch J, Rüßmann H (1982) Juristische Begründungslehre. München
Kramer EA (2019) Juristische Methodenlehre. München
Krebs P, Becker M (2014) Entstehung und Abänderbarkeit von Gewohnheitsrecht. JuS, 98–101
Kriele M (1981) Besonderheiten juristischer Hermeneutik. In: Fuhrmann M, Jauss HR, Pannenberg W (eds) Text und Applikation, Theologie, Jurisprudenz un Literaturwissenschaften im hermeneutischen Gespräch. Munich, pp 409–412
Kuchinke K (1964) Grenzen der Nachprüfbarkeit tatrichterlicher Würdigung und Feststellungen in der Revisionsinstanz, Ein Beitrag zum Problem von Tat- und Rechtsfrage. Bielefeld
Langenbucher K (1996) Die Entwicklung und Auslegung von Richterrecht, Eine methodologische Untersuchung zur richterlichen Rechtsfortbildung im deutschen Zivilrecht. München
Larenz K (1991) Methodenlehre der Rechtswissenschaft. Berlin
Larenz K, Canaris C-W (1995) Methodenlehre der Rechtswissenschaft. Berlin
Larenz K, Canaris C-W (2002) Methodenlehre der Rechtswissenschaft. Berlin
Longino HE (2002) The fate of knowledge. Princeton
Luther C (2013) Die juristische Analogie. Jura, 450–452
Maunz T, Schmidt-Bleibtreu B, Klein F, Bethge H (2019) Kommentar zum Bundesverfassungsgerichtsgesetz. München
McMullin E (1983) Values in science. In: Asquith P, Nickles T (eds) Proceedings of the 1982 Bieenial Meeting of the Philosophy of Science Association, Symopsia. East Lansing, pp 3–28
Merton RK (1973) the normative structure of science. In: Merton RK (ed) The sociology of science, theoretical and empirical investigations. Chicago, pp 267–278
Möller C (1997) Die wirtschaftliche Betrachtungsweise im Privatrecht. Berlin
Müller F, Christensen R (2013) Juristische Methodik, vol 1, Grundlegung für die Arbeitsmethoden der Rechtspraxis. Berlin
Muthorst O (2019) Grundlagen der Rechtswissenschaft. München

Neupert M (2011) Rechtmäßigkeit und Zweckmäßigkeit, das Rahmen-Bild-Modell der verwaltungsgerichtlichen Kontrolldichte bei der Eingriffsverwaltung. Tübingen
Nierhauve C (2016) Rechtsklugheit – Beitrag zu einer Rhetorischen Rechtstheorie. Frankfurt/Main
Okasha S (2016) Philosophy of science, a very short introduction. Oxford
Rapp C (2002a) Rhetorik. Berlin
Rapp C (2002b) Rhetorik, übersetzt und erläutert von Christoph Rapp. Berlin
Rapp C (2012) Aristoteles zur Einführung. Hamburg
Riehm T (2006) Abwägungsentscheidungen in der praktischen Rechtsanwendung, Argumentation – Beweis – Wertung, München
Rödig J (1973) Theorie des gerichtlichen Erkenntnisverfahrens. Berlin
Rüthers B, Fischer C, Birk A (2019) Rechtstheorie, mit juristischer Methodenlehre. München
Säcker F-J (1971) Zur demokratischen Legitimation des Richter- und Gewohnheitsrechts. ZRP, 145–150
Scheuerle WA (1958/1959) Beiträge zur Trennung von Tat- und Rechtsfrage. AcP, 1–85
Schnapp FE (2016) Logik für Juristen. München
Schünemann B (1993) Zum Verhältnis von Norm und Sachverhalt bei der Rechtsanwendung, von Ober- und Untersatz im Justizsyllogismus und von Rechts- und Tatfrage im Prozessrecht. In: Festschrift für Arthur Kaufmann zum 70. Geburtstag, Heidelberg, pp 299–320
Simon D (2011) Alle Quixe sind Quaxe, Aristoteles und die juristische Argumentation. JZ, 397–703
Sodan H (1999) Das Prinzip der Widerspruchsfreiheit der Rechtsordnung. JZ, 864–873
Stein F, Jonas M, Roth H (2016) Kommentar zur Zivilprozessordnung: ZPO. Tübingen
Thiel M (1980) Interpretation, Philosophie, Jurisprudenz, Theologie. Heidelberg
van Aaken A (2008) Funktionale Rechtswissenschaftstheorie für die gesamte Rechtswissenschaft: Eine Skizze. In: Jestaedt M (ed) Rechtswissenschaftstheorie. Tübingen, pp 79–104
von Schlieffen K (2011a) DAS ENTHYMEM, Zur Rhetorik des juridischen Begründens. Interdisziplinäres Symposion zur Methode und Theorie der Rechtsrhetorik an der FernUniversität Hagen vom 29. bis 30. April 2011, Sonderheft Rechtsrhetorik, 377–619
von Schlieffen K (2011b) Wie Juristen begründen, Entwurf eines rhetorischen Argumentationsmodells für die Rechtswissenschaft. JZ, 109–116
Wendel M (2019) Verwaltungsermessen als Mehrebenenproblem, Zur Verbundstruktur administrativer Entscheidungsspielräume am Beispiel des Migrations- und Regulierungsrechts. Tübingen
Wrigley C (2002) Winston Churchill, a biographical companion. Santa Barbara
Würdinger M (2006) Die Analogiefähigkeit von Normen. AcP, 949–953
Zabel B (2017) Philosophie der Rechtswissenschaft. Hamburg, pp 167–200
Zippelius R (2012) Juristische Methodenlehre. München

Part II
Theory of Law Put in Contact with Evidence Issues and Scholarship

Why Are We Bound by Evidence? On The Normative Stance of Legal Proof

Weronika Dzięgielewska

Abstract The article aims at identifying the relationship between legal and epistemic normativity that determines the normative nature of legal evidence. For this task, the categorial tools developed on the grounds of contemporary metaethics are being applied, exposing the polysemic nature of the notion of normativity. It leads to the conclusion that legal normativity functions as metanormativity for epistemic normativity, as in the legal practice, evidence attains its epistemic significance within the course of the inferential interactions between participants of the 'legal game'. Therefore if epistemic correctness is seen as a subset of legal correctness, at least within the legal evidence-finding process, different aims of both practices could reconcile. In this account epistemic normativity participates in forming the assertibility conditions for legal practice. Legal normativity, understood in terms of the mutual accountability of commitments of the participants of legal practice, gains objectivity in relation to its aim of arriving at a resolution based on factual findings. This objectivity, due to the history of past ascriptions and commitments, is able to give rise to the propositional content of evidence and thus it exceeds formal account of evidence based on coherence to legal standards only.

The paper was prepared within the framework of a research project funded by the National Science Centre (Narodowe Centrum Nauki) (PRELUDIUM 17 2019/33/N/HS5/01418).

W. Dzięgielewska (✉)
Adam Mickiewicz University, Poznań, Poland
e-mail: weronika.dziegielewska@amu.edu.pl

V. Klappstein, M. Dybowski (eds.), *Theory of Legal Evidence - Evidence in Legal Theory*, Law and Philosophy Library 138,
https://doi.org/10.1007/978-3-030-83841-6_4

1 Defining the Legally Normative: Between Epistemic and Legal Normativity

1.1 Preliminaries

The primary concern of this paper is the concept of normativity, and, specifically, the interrelation between normativity of belief and legal normativity. The assumption is, therefore, that both epistemic normativity and legal normativity are relevant for establishing the non-arbitrary character of legal evidence. Thus, they serve an explanatory purpose as to the concept of evidence. However, there are reasons for skepticism as to the possibility of interlinking both types of normativity, mainly due to the view that legal normativity, if there is such a concept, substantially differs from its epistemic equivalent.

My hope is that a possible ground for reconciliation lies within metanormative theory that enables to set forth an interpretation of the interconnection between legal and epistemic normativity. For this aim, the methodology provided by practice theory will be adopted, since the legal practice is to be understood as a case of a more general discursive practice of exchanging reasons. In this view, normativity of the practice derives from the mutual recognition of deontic statuses between its participants. Due to the inferential relations of ascribing, demanding and expressing these statuses, the practice is capable of giving rise to the conceptual content.

In such context, the notion of evidence is to be positioned within the core of the discursive practice and described as a premise in the inferential chain of giving and asking for reasons, where its content is being established. Next, it is to be claimed that the singularity of legal evidence rests on the fact that the legal practice exceeds certain primacy over the practice of forming belief. The key moments of legal proceedings, such as admission of evidence, are interpreted as metanormative to the general discursive practice. Also, the important thread of these considerations is perceiving the legal process of evidence-finding as aimed towards establishing proof. Thus, the conclusion becomes an attempt at disputing the sources of non-voluntary status of legal evidence.

1.2 Debating Normativity

However, as a starting point, one may put the fecundity of the endeavor itself under question. Why contrast epistemic normativity with its legal analogue? The answer is mainly due to the engagement in the growing area of philosophical interest that is applying the results of metaethical reflection onto the grounds of general jurisprudence. As it is said, whence metaethics concerns foundational disputes on how ethical facts fit into reality, general jurisprudence, analogously, discusses second-order questions *about* legal thought and talk, and thus how legal facts fit into reality.[1] Consequently, this approach leads to the focus on normativity of law as an explanatory source for the non-voluntary character of law as a social practice.

Attention to the topic of legal normativity has been famously drawn with the formulation of the so-called 'Normativity Thesis' by Postema,[2] according to which, law can only be fully understood when one understands how it is that laws give members of a community, officials and law-subjects alike, reasons for acting. Thus, any adequate general theory of law must give a satisfactory account of the normative (reason-giving) character of law. What is worth emphasizing is that in this view, law is being treated as a form of practical reasoning that enables describing the legal practice in terms of reasons.

Applying this approach to furthering the explanation of the notion of evidence demands treating evidence-finding as a particular case of a more general legal practice of exchanging reasons. Evidence-finding is situated within a certain time and space during individual instances of legal proceedings that involves individual participants, with distinctive participation of the official authority conducting the process. These proceedings can be perceived as a match within the game of law, to use the famous metaphor endorsed by Marmor,[3] because they include making moves that are constitutive for the practice in general and that could be subject to the test of correctness. Describing a singular case of legal proceedings, using the above described tools, enables not only to verbalise the dynamic character of the notion of evidence but also to shed some light on one of the most common truisms about law—that law application concerns determining the legal consequences of the occurrence of actual (true) states of facts, which are examined during these proceedings. This truism is not only declaratory, as it is reflected in the texts of the continental law statutes.[4]

Examining the possible implications of such a statement—that legal consequences are being decided on the basis of factual states of affairs—calls for a theory of belief that would adequately supplement the considerations on legal practice. It is therefore essential to reflect on how these states of affairs are being asserted; basing on which evidence true beliefs are being formed.

I am interested in pursuing the consequences of a standpoint in the theory of belief that emphasizes the normative dimension of belief, in the sense of stating that what is central to a mental state being a belief is that it is subject to certain standards of correctness, and necessarily defective in a certain way if false, a view called by Nolfi[5]

---

[1] Plunkett et al. (2019), p. xi.

[2] Postema (1982), p. 165.

[3] Marmor (2006).

[4] With an example of article 7 of the Polish Code of Administrative Procedure (Journal of Laws 1960 No. 30, item 168), called the "Principle of Objective Truth", that states: 'Public administration bodies shall uphold the rule of law during proceedings and shall take all necessary steps to *clarify the facts of a case and to resolve it*, having regard to the public interest and the legitimate interests of members of the public'.

[5] Nolfi (2015).

'normativism about belief'.[6] This view has been identified as a version of epistemic constitutivism, understood as a strategy of grounding epistemic normativity. Epistemic constitutivists believe that epistemic norms necessarily entail good reasons to conform to these norms—in virtue of the fact that belief constitutively aims at truth.[7]

Normativism about belief could be associated with a view that a belief has a 'direction of fit', in the sense that beliefs ought to fit with, or get right, the states of affairs they describe or represent.[8] These standards of correctness, legitimizing talk about epistemic normativity, are usually perceived as epistemic norms, such as norms of epistemic rationality. I follow Kelly[9] here in claiming that, roughly, one displays this kind of rationality when one conforms to the norm of believing propositions that are strongly supported by one's evidence and refraining from believing propositions that are improbable given one's evidence.[10]

For the current task, I find a version of this standpoint endorsed in Wedgewood[11] especially supportive for explaining legal practice in terms of reasons, as it situates the normativity of belief within a social practice that determines the correctness of this belief. Stating that a belief is correct if and only if the proposition believed is true discerns correctness of this belief as expressing a normative concept, constitutive for the practice of forming belief. Normativity of this concept derives from the fact that it constitutively plays a regulative role in certain practices, such as practice of reasoning that is central for the formation of a belief. A belief counts as correct in this sense when it satisfies the fundamental epistemic norm—the principle that a belief is correct if and only if the proposition believed is true. For the practice of practical reasoning, choices and intentions are correct when complying with the universal practical norms—principles specifying when choices satisfy the concepts that are normative for the practice of practical reasoning.[12]

---

[6] I am aware of the fact that normativism about belief is not an uncontroversial view. For critical examination see Glüer and Wikforss (2018). However, for the purposes of this paper, I decide not to advocate this view, but consider consequences of adopting normativists outlook on belief for the relationship between normativity of law (which is controversial itself, of course) and the normativity of belief, assuming there is one.

[7] Côté-Bouchard (2016), p. 3183. I am aware of the debatable character of epistemic normativity, especially followed by a strategy of epistemic constitutivism. I decide to make it a point of departure for a discussion on the topic of the interrelation of both types of normativity, with the assumption that there are such. For a discussion of epistemic constitutivism see Côté-Bouchard (2016), for strategies of grounding epistemic normativity see Grimm (2009). However, as Côté-Bouchard claims, his criticism of epistemic constitutivism leaves open the possibility of deriving the content of epistemic norms from the constitutive aim of belief. I consider the topic of how the content of these norms are being determined as central for the present task.

[8] E.g. Searle (1983).

[9] Kelly (2003), p. 612.

[10] I think it is not necessarily the case that the argument that is about to follow has to rest on the assumption that normativity of epistemic reason derives from epistemic rationality. An instrumentalist view on epistemic normativity is also possibly understood as being guided by norms of instrumental rationality, such as taking the means to one's (epistemic) ends, although I don't want to develop it here; for a discussion see Kelly (2003, 2007).

[11] Wedgewood (2002).

[12] Wedgewood (2002), pp. 268, 272.

Extending this approach, making moves in a practice is not voluntary in the sense that if one engages in the practice and recognizes that certain concepts are normative within this practice, it could be deemed irrational to make a judgment about the content of this concept—so as commit oneself to the content of this concept—and yet to make a move that is contrary to this previous commitment.[13] Therefore, one has a decisive reason against making a certain move if one judges another move as normative due to her previous commitments (at least if one judges between moves and there is an alternative move that one judges to be normative). 'Having a normative reason' means that if an agent judges move x to be a normative concept, she 'ought not' make a move that is not x. The process of making belief thus becomes a case of a process of reasoning that includes forming and abandoning beliefs that become moves within this practice.[14]

Such understood epistemic normativity, deriving from a certain norm of correctness—that a move in the practice, such as forming a false belief, is incorrect when false and thus subject to criticism—complements an approach to legal normativity rooted both in the accountability of the commitments of the participants in the legal practice and in the exchange of reasons taking place accordingly—a view that is to be discussed later. What is more, it legitimates introducing evidence as a normative concept. It is thus essential to observe that evidence could be perceived as a reason to believe. As Kelly claims: "Indeed, one might think that 'reason for belief' and 'evidence' are more or less synonymous, distinguished chiefly by the fact that the former functions as a count noun while the latter functions as a mass term".[15] Evidence can therefore be perceived not only as a normative concept, but also one gaining its content in the course of the discursive practice of exchanging reasons. Therefore, it may be fruitful for determining how facts in legal practice are being established in a way that does not reduce the process of 'legal cognition' to rule-following only.

Therefore, if assuming that both the process of evidence-finding and the legal practice have a non-voluntary character, in the sense of involving relevant reasons, it may seem vital to discuss the relationship between these obligations. I propose to analyze this interconnection in terms of normativity and try, as stated at the beginning, to discuss interconnection between both epistemic (of belief) and legal normativity.

---

[13] "Suppose that a certain concept 'F' is normative for a certain practice. Then it is a constitutive feature of the concept 'F' that if one engages in this practice, and makes judgments about which moves within the practice are F and which are not, one is thereby committed to regulating one's moves within the practice by those judgments" (after Wedgewood 2002, p. 268).

[14] Wedgewood (2002), p. 269.

[15] Kelly (2007), p. 468 (in the footnote).

1.3 *Different Purport and Different Aim Theses*

In a recent debate on normativity, there are two claims I find especially challenging for the view of the interconnection between epistemic and legal normativity—one of them is associated with discerning between robust and formal sense of normativity, the other with separating aims of the process of forming belief and the legal practice. I think of these challenges as the Different Purport and Different Aim Theses, respectively.

Following the Different Purport Thesis, legal normativity is ubiquitous and has essentially weaker—that is formal—sense, in contrast to the full-blooded, robust normativity of epistemic normativity. The weakness of legal normativity lays within ensuring coherence with certain standards of correctness which means that, if at all, it can import only institutional reasons. In this view, legal norms are seen as standards that can only be used to assess whether something (e.g. an action) accords with it.[16] Robust morality, on the other hand, necessarily possesses the ability to provide autonomous reasons, not relative to any external standards. Terminology of robust and formal normativity is usually traced back to McPherson,[17] although the idea of the distinction itself is already relatively grounded. Other philosophers tend to label formal normativity 'pseudo', 'instrumental',[18] and 'generic',[19] while robust normativity has been labeled 'genuine',[20] 'true'[21] and 'authoritative'.[22] Noticeable characteristic is given by Parfit[23] who considers formal normativity as 'rule implying' in contrast to 'reason-implying' robust normativity. Robust normativity demands a positive answer to the so-called normative question posed by Korsgaard[24] of whether there are good or genuinely normative reasons to conform to certain standards. Therefore, the problem posed by the Different Purport Thesis is that epistemic normativity and legal normativity are normative in fully incommensurable senses (and thus having different purport).

According to the Different Aim Thesis, the aim of legal practice and forming belief have distinct constitutive aims and hence distinct success conditions.[25] There is a widespread claim that beliefs aim at the truth, endorsed, as it was already said, by epistemic constitutivists.[26] Côté-Bouchard[27] discerns three versions of the strategy

[16] Plunkett and Shapiro (2017).
[17] McPherson (2011).
[18] Joyce (2011).
[19] Copp (2007).
[20] Joyce (2011).
[21] Broome (2013).
[22] Copp (2007); after Finlay (2019), p. 205.
[23] Parfit (2011).
[24] Korsgaard (1996), pp. 7–48.
[25] Lindeman (2019), p. 88.
[26] For literature, see Côté-Bouchard (2016).
[27] Côté-Bouchard (2016).

of epistemic constitutivism, namely its functional, personal and normativist interpretation. According to functionalists, being true is a constitutive function or purpose of a belief.[28] For personalists, aiming at truth is as an aim that agents themselves necessarily possess. As indicated earlier, I decide to follow here the normativist path set forth in Wedgewood (2002) in claiming that this is to be interpreted as a normative claim, that a belief is correct if and only if the proposition believed is true, as it echoes corresponding theses about the constitutive character of legal norms for legal practice as such. However, in this light, the Different Aim Thesis becomes a consequence of the Different Purport Thesis, as it identifies necessary, and thus 'genuine', aim of belief.

For the aim of law, although debatable in itself, the obvious candidate would be probably, at least, variously understood coordination of people's social behavior. However, some ascribe to law a distinctive moral aim. According to the Moral Aim Thesis endorsed by Shapiro, it is an essential feature of law that it has a moral aim. For Shapiro, it means that what is constitutive for law as a social phenomenon is its aim of providing morally good solutions of solving moral disputes of a community when other methods of coordinating agents fail in this respect.[29] A modification of this thesis was proposed by Plunkett[30] in the form of the Represented-as-Moral Thesis that is supposed to better comply with the requirements of legal positivism.

Therefore, whatever the aim of law might be, the aims of both practices, as Different Aim Thesis advocates would want, are constituted by separate direct that make their standards for correctness irreconcilable.

The solution for the difficulties posed by the Different Purport and Different Aim Theses that I try to examine will come in two steps. First, after Lindeman,[31] I assume that although what distinguishes normative domain is a matter of controversy, a domain is normative when it can be understood in terms of reasons, and even though legal reasons may not prove autonomous, normativity of law has distinctly stronger features than mere formal one. Second, different aims of the practices can be reconciled at least within the course of a separate 'legal game' that would be an individually understood case of legal proceedings. In this perspective, the aim of a 'legal game' rests on issuing an individual a concrete legal norm and, at the same time, both settling the dispute and finalizing the process of belief-making.

---

[28] E.g. Velleman (2000).

[29] Shapiro (2011), p. 213.

[30] Plunkett (2013), p. 568.

[31] Lindeman (2019), p. 88.

2 Need for Reconciliation: Legal Normativity Revisited

As previously indicated, formalist accounts of legal normativity tend to reduce its normative force only to ensure norm coherence, irrespective of the content of these norms. Therefore, even if a formalist grants law reason-giving character,[32] the only reasons law may provide an agent with would be reasons in a norm-relative sense, as entailed by legal norms and relative to these norms. Côté-Bouchard[33] defines these norm-relative reasons as 'the considerations that favour φ-ing according to or from the point of view of these norms'.

An alternative account for perceiving legal normativity that I consider appealing is the one provided by analytical neopragmatism. In this context, legal normativity would be seen, following Joseph Rouse, as a structure aroused on more extensive, mutually supportive normative patterns. The temporally extended character of the discursive practices that articulate conceptual understanding is based there on the prospective, constitutive performances undertaken by the participants of the practice.[34] This perspective is aided by Robert Brandom, who elucidates what it means for a discursive performance to be constitutively normative. For language in the proper sense, according to Brandom, has the core of its practices—it is a basic ability necessary for action to be considered as saying something. This ability is to make a claim—assertion—that has a propositional content. The ability to assert has, in this respect, a pragmatic dimension, as a minimal action which, together with inference, determines the rationality of the discursive practice. This is because, as Brandom says, assertions can serve as premises and conclusions in inferences, and language games must include the practice of giving and demanding reasons. The normativity of the movements of the game—assertions—rests therefore on their implicitly normative character as based on the practices of giving and demanding reasons.[35] Making assertion is an expression of *commitment* to the content of this assertion, and it *entitles* others to verify its premises.

Normative practices described from this commitment-oriented perspective establish an intentional semantic relationship between the subject and the world, manifesting the expressive role played by the normative vocabulary related to both giving and demanding reasons. It should be emphasized that this role is revealed in the world's reaction to using concepts by the subject—the representational and objective dimension of intentionality is manifested in this approach by assigning to subjects doxastic commitments concerning objects. By interacting with other language users who can claim reasons for using a particular concept (as a reason

---

[32] Depending on the concept of reasons that is being adopted. Some grant reason-giving character only to robust normativity, as Parfit (2011) who discerns between reason-giving and rule-implying normativity. Côté-Bouchard (2016) suggests a descriptive reading of 'reasons' that are norm-relative.

[33] Côté-Bouchard (2016), p. 3183.

[34] Rouse (2016).

[35] Brandom (2008).

for undertaking a specific action), it is possible to verify the material obligations of the entity related to the content of concepts.[36]

For Brandom, the most basic form of intentional activity is the practice consisting of an open-ended sequence—a Test-Operate-Test-Exit (TOTE) 'cycle of perception, performance, assessment of the results of the performance, and further performance'.[37] These feedback-governed performances are 'thick' practices in the sense of essentially involving objects, events, and worldly states of affairs. Interestingly, as Brandom says, '*bits of the world* are incorporated in such practices, in the exercise of such abilities'.[38]

To illustrate the socially determined objectivity of conceptual content Brandom introduces an analogy deriving from common-law systems of law application and determination of legal concepts. Accordingly, when resolving each case, the judge adopts a practical attitude of 'recognising the authority exercised by the commitments of previous judges whose decisions have provided precedents for the application of the same legal concept'. Furthermore, the judge also exercises authority over the content of the legal concepts being applied and thereby over future judges.[39] Therefore Brandom underlines the normative stance of the social verification of the conceptual content. Therefore, in this account, reasons do not only derive from coherence with certain standards but rather from the verification of the content of the normative attitudes expressed by the participants of the discursive practice. As Lewis observes, in this view the norms implicit in the practice 'are not only made up of those we acknowledge but also ones that are attributed to us by others ' in an 'inferential context of responsibility and authority, recognition and acknowledgment'.[40] Moreover, this practice is not purely conventional as it concerns wordly states of affairs.

Transferring account of analytical pragmatism to the grounds of legal practice was proposed by Canale and Tuzet[41] and Dybowski,[42] for several good reasons. Primarily, in the pragmatist narrative endorsed by Brandom, the classical project of analysis based on the translatory relation between base and target vocabularies can be applied to the studies revealing empirical and analytical commitment, such as general jurisprudence. Secondly, pragmatist account of normativity of the social practice directs attention to the human being as a subject of discursive practices and abilities forming a certain anthropology rooted in rationality and intentionality.[43]

Pragmatist position enables to consider legal norm as a license for substantive reasoning, one that is significant in inferential exchange of reasons derived from the

[36] Dybowski (2017), p. 25.

[37] Brandom (2008), p. 177.

[38] Brandom (2008), p. 178.

[39] Lewis (2018), p. 9.

[40] Lewis (2018), p. 9.

[41] E.g. Canale and Tuzet (2007), pp. 32–44.

[42] E.g. Dybowski (2017, 2018).

[43] Dybowski (2017), p. 32.

statuses adopted by the participants of the legal practice.[44] The addressee is obliged to give reasons for deviating from the standard, as well as for complying with it, but also for the content of this standard. Reason-giving character is stronger because it is based on interactions that are additionally institutionally mediated.

An observation traced back to Lewis is that Brandomian perspective may serve as a 'meta' level for other systems of social validity. Although Lewis claims only that Brandomian perspective cannot do without first-level assumptions on the character of ethical relations grounding social recognition, I propose to perceive legal practice as a special case of a general discursive practice, including substantive reasoning that may serve as verification of the first order; epistemic reasons.

Therefore legal normativity, understood in pragmatist terms, would rest on the fact that actions of its participants are not solitary, and thus normative, respective to their content. That is because they become subject to verification by the other participants who are entitled to demand justification (reasons) for their conduct. What is interesting, perceiving law as a discursive practice directs attention to the content of legal norms that is being verified in the process of law application.

3 Metanormativity and the Law

To develop the argument on the interconnection between epistemic normativity and such pragmatically-understood legal normativity, I turn, as promised at the beginning, to the metanormative account developed on the grounds of metaethics by Finlay.[45]

Before I expand this view, I'd like to take a step back to comment on the fruitfulness of the metaethical domain for legal philosophy, especially in relation to Enoch, who expressed the view that general jurisprudence is just not interesting as an area of metanormative philosophical enquiry, as law does not provide, unlike ethics or epistemology, *genuine* reasons for action.[46] Overcoming this statement is therefore connected to challenging the Different Purport Thesis. However, Enoch excluded, metanormative enquiry is usually seen as an especially promising ground for general jurisprudence, which is seen as parallel to another well-known part of that project, namely, metaethics. As Shapiro and Plunkett claim, 'metalegal inquiry aims to explain how legal thought and talk fit into reality'.[47]

Metanormative inquiry may therefore serve an explanatory purpose for legal practice, and I follow this line here. However, I decide to leave aside the question whether this goal, in itself, suffices to ground metalegal considerations as

---

[44] Dybowski (2017).

[45] Finlay (2019).

[46] See: Enoch (2019).

[47] Plunkett and Shapiro (2017), p. xi.

philosophically interesting (but, challenging Different Purport Thesis may turn out otherwise).

Therefore, following Finlay and using his metaethical considerations on the meaning of normativity, I would like to distinguish two senses of normativity. The distinction is cognitivist in nature, and for the sake of the argument, I assume that there is a property of normativity, and that law possess it (although distinguishing these senses does not necessarily involve a claim that such property *exists*). The distinction is grounded in the observation of the *polysemic* nature of the notion of normativity, which means that among philosophers there is a tendency to use the notion in closely related, yet diverging senses. It may prove explanatory as to the theme relation between epistemic and legal normativity.

The first sense of normativity therefore being:

- $\text{normative}_{\text{ont}}$: (As of facts and properties); Having a property P of some special kind.

And the second:

- $\text{normative}_{\text{rep}}$: (As of expressions and judgments); Being about something $\text{normative}_{\text{ont}}$.

To illustrate how these two senses are used, Finlay gives examples of the adjectives 'esthetic' and 'mythological'—mythological_1 language (=language about mythology) need not itself be mythological_2 (=existing only in cultural imagination).[48]

What I am inferring from polysemic assumption on normativity is that the interrelation between epistemic and legal normativity may rest on their functioning in the above mentioned, dissimilar senses. For, as it was already implicitly suggested, epistemic normativity *genuinely* concerns facts and properties. It is thus normative in a sense that it is subject to certain norms of correctness. As Wedgewood suggests, on this view, a 'belief' is not just a proposition that is believed, it is a particular mental state, which could be subject to criticism if not satisfying epistemic norm that ascribes correctness to the true propositions only. It was said that the belief is incorrect, and as such criticisable, if it fails to aim at the truth.

In legal fact-finding, expressing assertions that consider assessments as to the state of affairs by participants of the practice—the fact-finders—would be therefore $\text{normative}_{\text{rep}}$ and thus *about* what is $\text{normative}_{\text{ont..}}$ Importantly, the conclusion that $\text{normative}_{\text{rep}}$ propositions are merely descriptive, would be too quick. I endorse the view that $\text{normative}_{\text{rep}}$ statements are subject to practical normativity of legal practice that verifies correctness of forming certain beliefs. Normativity of law would thus function as metanormativity for epistemic findings, at least within the process of legal fact-finding.

[48] Finlay (2019), p. 192.

4 Between Legal Evidence and Proof

4.1 (Legal) Objectivity of Evidence

The final point demands further discussion of the interrelation between epistemic and legal normativity, referred to the process of legal evidence-finding. The attempt in question resembles Haack's statement that 'Every legal system needs, somehow, to determine the truth of factual questions'.[49] However, it should be noted that the notion of evidence itself can be used in close, yet diverging senses, and it may be misconceived, as it is usually claimed that it has different meaning on the grounds of epistemology and law. As Haack writes, one primary meaning of legal evidence is that it is an 'object of sensory evidence that is presented before the court',[50] a meaning that is alien to solely epistemic disputes. Therefore, in relation to the previous comments to both types of normativity, for the next step I adopt the meaning of evidence in terms of a claim—assertion—as to the fact or as to the evidence in this basic sensory sense. In this sense, evidence acquires its status as evidence when it enters the course of inferential normative relations of the participants of the discursive practice and may be of use both for epistemology and the law.

Consequently, the concept of evidence possesses pragmatistically understood objectivity as to the aim of the legal proceedings, that is issuing an individual and concrete legal norm basing on certain factual findings. It is worth observing that 'a game' of individual legal proceedings becomes a case of a more general discursive practice, where subjects of different statuses participate, presenting the official authority—the legal fact finder—with evidence. Such understood evidence becomes an epistemic reason for acquiring a certain standpoint by the fact-finder in the course of establishing facts. Then what may serve as good, worthy or sufficient evidence, in relation to the aim of the proceedings, is determined by the legal fact-finder who decides the admission of evidence and grants it its worth. Importantly, the legal fact-finder may simultaneously verify the content of epistemic norms. However, her assessment may be criticized by the other participants of the legal game and also by other (future) judges (to use Brandom's common-law analogue). Therefore, legal claims on $\text{normative}_{\text{ont}}$ facts (so as evidence), subject to epistemic norms of correctness, are solitarily $\text{normative}_{\text{rep}}$, but they gain their own normativity in the process of the exchange of reasons by the participants of legal practice, who may question their correctness and give reasons for contrasting assessments. In this view, the crucial point of establishing normative status of evidence, however, would be determining what, in the proposed terms, establishing proof means.

---

[49] Haack (2004).

[50] Haack (2004), p. 48.

4.2 Establishing Proof

Ascribing significance to evidence within the course of the proceedings becomes definite when the legal fact-finder assesses its weight and sufficiency. It takes the form of asserting as to what facts, basing on which evidence, the fact-finder considered proven, and thus establishing proof. In this act of categorical statement as to the weight and quality of evidence, the authority simultaneously determines which evidence has significance for this individual case of legal practice. Therefore, the legal fact-finder both specifies the content of 'legal evidence', committing herself to its assessed meaning, but also determines the content (in a sense of concretization) of the relevant epistemic norms. A worth-considering example of such norms is provided by Kelly: one is epistemically rational when one believes propositions that are strongly supported by one's evidence and refrains from believing propositions that are improbable, given one's evidence.[51] It has to be observed that it is not yet clear what, in this context, probability means; as whether some evidence can overrule against support provided by the other or what weight is to be ascribed to each set of evidence. This remark is connected to the reflection on the gradational character of evidence in Haack (2004), who 'construes the quality of evidence (and hence of epistemic justification), not as categorical, but as a matter of degree: evidence with respect to a claim may be stronger, or weaker; a person may be more, or less, justified in believing something'.[52]

It is therefore essential for the participants of the practice to commit themselves to reasons for adopting certain standpoints as to the factual state of affairs. The judge has institutional power to settle the dispute, as the agent leading the process of evidence-finding. Thus, the process of legal fact-finding can also be seen as the process that concretizes, as normativists would want, the fundamental epistemic norm—the norm of correctness that requires that every belief aim at the truth.

For that reason, within the grounds of pragmatist interpretation of the legal evidence-finding practice, I assume that establishing proof comes in the form of an assertion as to the evidence and that it is *about* $\text{normative}_{\text{ont}}$, epistemological facts and properties, and so this assertion is itself $\text{normative}_{\text{rep}}$. The content of this assertion concerns the fact that could be asserted as true on the basis of the gathered evidence. However, the assertion being made, it enters the game of exchanging reasons, which the legal practice consists of. Therefore, legal practice becomes practically metanormative as to the epistemic normativity of belief because the correctness of epistemic assessment is verified legally, and as such institutionally. The meaning of evidence actualizes during legal proceedings understood as a norm-driven practice of the exchange of reasons of its participants, which is guided by the reasoning performed by a legal fact-finder (the official authority). It illustrates the thesis that the practice becomes normative in relation to the accountability of assertions undertaken by the participants because it enables ascribing commitments,

[51] Kelly (2003), p. 612.

[52] Haack (2004), p. 13.

not only to the legal fact-finder, but also to the parties of the case. However, if not viable, the participants' assertions may become subject to criticism.

This proposition could be seen as a variation of an idea traced back to Dummett, that is of the relationship between truth and language, namely that truth is the aim of the assertion.[53] This account considers assertion as a constitutive practice, which makes any assertion that fails to be true, *ipso facto,* liable to criticism. There are of course certain reservations as to the fact that this criticism proneness is determined by the legal rules also, and the possibility of verifying legal assertions institutionally (when subject to judicial review).

Clearly, the above standpoint requires certain presuppositions, with the obvious example of the assumption that official authorities are actually interested in resolving the case basing on actual facts. In similar context, Haack (2004) recalls a reservation made by Rorty[54]; that if standards of epistemic correctness were solely conventional—not universal and not truth indicative—law application would become deprived of any resemblance to justice. In this light, a question of whether Brandomian account of normativity reduces discursive practices to the conventional phenomenon only seems well justified. Roughly, it is worth noting that Brandom, although not entirely clear on this subject, introduces an idea of *incorporating* to the practices bits of the world, which this statement prevents from seeing it as a purely formal account. The factual state of affairs is but actually vital for verifying the content of the commitments. Moreover, within modern evidentiary procedures, findings as to the facts are not contrary to what evidence suggests, hence they are based on the assumption that the more evidentiarily justified the claim, the likelier it is to be true. Therefore, law that aims at true findings does not contradict epistemic norms, even if it functions as a metalevel for verifying the quality of epistemic reasons. The perspective of meta-character of epistemological consideration within legal practice are somehow reflected in what Haack says when she says she understands legal epistemology as '*epistemological work relevant to issues that arise in the law*'.[55]

5 Conclusions

Summing up the above concerns, four conclusions are set forth—the first concerns the normative nature of legal evidence, the second concerns the Different Aim Thesis and the third—a cautious, yet possible answer to the Different Purport Thesis. The last conclusion is a remark on the relationship between theoretical and practical reasoning.

[53] Dummett (1959).

[54] Rorty (1979).

[55] Haack (2004), p. 8.

Firstly, I claimed that legal evidence is *about* normative$_{ont}$ facts and its normative character is being determined in the course of the exchange of reasons taking place during legal proceedings that also specifies its propositional content. Statements concerning evidence are therefore of normative$_{rep}$ character and are subject to pragmatistically understood normativity within the normative practice of the exchange of reasons. Legal normativity functions as metanormativity for epistemic normativity, as in the legal practice, evidence attains its epistemic significance within the course of the inferential interactions between participants of the 'legal game'.

Secondly, challenging the Different Aim Thesis requires assuming, following Haack, that law is concerned with materially correct verdicts that are based on factual findings.[56] Therefore, if epistemic correctness is seen as a subset of legal correctness, at least within the legal evidence-finding process, different aims of both practices could reconcile. Of course, this conclusion would not follow without any substantive assumption about the law in question. It is only legitimized within a legal system that is actually concerned with arriving at legal consequences on the basis of factual findings. However, it does not undermine the thesis that the normativity of legal practice exceeds verifying coherence with certain standards. The legal practice diverges from other formal norms of fashion or etiquette because its organization is institutional and the consequences of the epistemic assessments are actually practically enforced.

Thirdly, the Different Purport Thesis—the assumed full-blooded normativity of epistemic normativity—in this account, participates in forming the assertibility conditions for legal practice. Hence, legal practice forms stronger reasons than just based on rule-coherence, at least within the process of legal evidence finding. Legal normativity, understood in terms of the mutual accountability of commitments of the participants of legal practice, gains objectivity in relation to its aim of arriving at a resolution based on factual findings. This objectivity, due to the history of past ascriptions and commitments, is able to give rise to the propositional content (also to the content of *evidence*) and thus it exceeds formal account of reason-giving based on coherence only.

Finally, I claimed that epistemic reasons may serve as reasons for adopting practical attitudes and that they are verified within the social interaction undertaken on the grounds of a discursive practice. I suggested that both epistemic and legal normativity is concerned with reasons that are stronger than mere formal ones. With the last conclusion I would like to address the reservation on whether, and how, it is possible to narrow the gap between theoretical and practical reasoning. For it is said that the first type of reasoning concerns revising one's belief, whilst the other consists of revising choices or intentions.[57]

The reservation itself is connected to the so-called Incommensurability Thesis, introduced by Feldman,[58] that expresses skepticism as to the question of what is

[56]Haack (2004), p. 50.

[57]Wedgewood (2002), p. 269.

[58]Feldman (2000), pp. 14–15.

epistemically rational to believe, all things considered, when what is epistemically rational to believe clearly diverges from what it is practically advantageous to believe. It is possible to discern a rational standard of belief only from one chosen perspective—theoretical or practical, never both.

I find plausible what Harman indicates in stating that only in the first instance do we consider sharp the distinction between theoretical reasoning, as concerned with what to believe, and the practical—concerned with what-to-do questions.[59] It means that theoretical reasoning, only in the first instance, becomes a process of changing belief and practical reasoning, only in the first instance as well, directs changing choices, plans and intentions. At second glance, it is easily observed that 'changing what you plan to do can affect what you believe will happen and changing your beliefs may lead you to change your plans'.[60] Harman concludes that practical reasons can be relevant in cases when further epistemological inquiry is to be concluded, as it is 'not worth further effort'.

Although Harman refrains from claiming that practical reasons can be used to choose between competing theoretical conclusions, in legal practice the gap between both types of reflection becomes nearly unintelligible, especially within the process of law application. Inquiry that is undertaken during a singular case of legal proceedings requires a specific end—issuing an individual and concrete legal norm and thus finalising the process of fact-finding. Satisfaction qua determination of legal concepts requires practical verification of theoretical reasons. Therefore, on the grounds of legal practice, it is possible to consider the value of epistemic reasons and, thus, for the legal practice to acquire a 'meta' character in relation to the epistemological investigations taking place during legal proceedings.

References

Brandom R (2008) Between saying and doing: towards an analytic pragmatism. Oxford University Press, Oxford

Broome J (2013) Rationality through reasoning. Wiley, Hoboken

Canale D, Tuzet G (2007) On legal inferentialism. Towards a pragmatics of semantic content in legal adjudication? Ratio Juris 20(1):32–44

Copp D (2007) Morality in a natural world. Cambridge University Press, Cambridge

Côté-Bouchard C (2016) Can the aim of belief ground epistemic normativity? Philos Stud 173 (12):3181–3198

Dummett M (1959) Truth. Proc Aristotelian Soc 59(1):141–162

Dybowski M (2017) Legal theory and challenges of analytical pragmatism. Archiwum Filozofii Prawa i Filozofii Społecznej - Journal of the Polish Section of IVR 2017(1)

Dybowski M (2018) Articulating Ratio Legis and practical reasoning. In: Ratio Legis - Philosophical and theoretical perspectives. Springer, Berlin

[59] Harman (2004), p. 48.

[60] Harman (2004), p. 48.

Enoch D (2019) Is general jurisprudence interesting? In: Plunkett D, Shapiro S, Toh K (eds) Dimensions of normativity. Oxford University Press, Oxford
Feldman R (2000) The ethics of belief. Philos Phenomenol Res LX:667–695
Finlay S (2019) Defining normativity. In: Plunkett D, Shapiro S, Toh K (eds) Dimensions of normativity. Oxford University Press, Oxford
Glüer K, Wikforss Å (2018) Reasons for belief and normativity. In: Star D (ed) The Oxford handbook of reasons and normativity. Oxford University Press, Oxford
Grimm SR (2009) Epistemic normativity. In: Haddock A, Millar A, Pritchard D (eds) Epistemic value. Oxford University Press, Oxford
Haack S (2004) Epistemology legalized: or, truth, justice, and the American way. Am J Jurisprud 49 (1):43–61
Harman G (2004) Practical aspects of theoretical reasoning. In: Mele AR, Rawling P (eds) The Oxford handbook of rationality. Oxford University Press, Oxford, pp 45–56
Joyce R (2011) The myth of morality. Cambridge University Press, Cambridge
Kelly T (2003) Epistemic rationality as instrumental rationality: a critique. Philos Phenomenol Res LXVI(3)
Kelly T (2007) Evidence and normativity: reply to Leite. Philos Phenomenol Res LXXV(2)
Korsgaard C (1996) The sources of normativity. Cambridge University Press, Cambridge
Lewis J (2018) Hegel and the ethics of Brandom's metaphysics. Eur J Pragmatism Am Philos X-2
Lindeman K (2019) Legal metanormativity: lessons for and from constitutivist accounts in the philosophy of law. In: Plunkett D, Shapiro S, Toh K (eds) Dimensions of normativity. Oxford University Press, Oxford
Marmor A (2006) How law is like chess. Leg Theory 12(4):347–371
McPherson T (2011) Against quietist normative realism. Philos Stud 154(2):223–240
Nolfi K (2015) How to be a normativist about the nature of belief. Pac Philos Q 96(2):181–204
Parfit D (2011) On what matters, vol 2. Oxford University Press, Oxford
Plunkett D (2013) Legal positivism and the moral aim thesis. Oxf J Leg Stud 33(3):563–605
Plunkett D, Shapiro S (2017) Law, morality and everything else: general jurisprudence as a branch of meta-normative inquiry. Ethics 127(4)
Plunkett D, Shapiro S, Toh K (2019) Introduction. In: Plunkett D, Shapiro S, Toh K (eds) Dimensions of normativity. Oxford University Press, Oxford
Polish Code of Administrative Procedure (Journal of Laws 1960 No. 30, item 168)
Postema GJ (1982) Coordination and convention at the foundations of law. J Leg Stud 11(1)
Rorty R (1979) Philosophy and the mirror of nature. Princeton University Press, Princeton
Rouse J (2016) Practice theory. In: Turner S, Risjord M (eds) Handbook of the philosophy of science, vol 15: Philosophy of anthropology and sociology. Elsevier (North Holland Publishing Co.), Amsterdam
Searle JR (1983) Intentionality. Cambridge University Press, Cambridge
Shapiro S (2011) Legality. Harvard University Press, Harvard
Velleman JD (2000) On the aim of belief. In: The possibility of practical reason. Oxford University Press, Oxford, pp 244–281
Wedgewood R (2002) The aim of belief. Philos Perspect 36(s16):267–297

A Good Enough (Meta) Theory of Evidence in Law: An Inferentialist Account

Maciej Dybowski

Abstract The chapter explores the meta-theoretical possibilities of a good theory of evidence in law in order to explain how it is possible to think of bridging the detached accounts of knowledge and of law in the field of legal evidence. Section 1 is a critical discussion of detachment between theories of legal evidence and those of law and looks into factors responsible for this detachment. Among those factors, the alleged dualism of 'facts' and 'norms' and ambiguities about judges' epistemological theories are examined, concluding that there is no strictly nonnormative realm and that a normative metalanguage could be employed to specify both what happens and what is done. Section 2 focuses on the preconditions of a good-enough legal evidence theory which both accounts for acquiring knowledge and is compatible with one's theory of law. Drawing on how foundationalism, externalism, internalism, coherentism and reliabilism bear on accounts of knowledge and law, a shift of focus with regard to epistemological theories is advanced: instead of (or alongside) thinking of epistemological accounts as accounts of knowledge, one can think of them as accounts of when it is proper to attribute knowledge. Likewise, if the gap between the detached theories is to be bridged, a perspective on law which is sensitive to the problems shared by the accounts of law and knowledge is sought and found in Robert Brandom's inferential pragmatism. This theory is particularly useful to any account that intends to make sense of both our thoughts and actions (i.e. our cognitive and practical commitments). Section 2 closes with an exposition of the inferentialist account of law. Section 3 explains how the detached accounts of knowledge and law in the field of legal evidence can be brought together, following the common inferentialist lines connecting the pragmatist models of our cognitive activities of legal discursive practices. Finally, the legal syllogism is used as a test site for putting these ideas to work and is reinterpreted as a shortcut for the social route from legal reasoning to representing legal evidence. Following inferentialist lines, Sect. 3 shows how legal syllogism holds within nine implicit moves in the legal game of giving and asking for reasons. Each of these moves is

M. Dybowski (✉)
Legal Theory and Philosophy Department, Adam Mickiewicz University, Poznań, Poland
e-mail: dybowski@amu.edu.pl

V. Klappstein, M. Dybowski (eds.), *Theory of Legal Evidence - Evidence in Legal Theory*, Law and Philosophy Library 138,
https://doi.org/10.1007/978-3-030-83841-6_5

made of commitments capable of serving both as premises and as conclusions of inferences relating it to other commitments and of related entitlements. Each of these moves is also inferentially connected with any other one and offers means for eliminating incompatibilities.

1 Evidence Theory Not Good Enough for Law

Much is at stake in theorizing about evidence theories in the domain of legal science. On the one hand, one may adopt an evidence theory which is detached—possibly to a degree—from an account of law. On the other hand, one may endorse a theory of law which—again, to a degree—has little consideration for evidence theories. What is at stake here is **whether one should be satisfied with one or another version of detached theories in the realm of evidence in law**. To be sure, the actual detachment or separation between theories comes in degrees, but the problem remains as long as a theorist of law or, respectively, a theorist of evidence, implicitly or explicitly endorses some version of irreconcilable ontological or epistemological separation.

1.1 Two Kinds of Detached Theories

Theories of legal evidence are generally distant from theories of law and, conversely, most theoretical accounts of law are disconnected from the issues of legal evidence.

The received view is that theories of legal evidence are concerned with resolving **matters of fact** by some institutional entities.[1] Other determinations, such as the content of applicable law, according to Alvin Goldman, "fall outside the scope of the theory of evidence as usually understood, mainly because they address the nature of law (. . .)".[2] Of course, to the extent that theories of evidence are theories of *legal* evidence, they cannot enjoy absolute detachment from the law. More often it is the case that they remain mute about the legal part, concerning which they hold some implicit assumptions. Instead, evidence-handling procedures and, consequently, theories of legal evidence in their core are dedicated to the search for truth, which they treat as the most plausible rationale of their enquiries.[3]

Reaching agreement as to truth being the unifying rationale of evidence theories does not resolve the detachment issue. On the contrary, it seems to contribute to an even firmer entrenchment of evidence theories in their separation from more general accounts of law and leaves them focusing on their criteria of accuracy or

---

[1]Evidenced theorists devoted to this view may disagree whether the legal evidence topic is restricted to admitting or excluding evidence at trial or extended to pretrial proceedings.

[2]Goldman (2005), p. 163.

[3]See Goldman (2005), p. 169.

truthfulness. In other words, as long as evidence-handling is expected to produce true outcomes, most discussion in detached evidence theories is concerned with establishing what it is for such outcomes to be true. The question of truth is thus delegated to specialized theories of legal evidence which, in turn, apply or modify the tenets of different epistemological theories, typically without being explicit about their principles or origins.[4] This, I think, applies both to the theories developed by evidence theorists and to theories in a less rigorous sense, such as those adopted by fact-triers.

As far as theories *sensu stricto* are concerned, the most notable example of the tendency described here would be the emergence and growth of what Richard Lempert has labelled "the new evidence scholarship".[5] The resulting evidence scholarship, which was initiated in the common-law legal culture and has spread throughout the world,[6] largely focuses on analyzing a legal proof process in the light of mathematics (especially probability and statistics) and psychology. Among the issues researched by more recent scholarship, Pardo lists such problems as basing legal judgments on explicitly statistical evidence, using statistical evidence in the proof process, defining relevance and probative value in probabilistic terms, analyzing the probative value of particular items of evidence, particular rules of evidence, particular standards of proof, as well as various "proof paradoxes".[7] The founding insight of many different probabilist approaches to what constitutes relevant evidence can be traced to Bayesianism's focus on conforming one's degrees of belief to the probability calculus. Despite many and various refinements, "the new evidence scholarship" is bound to remain a detached theory. Moreover, it remains a theory whose main subject is ultimately explaining the legal decision-makers' subjective processes of assessing the evidence. As Goldman notes: "Since different people may have different subjective likelihood ratios, whose subjective likelihood ratio should be used in deciding whether evidence meets the relevance test? In practical terms, of course, judges will use their own subjective likelihood ratio".[8] To provide an account for such cognitive acts of the magistrates is a quick recipe for producing a detached theory of legal evidence.

Supposedly, similar arguments could be made against **the second type of detached theories** pertaining to theories of law. As this chapter is concerned with evidence theories, I will not attempt to describe them at length. Suffice it to say that mainstream positivist theories seem to be comfortable with delegating extralegal fact or legal evidence issues to epistemological theories, or they take such notions for granted. Not that positivism is disinterested in facts. On the contrary, it is almost exclusively interested in social facts being something constitutive of law, as attested

[4] See Pardo (2005), pp. 327ff.

[5] See Lempert (1986).

[6] See Jackson (1996).

[7] See Pardo (2013), pp. 549–551.

[8] Goldman (2005), p. 169.

by such theorists as Hart[9] or Raz,[10] but this interest is not extended to the facts dealt with in adjudication. Legal positivists often tend to be also philosophical positivists, which involves delegating their epistemological concerns with facts of the case to the natural sciences. Theorists of anti-positivist creed may fundamentally differ in their accounts of the knowledge of facts, but they will remain in favour of one or another version of detachment theory. Legal realists, for instance, claim that "judges reach decisions based on what they think would be fair on the facts of the case, rather than on the basis of the applicable rules of law",[11] which makes them embrace a singular account of law, according to which the focus is shifted from legal rules to facts, at the expense of the former. Dworkinian anti-positivism goes in a different direction, where neither facts nor rules seem to matter all that much since judges "actually decide cases according to their own political or moral tastes, and then choose an appropriate legal rule as a rationalization".[12]

For the limited purpose of the present analysis, it is sufficient to present two alternative types of detached theories concerning their interest in legal evidence. The question remains as to what motivates this kind of separation.

1.2 What Lies Behind the Detachment?

If the discussed detachment between theories of legal evidence and those of law is to be held responsible for producing insufficiently good theories of evidence in the domain of law, one wonders about the reasons lying behind it. It would be impossible to provide a list of reasons equally applicable to each of the detached theories. Given the actual social division of labour between theories of legal evidence and theories of law, any critical assessment of their separateness has to proceed with great caution. And yet, in my opinion, it is something to be assessed in principle as disadvantageous to either type of theorizing. Some general points may help speculate about what motivates the chasm.

First, the actual detachment of the two types of theories may reflect **a deeper distinction between "legal" and "factual"**. Allen and Pardo tend to oversimplify the problem by claiming that there is no epistemological or ontological distinction between legal and factual questions and that there could be one epistemological

[9]As H.L.A. Hart puts it: "(. . .) I think (though I cannot prove) that insistence upon the distinction between law as it is and law as it ought to be has been, under the general head of 'positivism,' confused with a moral theory according to which statements of what is the case ('statements of fact') belong to a category or type radically different from statements of what ought to be ('value statements'). It may, therefore, be well to dispel this source of confusion." (Hart 1983, p. 82).

[10]According to J. Raz, "(. . .) law is source-based if its existence and content can be identified by reference to social facts alone, without resort to any evaluative argument." Raz (1994a), p. 211.

[11]Leiter (1997), p. 275.

[12]Dworkin (1978), p. 3.

theory to bind them all.[13] It is quite obvious that a distinction can be drawn between social facts (including legal ones) and natural facts, certainly on the level of respective vocabularies. Some thinkers believe that the ontological difference, as famously offered by Searle,[14] can be based on the human factor: while natural (brute) facts can exist without humans, social facts are ontologically subjective, but they are objective epistemically due to being collectively recognised. Another epistemological difference could be made using the distinction introduced by Ian Hacking[15] between indifferent classifications which make no difference to what is represented (e.g. quarks) and interactive classifications which relate accordingly or contrastively with the manner of representation (e.g. criminals). Hence, contrary to Allen's and Pardo's claim, even if an ontological distinction could be questioned, there is a clear epistemological difference between natural and social facts, and consequently, between "factual" and "legal". Whether the difference explains the distinction between "legal" and "factual" adjudicative questions is a different, albeit important, matter. Still, it does not seem to be a good idea to separate evidence theories from theories of law because the former are allegedly dealing with natural or indifferent kinds and the latter are operating solely within the realm of social or interactive kinds.

Second, the detachment of evidence theories might be connected with an underlying **picture of judges being at relative liberty to choose their own epistemological theory.** Returning to Goldman's point[16] about the ultimate subjectivity of judges' decisions concerning evidence, the abundant evidence scholarship, rooted mainly in probability and statistics, seems to conform to the idea espoused by traditional legal thought, especially in continental "legal dogmatics". The idea is that judges as factfinders—within the constraints of legal rules—must be viewed as ultimately bound by their private theories of truth. Consequently, evidence theories could only serve the purposes of *ex-post* rationalizations or *ex-ante* guidelines for judges to choose from. Such ideas can be illustrated by a comment from Polish criminal procedure scholars who claim that in the context of judicial proceedings, "[t]he accepted [concept of] truth depends upon an assessment of evidence that was used – whether it was free or formal".[17] This point seems to relate the epistemological issue of truth in legal trials to the scope of liberty (or the scope of constraint) a judge might enjoy in assessing the evidence. In the end, is the image of the cognitive realm of an individual judge where the truth emerges; the image to which older and newer evidence scholars are attached, albeit with the tools of different epistemological theories.

Third, but related to the second, the image of a judge as solitary truth-seeker is strengthened by the ambiguity expressed by some continental authors, at least the

[13] See Allen and Pardo (2003).

[14] See Searle (1995).

[15] See Hacking (1999).

[16] See Sect. 1.1.

[17] Waltoś and Hofmański (2018), p. 219.

Polish ones, as to **what judges must know in order to decide cases and, more importantly, how they acquire their knowledge**. On the one hand, these authors admit that judges decide the cases on the basis of the facts they have established in the course of the proceedings. They add, however, that "finding the factual grounds for the decision is, next to finding the validity and content of applicable provisions of law, a necessary condition for making any decision during the trial".[18] The ambiguity seems to be self-imposed, as if the two cognitive processes—as to the facts and as to the law—were conducted in total isolation. There can be important legal and functional reasons for separating those two processes, but certainly not in the typical continental model of an active judge. The discussed ambiguity can easily be extrapolated from two detached and not necessarily related types of theories of evidence and law. A similar point is made by Pardo[19] who observes in the common-law context that an epistemological theory of legal evidence, even a correct one, typically assumes that the epistemic work of legal evidence factfinders is done separately in the realm of law and in the realm of facts of a case. Not that such theories are unaware of legal constraints, but they delegate the first part of the epistemological work to legal theory. This results at best in duplicate theories: one of the rules of legal evidence, the other of the evidence itself. The problem tacked from the perspective of the theory of legal evidence is often described in terms of the assumptions hidden behind the fact-finding. However, according to Pardo, the solution to the problem is not to work out two separate theories, even if they correspond, but one epistemological theory which combines the cognitive aspects of legal rules and legal fact-finding.

Fourth, and last, it is worth mentioning a deeper **philosophical misunderstanding** which may lie behind the detached theories of evidence in law. Thus far only the candidates for motivating the discussed detachment which emerged within the field of legal and evidentiary scholarship have been discussed. Now, with the insights from Robert Brandom's reading of Kant, we can also grasp how the detachment might have originated from associating the not-good-enough accounts of evidence with the realm of regularity, while identifying the province of law with the realm of responsibility.[20] However, distinguishing between that to which concepts apply, i.e. the realm of regularity and those who use concepts, i.e. the realm of responsibility, must not commit us to the dualism of fact and norm; the dualism which in my view is an implicit—and the deepest—factor leading to working out the two separate types of theories. The Kantian lesson is, according to Brandom, that there is strictly no nonnormative realm and that **a normative metalanguage could be employed to specify both what happens and what is done**.

[18] Hofmański and Zabłocki (2011), p. 142.

[19] See Pardo (2005), section III.

[20] See Brandom (1994), pp. 623–626.

2 Evidence Theory Good Enough for Law

Section 1 has shown that accounts of legal fact-finding and evidence in the legal scholarship seem to enjoy a high, perhaps too high, degree of autonomy from legal theory. This, in turn, results in the former being disconnected from distinctly legal accounts of legal systems and practices. The damage is collateral, because legal theories, particularly in the versions which predominantly focus on rules, are less attached to the epistemological issues concerning the knowledge of facts. Building a bridge between legal theory and evidence theory is one of the most important, and most general, problems motivating the present chapter.

From the remarks in Sect. 1, a general requirement of a good enough evidence theory for the law also follows: such a theory should both account for acquiring knowledge and be compatible with one's theory of law. This requirement prompts two meta-theoretical questions: (1) how can knowledge in law be best accounted for?; and (2) how can a theory of knowledge be suitably connected with an account of law?

2.1 Knowledge in Law

2.1.1 Is There a Foundation?

There are different ways of conceptualizing knowledge, most of which have a direct bearing on the issues considered in bridging legal theory and evidence theory with the aim of specifying requirements of a good enough evidence theory for the law. Under the traditional approach—from Descartes to the logical positivists—knowledge is identified with a justified, true belief. With the focus on justification, a classic problem of infinite regress arises. Again traditionally, this problem was solved by purporting to set an infallible foundation for knowledge. Foundationalism had to fail since it had to presuppose some prior concepts and premises and hence it was regressive itself. Moreover, as shown by Sellars, to know something requires not only justification but also inferential understanding of the content being justified.[21] According to Brandom, "the rock on which foundationalism founders is (. . .) its incapacity to explain what it is to *understand* the significances of elements in the observational justificatory basis. For in order to be able to apply one concept noninferentially, (. . .) one must be able to apply others inferentially".[22] The classical view was also famously exposed by Edmund Gettier as unable to provide sufficient conditions to establish knowledge because one can accidentally believe something to be true without having the right reasons.[23] As W.V.O. Quine noted, foundationalism

[21] See Sellars (1956).

[22] Brandom (1994), pp. 90–91.

[23] See Gettier (1963).

wanted to provide a certain basis for knowledge, including scientific practices, but to the extent that it appealed to science it ended up circular.[24] According to Quine, the upshot of this circularity was a license for epistemology to rely on scientific results, without being troubled by the foundational issues. Brian Leiter famously claimed that Quine's proposed naturalization of epistemology is a model for the philosophy of law which should follow in the footsteps of American Legal Realists and abandon foundationalist concerns with the justification of judicial decisions in favour of empirical investigation of the actual decision processes.[25] It is highly debatable, nevertheless, whether Leiter's analogy between the justification of belief in scientific theories and the justification of decisions in legal cases is a sound one.[26]

2.1.2 Internalism and Externalism

Another aspect of the problems concerning the epistemic justification of beliefs is the internalism–externalism distinction.[27] Internalism holds that only what the subject can easily become aware of (e.g. by reflection) can constitute the justification of her beliefs and thus reasons are relative to that particular subject. Externalism denies this restriction and advocates reliance on objective, external practices of producing justified beliefs, whether or not the subjects have reasons to believe they are true. The bearing of this distinction on theories of law and evidence is manifold.

In legal theories, the internalism–externalism distinction in epistemology is usually transferred from an individual subject to legal practice seen as a social or institutional entity of a kind. Drawing on Hart's distinction between the external and internal point of view,[28] contemporary legal theorists can be externalists to the extent they identify justification of legal decision-making or, more broadly, the normativity of law with factors external to judicial practice and found outside of the law, e.g. in morality, economics or literary criticism.[29] Internalist legal theorists advance analysis of the practice of legal decision-making restricted to the interpretative techniques and linguistic resources used by the practitioners. They argue that the best way to evaluate legal decision-making is by internal investigation of judicial practices[30] or, more broadly, they seek to work out the implications of law from a

[24] See Quine (1969).

[25] See Leiter (1997).

[26] See Greenberg (2011).

[27] See Alston (1986) and Bonjour (2002).

[28] See Hart (1961), pp. 55–56.

[29] In contemporary legal theory, most important forms of externalism are exclusive legal positivism, moral realism, law and economics, Critical Legal Studies. See Shiner (2010), p. 418.

[30] A prominent proponent of narrow internalist approach in the philosophy of law is Patterson (1996) with his, inspired by the later Wittgenstein, anti-philosophical jurisprudence that supports the view of legal discourse as autonomous.

viewpoint internal to law.[31] In legal evidence theory, the internalism–externalism distinction in epistemology seems to be carried out more straightforwardly since such theories are typically concerned with what justifies the beliefs of an individual or institutional factfinder. For example, evidence scholars research how internalism and externalism might approach the question of how to construe the justification provided by different types of evidence (e.g. testimony).

2.1.3 Coherentism

Next to the foundationalist aim of finding some self-evident or indubitable base for knowledge, knowledge can also be conceptualized in term of the coherence of a given system of beliefs.[32] Such epistemological coherentism, championed in contemporary philosophy by, among others, Laurence BonJour[33] and Keith Lehrer,[34] is not to be confused with the coherence theory of truth. Coherentism concerns the justification of beliefs and it claims (in the strongest form) that belonging to a coherent system of beliefs is both necessary and sufficient for a belief to be justified. In the latter case, a belief is justified to the extent it is connected with other beliefs through inferential and justificatory relations. Coherentist theories differ as to such notions as a system of beliefs or belonging to a system of beliefs. A coherentist theory of knowledge justification may be required to be logically consistent and contain a sufficient degree of inferential, evidentiary and explanatory relations, but in order to meet the criterion of being true, the system of beliefs must also be relatively complete and dynamically responsive to the world. Internalist coherentism seems to be doomed to failure, because of the infinite regress which arises from the assumption that if agents know their own beliefs, they must also therefore hold some beliefs about those beliefs, and so on. However, coherentism's holism and common sense in describing how we justify our beliefs by appealing to other beliefs and how unreliable but cohering reports may increase probability seem plausible.

Coherence is a concept broadly used in the philosophy of law[35] and in legal theories, but stressing the idea of coherence between the asserted elements which

[31] Among legal theories embracing internalism in the broader sense indicated here, Shiner (2010) lists classical natural law, Ernest Weinrib's legal formalism, Lon Fuller's account of the inner morality of law, the 'legal principles' approach (Dworkin, Alexy), inclusive legal positivism and conventionalist theories of law.

[32] A hybrid or intermediate epistemological theory which combines the alleged advantages of foundationalism and coherentism is Haack's (1993) foundherentism. I favour Tramel's (2008) view that foundherentism is a version of foundationalism.

[33] See BonJour (1985).

[34] See Lehrer (1990).

[35] A good overview of more or less recent coherence debates in the philosophy of law, including problems posed by AI, is provided by Araszkiewicz, Šavelka (2013).

make up law[36] is not identical with adopting an epistemological coherentist stance. The latter, labelled as "legal coherentism",[37] applies to the coherence of propositions about the law to statements and beliefs about the law.[38] In the field of legal evidence theory, a coherentist theory of evidence and legal proof has emerged.[39] This theory, highly critical of probabilistic theories, is on the right track of bridging the theory of law and theory of legal proof to the extent it connects epistemic justification to the dynamics of justification in adjudication, and thus it marks a step towards the hope of providing a unified account of the justification of conclusions about both questions of fact and questions of law which seems to have motivated the coherentist project of Amalia Amaya.[40]

2.1.4 Reliabilism

According to the reliabilist view, beliefs are justified to the extent they are reliably formed. Goldman proposes the best-known account of process-related reliabilist justification of knowledge.[41] He sees beliefs as having causal history, whereas traditional justification theories restrict justification to a function of the current mental states of a subject. Generally speaking, Goldman advocates the view that belief is doxastically justified for a subject if it is formed from a reliable (i.e. truth-conducive) belief-independent process or from a conditionally reliable process dependent on basic beliefs. Brandom[42] identifies three insights of reliabilism: the founding one, according to which reliably formed true beliefs can qualify as knowledge even if the subject cannot justify them; and Goldman's implicit insight that the attribution of reliability must be relativized to reference classes. He also warns against two blindspots of reliabilism: the conceptual one, i.e. extrapolating reliabilist epistemology to semantics, which results in the mistaken conception that the content of knowledge claims can be understood without appeal to inference; and the naturalistic one, i.e. seeing reliabilism as the basis for naturalized epistemology which allegedly could do without reasons. **For Brandom, the only way to salvage reliabilism is to understand it in terms of the goodness of inference.**

---

[36] As prominent instances of this approach to coherence in legal theory which, in my view, has more to do with a coherence theory of truth, see e.g. MacCormick (1984) and Raz (1994b).

[37] See Zipursky (1997).

[38] According to Zipursky (1997), pp.1681–1682, there are similarities between his view and other views, e.g. Dworkin's or Coleman's.

[39] See Amaya (2013).

[40] See Amaya (2011).

[41] See Goldman (1979, 2008).

[42] See Brandom (1998/2000). For quotations, I shall use the version of the 1998 article which appears as chapter III in Brandom (2000).

In the field of theory of legal evidence, Goldman himself is the best exponent of his own version of reliabilism.[43] The main question he tacks is how reliable belief-forming procedures are in the area of law, and the main answer he offers is a reliabilist perspective for assessing Bayesian methods, simple heuristics or coherent explanations. Goldman's ideas applied to legal knowledge could specify it as a type of belief-dependent process whose reliability is dependent on legal procedures which are assigned the task of being truth-conducive. It has been noted by Marrero that Goldman's external point of view does not suffice to evaluate the acquisition of knowledge in the field of law, because although Goldman assesses the impact of legal institutions in the epistemic performance of legal actors, he overlooks the impact that individual legal agents have in legal systems.[44]

2.1.5 How Is Knowledge in Law To Be Accounted For?

The above panorama, certainly not inclusive of all epistemological options, leaves one with an open question. At this point, it would be a good idea to summarize the lessons which can be learnt from the current debates about knowledge. For one simple reason which requires an important shift of focus with regard to epistemological theories, I suggest that such a summary should proceed along Brandomian lines: instead of (or next to) thinking of epistemological accounts as those of knowledge, we can think of them as accounts of when it is proper to *attribute* knowledge.[45]

The first lesson from describing how foundationalism, internalism, externalism, coherentism and reliabilism account for **knowledge is**, therefore, that it is always someone's (knower's) knowledge in the sense of being **attributable**. The knower's belief matters only in so far as it can be attributed to him or her since there are no free-floating beliefs that epistemological theories can make sense of. **With regard to law, and particularly to adjudicating as the proper context for legal evidence, attention should be paid to whom (e.g. legislator, judge, court jury, witness, expert, etc.) and by whom the knowledge is attributed (e.g. legislator, judge, court jury, witness, expert, etc.).**

The second lesson from the above-described epistemological accounts of knowledge is that they all have to address the problem of justification or **offering reasons** in order to explain what it is for a belief not to be true only accidentally.[46] The notion of reliability or coherence cannot replace that of reasons. No doubt, reliability could be cited as a reason for believing something if the knower knew or believed that some reliability indicators available to her made it a good reason, one among others, for that belief. Similarly, a belief's belonging to a coherent system of beliefs, i.e. a

---

[43] See Goldman (2002, 2003, 2005).

[44] See Marrero (2011).

[45] See Brandom (1998/2000), pp. 117–118.

[46] See Brandom (1998/2000), p. 98.

result of the knower's and/or attributor's ability to treat it as such, is just as good a reason for that belief to be justified. Even though having beliefs for which one is not able to produce reasons may appear to count as instances of knowledge,[47] especially from the perspective of justificatory internalism, such episodes do not constitute a plausible explanation of what it is to attribute knowledge globally. Rather, such local cognitive states become understandable against the background of a broader set of reason-giving practices. **An account of knowledge with regard to law should, therefore, be able to provide some perspective on reasons or justificatory practices which pertain to the legal domain**.

The third lesson, which also follows from the previous ones and is implicit in any account of knowledge theory under scrutiny, is that epistemological conditions of justification (regardless of the epistemological family they belong to) entail or presuppose semantics. Not just any semantics. Since only attributable cognitive states, i.e. those which can serve as reasons one for another, can be recognizable as beliefs,[48] there are some semantic restrictions on what counts as beliefs. Namely, if beliefs are to be the moves in the game of giving and asking for reasons, they have to have propositional content which can be inferentially articulated. This inferential articulation is nothing less than the application of concepts. Sensitivity towards semantics is implied respectively by internalism, coherentism and reliabilism. As can be learnt from internalism, the relevant knowledge in a legal evidence context is propositional, which requires the agent to have beliefs that are imbued with propositional content. The coherentist lesson also leads to the requirement for evidence to be a proposition because only a propositional form enables beliefs to enter the "space of reasons" and to function in such interconnections that propositionally articulated beliefs can be inferentially connected with other premises and further conclusions. In brief, a good **account of knowledge in law cannot ignore semantics** because, as is generally the case, our epistemic endeavours in law and elsewhere are non-accidentally connected with our discursive practices, i.e. those of using concepts.

The fourth lesson offered by epistemological theories is that an account of knowledge should have a say on **how the attribution of knowledge takes place and whether these practices are normatively constrained**. The problem of knowledge both in law and in the evidence must be seen, according to the Brandomian thought which I am developing in this paper, in the broader perspective of our discursive practices. Hence an account of knowledge in law should be able to provide some explanation for the social mechanism of attributing beliefs, justifying them and vindicating their truth-conduciveness.

[47] E.g. I can be claiming to know what the Polish constitution says about this or that without being able to produce a sufficient reason, due to not remembering the number or wording of the relevant provision.

[48] See Brandom (1998/2000), p. 108.

2.2 *A Theory of Law Suited to Capturing the Advantages of a Good Enough Theory of Knowledge*

If learning from different accounts of knowledge in law is to be made sense of, a good enough theory of knowledge should be matched by a good enough account of law; and if the gap between the two is to be bridged, one must look for a perspective on law which is sensitive to the problems which accounts of law and knowledge may share. In my opinion, such common problems which find their way into a theory of law and enable developing a common methodological framework include: (1) the need to adopt a perspective on reasons or justificatory practices which pertain to the legal domain; (2) an account of semantics which is suitable for explaining what we do as seekers of epistemic and legal reasons, i.e. an account of our discursive practices—those of using concepts; and (3) an account of how those practices are normatively constrained in social contexts.

2.2.1 Inferential Pragmatism

Inferential pragmatism seems to address all of the above-mentioned problems and more. It is an explanatory strategy which, in understanding conceptual content in an autonomous discursive practice (ADP) in a natural language, gives precedence to what is implicit in the practice or activity of applying concepts; moreover, it recognizes **the practice of making material inferences, which is constitutive for grasping the content.**[49] Accordingly, the meaning of a linguistic unit is fixed by the set of materially correct inferences in which it is used.[50] Conditions for correct material inferences have a normative dimension which can be accounted for in the normative vocabulary of deontic statuses: commitment and entitlement. Such an inferentialist point of departure seems promising for an account of law which might be able to address the epistemological challenges discussed above since it begins with an underlying account of semantics which deals with both the reasons and social dimensions of normativity.

According to Brandom, "expressions come to mean what they mean by being used as they are in practice, and intentional states (...) have the contents they do in virtue of the role they play in the behavioural economy of those to whom they are attributed. Content is understood in terms of proprieties of inferences, and those are understood in terms of the norm-instituting attitudes of taking or treating moves as appropriate or inappropriate in practice".[51] Consequently, if one wants to understand what concepts are, one needs a pragmatic theory of that practice, an explanatory strategy starting with what people do rather than with what they mean. Brandom's

---

[49] See Brandom (2000), pp. 4, 49.

[50] See Sellars (1956).

[51] Brandom (1994), p. 134.

account of discursive practices in natural language focuses, in my opinion, on two dimensions: inferential and normative.

The inferential dimension of using concepts has to do with the practice of treating some inferences as materially correct. This is what we do in our epistemic endeavours, in law and in any discursive practices which, according to inferentialism, are based on both our beliefs and actions having specific propositional content: they are about something, and it can be put in the form of a sentence. Their meaning can be fully grasped and articulated only in their inferential relations.[52] This approach to semantics underlines the essential rationality of humans as sapient, bound by the force of better reasons, rather than merely as sentient creatures.

Our beliefs and actions, according to inferentialism, also have a normative dimension as far as they can be ascribed to agents and believers, either correctly or incorrectly. The moves in the game of applying concepts must follow the criteria of appropriateness. Conditions for correct material inferences can be accounted for in the normative vocabulary of deontic statuses: commitment and entitlement. By using concepts, participants of discursive practice adopt discursive commitments for specific conceptual contents. Such commitments result in the entitlements of other participants to verify them, and—on the part of those who undertake them—to justify them.[53] In standard cases, commitments are inherited from premises, because being committed to premises in material inferences leads to being committed to conclusions. Being committed to certain contents may exclude commitments to other contents. Public acts of speech or actions are treated as assertions by those who can assess their inferential significance in the light of their own discursive commitments. Assertions can be supplemented by other acts of speech such as deferral, disavowal, query or challenge. Such discursive moves are normative precisely because they produce the normative statuses of those who participate in discursive practice; not because of some antecedent rules. Keeping track of one's own and others' deontic statuses—that is, commitments and entitlements—is what Brandom calls 'deontic score-keeping'.

Inferential pragmatism is particularly useful to any account that intends to make sense of both our thoughts and actions (i.e. our cognitive and practical commitments). This is exactly the intersection of knowledge theory and legal theory. The theoretical account of law which could tackle the problems of epistemological theories would also have to make sense of our thoughts and actions. It would have to develop, with regard to law, Brandom's claim that "there are two species of discursive commitment: the cognitive and the practical. (...) practical commitments

[52] "For a response reliably differentially elicited by [for example] red things to qualify as the application of a concept, it must have a significance of a move in the game of giving and asking for reasons. It must be available as a premise for drawing further conclusions and be liable to challenge by inferences from premises with incompatible consequences. Grasping the concept 'red' requires practical mastery of its inferential role, as well as its non-inferential role as an appropriate response to certain sorts of stimuli" (Brandom 2009, p. 184).

[53] See Brandom (1994), p. 172.

are like doxastic commitments in being essentially inferentially articulated".[54] This is precisely where accounts of knowledge and accounts of law may find common ground.[55]

2.2.2 An Inferentialist Account of Law

As I explained elsewhere,[56] the Brandomian philosophical framework gives explanatory precedence to pragmatics before semantics, and ultimately allows semantics to be combined with practical reasoning. It is thereby suitable to complete the task of explaining the relationship between what we say (i.e. semantic problems at large) and what we do, with regard to bridging evidence theory and legal theory. Completion of this task, however, requires some preliminaries to demonstrate the framework's adequacy for theorizing about law and to introduce the vocabulary deployed in the final part of this article. There are some important similarities and differences between an autonomous discursive practice (ADP) in a natural language and legal discursive practices (LDP).

Law fits into this broadly inferentialist picture of semantics, provided that when legal practitioners use legal concepts (when they engage in LDP), they remain within given ADP. It must be assumed, however, that such practitioners have discursive skills and abilities which extend in some respect beyond those of any participant of ADP. Legislatures, administrative bodies, courts, solicitors, counsels, prosecutors, and so on, are all institutional users in the sense that their discursive moves in that practice count only in so far as they take place when such users act in their official, status-related, capacity. It must also be assumed that practitioners are reasonable in LDP, just as they are in ADP. LDP is built on the ability to use legal concepts in order to form beliefs and/or actions which can be treated by other participants of that LPD as having determinate content. One can easily, but unconvincingly, associate law exclusively with LDP since it is inconceivable without linguistic utterances, legal rules or norms having pride of place among them. However, the central case of human action is acting on reasons, and not on linguistic utterances which may articulate them. We would not have developed our ability to prescribe and assess our own conduct and the conduct of other people unless we were first able to treat at least some of our behaviour as prompted by reasons. This is why, apart from common features of ADP and LDP, attention has to be paid to important differences between them.[57]

---

[54] Brandom (1994), p. 233.

[55] More on relations between doxastic commitments (beliefs) and intentional actions, see Dybowski (2018).

[56] See Dybowski (2018).

[57] The following exposition of distinguishing features of LDP is a shortened but significantly revised version of the account offered in Dybowski (2017), pp. 58–64.

First, it is **a commitment to action in law** that in the pragmatist order of explanation precedes deontic statuses acquired in LDP. Admittedly, it could be tempting for legal theorists to focus on the normative vocabulary used by Brandom since the language of commitments, entitlements and rules is all too familiar. However, deontic statuses in ADP (paradigmatically, commitment to semantic content) must not be confused with deontic statuses in LDP (commitment to *legal* semantic content). What is more, those LDP statuses must not be confounded with specifically legal deontic statuses (commitment to *legal* action) which underlie what takes place in LDP. In the socio-legal world known to us there have to be social structures of specific legal authority and legal responsibility. It is by reference to the practices taking place within the frame of these structures that we assign deontic statuses with regard to legal concepts and legal actions.[58]

Second, following from the first, **legal practical reasoning (LPR) sets the proper explanatory context for dealing with action in law**. The problems of deploying concepts (by forming beliefs) have a particular connection with those of action in law, namely with LPR. Different philosophical traditions accept that practical reasoning is about what one ought to do (it is about action) but differ on the epistemic grounds for action. In the classical tradition, the major problem in this regard is that of knowing the good, and how that knowledge relates to the right action. The modern tradition often replaces knowing the good in practical reasoning with wanting something, or focuses on purposive behaviour and action in general. Briefly, received views of practical reasoning focus either on premises (reasons or other possible grounds for action) or on conclusions (action). Brandom's account of practical reasoning may be able to escape the risk of such a one-sidedness, since it is based on the fundamental idea that "giving and asking for reasons for actions is possible only in the context of practices of giving and asking for reasons generally – that is, of practices of making and defending claims or judgments".[59] It can be claimed that within an account of law, this approach to practical reasoning applies to LPR: to the extent that legal reasoning is about what one ought to do, it falls within the scope of practical reasoning. However, an accurate account of specifically legal reasons for action remains a bone of contention among legal scholars. Drawing on Brandom's account of ADP, it can be noted with regard to law that acquiring and ascribing deontic statuses in LDP presupposes a more primitive ability to engage in LPR, to give and ask for specifically legal reasons. This ability to distinguish between legal and non-legal reasons for action can only develop in a given natural language, and a particular socio-legal setting.

Third, if LPR is to be made sense of, its account has to tackle **the nature of legal reasons qua practical reasons**. Brandom identifies three types of practical reasons,

---

[58] To illustrate this point: one could be discursively committed to a certain legal meaning of a linguistic expression (e.g., as a legal historian of an ancient legal system), and thereby 'picture' assuming one's deontic status, within that historic LDP, but this is not identical with one's treating it as a legal reason for action.

[59] Brandom (2000), p. 81.

exemplified by preferences or desires, social statuses and unconditional duties. What follows are three types of practical inferences: instrumental, institutional and unconditional. Each of these can be expressed in the form of a rule or norm. Yet, according to Brandom, a proposition expressing that norm does not prescribe conduct in the first place, but rather explicitly endorses the material proprieties of practical reasons. In other words, normative or evaluative vocabulary is to practice as conditionals are to theory. While instrumental inferences are based on preferences acknowledged or attributed to the agent, unconditional inferences, in Brandom's account, are characterized by agent-neutral moral reasons. In the case of institutional inferences, however, premises are articulated by recognizing *the particular institutional status of an agent*—that status serving as the main premise. Alternative institutional inferences are usually not available, because it is from a given social status that particular practical conclusions follow. Moreover, the 'goodness' of institutional inferences is not licensed by the norm implicit in such inferences, but "by others associated with the same social institutional status".[60] I endorse the idea that legal reasoning, albeit not identical, can be assimilated to the institutional pattern of reasoning, with obvious benefits: (1) it saves the realm of law from being confused with instrumental or unconditional reasoning, without leaving it totally disconnected from either; (2) it affirms the connection of law with social world through institutional legal statuses, being essentially social constructs; and (3) it grounds law's claims to both rationality and objectivity.

Fourth, without falling into the pitfalls of settling either on regulism or regularism,[61] **an inferentialist account of law has the resources to work out a plausible stance on legal rules or norms**. In legal theory, particular attention is paid to explicitly normative statements which prescribe conduct (legal rules or norms, depending on convention), and so theories of legal interpretation have developed methods of elaborating more or less unambiguous prescriptive statements from legal texts. What we are usually particularly oblivious to, however, is the fact that the ability to generate such prescriptions—whether by legislators or by law-applying agents—presupposes the ability to deploy their content in practical reasoning. To be precise, much of contemporary legal theory is about language, pragmatics included, and about practical reasoning. Yet seldom are these problems connected. Inferential pragmatism, in my view, offers a connection between law and language. It does so by setting an order of explanation which does not proceed from words (refined in LDP into prescriptive legal statements) to actions but from practices of finding specifically legal reasons for actions to *statements which codify such practices by licensing certain inferences as distinctly legal*. This is where legal rules or norms come to the fore. One may take as an example the concept of the norm of conduct

[60] Brandom (2000), p. 91.

[61] Brandom's Wittgensteinian argument against 'regulism' is that no account of the existence of rules that relies entirely on their existing explicitly and antecedently to a rule-guided behaviour can work. What he calls 'regularism', on the other hand, is an equally unworkable claim that the normative rules that an agent's behaviour is guided by can be read off from regularities in the way that agent (or others) behaves. See Brandom (1994), pp. 24–30.

(a master concept for distinguishing legal norms), adopted by a prominent twentieth-century Polish legal theorist—Zygmunt Ziembiński. According to this author, such a norm is "a non-descriptive utterance which is linguistically adequate to suggest its addressees a given active or passive behaviour in some circumstances".[62] Legal norms of the same structure are typically 'coded' in various legal provisions and 'decoded' in the process of legal interpretation, performed under a set of directives that have a linguistic and/or axiological basis.[63] Assuming that to 'decode' such elements of the norm as its addressee and the circumstances amounts to recognizing *a particular institutional status of an agent,* and to 'decode' an active or passive behaviour amounts to recognizing *an action*, a given legal norm can be seen as a particular LPR pattern, with that status serving as the pattern's premise in which a distinctly legal reason for action is articulated. However, one important note must be added. Assimilating a legal norm to a pattern of LPR does not commit one to an order of explanation which proceeds from words ("utterances" or "expressions" in the vocabulary of Ziembiński and Zieliński) to action. On the contrary, the practice of 'coding' and 'decoding' explicit wordings which prescribe lawful conduct can be better understood against the background of practices which license certain inferences as distinctly legal.

These are also, it may be added, the practices in which the content of legal concepts is ultimately determined within the overall aim of law's practice, i.e., prescribing the right conduct by providing reasons for acting. A feature of law as a discursive practice, different from universal ADP, is applying and forming reasons which are explicit rather than implicit. This explicitness is due to rational justification being required and pertinent to legislative and judicial decisions.[64] Another property of institutional moves in LDP is the existence of special rules for ascribing meaning, particularly through applying the legal definitions and decisions of other institutional bodies, with regard to identifying conceptual content through the decisions of courts or legal doctrine. While using legal concepts, "judges are responsible for the law, and (. . .) judges are responsible to the law"[65] because they further determine the content of the legal concepts *for* future judges and become responsible *to* the conceptual contents inherited from prior users.

---

[62] Ziembiński (1987), p. 51.

[63] This is a brief formulation of the 'derivational' theory of legal interpretation developed by Maciej Zieliński on the basis of Zygmunt Ziembiński's account of legal norms of conduct. See Zieliński (1972).

[64] See Brandom (2014), p. 20.

[65] Brandom (2014), p. 32.

3 Towards a Good Enough (Meta) Theory of Evidence in Law

3.1 Bridging Along Inferentialist Lines

In order to sketch the meta-theoretical lines along which the bridging of epistemic problems in evidence theories and theories of law could proceed, it is useful to recall Brandom's point about the central issue of knowledge:

"In calling what someone has 'knowledge', one is doing three things: *attributing* a *commitment* that is capable of serving both as a premise and as a conclusion of inferences relating it to other commitments, *attributing entitlement* to that commitment, and *undertaking* that same commitment oneself. Doing this is adopting a complex, essentially *socially* articulated stance or position in the game of giving and asking for reasons".[66]

The final part of this chapter attempts to provide a model of knowledge acquisition and, consequently, of producing evidentiary output in a legal context. This model, imperfect as it is, intends to unveil the acquisition of evidentiary knowledge in law as a complex set of moves in the game of exchanging reasons. To be sure, it is a model in a loose sense of the word. Its main focus is on solving one particular problem to which this paper is dedicated: **how it is possible to think of attaching the detached accounts of knowledge and law in the field of legal evidence**. In my view, not only is this model open for revisions; it is also, and more importantly, inclusive of different epistemological approaches to legal evidence. Any particular theoretical solution to the detachment problem may treat the following model as a checklist for mapping the knowledge attribution issues it finds relevant but it may also see it as a helpful tool for working out its own meta-theoretical model in which the contents of this or that theory can be rooted.

It should be clear by now how a more bridging and more coherent account of evidentiary knowledge in law could proceed. On the one hand, the crucial elements of a pragmatist model of our cognitive activities[67] and, on the other, the model of legal discursive practices[68] reveal the common inferentialist lines along which some proposals for a theory of legal evidence could develop. First, both our cognitive and action-oriented practices are based on reasons: they call for justification. Therefore,

---

[66]Brandom (2000), p. 119. Brandom further explains that undertaking a commitment makes it appropriate for others to attribute it. This can happen in two ways: (1) one may acknowledge the commitment, paradigmatically by being disposed to avow it by an overt assertion; or (2) one may acknowledge it by employing it as a premise in one's theoretical or practical reasoning. Acknowledgement by employing a premise may include: (1) being disposed to act on it practically; (2) undertaking the commitment consequentially, as an inferential consequence of what one acknowledges. Attributing beliefs or commitments is a practical attitude that is implicit in the scorekeeping practices while ascribing beliefs or commitments is making that practical attitude explicit in the form of a claim. See Brandom (2000), p. 174.

[67]See Sect. 2.1.

[68]See Sect. 2.2.

in analysing those practices, tracking inferential connections between the contents of appropriate assertions serves the aim of making explicit how non-accidentally interrelated and inseparable those contents are. Second, the deontic scorekeeping with regard to doxastic commitments (knowledge) and practical commitments (law) provides a useful framework for developing a model which combines attribution of knowledge with LPR, including the semantic dimension of the moves in the legal-evidentiary game of giving and asking for reasons. Three, inferential pragmatism offers the resources necessary to explain the social division of labour taking place when epistemic issues are settled in a process of legal adjudication, including its legal-normative constraints. Making use of those resources can be a way of explaining how the collective labour of participants produces outcomes which meet the epistemological requirements of justification and truth-conduciveness.

3.2 *The Insight and the Blindspot of Legal Syllogism*

Legal syllogism[69] can be used as a test site for putting to work the ideas about a good enough theory of knowledge and about a good enough account of law. A structure of this kind of subsumption, certainly not identical with adjudication, can be presented as follows[70]:

- It ought to be the case that every person having properties P does ф
- Person N has the properties P
- It ought to be the case that N does ф.

Legal syllogism, with a factual premise ‘compressed’ between a major normative premise and a normative conclusion, is an understandable but largely failed, and unjustly ridiculed, attempt at providing rational justification required by and pertinent to judicial decisions. The controversies surrounding it (e.g. logical or sociological) should not overshadow an interesting insight of legal syllogism: it recognizes the inferential structure of legal evidence. What is it for a statement of the minor premise to be a true claim, and as such, to be treated as evidence? The very way this

[69] Legal syllogism is traditionally treated as an argument based on deductive reasoning and seeking to establish whether a specified act is lawful and built of a major premise (“proposition of law” or “law finding”), a minor premise (“proposition of fact” or “fact-finding”) and a conclusion (“judgment” or “law applying”). E.g. (1) For every x: if x at a parliamentary election takes a ballot paper out of a polling station, then x ought to be found guilty of an offence. (2) The accused took a ballot paper out of a polling station at a parliamentary election. Therefore (from (1) and (2)), (3) The accused ought to be found guilty of an offence. See Guest (1961). For vast literature on the legal syllogism and recent revival of interest in it, see Duarte d’Almeida (2019).

[70] See Nowak (1970), pp. 164, 166. If it is assumed that legal norms have a truth value, the legal syllogism would be a trivial case of $\forall x((Fx \rightarrow Gx) \wedge Fa) \rightarrow Ga)$. If, on the other hand, the truth value is ascribed to validity statements, the legal syllogism can be presented as: (1) There is a valid legal norm: ‘It ought to be the case that every person having properties P does ф’; (2) A person N has properties P; (3) There is a valid legal norm: ‘It ought to be the case that N does ф’.

question is posed reveals something unique about the practice of law: picking out the propositional content of this claim (when referring to a particular person under particular circumstances) emerges as secondary to the statement's role in practical legal reasoning. Indeed, one (e.g. a judge) can only be committed to such content if one is first inferentially committed to the LPR pattern expressed in the major premise to which the sentence conjoins, and thus to the last sentence whose content is the action prescribed.[71] Of course, it is not unlikely that propositions about facts can figure in other discursive practices as elements of practical reasoning, instrumental or moral ones, but there they usually acquire their content independently of those reasonings and independently of the asymmetries of institutional authority. Somewhat metaphorically, but importantly, the insight of legal syllogism is that in the sea of our assertions, legal practical reasonings are fishing for specific propositional (and conceptual) contents, and not the other way round.

What is lost from the sight of legal syllogism, nevertheless, is that legal syllogism is better thought of as a shortcut for a far more complex interplay of many epistemic agents who attribute knowledge by acquiring and ascribing the appropriate deontic statuses of commitments and entitlements.[72] It is through sequential attribution of those deontic statuses that the dynamics of knowledge acquisition implicit in the premises and conclusion of legal syllogism can be made explicit. Static rule-deductivism and, consequently, conceiving of the legal syllogism as one person's job (i.e. the judge's) is precisely the source of the syllogism's inaccuracy. However, on the legal syllogism-friendly reading proposed below, it can be reinterpreted as an abbreviated examination of—to borrow one of Brandom titles—**the social route from legal reasoning to representing legal evidence**. Following along inferentialist lines, I will try to show how legal syllogism holds within nine implicit moves in the legal game of giving and asking for reasons. Each of these moves is made of commitments capable of serving both as premises and as the conclusions of inferences relating it to other commitments and of related entitlements. Each of these moves is also inferentially connected with any other one and offers means for eliminating incompatibilities.

The following model of legal syllogism, which in my view applies to adversarial and non-adversarial as well as criminal and private law proceedings, is meta-theoretical in the sense that it does not determine which theoretical solutions with regard to specific accounts of knowledge or evidence and specific accounts of law should be recommended. In other words, what theoretically motivates distinct moves which produce cognitive outcomes is beyond the scope of the model as long as the compatibility of those moves is preserved. The model assumes a moderate

[71] Following Brandom, I assume that not only our beliefs but also our actions have specific propositional content: they are about something, and it can be put in the form of a sentence.

[72] In the Brandomian sense described above (see Sect. 2.2.1), not in the sense of legal commitments and entitlements.

reconstructionist[73] approach to the abilities or dispositions that participants of the net of interactions must exhibit in order to provide the knowledge they have. This reconstruction is not about their actual actions but about the abilities they must display in order to have relevant knowledge, which the model renders in the vocabulary of deontic statuses.

3.3 Legal Syllogism Made Explicit

The following nine moves implicit in the legal syllogism game of giving and asking for reasons correspond to the major premise ((1)–(4)), minor premise ((5)–(6)) and conclusion ((7)–(9)). Each of the moves is supplemented with comments in small font.

(1) Community members **acknowledge** the legislator's **commitment** to licensing LPR patterns for those members.

The legislator is **attributed an entitlement** to license LPR patterns for community members.

Community members **undertake a commitment** to the LPR patterns licensed by the legislator.

The first move, presupposed within the legal syllogism game of giving and asking for reasons (more precisely, within its **major premise**), concerns the general problem of **attributing the legislator's knowledge sufficient and necessary to make law**. According to the inferentialist pragmatist assumptions adopted under this model, the problem can be formulated in a following question: what must one be able to do in order to license an LPR pattern. The answer, for the present purpose, is that it takes the ability to perform a semantic task of formulating something like a classical Russellian indefinite description[74]: $\exists x(Fx \wedge Gx)$. This reads informally: there is an x such that (1) x holds status S in circumstances C and (2) x does ϕ. A further sequence of moves[75] will result in fixing the content of a definite description[76] in a transition from the indefinite description contained in a particular LPR pattern under scrutiny. Such a definite description can be formalized as: $\exists x((Fx \wedge \forall y(Fy \rightarrow x=y)) \wedge Gx)$. This reads non-technically: (1) There is an F (such that x holds status S in circumstances C); (2) at most one thing is F and (3) something that is F is G (does ϕ). The first move, however, concerns only an

[73] In theoretical and legal analyses of language, descriptivism and reconstructionism are two classical methodological approaches stemming from linguistics. The moderate reconstructionism adopted here is close to descriptivism in connecting pragmatics with semantics, but it embraces reconstructionist interest in logical, formal and ideal qualities of language. For Polish contributions to these three approaches, see Woleński (1967), p. 148; Gizbert-Studnicki (1985), pp. 71–72; Ziembiński (1985), pp. 330–337. For a recent overview of the debate see Andruszkiewicz (2016), pp. 218–222.

[74] The very idea of introducing indefinite and definite descriptions comes from Maciej Zieliński's account of facts, where indefinite descriptions are loosely mentioned with regard to 'imagined facts' and definite descriptions (I presume) can be associated with 'facts thought of by a judge as real'. See Zieliński (1979), pp. 77, 85, 87.

[75] See especially (6) and (7).

[76] For the sake of clarity and simplicity it is accounted for as a single definite description.

indefinite description since any LPR pattern structurally presupposes that there is someone who in virtue of their status and circumstances behaves in a certain way. Of course, any LPR pattern can be articulated as a legal rule or norm which involves the problem of its normativity. However, this question of deontics and semantics (e.g. of what it is for x to have a legal duty to ϕ) can be left aside. First, because semantic content of an LPR pattern and its binding force, though interrelated, can be treated separately. Under the present approach, the normativity problem may be seen as dependent on the attitudes (or normative stances) of those who engage in LPR practices (or the attitudes of the magistrates, in Hartian terms of the rule of recognition). Second, the epistemological concern with the game of giving and asking for reasons which takes place within the legal syllogism can be said to assume that validity or justificatory criteria for any given LPR pattern are actually met by a given legal system. With this assumption in place, the main knowledge-related problem is that of discursive practices which lead to representing the content of such patterns. The knowledge attributed to the legislator is traditionally accounted for in the constitutional vocabulary of the rule of law and the principle of legal certainty following from it.

(2) Community members **attribute** to one another a **commitment** to follow LPR patterns.

Each community member is **attributed an entitlement** to every other community member's following LPR patterns.

Each community member **acknowledges** practically a **commitment** to follow LPR patterns.

The second move makes explicit another attribution of knowledge: socially recognized **self-attribution of epistemic access to LPR patterns** by those who may follow them. Apart from knowledge attributed with regard to licensing LPR patterns, the major premise of legal syllogism presupposes that before institutional legal knowers (*scil.* courts) perform their evidentiary or fact-finding work, community members who can be addressees of legal norms expressing LPR patterns have to be thought of as self-assessing (possibly to a degree) knowers. This implicit presupposition is articulated in a consequential maxim *Ignorantia iuris nocet.* It is also assumed by *impossibilium nulla est obligatio* maxim since one must be able to apply modal vocabulary to the content of LPR patterns. For those accounts of law which associate minimal social effectiveness with legal validity, this attribution of knowledge is also pertinent. Moreover, the symmetricity of this attribution is based on the assumption that knowledge of the law is implicitly conceived of as equally accessible; this is an epistemological reflection of the principle of equality before the law.

At this point one could start talking of **legal-status-holders** instead of community members, because once the social practice of attributing and undertaking the commitment to LPR patterns is established, those attributors must be disposed to treat themselves as committed to the LPR patterns in which their legal status can become a premise. However, since the present model's concern is with the social division of epistemic labour, they can be referred to as community members. Most of them will retain that more primary communal role which, in my view, better characterizes them with regard to any other type of practical reasoning than any reduction, but it has to be borne in mind that apart from the presupposition (1), community members in the legal game of giving and asking for reasons are expected to identify themselves and are identified by reference to those legal statuses. However, the conclusiveness of such identifications depends ultimately on decisions of law-applying agents (i.e. the exit solution of the whole legal syllogism game), whereas it can be assumed that community membership is an independent given.

(3) The legislator **attributes** to himself a **commitment** to license distinct LPR patterns for institutional legal knowers to assess whether LPR patterns licensed for community members are followed.

Legislator **undertakes a commitment** to license distinct LPR patterns for institutional legal knowers to assess whether LPR patterns licensed for community members are followed.

Institutional legal knowers are **entitled to the commitment** undertaken the by legislator to provide them with distinct LPR patterns for assessing whether LPR patterns licensed for community members are followed.

The third move within the major premise of legal syllogism game of giving and asking for reasons concerns the **attribution of knowledge of LPR patterns pertinent to institutional legal knowers**. It goes beyond the legislator's knowledge (1) and the norm-addressees' self-assessment knowledge (2) and concerns filling the epistemic gap between the two. On the one hand, there is knowledge attributed to formulating what can be articulated in an indefinite description $\exists x(Fx \wedge Gx)$, while on the other there is knowledge attributed to those who by trial and error employ their cognitive skills with regard to such descriptions in their daily practices of LPR. However, there is also another knowledge-attribution assumed in the major premise. Since 'it ought to be the case that every person having properties P does ϕ', there has to be someone disposed to have the **knowledge qualified as non-accidental and reliable** (unlike that stemming from self-assessment which can be caught in the traps of internalism). To attribute knowledge thus qualified, it takes the legislator's commitment to establish and provide **institutional legal knowers** (paradigmatically judges or courts and/or juries[77]) licensed with special LPR patterns which guarantee those qualities. Institutional legal knowers belong to a broader category of legal knowers (e.g. witnesses, experts or norm-addressees) distinguished with regard to the cognitive input they bring into legal evidentiary practices, but in developed Western legal systems they form a constitutive category of legal knowers in terms of which other legal knowers are thought of. LPR patterns pertinent to institutional legal knowers provide them with epistemic and meta-epistemic resources for assessing whether community members follow the LPR patterns they are committed to. Admittedly, alternative explanations are available. E.g. it could be assumed that community members themselves attribute that commitment to institutional legal knowers. It seems more convenient, however, to see the legislator's commitment of both the legislator's primary commitment to license LPR patterns and of the mutual commitments of community members as following those patterns. To account for the major premise of legal syllogism assumes accounting for what it is to apply it, including who and how to do it, but this attribution to legislator is optional since in primitive legal systems the legislator can be practically identified with a legal knower. An **entitlement of institutional legal knowers,** resulting from a commitment attributed to the legislator, may seem to be under the threat of falling in a vicious circle since those knowers have to do for themselves what in virtue of the reasons inherited from the legislators they have to do for the community members, i.e. follow LPR patterns in order to see if others follow theirs. This, however, is precisely the subset of the game of legal reasons the legal syllogism presupposes. Hence, readers of this comment may either follow the rest of the reconstruction and come back to the present move or, preferably, accept that the legal

[77] Court and jury findings can be treated as involving group judgments rather than individual ones, but I do not accept the claim that groups might have beliefs. In my view, the fact that knowledge can be ascribed to institutional entities or groups does not commit one to the claim that they actually acquire knowledge, just like ascribing statements to them does not mean that they speak.

syllogism assumes under the major premise that institutional legal knowers have been properly identified unless the assumption can be reasonably challenged.

(4) Community members **attribute** to the legislator a **commitment** to a *particular* LPR pattern provided for them to be followed.

The legislator is **entitled** to community members' following a *particular* LPR pattern.

Community members **undertake a commitment** to a *particular* LPR pattern provided for them to be followed.

The fourth move is as close as can be to the original major premise in a traditional reading of legal syllogism but it must be read in the light of the preceding moves. The **knowledge-commitment attributed and undertaken with a particular LPR pattern** is analytically woven out of the fabric of other deontic statuses, but one cannot know just one LPR pattern unless one knows about the other moves associated with that pattern: those of the legislator, other community members and institutional legal knowers. To master the interplay of commitments and entitlements with regard to LPR patterns attributed among the legislator, community members and institutional legal knowers is the condition of knowing a particular LPR pattern with its underwriting indefinite description.

(5) An individual community member **attributes** to institutional legal knowers a **commitment** to assess whether she follows a particular LPR pattern.

An individual community member is **attributed an entitlement** to the assessment by institutional legal knowers of whether she follows a particular LPR pattern.

A community member **undertakes a commitment** to the assessment by legal institutional knowers as to whether she follows a particular LPR pattern.

The fifth attribution move serves the aim of reconstructing in the most general way a set of social practices in which the **minor premise** of legal syllogism can be articulated. This articulation amounts roughly to explicating what it is for something to become cognitively accessible as 'facts of a case'. A community member's[78] commitment, attributed and undertaken with regard to **institutional legal knowers'** assessment of her following a particular LPR pattern, provides the necessary frame for discursively **singling out a concrete and individual representation associated with an indefinite description**. Traditional legal wisdom rightly associates what corresponds to this move in the legal syllogism game of giving and asking for reasons with evidence-collecting and fact-finding procedures prescribed by distinct legal systems. However, there is a strong epistemic claim which underwrites a variety of different procedural moves involved in legal fact-finding. This claim is articulated by the '*iura novit curia*' maxim which can be treated as an explicit knowledge-attribution. Seemingly the maxim restricts the knowledge to legal matters, but it is precisely the content of the commitment attributed to institutional legal knowers that distinguishes *their* knowledge as to the facts from any other type of anyone else's knowledge. This commitment can be seen as following from the assumptions made explicit with regard to the syllogism's major premise, but it can

[78] For sake of simplicity, an attributor is identified with a community member whose case is being decided but it must be noted that (1) this is not necessarily a natural person, and (2) this is not necessarily the person whose following of an LPR pattern is under scrutiny (e.g. it can be a public prosecutor or a plaintiff).

also serve as a premise for further moves in the exchange of reasons. The move, reconstructed as attributing to institutional legal knowers a commitment to assess how an attributor (or someone else) follows an LPR pattern, relates also to epistemic grounds for initiating legal proceedings, whether by private individuals or entities or by those who act in their institutional capacities (e.g. prosecutors). Institutional legal knowers do not act *sua sponte*, they never activate themselves. Prompting them to cognitive actions assumes their epistemic authority as an integral part of their legal capacity to decide cases. As a consequence of attributing this commitment, a community member acknowledges her corresponding entitlement to the epistemic reasons which institutional legal knowers are expected to provide them with and undertakes a commitment to those reasons.

(6) Both legal knowers and community members **attribute** to the legislator a **commitment** to provide them with coordination schemes for assessing whether community members follow the LPR patterns.

Legal knowers and community members **attribute** to themselves respectively an **entitlement** to the coordination schemes for assessing whether community members follow the LPR patterns.

Legal knowers and community members **undertake** respectively a **commitment** to the coordination schemes for assessing whether community members follow the LPR patterns.

The sixth move is a **collective attribution of a commitment to coordinated restrictions on available attributions of knowledge**. As can be seen from the presuppositions which underlie the major premise of legal syllogism, the epistemic work related to LPR patterns is distributed among those who formulate those patterns, those who are expected to follow them, and those who assess whether they are followed. The parallel distribution of attributing practices at the fact-finding stage is epitomized by the minor premise. What the preceding move (5) expresses, namely that the overarching commitment for this stage is the one attributed to institutional legal knowers, could be treated as sufficiently reconstructed. A long-standing feature of Western legal systems, however, has developed complex nets of interrelated epistemic moves oriented towards 'settling facts'. The latter, albeit rendered in different vocabularies, is the core of what legal evidence theories focus on. A plurality of agents with their often colliding knowledge-claims necessitates some explicit or implicit coordination of their actions. All of these actions can be treated as producing assertions, and as such they can be – just like other elements of a legal syllogism – characterized in the deontic scorekeeping idiom. According to the semantic idea underlying the present reconstruction, **the ultimate knowledge-related target of all those assertions made within the minor premise is fixing the content of a definite description**[79] **in a transition from an indefinite description contained in a particular LPR pattern**. Drawing on an indefinite description, the agents and knowers involved may, typically by adopting various and often incompatible commitments, formulate and test their assertions concerning the semantic content of each of the predicates which in conjunction make up the content of the definite description. The social division of labour involved in producing such assertions is standardly coordinated in our legal systems by such general schemes as the one expressed in the maxim: *Actori incumbit onus probandi*. That maxim reads in the deontic scorekeeping idiom as follows: once legal proceedings in a given case have been initiated, whoever makes claims with regard to the content of a

[79]For the sake of clarity and simplicity it is accounted for as a single definite description. See also my comment to move (1) in the main text.

particular definite description is thereby attributed a default commitment ('burden of proof'). That commitment results in all or some other participants' entitlement to the justification of that claim. However, legal systems impose specific restrictions on participants as to the contents they are committed to. The story of such restrictions can be told in the vocabulary of LPR patterns which guide and restrain the moves available to knowers and agents (legal knowers and community members) with a particular focus on the role ascribed to the institutional legal knower (court, judges) as a deontic scorekeeper. To illustrate this, several moves which give a more definite form to a general commitment attributed to legislator in (6) are mentioned below. Those moves can be associated with exclusionary rules (6.1), legal presumptions (6.2), witness testimony and expert opinions (6.3), and time frames for evidentiary proceedings (6.4).

(6.1) Both legal knowers and community members **attribute** to the legislator a **commitment** to provide them with LPR patterns which exclude or supplant certain types of relevant evidence in assessing whether community members follow the LPR patterns.

Legal knowers and community members **attribute** to themselves respectively an **entitlement** to the exclusion or supplanting certain types of relevant evidence in assessing whether community members follow the LPR patterns.

Legal knowers and community members **undertake** respectively a **commitment** to the exclusion or supplanting certain types of relevant evidence in assessing whether community members follow the LPR patterns.

(6.2) Both legal knowers and community members **attribute** to the legislator a **commitment** to provide them with LPR patterns establishing some epistemic conclusions which may or may not[80] be challenged by the attributors.

Legal knowers and community members **attribute** to themselves respectively an **entitlement** to be provided with LPR patterns establishing some epistemic conclusions which they may or may not challenge.

Legal knowers and community members **undertake** respectively a **commitment** to be provided with LPR patterns establishing some epistemic conclusions which they may or may not challenge.

(6.3) Both legal knowers and community members **attribute** to the legislator a **commitment** to attribute to institutional legal knowers an entitlement to formulate assertions relevant to assessing whether community members follow the LPR patterns, including assertions produced by additional knowers (e.g. witnesses, experts, etc.).

Institutional legal knowers **acknowledge an entitlement** to formulate assertions relevant to assessing whether community members follow the LPR patterns, including assertions produced by additional knowers (e.g. witnesses, experts, etc.).

[80] Depending on whether certain presumptions are treated as rebuttable or irrebuttable.

Legal knowers and community members **undertake** respectively a **commitment** to institutional legal knowers' assertions relevant to assessing whether community members follow the LPR patterns, including assertions produced by additional knowers (e.g. witnesses, experts, etc.).

(6.4) Both legal knowers and community members **attribute** to the legislator a **commitment** to set the time frame for collecting knowledge (i.e. attributing commitments, attributing entitlements and undertaking commitments) relevant to assessing whether community members follow the LPR patterns.

Legal knowers and community members **attribute** to themselves respectively an **entitlement** to being provided with the time frame for collecting knowledge relevant to assessing whether community members follow the LPR patterns.

Legal knowers and community members **undertake** respectively a **commitment** to being provided with the time frame for collecting knowledge relevant to assessing whether community members follow the LPR patterns.

(7) A community member **attributes** to institutional legal knowers a **commitment** to an assertion stating whether a definite description relevant to a particular LPR pattern applies to her.

A community member **acknowledges** her **entitlement** to an institutional legal knowers' assertion stating whether a definite description relevant to a particular LPR pattern applies to her.

A community member **undertakes a commitment** to an institutional legal knowers' assertion stating whether a definite description relevant to a particular LPR pattern applies to her.

The seventh move in the legal syllogism game of giving and asking for reasons opens the space of reasons available within the syllogism's **conclusion**. That move is the **attribution of knowledge necessary to assert a completion of the transition from an indefinite to a definite description with regard to the legal qualification of the content of the definite description**. Once the crucial problem of adjudication concerning fact-finding, i.e. fixing the content of a definite description, has been settled in the moves (5) and (6), it has to be addressed by institutional legal knowers from the perspective of the moves (1) through (4). This is traditionally put in terms a subsumption but, as shown above, it takes a far more complex network of inferential connections to produce an assertion which collects all the knowledge concerning the institutional legal status holder and the circumstances of her behaviour. Needless to say, such a qualifying assertion may confirm or disconfirm the propriety of applying a definite description to this or that particular subject. From the perspective of a community member whose case is under scrutiny, it is important to note that she acknowledges an entitlement which corresponds to a commitment attributed to institutional legal knowers: an **entitlement to be provided with reasons for such and such an assertion.** Unlike in universal discursive practice where one typically exercises one's entitlement to someone else's justification by express challenge or demand for relevant reasons, in LPD – including the game of giving and asking for reasons within legal syllogism – a requirement of justification is not an optional move, but rather a default position. Asserting a specific content of a definite description involves supplementing it with explicit reasons.

(8) Institutional legal knowers **attribute** to a community member an **entitlement** to have the assertion stating whether a definite description relevant to a particular LPR pattern applies to her reviewed by an appellate court.

Community members **acknowledge** their **entitlement** to have assertions stating whether definite descriptions relevant to particular LPR patterns apply to them reviewed by an appellate court.

Institutional legal knowers **undertake a commitment** to have their assertions stating whether definite descriptions relevant to particular LPR patterns apply to community members reviewed by an appellate court.

In the eighth move, **attribution of a commitment concerns an additional resource of knowledge** which a community member whose case had been decided may activate through such actions as appeal or application for revision. The additional knowledge stems from reviewing the epistemic moves of former institutional (and to some extent other) legal knowers. Since this move is optional, it seems more adequate for reconstructing the game of giving and asking for reasons within legal syllogism to see it as an entitlement of those whose legal status, circumstances and conduct had been subject to fixing a content of a definite description (or those others who might have been affected) The point of this move is that there can be an additional resource of knowledge prompted by actions of community members to perform or to delegate some epistemic work. The very possibility of this move has an impact on the epistemic work and its outcome ('the conclusion') on the part of institutional legal knowers who face a perspective of their assertions being reviewed. Such a review typically involves additional restrictions, e.g. *reformatio in peius iudici appellato non licet.*

(9) Community members **attribute** to institutional legal knowers a **commitment** to close the epistemic findings performed by those knowers.

Institutional legal knowers are **attributed an entitlement** to the closure of their epistemic findings.

Community members **undertake a commitment** to institutional legal knowers' closure of their epistemic findings.

The final move in the game of giving and asking for reasons within legal syllogism may not be, strictly speaking, based on knowledge attribution since the constellation of commitments and entitlements made thus far does not allow for producing any additional knowledge. However, the move which can be summarized by a principle of *res iudicata* marks a specifically legal dimension of putting an end to all epistemic endeavour concerning a particular case. This move has the consequence of an authority's assertion that **no further attributions of knowledge are available with regard to a particular definite description** which has to be taken into consideration in the preceding moves.

4 Conclusion

Throughout this chapter, I have endorsed the thesis that bridging the detached accounts of knowledge and law in the field of legal evidence is possible by following the inferentialist lines which connect the pragmatist model of our cognitive activities with the pragmatist model of legal discursive practices. A particular conclusion which emerges from the reconstruction of legal syllogism reinterpreted as a shortcut for the social route from legal reasoning to representing legal evidence is that the legal concept of evidence can theoretically dispense with fact-talk. Even though, I am sure, 'facts' will not be replaced in the vocabulary of legal evidence scholars by accounts of what legal knowers are committed to, a new light on those facts' specifically legal normativity might be shed as a result of this discussion. In fact, 'facts' from the realm of regularity are as far as they can be from 'legal facts' which dwell in the realm of responsibility. Noticing how different they are prompts a more general but striking conclusion about the law: in law's practices we are responsible to the law and for the law, and not to the world. Our responsibility to the law can be seen in justifications, precedents and considerations with regard to the 'facts' which rely on prior decisions which had conferred a specific content on the 'facts' in question. Our responsibility for the law with regard to the 'facts' has to do with exercising authority over the decisions of future legislators in conceptualizing current facts. The implicit two-ply normativity of this kind of responsibility (and how it structures the coherence and certainty of law) may be the ultimate explanation for such unique constraints for evidential contents in legal practice. If this picture is correct, that is, if practical legal commitments search the world for propositional contents as evidence (another way to put it is searching for 'facts' as reasons), then a theory of legal evidence cannot do without legal theory to the extent that the latter deals with practical legal reasoning. Roman lawyers developed a somewhat perplexing maxim: *quod non est in actis, non est in mundo*. It has been read as stating: what is not in the records, is not in the world, but now the ambiguity of *in actis* can be disambiguated. What is not in the legally relevant epistemic actions, is not in the world as lawyers know it.

References

Allen RJ, Pardo MS (2003) The myth of the law-fact distinction. Northwestern Univ Law Rev 97

Alston WP (1986) Internalism and externalism in epistemology. Philos Topics 14(1):179–221 (Papers on Epistemology)

Amaya A (2011) Legal justification by optimal coherence. Ratio Iuris 24:304

Amaya A (2013) Coherence, evidence and legal proof. Leg Theory 19:1–43

Andruszkiewicz M (2016) On some of the aspects of the linguistic theories of law. Stud Logic Grammar Rhetoric 46(59):211–229

Araszkiewicz M, Šavelka J (eds) (2013) Coherence: insights from philosophy, jurisprudence and artificial intelligence. Springer

Bonjour L (1985) The structure of empirical knowledge. Harvard University Press

Bonjour L (2002) Internalism and externalism. In: Moser PK (ed) The Oxford handbook of epistemology

Brandom RB (1994) Making it explicit. Reasoning, representing and discursive commitment. Harvard University Press

Brandom RB (1998/2000) Insights and blindspots of reliabilism. Monist 81(3):371–392. Reprinted in Brandom 2000: 97–122

Brandom RB (2000) Articulating reasons. An introduction to inferentialism. Harvard University Press, Cambridge
Brandom RB (2009) Reason in Philosophy. Animating Ideas. Harvard University Press
Brandom RB (2014) A Hegelian Model of legal concept determination: the normative fine structure of the judges' chain novel. In: Hubbs G, Lind D (eds) Pragmatism, law and language. Routledge, New York, pp 19–39
Duarte d'Almeida L (2019) On the legal syllogism. In: Plunkett D, Shapiro Scott J, Toh K (eds) Dimensions of normativity: new essays on metaethics and jurisprudence. OUP, New York, pp 335–364
Dworkin R (1978) Taking rights seriously, 2nd edn. Harvard University Press, Cambridge
Dybowski M (2017) Transition to democracy and determinacy of legal concepts. A Brandomian semantics view. In: Fekete B, Gárdos-Orosz F (eds) Central and Eastern European socio-political and legal transition revisited. Peter Lang GmbH, Frankfurt am Main, pp 57–74
Dybowski M (2018) Articulating Ratio Legis and practical reasoning. In: Dybowski M, Klappstein V (eds) Ratio Legis. Philosophical and theoretical perspectives. Springer, Cham, pp 29–55
Gettier E (1963) Is justified true belief knowledge? Analysis 23(6):121–123
Gizbert-Studnicki T (1985) Teoria prawa, filozofia, lingwistyka. [Legal theory, philosophy, linguistics]. Studia Filozoficzne 2–3:67–81
Goldman AI (1979) What is justified belief? In: Pappas G (ed) Justification and knowledge. D. Reidel, Dordrecht, pp 1–23
Goldman AI (2002) Quasi-objective Bayesianism and legal evidence. Jurimetrics 42:237–260
Goldman AI (2003) Simple heuristics and legal evidence. Law Probab Risk 2:215–226
Goldman AI (2005) Legal evidence. In: Golding MP, Edmundson WA (eds) The Blackwell guide to the philosophy of law and legal theory. Blackwell Publishing, pp 163–175
Goldman AI (2008) Immediate justification and process reliabilism. In: Smith Q (ed) Epistemology: new essays. Oxford University Press, Oxford, pp 63–82
Greenberg M (2011) Naturalism in epistemology and the philosophy of law. Law Philos 30:419–451
Guest AG (1961) Logic in the law. In: Guest AG (ed) Oxford essays in jurisprudence. Clarendon Press, Oxford, pp 176–197
Haack S (1993) Evidence and inquiry: towards reconstruction in epistemology. Blackwell, Oxford
Hacking I (1999) The social construction of what? Harvard University Press, Cambridge
Hart HLA (1961) The concept of law. Oxford University Press, Oxford
Hart HLA (1983) Positivism and the separation of law and morals. In: HLA H (ed) Essays in jurisprudence and philosophy. Clarendon Press, Oxford, pp 49–87
Hofmański P, Zabłocki S (2011) Elementy metodyki pracy sędziego w sprawach karnych [Elements of criminal judge's methodology]. Wolters Kluwer, Warszawa
Jackson JD (1996) Analysing the new evidence scholarship: towards a new conception of the law of evidence. Oxf J Leg Stud 16(2):309–328
Lehrer K (1990) Theory of knowledge. Routledge, London
Leiter B (1997) Rethinking legal realism: toward a naturalized jurisprudence. Tex Law Rev 76:267–315
Lempert R (1986) The new evidence scholarship: analyzing the process of proof. Boston Univ Law Rev 66:439–477
MacCormick N (1984) Coherence in legal justification. In: Peczenik A et al (eds) Theory of legal science. D. Reidel Publishing, Dordrecht
Marrero D (2011) Cognitive agendas and legal epistemology. University of Arkansas Theses and Dissertations, p 146
Nowak L (1970) O prawomocności prawniczych rozumowań subspumcyjnych [On the validity of legal reasoning based on subsumption]. Ruch Prawniczy Ekonomiczny i Socjologiczny 2:163–173
Pardo MS (2005) The field of evidence and the field of knowledge. Law Philos 24:321–392
Pardo MS (2013) The nature and purpose of evidence theory. Vanderbilt Law Rev 66(2):547–613

Patterson DM (1996) Law & truth. Oxford University Press, New York
Quine WVO (1969) Epistemology naturalized. In: Ontological relativity and other essays. Columbia University Press, New York, pp 69–90
Raz J (1994a) Authority, law and morality. In: Raz J (ed) Ethics in the public domain: essays in the morality of law and politics. Clarendon Press, Oxford
Raz J (1994b) The relevance of coherence. In: Raz J (ed) Ethics in the public domain: essays in the morality of law and politics. Clarendon Press, Oxford
Searle JR (1995) The construction of social reality. Free Press, New York
Sellars WS (1956) Empiricism and the philosophy of mind. Minn Stud Philos Sci 1:253–329
Shiner R (2010) Law and its normativity. In: Patterson D (ed) Blackwell companion to philosophy of law and legal theory. Blackwell
Tramel P (2008) Haack's foundherentism is a foundationalism. Synthese 160(2):215–228
Waltoś S, Hofmański P (2018) Proces karny. Zarys systemu [Criminal trial. Overview of the system], 14th edn. Wolters Kluwer, Warszawa
Woleński J (1967) Język prawny w świetle współczesnych metod analizy semantycznej. [Legal language in the light of contemporary methods of semantic analysis] Zeszyty Naukowe Uniwersytetu Jagiellońskiego. Prace prawnicze, 31
Zieliński M (1972) Interpretacja jako proces dekodowania tekstu prawnego. [Interpretation as a process of decoding legal text]. Wydawnictwo Naukowe UAM, Poznań
Zieliński M (1979) Poznanie sądowe a poznanie naukowe. [Judicial cognition and scientific cognition. A comparison] Wydawnictwo Naukowe UAM, Poznań
Ziembiński Z (1985) Deskrypcjonistyczna i rekonstrukcjonistyczna analiza języka w prawoznawstwie. [Descriptionist and reconstructionist analysis of language in legal science] Studia Prawnicze 3–4:329–341
Ziembiński Z (1987) The methodological problems of theory and philosophy of law: a survey. In: Ziembiński Z (ed) Polish contributions to the theory and philosophy of law. Rodopi, Amsterdam, pp 39–74
Zipursky BC (1997) Legal coherentism. SMU Law Rev 50:1679–1720

The Architecture of Evidential Justification Between Atomism and Holism

Daniela Accatino

> Marco Polo describes a bridge, stone by stone.
> - But which is the stone that supports the bridge? Kublai Khan asks.
> - The bridge is not supported by one stone or another—Marco answers—but by the line of the arch that they form.
> Kublai Khan remains silent, reflecting. Then he adds:
> - Why do you speak to me of the stones? It is only the arch that matters to me.
> Polo answers:
> - Without stones there is no arch
> Italo Calvino, Invisible Cities

Abstract This paper explores the debate between atomistic and holistic approaches to legal evidential reasoning, with two aims. The first is conceptual and analytical: it draws some distinctions to clarify in what senses a conception of legal evidential reasoning can be holistic or atomistic. The second purpose is normative: it defends a normative conception for justificatory reasoning about questions of fact in judicial fact finding that notwithstanding its predominantly atomistic character includes some holistic elements.

A previous Spanish version of this article was published in *Isonomia – Revista de Teoría y Filosofía del Derecho,* N° 40, 2014, pp. 17–59. I thank the publisher for permission to publish this revised version.

D. Accatino (✉)
Universidad Austral de Chile, Valdivia, Chile
e-mail: daccatino@uach.cl

V. Klappstein, M. Dybowski (eds.), *Theory of Legal Evidence - Evidence in Legal Theory*, Law and Philosophy Library 138,
https://doi.org/10.1007/978-3-030-83841-6_6

1 Two Approaches to Legal Evidential Reasoning

Discussions in the field of law about the structure of evidential reasoning usually draw a contrast between *atomistic* and *holistic* models.[1] This distinction has become commonplace since the nineteen eighties, when scholarship from the field of cognitive psychology began to critique the excessively analytical approaches taken by the two theoretical currents then predominant in the study of judicial proof. These were, respectively, the 'Bayesian' and the 'Baconian' currents. Bayesians favoured the application of models of mathematical probability to legal evidential reasoning, particularly, the use of inverse probabilities via 'Bayes' theorem'. Baconians, by contrast, argued for a logical rather than mathematical understanding of probability.[2] According to the holistic critique, a flaw shared by both currents was that they dealt separately with elements that needed to be considered together. First, by establishing the probative force of each item of proof on an individual, item by item, basis. Secondly, by establishing degrees of probability in a similarly disaggregated way: once it had been established which elements of a case should be considered legally significant, probability assessments would be assigned element by element. According to the holistic critique, in dealing separately with each item, or with each assessment of probability, Bayesians and Baconians neglected the decisive role of global or comprehensive consideration of the accounts of the facts of the case, constructed and compared on the basis of the totality of available evidence.

A similar objection could be raised to the 'chart method' of analysis, first developed by Wigmore (1913), which was being recovered and revised by William Twining and Peter Tillers during the 1980s.[3] This analytical method proceeds, firstly, by formulating an exhaustive key list of propositions for any given case. This list names each principal event (*penultimate probandum*), every relevant evidentiary datum, every intermediate proposition that is necessary to justify the relevance of that datum, and every proposition that could contradict or weaken an inferential step. The relationships between the elements are then charted on a diagram. In this model, as in the Bayesian and Baconian approaches, consideration of the 'case as a whole' is not particularly significant.[4]

---

[1] Abu-Hareira (1986) was the first to introduce this distinction, later developed by various authors including Peter Tillers (1989), p. 1251–1252; William Twining (1990), pp. 238 ff.; Damaska (1990); Taruffo (1992), pp. 307 ff.; Anderson et al. (2005), p. 156. Vid. also Accatino (2020).

[2] The most significant studies in this line were those of Bennett and Feldman (1981), and by Pennington and Hastie (1986, 1991 and 1993). At around the same time, Abu-Hareira (1986) was also a proponent of a holistic approach to proof, although drawing on a different source, namely, James Glassford's 1820 study on judicial proof (*An essay on the principles of evidence and their application to subjects of judicial inquiry).* Glassford was a member of the Scottish School of Common Sense.

[3] Cf. Twining (1982, 1985); or Anderson and Twining (1991) (whose second edition appeared as Anderson et al. 2005). See also Tillers (1983).

[4] In fact, Wigmore himself presented his analytical model as "the only thorough and scientific method", presenting it as a preferable and superior alternative to what he called the "narrative

Some years on from when this debate began, the scenario in regard to theories of legal evidential reasoning has changed. Today, holism appears to be in favour, particularly those variants of it which posit some similarity between narrative-based reasoning and abductive reasoning, and which apply the model of inference to the best explanation.[5] In addition, other approaches to legal evidential reasoning, closer to atomism insofar as they centre on the analysis of chains of argumentation, have begun to recognise to a greater or lesser degree the relevance of narrative elements in the judicial establishment of facts.[6] Notwithstanding, it would be an error to draw too close an analogy with what was said at one time with respect to legal realism, and thereby conclude that 'we are all holists now'. Various recent works show that the controversy between the two approaches is very much alive, with holism being particularly questioned in regard to its solidity as a normative guide for judicial deliberation and decision-making about proof.[7]

The present paper evaluates the current status of this debate, aiming principally to assess the contributions and weaknesses of holistic approaches to the architecture of evidential justification. My analysis of the difficulties faced by such an endeavour lead me to argue that this architecture is best constructed in a principally, though not exclusively, atomistic fashion.

2 A Model for (Re)constructing the Atomism-Holism Distinction

A first step is to sketch out the various, theoretically distinguishable, front lines on which the contention between atomism and holism could take place. This is necessary since when we speak about a conception of, or group of hypotheses about, legal evidential reasoning we could mean different things. To this end, I propose to draw the following three distinctions:

---

method": Wigmore (1913), pp. 858 and 821. The latter was characterized by the integration of evidentiary facts into a framework relating the sequence of events in a case.

[5] Cf. Allen (1994); Pardo (2000); Pardo and Allen (2008); Allen and Stein (2013); Amaya (2009, 2013).

[6] Cf. Twining (1990); Anderson et al. (2005), pp. 145 ff.; Bex (2011); Bex et al. (2010) and Bex and Walton (2012). On the distinction in evidentiary reasoning between approaches based on probabilities and those based on narratives or argumentation, see. Kaptein et al. (2009), pp. 5 ff.

[7] See, for example, Menashe and Shamash (2005); Taruffo (2009), pp. 79 ff.; Aguilera (2009), pp. 275 ff.; Coloma (2011), pp. 78 ff.; Griffin (2013); Mnookin (2013) and Schweizer (2014).

2.1 *Distinguishing Between Various 'Moments' of Legal Evidential Reasoning*

Adopting a theatrical metaphor, we can think about the process of fact finding as a play in various acts.[8] In each act, various forms of legal evidential reasoning come into play. These correspond to various actors in the process and can be differentiated as objects of study. We may usefully distinguish between:

(a) Conceptions of legal evidential reasoning in the investigative phase or case preparation phase, during which probative elements are collected and hypotheses are generated.
(b) Conceptions of legal evidential reasoning in the phase of decision-making about admissibility of evidence. Various procedural systems conceive of this phase as the stage immediately before evidence is presented at trial. In this pre-trial phase, the court must decide on the relevance of the proofs and whether they are compatible with the legal rules of exclusion (in regard, for example, to illicitly obtained evidence).
(c) Conceptions of legal evidential reasoning at the stage of final decision-making (verdict). In this stage, as Ferrer (2007, pp. 45 ff.) suggests we can distinguish two moments. First, assessment of the probative force of the items of evidence that are to hand. Second, decisions about their sufficiency when measured against the applicable standard of proof. It is therefore possible to distinguish between:

   – Conceptions of judgement of the probative force of available evidence
   – Conceptions of judgement of the sufficiency of evidence in accordance with the applicable standards of proof.

As we will see, the holistic critique of atomism has mainly centred on legal evidential reasoning in the stage of jury or court deliberation towards a verdict. This paper takes the same focus, and therefore the distinction drawn here between (a.3.1) and (a.3.2) is key.

[8]The theatrical metaphor is used by Schum (1986, pp. 830 ff.), who distinguishes between three acts during which "inferential drama" is performed in the field of law: discovery, evidence, and deliberation and decision (these last two treated as one act). This tripartite distinction does not consider the possibility that potentially relevant proofs uncovered at the investigative stage may not make it into the trial proper, falling victim of filters provided by the rules of exclusion, whose application may be the subject of a prior judicial decision.

2.2 Distinguishing Between Descriptive and Normative Perspectives on Legal Evidential Reasoning

We can identify differences between these two points of view regarding each of the three moments or stages of legal fact finding set out above. In specific reference to the phase of decision-making about facts, which is the principal concern of this paper, we can discern:

(a) Descriptive conceptions of judicial evidential reasoning, which aim to reconstruct the ways in which judges—or juries—actually reason when they weigh evidence and decide on it sufficiency in a particular trial.
(b) Normative conceptions of evidential justification, which aim to determine how judges or juries should reason if their findings of fact are to be considered adequately justified.

The determination of the possible objects of study of both descriptive and prescriptive approaches to legal evidential reasoning admits further differentiation if we take into consideration the institutional characteristics of the fact-finding practices under study. Specifically, we can consider whether the decision about facts is being made by an individual judge or a collegiate body; and whether decisions are or are not reasoned (i.e. are accompanied by an explicit account of the grounds that support it). When decisions are not explicitly reasoned, descriptions of legal evidential reasoning may limit themselves to seeking to account for the psychological process of decision-making—by single-member tribunals or by individual members of a collegiate body—and/or the process of deliberation to arrive at a common verdict, in the case of collegiate bodies. Where decisions are explicitly reasoned, a third element can be descriptively examined: the reasoning that supports the findings of fact as delivered. In this sense, if we assume that judicial statements of reasons should be interpreted as justificatory,[9] we can approach to evidential justification not only from a descriptive point of view, but also from a normative perspective.

This last should not lead us to conclude that normative conceptions of evidential justification can only be developed where decisions are explicitly reasoned, i.e. as models for the kind of justificatory discourse that such decisions should—or if the statement of reasons is a legal requirement, must—contain. We can also use the language of evidential justification in regard to decisions for which a statement of reasons is not required—typically, jury verdicts. This is possible because here too we can speak in terms of justificatory reasons considered sufficient to allow certain facts to be treated as proven. It is, after all, not only possible but expected that a jury verdict should be justifiable. That is, there is an expectation that the decision reached is congruent with available evidence, and that facts are considered proven only when

[9]For a defense of the justificatory conception of the statement of reasons, and a critique of the "psychological conception"—which understands statement of reasons as a mere recounting of the mental processes of decision-making—see Gascón (1999), pp. 211 ff.

the evidence for them is sufficient according to the applicable standard. This holds true even when the jury is not expected or required to make its justification explicit in a written statement of reasons.

Whether statements of reasons for decisions are required or not, a normative conception of evidential justification ought to offer a guide for determining, firstly, what should count as a valid justificatory reason, and, secondly, how that justificatory relationship should be established. What will vary according to the institutional conditions within which judicial decision-making takes place is the mode of operation of any such normative orientation. It may serve variously as a guide for individual deliberations (in individual and collegiate decisions contexts); as a guide for collective deliberations (in the case of decisions by collegiate bodies), and/or as a guide for the formal statement of reasons (in the case of reasoned decisions).[10]

In the next section of the paper, we will see that the holistic critique of atomism has been developed on both descriptive and normative fronts. The paper considers both of these variants of critique, although its main focus of interest is to determine how can each approach contribute to a legally and epistemologically appropriate model of justification of judicial decisions about proof.

2.3 *Distinguishing Between the Object of Proof (Probanda) and Evidentiary Reasons (Probans)*

Any conception of legal evidential reasoning in the phase of judicial decision-making, whether descriptive or prescriptive, must address how to establish a relationship between that which is the object of proof (and, therefore, the object of the decision) and the range or set of reasons that are considered relevant (either de facto, or through normative validation). This in turn requires that we specify what counts as an object of proof, and what constitutes an evidentiary reason. Standard holistic approach tends to represent evidential reasoning as a 'whole', as we will see further below. It may be useful here to differentiate—although this is not usually done—between the object of proof, which is taken to be the 'case as a whole', and the set of reasons considered relevant to decision-making. This will here be referred to as the 'whole system of beliefs' of the decision maker. This in turn allows us to distinguish between:

(a) An atomistic versus a holistic conception of the object of proof
(b) An atomistic versus a holistic conception of the structure of legal evidential reasons.

[10] A normative conception of evidentiary justification can provide criteria for an *a posteriori* check on decisions and/or their statement of reasons, depending on the structure of appeals in a particular legal system.

As we will see, the holistic identification of the case-as-a-whole as the object of proof contrasts with the atomistic identification of each penultimate *probandum*—corresponding to each of the legal elements required by relevant norms—as an independent *probandum*. With regard to the representation of legal evidential reasons, holistic approaches argue for a reciprocal, mutually reinforcing, interdependent, network-like, relationship between the totality of evidentiary data and the decision maker's other beliefs. Atomism, on the other hand, holds that there is or ought to be a linear and one-way relationship between each evidentiary data and the facts to be proven.

To sum up, we have established a threefold typology of conceptions of legal evidential reasoning—namely (a), based on distinguishing between moments or phases; (b), distinguishing between descriptive and normative perspectives, and (c), distinguishing between the object of proof and the evidentiary reasons. These will allow us to proceed, in parts III, IV and V below, to first identify and then to weigh the arguments advanced by the version of holism that began to take shape from the 1980s. (I will refer to this version henceforth as 'standard holistic theory'). The typology also allows us to admit the theoretical possibility of an approach to legal evidential reasoning that draws on both holistic and atomistic elements. As has already been suggested (and see part V, below), identification of the weaknesses of the standard holistic approach will lead me to argue for a principally, though not exclusively, atomistic approach to evidential justification. Such an approach recognises the contribution that holism has made in the field of description while drawing on the following normative suppositions: (a) an atomistic conception of the object of proof; and (b) a mixed conception of the structure of legal evidentiary reasons; one which combines an atomistic structuring of justification of judgements about the reliability and individual force of each element, with a holistic structuring of justification of judgments about the combined weight and sufficiency—meeting of the required evidentiary threshold—of all items relevant to each penultimate *probandum*.

It is important to note that the version of atomism that is suggested for adoption in this mixed conceptualisation is not the mathematical, Bayesian probabilities, approach that holistic theories usually treat as their principal antagonist. Rather, I propose the use of argumentative atomistic analyses such as the modified Wigmorian analysis proposed by Anderson et al. (2005).[11] Theories of mathematical probability may certainly have their place in understanding the statistical basis of a range of scientific and forensic proofs and weighing their utility. This paper however

[11] It is important to note that neither Wigmore's chart method, nor the revised version of it advocated by Anderson, Twining and Schum, were conceived of as a way to create a model of justification of evidentiary decision. They were, rather, designed as useful analytical aids to lawyers in the structuring their argument. However, they can still be relevant to a normative conception of evidentiary justification insofar as their advantages include—as Anderson et al. (2005, pp. 141–142) point out that they can be used to identify epistemic weaknesses in the evidence and in the evidentiary inferences that can be made from the evidence. I am grateful to Jorge Cerdio for alerting me to the need for this clarification.

discounts the notion that an entire theory of evidential justification can be constructed around the calculation of probabilities. Three of the various common objections to Bayesianism[12] have particular force as regards a theory of evidential justification. The first is the absolute subjectivity of the quantitative estimates of initial probabilities of a hypothesis—where there are no usable statistical frequencies that can be applied—and/or of the estimates of likelihood assigned to those items of evidence that cannot be expressed in probabilistic terms.[13] The second is the inability of Bayesianism to offer satisfactory interpretations of standards of proof—due to the 'conjunction paradox'—and the arbitrariness of the setting of the probability threshold required for the standard of criminal proof.[14] The third is the contradiction between Bayesian approaches and key legal principles such as the presumption of innocence—since Bayesianism requires us to assign an initial probability estimate to the hypothesis of guilt—and the requirement of individualised, case-specific evidence—since Bayesianism entertains the possibility that an event can be considered proven on the sole basis of statistical proof.[15]

3 Standard Holistic Theories of Legal Evidential Reasoning: The *Story Model* and Inference to the Best Explanation

The holistic approach to legal evidential reasoning was initially presented as a descriptive conception of psychological processes of fact-finding—and in particular, about the reaching of verdicts by juries in criminal trials-, formed on the basis of general theories of cognitive psychology and empirical research on judicial processes. One particular variant is known as the 'story model', because its working assumption is that juries impose a narrative structure onto the information they are given in the course of a trial, constructing one or more stories about the cause-effect relationships and intentionality involved in the events which are the subject of the trial.[16]

Stories about what happened are constructed by attributing meaning to the information that is presented in trial, on the basis of the background knowledge the jury already possesses. This model gives particular importance to general knowledge about the structure and composition of sequences of intentional human actions (*episode schema)*, and to knowledge about events similar in content to those at issue in the case (*memory stores*). The schema structure jurors' expectations about

[12] An overview of these difficulties can be seen in Twining and Stein (1992), p. xxii and in Allen and Pardo (2007).

[13] For discussion of the implications of this problem see Redmayne (2003).

[14] On these difficulties, cf. Tribe (1971) and Cohen (1977), pp. 49 ff.

[15] See Ferrer (2007), pp. 98–108.

[16] Cf. Bennett and Feldman (1981), pp. 41 ff.; Pennington and Hastie (1986, 1991, 1993, 2000).

narrations' integrity, while the memory stores provide a basis for their evaluation of their plausibility. The combination of integrity, plausibility and consistency offered by a particular story condition the coherence that is attributed to it, and therefore the likelihood that the jury will accept it.[17] Finally, this accepted version is compared against the range of possible decisions (*choice set*), which in the case of a jury corresponds to the categories of verdict available to them. These categories are defined by lists of elements derived from jury instructions about applicable legal norms. While the construction of the story is represented as a non-deliberative process of 'comprehension', its comparison to the categories of available verdicts is understood as a deliberative process. During this process, the meaning of unfamiliar legal concepts has to be decided and instructions about standards of proof has to be applied, in order to decide whether the attributes of some specified category of verdict are fully satisfied by the narrative they have already agreed upon as to what, exactly, took place.[18]

From this necessarily abbreviated sketch of the story model we can see that it proposes a holistic conceptualisation of the object of proof, in the form of a story or overall narration of the facts of the case, plus the reasons relevant to evidentiary decision-making. These are combined into a single whole, where evidence plus the decision makers' existing knowledge form an interdependent totality whose strength or persuasiveness is evaluated globally. This holistic representation of legal evidential reasoning includes both the appraisal of the probative force or value of the items of evidence, and their sufficiency evaluation according the legal standard of proof. Both of these deliberative moments are incorporated into the overall assessment of the coherence of the stories told about the events.

A similar image emerges from later work in cognitive psychology on processes of decision-making in complex contexts. Research in this area has led to the development of a general model of what is known as coherence-based reasoning, which has developed specific applications in the area of judicial decision-making.[19] The central thesis is that decision-making about facts proceeds via the gradual formation of a coherent mental model which integrates evidence and the subject's background knowledge. This process proceeds via unconscious or subconscious 'coherence shifts', which modify the mental representation of relevant factors or variables so as to better adapt them to the state of coherence that is emerging. This research, according to at least one of its authors, "fits with the *story model*" (Simon 2004, p. 563) in its holistic characterisation of the decision-making process. Moreover, by introducing the broader notion of coherent mental representations, it allows the story model to be applied also to judicial cases which do not deal with a sequence of intentional actions, but rather with a situation or state of affairs that does not lend itself to being structured as a story.[20]

[17] Cf. Pennington and Hastie (1993), p. 294 and (2000), p. 217.

[18] Cf. Pennington and Hastie (1993), pp. 294 and (2000), pp. 213 and 219.

[19] See, for all the issues mentioned, Simon (2004).

[20] Twining (2000), p. 85, draws attention to the existence of cases of this kind.

These efforts to apply the story model to legal evidential reasoning awoke interest, and a range of reactions, among scholars who worked on evidence law. Some of these reactions recognised the model as extremely relevant for detecting possible dangers in the process of evaluation of evidence. These dangers include, for example, the effects of prejudices in the form of stereotypes or archetypal 'scripts', or the possibility that narrative plausibility would prevail over attention to the particular evidence offered in a case.[21] Other scholars built on the story model to develop an alternative theory of legal evidence, one which they considered more 'realistic' than the Bayesian theory that predominated at the time in Anglo-American New Evidence Scholarship. The added realism came, for these authors, from the greater capacity of the new theory to explain the actual practices of decision-making about facts as well as actual interpretations of evidence law. On the other hand, this new approach is intended to be free from the theoretical and normative objections commonly made to Bayesianism. The resulting approach—that represents the last step in the formation of the standard version of the holistic view of legal evidential reasoning—has been particularly developed in the work of Ronald Allen and, later, Michel Pardo.[22]

This theory views the process of decision-making about facts as an evaluation of the relative plausibility of the narratives presented by the parties or constructed by decision makers. In its most recent versions, it also assumes that this evaluation can be understood as a process of inference to the best explanation, or a type of abductive reasoning. The greater or lesser explanatory plausibility of a story is a function of its consistency, simplicity, coverage (capacity to explain more, and other types of, facts or events) and coherence (concordance with the decision maker's background knowledge).[23] These criteria are weighed against one another, with no explicit formula governing how they are combined. How the plausibility of various alternative narratives will be comparatively evaluated will vary depending on the standard of proof that is to be applied to the case. In a civil case, for which the standard is the preponderance of the evidence, comparative analysis will opt for the best available explanation. If, however, the case is a criminal one in which the threshold is set at 'beyond reasonable doubt', comparison will seek to test whether a plausible explanation exists that is consistent with the innocence of the accused, even where this explanation is less plausible than another that is consistent with his or her guilt. In

[21] Cf. Twining (1990), pp. 220 ff.; Anderson and Twining (1991), pp. 165 ff.; Taruffo (1992), pp. 312 ff.; Wagenaar et al. (1993) and Menashe and Shamash (2005). For a suggestive analysis of the impact of the construction of profiles or stereotypes of victims or the accused in criminal trials, see Coloma (2010).

[22] Cf. Allen (1994); Pardo (2000); Allen (2008); Pardo and Allen (2008); Pardo (2013); Allen and Stein (2013).

[23] The identification of, and nomenclature applied to, criteria that determine the choice between conflicting explanations differ widely across various texts by the same authors: cf. Allen (2008), p. 326; Allen and Stein (2013). Nor do the texts contain precise definitions of the criteria applied. The authors justify this lack of precision with the claim that their interest is practical, rather than conceptual or philosophical: Allen (2008), p. 321; Pardo and Allen (2008), p. 230.

circumstances where a case requires the existence of 'clear and convincing' evidence, comparative judgement focuses on determining whether the version advanced by the party which carries the burden of proof is more plausible than that offered by their counterpart to a sufficient degree.[24] Once a particular version of events has been accepted as either the best or the only plausible explanation—depending on the type of case—a final decision will be made as to whether this version contains all the formal elements required by the legal norms that apply to the case.

The relative plausibility theory agrees with the story model's holistic approach to legal evidential reasoning. In both of them the object of proof is an overall narrative of the facts. And the evaluation of reasons—evidence and background knowledge—, to ascertain both relevance and probative value and sufficiency, is globally depicted in each.[25] It is however less clear if relative plausibility theory shares the purely descriptive character of the story model. Relative plausibility theory certainly claims or aims to be a life-like representation of how facts are determined in actual legal cases. In this respect, its characterization of legal evidential reasoning coincides with that of the story model. An additional normative dimension of relative plausibility theory is however more ambiguous.[26] In some works, its proponents explicitly renounce any prescriptive pretension. Allen, for example, stipulates that his theoretical project aims only to offer a detailed description of the nature of juridical proof, and is accordingly "purely positive rather than normative" (2008, p. 321). However he goes on to claim that various existing rules of evidence "reflect the comparative plausibility structure" (2008, p. 326) and that his theory offers a better explanation than theories of mathematical probability of concepts and institutions of evidence law including relevance, probative force or weight, and standard of proof.[27] These affirmations suggest that the 'positive' character that Allen attributes to relative

---

[24] Although the vagueness of this expression is acknowledged by Pardo and Allen (2008), p. 240, this is attributed to a lack of precision in the standard per se rather than any flaw in the theory.

[25] The three moments of evidentiary reasoning are analysed in Pardo and Allen (2008) and in Pardo (2013). Explicit reference to the ascendancy of a holistic conception of evidentiary reasoning can be found in Pardo (2000) and in Allen and Stein (2013), pp. 576–577.

[26] It is possible to establish a relationship between this ambiguity and the conception of "naturalized epistemology" that Leiter and Allen (2001) accept insofar as it may "fruitful way of understanding evidence law" (2001, p. 1497)". In this piece, the authors claim to be following Alvin Goldman in adopting an approach which "retaining the distinctively *normative* element of epistemology –the regulation of our cognitive activities so that they result in knowledge" (2001, p. 1497, italicised in the original), but which also holds that information about how cognitive processes really operate (individual epistemology) and, above all, about how social practices and processes of formation of beliefs operate (social epistemology) are necessary if normative orientations are to be offered. However, when the authors apply this conception to the area of proof, they adopt a normative perspective only in order to evaluate whether the norms of evidence law are instrumentally adequate for the effective acquisition of knowledge. As far as reasoning processes are concerned, they restrict themselves to defending the theory of relative plausibility because "it appears to explain what factfinders actually do", "it unmistakably explains what advocates actually do at trial" and because of its "better explaining the basic structure of trials than its competitors (2001, p. 1528).

[27] Cf. Allen (2008), p. 326; and, in the same line, Allen (2005).

plausibility refers not only to the claim that it corresponds to actual decision-making processes, but also to its capacity to account for the way in which law defines those processes when it establishes rules of admissibility and standards for decision-making. From this point of view, the theory of relative plausibility should only be considered normative in a weak sense, by virtue of its reference to positive evidence law.

Other works however defend relative plausibility theory from a strong normative stance, with reference to the requirements of epistemic rationality. This can be seen, for example, in work by Pardo and Allen which specifically counters the objection that relative plausibility is nothing more than a description of actual decision-making practices, with no normative component: "inferences based on explanatory considerations may be justified as well, indeed more so than the conclusions generated by a probability approach" (Pardo and Allen 2008, p. 225). In the same text, the model of inference to the best explanation is defended against general objections to its supposed lack of epistemological soundness (Pardo and Allen 2008, p. 245).[28] A similar defense of the epistemic quality of conclusions obtained via the relative plausibility model can be found in another article by Allen and Stein (Allen and Stein 2013, pp. 572 ff.), which therefore offers stronger grounds for attributing normative pretensions to this model.

The rise of a strong normative pretension can meanwhile clearly be detected in other approaches to legal evidential reasoning, which resort to the model of inference to the best explanation to define what counts as adequate evidential justification. Thus for example the work of Amalia Amaya (2009, 2013), which is explicitly grounded in a coherentist theory of epistemic justification, as that of Bex et al. (2010, pp. 127, 132 and 134), who assume that a model of legal evidential reasoning should also allow discernment of whether a conclusion can be rationally justified. Although both of the last two approaches cited may be considered holistic in some senses, each departs in various ways from what this paper has called the standard holistic approach to legal evidential reasoning. Amaya, for example, develops a more articulated version of the requisites of coherence that must be met before a hypothesis can be accepted. She also incorporates additional justificatory requirements derived from a consideration of the specific context in which judicial proof is generated, and from the standards of epistemic responsibility that should therefore apply. In the case of Bex et al. (2010), the authors develop a 'hybrid theory' that incorporates holistic narrative elements alongside with atomistic argumentative elements. As we will see below, both approaches—that of Amaya and that of Bex et al—contribute in significant ways to the development of an epistemically and legally adequate conceptualisation of legal evidential reasoning. The proposal sketched out in the present paper however departs from these, in particular, insofar as they maintain, firstly, a holistic conceptualisation of the object of proof—the global narrative of the facts of the case—and, secondly, a related, strongly holistic,

[28] Pardo and Allen (2008), p. 245.

notion that probative sufficiency is best judged by application of inference to the best explanation to the overall stories of the case.

4 Holistic Dimensions of Evidential Justification

Holistic approaches to judicial proof have without a doubt improved our understanding of psychological processes of decision-making. The descriptive theses that holism sets out are significant, therefore, for a normative project, in offering a potential basis for detecting and critiquing the risks of prejudice or cognitively determined error. They are also important for establishing to what extent a normative model of evidential justification can be effectively applied in practice, an issue to which we will return in the final part of the paper.

Their contribution is, moreover, not limited to reminding us of the psychological need for stories in understanding proof; or to explaining the consequent rhetorical advantages of the narrative strategies often used by lawyers in the courtroom. Holistic conceptions of legal evidential reasoning can also throw light on various issues that are important in any normative theory of justification of judicial decisions about facts.

First, holistic approaches to judicial proof highlight the fact that, even while the facts that are at issue in a case can—and as we will see below, should—be disaggregated into a set of propositions, their meaning as objects of proof depends on their integration into a coherent whole.

In other words, a single event (or, to be more precise, the proposition that affirms that such an event took place) is relevant as the object of proof in a case insofar it can be coherently incorporated into a particular case narrative which, when considered overall, can be held to constitute a concrete example or manifestation of the generic case regulated by the applicable legal rules. Each individual ultimate *probandum*, considered in isolation, lacks legal significance. Thus for instance the existence of a harm or loss suffered by a specific person constitutes a legally significant fact, one that can constitute a *probandum* in a trial, because it can be coherently incorporated in a story involving a set of events that could be classified as a case of harm caused to a third party through negligence.

We can say, then, drawing on a term often used in the literature on legal proof, that a 'case theory' is a prerequisite for the justification of a judicial decision. A case theory is necessary because it allows each proposition to become intelligible as legally significant, allowing it to be subsumed into the generic case to which the applicable legal rules refer. The coherent integration of the propositions that are the object of proof into a case theory is therefore a first and particular sense in which the architecture of evidential justification needs to pay attention to the issues of overall coherence which holistic conceptions of legal evidential reasoning seek to highlight.[29] Recognising that an overall narrative is a precondition if penultimate probanda are to be considered legally intelligible does not, however, imply acceptance of a holistic conception of the object of evidential justification. Nor does it signal acceptance of a holistic conception of evidential reasons. The recognition of the need for overall narrative implies, rather, a kind of limited semantic holism. In it, the overall narrative of the case becomes the context within which each proposition that is the object of proof acquires legal meaning.

Second, we ought also to consider the potentially justificatory value of considerations of plausibility. According to holistic conceptions, plausibility, which occurs when a case narrative appears coherent with widely held knowledge or common sense, plays a central role in the acceptance of a proven fact.[30] In general terms, holistic conceptions emphasise the importance, but also the diversity and complexity, of the whole system of beliefs held by the person who is emitting judgement. Holistic conceptions therefore set particular store by the significant role that certain elements of a person's *stock of knowledge* will play in determining plausibility, irrespective of the specific evidence advanced regarding a story. This is the case for example with elements such as stereotypes, certain standardised narrative schema, or generalizations about what usually happens in certain types of relationships or situations.

These elements, which for the sake of clarity I will refer to as 'narrative generalisations', should be distinguished from the concept of empirical generalisations as dealt with by atomistic conceptions of legal evidential reasoning. Atomism treats empirical generalisations as premises of inductive inference, used to connect a particular piece of information with its corresponding evidentiary conclusion.[31] By contrast, narrative generalisations can lend plausibility to a narrative independently

[29]The coherent integration of a theory of the case corresponds to the condition of "internal consistency" that was identified in the story model as one of the criteria of narrative coherence, and in Allen and Pardo's theory as one of the criteria of explanatory plausibility (see also, in a similar vein, Bex et al. (2010), pp. 143 and 145. We might agree that, just as the integration of statements about the facts into an overall narrative of the case is a precondition for their individual justification, the construction and comparison of global hypothetical narratives plays a significant role in the investigative stage: cf. Schum (2001b), pp. 178 ff.

[30]Pennington and Hastie treat plausibility as the congruence of a story with the set of generally accepted pieces of knowledge about the world, or common sense. Allen and Pardo, by contrast, use the term 'coherence' for this concept, and reserve the concept of plausibility to refer to the quality that results from the application of the complete set of criteria relevant to the acceptance of an explanation. For present purposes I have preferred that of Pennington and Hastie, given that the notion of coherence also has a broader meaning and usage in discussions of general and legal epistemology.

[31]On the uses of generalisations as a guarantee (in the sense proposed by Toulmin), or as a 'glue' in evidentiary inferences, see Schum (2001a), pp. 81 ff.; Anderson et al. (2005), pp. 100 ff; González (2003), pp. 36 and 42.

of, and indeed in the absence of, specific evidentiary data about a particular action or state of affairs that is the object of proof.[32]

An example used by Wagenaar et al. (1993, pp. 44 ff.), and also taken up by Bex et al. (2010, pp. 126 and 146–147), may assist us in understanding the operation of narrative generalisations. The example deals with the case of Danny Rijkbloem, a 23 years old Surinam-born resident of Holland. Rijkbloem had a long criminal record, stretching back to when he was 15 years of age, including convictions for robbery and theft. His 20 years old live-in girlfriend Nicole Lammers, daughter of a Dutch baker, decided under parental pressure to end their relationship and move out. A few days later, she and her parents went to Rijkbloem's flat to recover her possessions. An altercation broke out, which ended with Nicole's father dead from a gunshot wound to the head. The version of events offered by Nicole and her mother, and later advanced by the prosecution, portrayed Rijkbloem as the author of the fatal shot. Rijkbloem however insisted that Nicole's mother had produced a firearm from her handbag and threatened him with it, causing him to throw himself at her to avert the gun's aim. The gun had, he claimed, gone off accidentally in the ensuing struggle, causing Nicole's father's accidental death.

As Wagennar et al. suggest (1993, p. 44), the narrative by which Rijkbloem is the guilty party has a certain familiar ring to it. A young woman from a good family falls in love with the wrong man; her parents try to save her; but the miscreant, used to resolving problems in his own underhand way, ends up killing the father and blaming the mother. The version put forward by the accused is scarcely credible by comparison, it being hardly usual, at least in Holland, to conceive of a respectable mother carrying a gun around in her handbag. This sense of a template of normality, and the resulting generalisation based on common sense, lend greater or lesser degrees of plausibility to the alternative narratives irrespective, again, of the specific evidentiary data available in the case.

Holistic conceptions of legal evidential reasoning in general, and the story model in particular, foreground the psychological relevance of assessments of plausibility in the acceptance or rejection of a version of events in a case. A separate issue, of interest here, is whether such assessments can also have justificatory relevance: that is to say, whether assessments of plausibility should also be admitted as epistemic reasons for inclining toward one or another conclusion about evidence.

Might we, for example, attribute justificatory value to the narrative generalisations identified as operating in the Rijkbloem case? Can the generalisation that miscreants with a criminal history 'are likely to react violently to the smallest provocation' lend weight to the hypothesis that Rijkbloem, with just such a history, shot Nicole's father in the heat of an argument? Can the generalisation that respectable Dutch matrons are unlikely to carry guns in their handbags be deployed as a

[32] Also Wagenaar et al. (1993), in a chapter aptly entitled "Proof by narrative only", pp. 44 ff., Bex et al. (2010), pp. 136 and 146 ff. and Bex and Walton (2012), p. 116, make reference to the use of arguments related to the plausibility of a narrative based not on specific proof, but directly on general appreciations of common sense.

valid argument against the hypothesis that it was Nicole's mother who fired the fatal shot?

We must conclude that this type of argument can indeed provide some inductive justification toward one or another conclusion, as long as the generalisations involved do have some empirical foundation, rather than being based on entirely unfounded prejudice or some other form of erroneous belief (see Menashe and Shamash, 2005, on the danger of the latter).[33] As a general principle—that is, setting aside the question of specific evidence—a hypothesis that is more plausible according to related narrative generalisations can be considered more likely to be true than can an alternative, less plausible or implausible, hypothesis.

The degree of epistemic justification provided by this type of inference, founded as it is on narrative generalisations, is relatively low when compared with inferences which do take into consideration evidence related to the case at hand (always supposing, of course, that the information provided by that evidence is reliable). In the area of juridical proof, however, the decision about facts must be founded on information related specifically to the actions or state of affairs that is at issue in the case (a differentiating element to which we will return in Sect. 5, below). Accordingly, the plausibility of a narrative about the facts is not in itself sufficient to justify accepting that narrative as proven. This does not altogether prevent plausibility from being afforded some justificatory weight, insofar as it may refer to a principal proposition that is also an object of proof (viz., in the case of Rijkbloem, the participation of the accused in the homicide of Nicole's father).

Finally, holistic approaches also prove to be important for understanding the ways in which the full set of evidentiary reasons combine to justify a decision about their sufficiency for considering an event to be proven.

We have already ruled out, in Sect. 2 above, the idea that the evaluation of the probative sufficiency of a body of evidence can be justified by some form of mathematical calculation. Atomistic argumentative approaches such as Wigmore's chart method do not, for their part, offer an alternative, non-quantitative model of proof integration with a pure, linear, logical structure.[34] Holistic approaches, on the other hand, can correctly represent the network-like character of interdependent relationships between relevant evidentiary reasons.

This holistic moment of integration between evidentiary data should be recognised even if it is accepted that certain aspects of evidential justification are necessarily atomistic—as will be argued in the following section. The holistic moment is the one at which it is determined what degree of evidentiary support the overall set of evidence provides to each principal factum *probandum* (and to the alternative, competing, hypotheses that may be advanced).

---

[33] See, in the same vein, Twining (2000), pp. 76–77 and Bex et al. (2010), pp. 146–147. Although it is not possible to develop the point fully here, it is interesting to note that arguments based on narrative generalisations operate in a similar way to naked statistical evidence. See, in this regard, Schauer (2003), pp. 79 ff.

[34] Cf. Twining (1985), p. 183.

Atomistic analysis may allow us to identify various chains of argument and counterargument for each penultimate *probandum*, constructed on the basis of evidence and generalisations. However, the overall evaluation of the force of body of available evidence, the measuring of it against the degree of inductive support that any alternative hypotheses may enjoy, and the evaluation of it sufficiency according to the legal standard of proof, do not seem to lend themselves to a new, linear, chain of inference. Instead, such tasks require weighting of the explanatory fit between the body of available evidence and the competing hypotheses regarding each penultimate *probandum*. This evaluation must also consider the relative epistemic soundness of the evidentiary reasons, determined using atomistic analysis.

One model which offers an illuminating illustration of the structure of this kind of reasoning is that proposed by Susan Haack (1993, pp. 73ff.; 2012, p. 215 ff.; 2013, pp. 78–79), in what is called a 'foundherentist' theory of epistemic justification.[35] The model uses the metaphor of a crossword puzzle to explain how the degree of epistemic warrant of a proposition depends on the quality of evidence that exist regarding it. Following this image, the structure of proof is not linear but rather branches out, as does a crossword. What makes the quality of evidence regarding a particular affirmation better or worse is analogous to what makes the possible answers to a crossword puzzle more, or less, reasonable:

(i) The level of support offered by the evidence; something akin to the level of fit of one possible solution to a crossword entry with the clue and with intersecting completed entries. In other words, "how supportive evidence is depends on the contribution it makes to the explanatory integration of evidence-plus-conclusion" (Haack 2013, p. 79).
(ii) The security of the reasons, independently of the claim in question. This would be analogous to the reasonableness of the completed intersecting entries, independently of the entry in question.
(iii) The comprehensiveness of evidence; which may be likened to the proportion of the crossword that has already been completed.

This model appears preferable to the 'inference to the best explanation' model resorted to by various holistic approaches to juridical proof. This latter is moreover applied not to the justification of each factual element of the case, as is assumed here, but rather to the relationship between the total set of evidentiary reasons and the global narrative of the case. On the one hand, the concept of explanatory integration is more precise, avoiding the risk of resorting to optimisation criteria other than that of explanatory coherence. This is a risk which arises with the model of inference to the best explanation—different variants of which moreover disagree about how the 'best' explanation is to be identified. Thus for example, an explanation may be considered better or best because it appears more plausible, even when it actually finds less support in the evidence than an alternative. In the Haack crossword model,

[35] As the name suggests, this theory offers an original synthesis of foundationalist and coherentist elements, in what its author calls "a kind of articulated holism": Haack (2013), p. 79.

on the other hand, explanatory integration is only one amongst various dimensions of the quality of evidence, and is evaluated separately from assessment of the independent security of each data. In this way, a clear and specific place is set aside for assessment of individual reliability and probative force: something that, as we shall see below, does not take place in standard holistic approaches. Finally, since this is a gradual rather than an optimisation model, it allows for an analytical distinction to be drawn between assessment of the quality of the set of proofs available and decisions as to their sufficiency with respect to the relevant legal standard. In this way, it is possible to develop a tailored, separate interpretation of each of the standards of proof that law sets out for different kinds of legal procedures. Thus the particular challenges and difficulties of attempting to bring all of these thresholds—in particular, the criminal law threshold of 'beyond reasonable doubt'—together in a single, best explanation, model are avoided.[36]

5 Atomistic Aspects of Legal Evidential Reasoning

As we have seen, it is possible to recognise some holistic aspects to evidential justification without necessarily endorsing the unqualified validity as a normative model of standard holistic conceptions of legal evidential reasoning. On the contrary: a central aim of this paper is to argue for the central place that atomistic analyses of proof must have in any theory of legal evidential justification that is

[36]Cf. Laudan (2007) on this point. It is not possible to examine in depth here how traditional standards such as preponderance of the evidence, or proof beyond reasonable doubt, are interpreted from within this particular conception of evidential justification. In general terms, we might observe that the standard usually applied to civil claims should be considered to have been met, with regard to each principal fact, where the following conditions obtain: first, specific proofs exist which are a good explanatory fit with the hypothesis that the event did take place (in this case, arguments of plausibility based on narrative generalisations or purely statistical reasoning would not be sufficient.) Second, this hypothesis better explains a set of reliable evidence than does any contradictory or contrasting hypothesis that exists (in this second, comparative, evaluation arguments of plausibility based on narrative generalisations could potentially be accepted as decisive). Where 'beyond reasonable doubt' is the standard of proof, there must again be a set of specific proofs that offer an explanatory fit with the hypothesis that each principal fact on which the charges are based did take place. Thus, once again, plausibility arguments based on narrative generalisation or statistics cannot be sufficient in and of themselves. There is, however, an additional requirement: any contradictory or contrasting hypotheses that postulates the innocence of the accused must be actively incompatible with the evidence, due to the existence of proofs that eliminate or refute such hypotheses. In common law systems, as is widely known, a third standard, known as 'clear and convincing' evidence, may apply in some civil cases. Interpretation of this standard requires the establishment of some sense in which the hypothesis that a principal fact did occur can be considered to provide a 'sufficiently' better explanation of the evidence than that offered by any counter-hypothesis. The model of evidential justification that I put forward in the paper would permit an interpretation in the case of this standard which would, in essence, state that plausibility arguments based on narrative generalisation would not be considered sufficient to tip the balance where two hypotheses were otherwise evenly matched in terms of the specific evidence base of each one.

sufficiently epistemologically rigorous, and sufficiently sensitive to the context of juridical proof.

A distinctive characteristic of juridical proof is that decisions about proven facts must be based on evidence that has been presented in trial. On the other hand, since adjudication relates to particular facts, judicial proof requires individualized evidentiary data, referred specifically to the case under scrutiny.[37] Nonetheless, in the standard holistic model evidentiary data do not enjoy a clear and distinct place, as is highlighted critically by the hybrid theories of legal evidential reasoning developed by Bex et al. (2010, p. 134).[38]

In the first place, the holistic model of the weighing of evidence, in terms of their global coherence or fit with a story of the case, does not allow for any critical examination of it epistemic quality. There is therefore no guarantee that sources of potential doubt as to the reliability of particular pieces of information are given due consideration. Indeed, the cognitive psychological research on which the story model is based suggests that holistic evaluations of proof tend to favour the overestimation of evidence which benefit whatever narrative has begun to suggest itself as the most coherent.[39] Against this backdrop, the assimilation of a new piece of evidence that bolsters the perception of coherence can modulate attitudes about previously admitted or studied proofs: reinterpretations may take place which placate initial doubts about the earlier proof.[40] This type of bias, operating in favour of whichever narrative can be perceived as the most coherent (confirmation bias or coherence bias), enhances the decision maker's confidence in the rightness of his or her decision by taking ever more distance from the other, contending, narratives.[41]

In second place, the integration of the weighing of evidence into an overall appreciation of the general coherence of a narrative is what may allow the decision maker to accept as proven a version that, while offering greater overall coherence, may enjoy less support in specific, evidentiary data (being potentially supported, rather, by elements such as its plausibility as per common narrative tropes or genres, as discussed in Sect. 3, above). The notion that a "true story" can be displaced, in this way, by a "good story" (Bennett and Feldman 1981, pp. 66 ff.) may be uncontroversial as a description of the psychological process of decision-making. It is, however, wholly unacceptable as a prescriptive conception of evidential justification.[42] Even if we were to concede a possible epistemic value to the plausibility of a story based on narrative generalisations, in the context of judicial

---

[37] On this requirement see Stein (2005), pp. 64 ff.; Ferrer (2007), pp. 98–108.

[38] Amalia Amaya, in the course of articulating her model of coherentist justification, also introduces a range of requisites that seek to guarantee that "some of the propositions that describe admissible evidence at trial, enjoy a degree of priority": Amaya (2013), p. 13.

[39] Cf. Simon (2004), pp. 522–523; Schweizer (2014), p. 2.

[40] Cfr. Simon (2004), pp. 536 ff.

[41] Also emphasised by Amaya (2013), pp. 19 and 34; and Griffin (2013), pp. 312–313.

[42] This same conclusion is defended by Simon (2004): "As defined, coherence is an empirical phenomenon, not a jurisprudential ideal" (p. 516) (. . .) "(p)recisely because the holistic account of human cognition is correct, its prescription is wrong (p. 569)".

proof it is surely unacceptable that a more plausible, but less specifically grounded, narrative should prevail over an other which has more specific evidence to back it up.

Rigorous attention to the specific proofs that are to hand accordingly seems to be a requirement if a decision about the facts of the case is to be considered legally justified. Accordingly, evidential justification must include a critical evaluation of the reliability of evidence and of the probative support it provide to the conclusion at stake. Any such evaluation requires a specific examination of the inductive inferences that can be constructed from each individual item of evidence and its corresponding counterarguments, related to its reliability or to the empirical basis or the applicability to the case of the generalisation on which the inference is based. All of this presupposes, therefore, assuming a normative, atomistic conception of the structure of legal evidential reasons when the probative force of an individual item of evidence is ascertained.

It presupposes additionally that the weighting of evidence should not be referred directly and globally to the overall narrative of the facts, but to each of the individual propositions that match the legal elements of the case. This "atomization" of the object of proof is necessary for two reasons. Firstly, because the inductive connection that empirical generalisations establish between an evidentiary data and a conclusion can only be critically examined if it is referred to a specific, identifiable proposition.[43]

Secondly, an atomistic conception of the object of proof is also necessary for judging the sufficiency of evidence. The analytical differentiation of propositions to be proved allows for guarantees to be given that each and every one of the elements of the generic case set out in the applicable legal rule is indeed present—that is to say, has been proven to the required standard—in the particular case. The object of proof becomes, therefore, each 'material fact'. i.e. every proposition advanced about a legal element of the case (although further determination may be needed in cases of complex propositions, as well as the individualization of intermediate propositions where evidence is indirect or circumstantial.)[44]

A nuanced, separate evaluation of the evidentiary basis for each one of these principal propositions allow us to guard against the danger that narrative plausibility will trump reasons grounded in specific evidence or will prevail in the absence of them. By contrast, a global or overall evaluation of the story of the case cannot offer guarantees that each penultimate *probandum* is sufficiently justified from actually existing proof. Even the modified (improved) version of the standard holistic model, proposed by Amaya (2008, 2013) and Bex et al. (2010), which requires that the version of events that is accepted as proven best integrates the totality of the evidentiary data presented in trial, cannot guarantee that sufficiency of evidence

---

[43] In a similar vein, Bex and Verheij (2012), p. 342 point out that the evidence base may be established differentially in regard to each element of the narrative.

[44] With regard to the concept of material facts, cf. Taruffo (1992), pp. 119 ff.

for the whole story implies sufficiency for each individual, principal, element.[45] Thus, to insist that all the elements required by the applicable legal rules are supported by sufficient evidence in a particular case solely because they are present in the overall narrative that has been globally accepted as proven risks straying into the fallacy of division.[46]

6 Can Atomistic Requirements Be Applied to Evidential Justification?

Holistic conceptions of legal evidential reasoning are often held up as models for guiding legal deliberation because of their close fit with how people naturally reason in fact finding.[47] They are also regarded as having explanatory capacity regarding procedural rules and practices.[48] From this point of view, it should be considered as misguided voluntarism to defend a conception of legal evidential reasoning that rescues the legal and epistemic value of atomism. This kind of conception would be directed, critics may say, at ideal-type judges rather than actual fact finders: ideal types who are moreover psychologically impervious to, and insulated from, real, effective, norms and practices of criminal law. Let us explore whether these objections can be overcome.

6.1 Psychological and Cognitive Viability of Integrating Atomistic Analysis to Evidential Justification

Here the interesting question, correctly adverted to by Allen and Leiter (2001) in the process of defining the notion of 'naturalised epistemology' to which they subscribe, is whether we are faced with "epistemic norms that are actually applicable by creatures like us" (p. 1499). In other words, whether we are in a situation of 'ought implies can'. Two comments ought to be made in this regard:

---

[45] Accordingly, Bex and Verheij (2012), p. 342, recognise that it is unusual for all the elements of a narrative to be grounded in specific proofs, affirming that 'good judgement' allows identification of which elements should be considered essential and which, given the range of evidence available and the type of case, should be expected to be based on proof. However, it is not clear how definitions of 'essential' are to be arrived at, or whether it is treated as a narrative category or—as I propose to treat it here—as a criterion defined by the interrelation between factual and normative premises of legal justification.

[46] For discussion of this fallacy see Van Eemeren and Garssen (2009).

[47] Cf, for example, Allen and Leiter (2001), p. 1528; Allen and Stein (2013), p. 575, and Amaya (2013), p. 40.

[48] Cf., for example, Allen and Leiter (2001), pp. 1534 ff. and Pardo and Allen (2008), pp. 261 ff.

Firstly, it is interesting to note that the psychological research on which the story model is based refer, according to its authors, to the form in which each individual juror arrives at a tentative decision, or forms a personal opinion, *before* any collective deliberation takes place. The effect that group discussion prior to a verdict may have on the final outcome is not captured, nor is the process by which any such deliberation takes place analysed. (Indeed, as Salerno and Diamond 2010, highlight, such processes have been much less extensively studied by cognitive psychologists). Story model researchers do not, either, consider whether their conclusions are also valid in the case of professional judges, another group little-studied by psychologists (see Schauer 2008). Judges are of course subjected to special forms of training and demands associated with their institutional role. Importantly, the latter include the requirement to offer a statement of reasons for their finding of fact. This is a duty required of judges in the civil law tradition, and also in some common law systems, when non-jury trials are held.[49] Accordingly, the mere fact that standard holistic theory seems to account for the reasoning processes of individual jurors does not automatically rule out the possibility that jurors, when deliberating collectively before delivering a verdict, can revise their preliminary opinions about competing narratives by considering the reliability and strength of the specific evidential base for each penultimate *probandum*. On the same basis, we cannot rule out the possibility that legally trained professional judges, under an obligation to reach reasoned decisions, can likewise critically scrutinize the evidence base for each penultimate *probandum*.

One objection to the preceding observation might be the claim that the overall impression, or coherent mental model, of a case inspires a high level of subjective confidence once it has been formed. In this view, the decision maker would be extremely unlikely to significantly revise his or her beliefs during any later stage of collective deliberation, or when drafting a judicial opinion. This problem is discussed by Dan Simon (2004, pp. 550 ff.), drawing on empirical research on juries. Simon concludes that critical concern about the risk of bias or error associated with adjustments of coherence in the formation of an overall narrative is not misplaced. Rather, having acknowledged the problem, Simon argues that there is a need to prevent such bias and error through a system of preliminary instructions to jurors, given before evidence is heard, designed to promote critical appreciation and avoid the premature discounting of alternative hypotheses. (Simon moreover adduces research evidence suggesting that this type of warning can be effective.)[50] Where professional judges are concerned, a similar effect may be achieved through constructing a model of reasoned opinions that requires them to justify their judgments about the reliability of proofs in a way which takes on board critical arguments, and makes explicit their reasons for discounting each of the alternative

[49] On the evolution in these systems of the requirement to give reasons for judicial decisions, see Ho (2000).

[50] Cf. Simon (2004), pp. 553 ff.

hypotheses that were presented over the course of the trial in regard to every penultimate probandum.[51]

6.2 *Viability of the Requirements of Atomistic Analysis in the Light of Current Procedural Rules and Practices*

We should recall at the outset that a normative conception of evidential justification would set little store by arguments based on the simple fit or coincidence with current procedural rules and practices. In the process of exploring the implications of adopting a normative social epistemology, Allen and Leiter (2001, p. 1498) recognise that the issue of whether that rules and practices are effective instruments for the acquisition of knowledge will still remain an open question (excepting, of course, situations in which the rules are justifiably oriented toward some external, extra-epistemic goal). With that reservation in mind, it is still possible to argue that a model of evidential justification with atomistic elements can be compatible with the institutional contexts within which legal fact finding takes place.

On the one hand, it is important to note that when the theory of relative plausibility is recommended as having superior explanatory capacity regarding various evidence law rules, the implicit or explicit point of comparison is usually Bayesian theories. The conclusion might be different if the comparison were instead being made with a model such as the one advanced in this paper: an atomistic, non-mathematical approximation that moreover incorporates some holistic aspects.

Thus for example, as argued in Sect. 5, above, the atomistic definition of the object of proof is consistent with the usual conception of legal subsumption, which distinguishes various legal elements defined by applicable rules that must be present in the case at hand. The atomistic definition, unlike the holistic one, allows evaluation of whether there is sufficient evidence, according with the applicable standard of proof, for each legally significant fact. Since no attempt is made—as it would be in Bayesian atomism—to evaluate or express the probabilities surrounding each element in mathematical terms, the problems presented by the Bayesian approach simply do not arise.[52]

---

[51] As Gascón (1999), p. 202, suggests, in this situation the requirement to give reasons may have a retrospective effect on the decisionmaking pathway, limiting the impact of considerations that can not be communicated. Various civil law legal systems show a tendency towards definition of an atomistic and dialectically complete model of reasoned opinions, in particular if we take into account the criteria of compliance control developed by courts of cassation: see Iacoviello (1997) and Accatino (2012).

[52] The difficulties arise because according to the rules of mathematical calculation of probabilities, the probability that two independent hypotheses both occur is equal to the product of the probability of each. Thus, if the probability of hypothesis A, and of hypothesis B, both equal 0.5, the probability of their both occurring is 0.25. As can be seen, then, the combined probability of two independent hypotheses is always inferior to the individual probability assessment of either one. Accordingly, in

Moreover, the atomistic definition also proves congruent with rules about the burden of proof, allowing their application as default rules for decision, to be systematically incorporated into a model of evidential justification. Indeed, the general tenor of rules about the burden of proof seem to require just this kind of individualised, sequential, examination of the sufficiency of proof regarding every *facta probanda*, when we recall that the main purpose of these rules is, precisely, to distribute responsibility among the parties for proving constitutive facts, on one side, and impeditive facts, on the other side. A similar dynamic is at work when we consider presumption rules which discharge the burden of producing evidence as to a fact (the presumed fact) when another fact (the basic fact) has been established, locating on the other party the burden of producing evidence to the contrary (in the case of rebuttable presumptions). The application of rules such as these also presumes separate consideration or determination of firstly, the sufficiency of evidence regarding the basic fact and secondly, whether sufficient evidence exists to contradict or refute the presumed fact.

It is sometimes argued that holistic conceptions usually correspond more closely than atomistic ones to the instructions that usually are given to US jurors.[53] However, this does not take into account the fact that other Anglo-American systems have gradually developed some practices to guide fact finding which seem to be inspired by some kind of atomistic notions about how juries ought to reason.[54] In practice, this comes down to three types of guidance that a trial judge is required to offer to the jury before they begin their deliberations.

The first one—offered in all common law jurisdictions except the US—consists of a summing up which spells out the legal elements of the crime (or, in general terms, elements of fact defined by the applicable legal rules), and sums up the evidence presented and arguments heard on both sides. While there is no single or universal model for the production of this summing up, one comparative study

a legal case, even if Bayesian evaluation of the relevant evidence has resulted in each principal fact being awarded an individual probability score superior to the ratio required by the applicable standard of proof, it is unlikely that the combined probability will meet the ratio. In consequence, facts which may be considered separately proven cannot be considered proven as a whole (cf. Cohen 1977, pp. 49 ff.).

[53] Allen and Stein (2001), p. 1534.

[54] See the critical appreciation of this asymmetry between the US criminal justice system and that of other Anglo-American systems provided by Marcus (2013) and by Griffin (2013). The pronouncement by the European Court of Human Rights on the compatibility of the due process rights enshrined in Art. 6 of the [European] Convention with non-justified jury verdicts, in the case *Taxquet v. Belgium* (2010), is interesting in this regard. The Court recognised compatibility on condition that proceedings offer "sufficient safeguards against arbitrariness and [make] it possible for the accused to understand why he was found guilty". It goes on to identify, as examples of mechanisms that meet these requirements, precisely the types of institution that we are discussing here (such as judicial summing up, or the putting to the jury, by the judge, of "precise, unequivocal questions put to the jury by the judge, forming a framework on which the verdict is based" (54 ECHR 26, paras. 92 and 93). See also commentary by Duff (2011) and Roberts (2011).

suggests that an atomistic conception of the object of proof is generally adopted.[55] A second type of guidance, regularly used in England, Wales, Canada and New Zealand, consists of a written guide for jury deliberation (known variously as a *route-to-verdict, question trail* or *decision trail).* This takes the form of a series of questions about the factual dilemmas or queries that the case hinges upon, structured in a tree-like formation whose branches take the jury step by step through the fact-finding process. When this 'decision tree' is followed, the answer given to each intermediate question leads either to a not guilty verdict or to a further question.[56] As we can see, this structure is congruent with the atomistic conception of the object of proof, since both assume that the various possible explanations for each material fact or *probandum* must be evaluated separately and stepwise. The final type of guidance betrays a similarly atomistic inspiration, this time regarding the need to separately determine the probative force of every evidentiary data presented in the case. This third type of guidance consist of 'judicial warnings' that alert juries to the particular challenges involved in correctly evaluating certain types of evidence, such as accomplice testimony, identification evidence, or certain kinds of scientific evidence.[57]

Doubts might be raised as to the capacity of jurors or professional judges to take on board the exigencies of these sets of guidance, or of a more analytical model of reasoned opinion, in the limited time and space available during an average trial. In answering this objection, it is worth considering how the dialectic dynamic already present in adversarial systems is not only compatible with atomistic analysis but may actually facilitates it.

On the one hand, as Twining (2000, p. 85) points out, the actual points of discrepancy or controversy between parties to a case usually refers to only some, or even only one, of the factual elements which the applicable legal rules require to be present. Disagreement rarely extends to the entire overall narrative, which usually contains elements in which the parties' versions coincide or about which their disagreements are limited to details of limited legal significance. Thus, the court, or the jury, is not usually confronted by a full-on contest between two entirely irreconcilable narratives, so much as by a set of arguments and counterarguments referring to specific *probanda.* It is therefore feasible to attempt a differential evaluation of the evidence base for those specific propositions, one which critically evaluates the arguments put forward by each side.

---

[55] A judge in Canada stated, for example, that "we aim to summarize the evidence as it relates to each issue that the jury must determine". And according to English judicial opinions "the judge is obligated to 'identif[y] succinctly those pieces of evidence which are in conflict . . . [in order to] focus the jury's attention on those factual issues which they must resolve'". Vid. Marcus (2013), pp. 6 and 10.

[56] Cf. Marcus (2013), pp. 53 ff.

[57] On such warnings see, in general, Roberts and Zuckerman (2010), pp. 676 ff. Those adopted in the UK, can be consulted in https://www.judiciary.uk/wp-content/uploads/2013/09/guidance-no10-warnings-to-juries-.pdf.

Moreover, contradictions or controversies between the parties during the trial will tend to draw attention to any possible sources of doubt that may affect the credibility of each item of evidence, or the evaluation of its probative force. This is particularly true where the system of instruction in force for jurors, or the particular type of statement of reasons that is required of judges, explicitly call for differential analysis of evidentiary data. In this sense, Anderson, Twining and Schum are right to claim that the adversarial system, "assigns primary responsibility for atomistic analysis and evaluation to the contending lawyers" (2005, p. 156). This makes subsequent judicial evaluation of the soundness of evidence easier, as the decision maker is presented with a set of pre-rehearsed arguments and counterarguments, usually prepared by the lawyers representing each side.

7 Conclusions

Atomism and holism are usually presented as mutually exclusive approaches to legal evidential reasoning. However, if we disaggregate fact finding into its various moments or phases, and if we also distinguish between the object of proof and legal evidential reasons, it becomes possible to articulate a normative conception of evidential justification that combines atomistic and holistic elements. A conception of this sort allows us to recognise the contribution made by holistic ideas not only to the understanding of the psychology of fact finding, but also the importance, for a well-grounded decision, of narratively integrating proven propositions, and of the fitting together of evidentiary reasons. At the same time, we can recognise the value of atomistic analysis in reducing the risk of error in evaluating the strength and reliability of evidence.

The notion that a combination of these two perspectives might prove fruitful is not a new one: it can be found, for example, in works by Twining and by Tillers, as well as in the 'hybrid theory' of legal evidential reasoning.[58] The contribution of this paper is therefore in proposing a specific mode for configuring this combination, one which sketches out a normative model of justification for findings of fact in judicial processes. The model is based on the following theses:

(a) An atomistic conception of the object of proof, which is identified as the singular proposition or propositions advanced with respect to each principal facts that matches de legal elements of the case. While the integration of these into a global narrative of the case is not afforded a necessary justificatory function as such, its semantic importance in rendering each proposition intelligible as legally significant is recognised.

[58] Cf. Twining (1990, 2000); Tillers (1989), pp. 1251–1253; Bex et al. (2010).

(b) An atomistic conception of the structure of evidentiary reasons for the justification of judgements about the reliability and individual probative force of each item of evidence.[59]

(c) A holistic conception of the structure of legal evidentiary reasons for the justification of evaluations of, first, the probative force of the body of evidence available regarding each principal fact, and, second, the sufficiency of that evidence when compared to the applicable legal standard of proof.

In sum, according to this conception, the architecture of evidential justification begins to resemble that of a stone bridge. In the style of the remarks that Italo Calvino attributes to Marco Polo, in an imagined dialogue with Kubla Khan, it is true that "the bridge is not supported by one stone or another, but by the line of the arch that they form". We must not forget, however, that "without stones there is no arch".[60]

References

Abu-Hareira MA (1986) An early holistic conception of judicial fact-finding. Juridical Rev:79–106

Accatino D (2012) La motivación de las decisiones judiciales como garantía de racionalidad de la valoración de la prueba. In: Bustamante M (ed) Derecho probatorio contemporáneo, prueba científica y técnicas forenses. Ediciones Universidad de Medellín, Medellín, pp 77–96

Aguilera E (2009) Sobre la estructura del razonamiento probatorio en sede judicial. Revista del Posgrado en Derecho de la UNAM 15(8):257–289

Accatino D (2020) Legal evidence theory: are we all "rationalists" now?. Revus (40):85–101

Allen R (1994) Factual ambiguity and a theory of evidence. Northwest Univ Law Rev 88:604–640

---

[59] As has already been stated, this paper does not develop a differentiated analysis of judgement of relevance. Insofar as judging the evidentiary force of an element of proof presupposes consideration of its relevance, we might deduce that if a normative, atomistic approach is taken to the former, the latter must be treated in an analogous way. Thus, relevance must be evaluated with regard to each individual element of proof, considering whether each may constitute or not the premise of an argument proving or disproving that a principal fact did in fact take place. In practice, this conclusion would be relatively easy to sustain if the judgement in question were always to determine, in a binary mode, the relevance or irrelevance of an element of proof. But legal norms regarding the admission or exclusion of evidence may require evaluation of the degree to which an element of proof is relevant, in order, for example, to weight this against the danger that its introduction may generate an unfair prejudice. Evaluation of the degree to which a particular element of proof is relevant is a complex judgement call, which appears to require simultaneous consideration of both the individual and the overall, or relative, weight of the element in the set of available evidence. All of this seems to point to the need for a holistic approach to judging evidentiary sufficiency, such as the one proposed in this paper. For an interesting discussion of this problem see Mnookin (2013).

[60] The full quote from *Invisible Cities* reads: "Marco Polo describes a bridge, stone by stone. "But which is the stone that supports the bridge?" Kublai Khan asks. "The bridge is not supported by one stone or another", Marco answers, "but by the line of the arch that they form". Kublai Khan remains silent, reflecting. Then he adds: "Why do you speak to me of the stones? It is only the arch that matters to me". Polo answers: "Without stones there is no arch" (p. 82).

Allen R, Leiter B (2001) Naturalized epistemology and the law of evidence. Virginia Law Rev 87:1491–1550
Allen R (2005) The narrative fallacy, the relative plausibility theory, and a theory of the trial. Int Comment Evid 3:1
Allen R (2008) Explanationism all the way down. Episteme 5(3):320–328
Allen R, Pardo M (2007) The problematic value of mathematical models of evidence. J Leg Stud 36:107–140
Allen R, Stein A (2013) Evidence, probability, and the burden of proof. Arizona Law Rev 54:557–602
Amaya A (2008) Coherence, justification and epistemic responsibility in fact finding. Episteme 5:306–319
Amaya A (2009) Inference to the best legal explanation. In: Kaptein H, Prakken H, Verheij B (eds) Legal evidence and proof: statistics, stories, logic. Ashgate Publishing, Aldershot, pp 135–159
Amaya A (2013) Coherence, evidence, and legal proof. Legal Theory 19(1):1–43
Anderson T, Twining W (1991) Analysis of evidence. Little, Brown & co., Boston
Anderson T, Twining W, Schum D (2005) Analysis of evidence, 2nd rev edn. Cambridge University Press, Cambridge
Bennett WL, Feldman M (1981) Reconstructing reality in the courtroom. Tavistock Publications, New York
Bex F (2011) Arguments, stories and criminal evidence – a formal hybrid theory. Springer, Dordrecht
Bex F, Verheij B (2012) Solving a murder case by asking critical questions: an approach to fact-finding in terms of argumentation and story schemes. Argumentation 26:325–353
Bex F, Walton D (2012) Burdens and standards of proof for the inference to the best explanation: three case studies. Law Probab Risk 11:113–133
Bex F, van Koppen P, Prakken H, Verheij B (2010) A hybrid formal theory of arguments, stories and criminal evidence. Artif Intell Law 18:123–152
Cohen LJ (1977) The probable and the provable. Clarendon Press, Oxford
Coloma R (2010) El debate sobre los hechos en los procesos judiciales. ¿Qué inclina la balanza? In: Accatino D (ed) Formación y valoración de la prueba en el proceso penal. Abeledo Perrot – Legal Publishing, Santiago de Chile, pp 87–117
Coloma R (2011) Las buenas y las malas historias. Criterios de validación del discurso de los hechos en las sentencias judiciales. In: Arenas F, Brunet P (eds) Cuestiones contemporáneas de teoría analítica del derecho. Marcial Pons, Madrid, pp 75–97
Damaska M (1990) Atomistic and holistic evaluation of evidence. A comparative view. In: Clark DS (ed) Comparative and private international law. Essays in Honor of John Merryman. Duncker & Humblot, Berlin, pp 91–104
Duff P (2011) The compatibility of jury verdicts with article 6: Taxquet v. Belgium. Edinburgh Law Rev 15(2):246–251
Ferrer J (2007) La valoración racional de la prueba. Marcial Pons, Madrid, Barcelona
Gascón M (1999) Los hechos en el derecho. Bases argumentales de la prueba. Marcial Pons, Madrid
González D (2003) Hechos y argumentos (Racionalidad epistemológica y prueba de los hechos en el proceso penal) (II). Jueces para la democracia 47:35–51
Griffin L (2013) Narrative, truth and trial. Georgetown Law J 101:281–335
Haack S (1993) Evidence and inquiry. Towards reconstruction in epistemology. Blackwell, Oxford
Haack S (2012) The embedded epistemologist: dispatches from the legal front. Ratio Juris 25 (2):206–235
Haack S (2013) El probabilismo jurídico: una disensión epistemológica. In: Vásquez C (ed) Estándares de prueba y prueba científica. Marcial Pons, Madrid - Barcelona, pp 65–98
Ho HL (2000) The judicial duty to give reasons. Legal Stud 20(1):42–65
Iacoviello F (1997) La motivazione della sentenza penale e il suo controllo in cassazione. Giuffrè, Milano

Kaptein H, Prakken H, Verheij B (2009) General introduction. In: Kaptein H, Prakken H, Verheij B (eds) Legal evidence and proof: statistics, stories, logic. Ashgate Publishing, Aldershot, pp 1–14
Laudan L (2007) Strange bedfellows: inference to the best explanation and the criminal standard of proof. Int J Evid Proof 7:292–306
Leiter B, Allen R (2001) Naturalized epistemology and the law of evidence. Virginia Law Rev 87:1491–1550
Marcus P (2013) Judges talking to jurors in criminal cases: why U.S judges do it so differently from just about everyone else. Arizona J Int Comp Law 30:1–64
Menashe D, Shamash ME (2005) The narrative fallacy. Int Comment Evid 3, 1, article 3
Mnookin JL (2013) Atomism, holism, and the judicial assessment of evidence. UCLA Law Rev 60:1524–1585
Pardo M (2000) Juridical proof, evidence, and pragmatic meaning: towards evidentiary holism. Northw Univ Law Rev 95(1):399–442
Pardo M (2013) Nature and purpose of evidence theory. Vanderbilt Law Rev 66(2):547–613
Pardo M, Allen R (2008) Juridical proof and the best explanation. Law Philos 27:223–268
Pennington N, Hastie R (1986) Evidence evaluation in complex decision making. J Personality Soc Psychol 51:241–258
Pennington N, Hastie R (1991) A cognitive theory of juror decision-making: the story model. Cardozo Law Rev 13:519–557
Pennington N, Hastie R (1993) The story model of decision making. In: Hastie R (ed) Inside the juror. The psychology of juror decision making. Cambridge University Press, Cambridge, pp 192–221
Pennington N, Hastie R (2000) Explanation-based decision making. In: Connolly T, Arkes H, Hammond K (eds) Judgment and decision making. An interdisciplinary reader. Cambridge University Press, Cambridge, pp 212–228
Redmayne M (2003) Objective probability and the assessment of evidence. Law Probab Risk 2:275–294
Roberts P (2011) Does Article 6 of the European Convention on Human Rights require reasoned verdicts in criminal trials? Human Rights Law Rev 11(2):213–235
Roberts P, Zuckerman A (2010) Criminal evidence, 2nd edn. Oxford University Press, Oxford
Salerno J, Diamond S (2010) The promise of a cognitive perspective on jury deliberation. Psychonomic Bull Rev 17(2):174–179
Schauer F (2003) Profiles, probabilities and stereotypes. Harvard University Press, Cambridge
Schauer F (2008) Is there a psychology of judging? In: Klein D, Mitchell G (eds) The psychology of judicial decision making. Oxford University Press, Nueva York, pp 103–120
Schum D (1986) Probability and the processes of discovery, proof and choice. Boston Univ Law Rev 66(3-4):825–875
Schum D (2001a) The evidential foundations of probabilistic reasoning, 2nd edn. Northwestern University Press, Evanston
Schum D (2001b) Evidence marshalling for imaginative fact finding. Artif Intell Law 9:165–188
Schweizer M (2014) Comparing holistic and atomistic evaluation of evidence. Law Probab Risk 13 (1):65–89
Simon D (2004) A third view of the black box: cognitive coherence in legal decision making. Univ Chicago Law Rev 71(2):511–586
Stein A (2005) Foundations of evidence law. Oxford University Press, Oxford
Taruffo M (1992) La prueba de los hechos (trans: Ferrer J). Trotta, Madrid, p 2002
Taruffo M (2009) Simplemente la verdad. El juez y la construcción de los hechos (trans: Accatino D). Marcial Pons, Madrid – Barcelona, p 2010
Tillers P (ed) (1983) Wigmore on evidence. Little, Brown and Company, Boston
Tillers P (1989) Webs of things in the mind: a new science of evidence. Mich Law Rev 87:1225–1258
Tribe L H (1971) Trial by mathematics, precision and ritual in the legal process. Harvard Law Rev 84(6):1329–1393

Twining W (1982) The rationalist tradition of evidence scholarship. In: Campbell E, Waller L (eds) Well and truly tried. Law Book Company, Sydney, pp 211–249 (re-published in Twining W, Rethinking evidence. Exploratory essays. Basil Blackwell, Oxford, pp 32–82)
Twining W (1985) Theories of evidence: Bentham and Wigmore. Weidenfeld & Nicolson, London
Twining W (1990) Lawyers' stories. In: Twining W (ed) Rethinking evidence. Exploratory essays. Basil Blackwell, Oxford, pp 219–261
Twining W (2000) Necessary but dangerous? Generalizations and narrative in argumentation about 'facts' in criminal process. In: Malsch M, Nijboer JF (eds) Complex cases. Perspectives on the Netherlands criminal justice system. Thela Thesis, Amsterdam, pp 70–98
Twining W, Stein A (1992) Introduction. In: Twining W, Stein A (eds) Evidence and proof. New York University Press, New York
Van Eemeren F, Garssen B (2009) The fallacies of composition and division revisited cogency. J Reasoning Argumentation 1(1):23–42
Wagenaar W, Koppen P, Crombag H (1993) Anchored narratives. A psychology of criminal evidence. Hervester Wheatsheaf, Hertfordshire
Wigmore H. (1913) The principles of judicial proof: as given by logic, psychology, and general experience, and illustrated in judicial trials. F.B. Rothman, Littleton, p 1988

Theories of Truth in Legal Fact-Finding

Viktor Gazda

Abstract Since the truth is always involved in determining the facts of a case, we as lawyers also need to ask a question, what it actually is to consider something true in a specific legal context. Simply, the truth is not legally described as something particular although we naturally want a court to decide on the ground of true facts. Once we know why the truth comes at the scene, we need to explore what it means—mostly in philosophy, and whether or how a judge could use this knowledge to issue a just decision based on a satisfying theoretical background.

1 Introduction

In this contribution, I shall discuss the relation between philosophical and legal concepts of determining the truthfulness of fact-findings. The main aim is to compare and decide whether these different kinds of concepts have something in common, and if the philosophical theories could somehow influence the decision, which factual conclusions are true or at least more probable to be true.

The decision to explore such a topic originates in one simple idea. Some judges may disagree, some of them usually say the aim of the process of finding the facts of a case is not to find the truth. Basically, as it is not a philosophical procedure but strictly a legal procedure. I do not think it is so simple. Would anyone want the court to decide on fact-findings that are false? I think even the most skeptical judges would refuse such an opinion. We then need to ask what the differences between the nature of truth in philosophy (as the main discipline exploring the phenomenon of truth) and in the application of law are. Once we admit we naturally think about the

This chapter was written with the support of the Charles University program SVV260494 "Integrating role of human rights in recent law".

V. Gazda (✉)
Charles University, School of Law, Prague, Czech Republic
e-mail: gazda@prf.cuni.cz

V. Klappstein, M. Dybowski (eds.), *Theory of Legal Evidence - Evidence in Legal Theory*, Law and Philosophy Library 138,
https://doi.org/10.1007/978-3-030-83841-6_7

truthfulness of fact-findings we also must count on the truth as a value of decision-making, or, at least, as an important criterion of right and just judgement. That means these two "worlds" must have something in common.

That is why, at first, a few key points of two important philosophical concepts, also being called "theories of truth", are shortly outlined. The correspondence theory and the coherence theory are not the only ones, there are many more in the philosophical and logical field. Anyway, it will be shown that these two concepts are probably the most important for decision-making solely concerning the stage of finding the facts. That is why I will not speak about pragmatic,[1] consensual,[2] semantic,[3] or any other concept having a great influence on the legal field.

After describing those philosophical basics, I move to outline two theoretical approaches to finding the facts of a case. These general concepts put a light on the requirements we demand from fact-findings to be true for the purposes of reaching a verdict. I should note that they were historically developed in the (post)soviet countries, therefore the legal grounds of this study are mostly situated in the central European legal context.

Section 4 is the key part of this chapter where I try to synthesize knowledge gained in the previous sections. I will stress the main points where philosophical and legal truth meet and design a conclusion of pros and cons of both legal approaches according to the elements of theories of truth, which mirrors in legal finding the facts of a case.

2 Basics of Theories of Truth

2.1 Correspondence Theory

In a simplified way, the key idea of this theory is that a statement is true when it corresponds with facts. That means it is also important to establish what the terms "fact" and "to correspond" stand for. The grounds of this theory were established by Aristotle, but he did not formulate it as a whole theory in the above-mentioned meaning. Aristotle was not using the word "fact".[4] He sometimes used the term "object" but more often he was talking about a state of things or a similar expression.[5] Nevertheless, the most important is Aristotle's concentration on outside reality.[6] Consideration of outside reality as a reference criterion of truthfulness

[1] James (1927).

[2] Habermas (2003).

[3] Tarski (1956).

[4] Crivelli (2006), p. 130.

[5] David (2016), available via https://plato.stanford.edu/archives/fall2016/entries/truth-correspondence/.

[6] Aristotle (2003), p. 180.

was later explored by other philosophers, mainly Thomas Aquinas,[7] and helped to develop a conception which has been the most commonly used even up to this day; mainly in the forms of the congruence and the correlation theories of correspondence.

The congruence correspondence theory of truth means that a statement is truth when its structure corresponds with the structure of a fact—as a relevant part of outside reality.[8] For instance, consider the statement "Paul is higher than Peter", in which we could see three elements. The first of them is "Paul", the second is "Peter" and the third is their relation. It is evident that if we change the first element for the third, the statement "Peter is higher than Paul", is of an entirely different meaning. That also means that for the validity of the congruence correspondence not just an accordance between those elements is important but also their order.[9]

Bertrand Russell, as the most significant representative of the congruence correspondence, introduces his theory with quite a natural idea; the groundings of this correspondence come out of a conviction of a thinking person, while the truthfulness of the person's statement is an attribute of such a conviction.[10] However, such a definition causes a problem with a false conviction which is not true despite a person's belief, so a real correspondence relation cannot exist.[11]

Russell realized that problem. His solution is based on looking out of an internal conviction and focuses on correspondence in external reality instead. If I am convinced of a historical event that did not happen, that does not mean I do not need to explore the fact itself, which is actually the other end of correspondence.[12] Thereby, Russell refuses a coherence theory of truth (see the next chapter) as a "monistic" theory in that regard.[13] Russell concludes that an existence of a conviction depends on our mind but the truthfulness of such a conviction is independent of mind.[14]

Let us introduce the second type of correspondence theory, the correlation correspondence theory of truth, also known as "Austin's theory of correspondence".[15] This second type of correspondence tries to come up with a solution of determining the truthfulness of more complicated or negative statements. This theory is not strictly built on a structural correspondence between facts and statements.

[7] Acquinas (2003).

[8] Kolář (2002), p. 71.

[9] Ibid., p. 73.

[10] Russell (1991), pp. 72–73.

[11] To prevent any ideas of the relativity of a conviction and difficulty of its determination (because truthfulness itself is a subject of exploring) consider for example physical laws. If a person is convinced that a thrown object does not fall down, we cannot talk about any correspondence, regardless of a person's conviction.

[12] Russell (1991), p. 75.

[13] Russell (2009), pp. 128–129.

[14] Russell (1991), p. 78.

[15] Kirkham (1995), p. 77.

Correlation correspondence understands that statements and facts are single units where the statement is true if it corresponds with the fact pursuant to a correlation as a language convention.[16] These conventions are either descriptive or demonstrative. Descriptive conventions correlate words with typical events and situations in the outside world. The demonstrative convention correlates statements with particular situations. Truthfulness of a statement is given by the mutual relation between individual components of a descriptive and demonstrative convention. I will try to explain these language conventions in the following text.

Representatives of the correlation correspondence prefer a language convention because they think it is unnatural to strictly compare the structure of the elements of statements and facts. The truthfulness of statements is given by a language convention as a result of the historical development of language.[17] The key difference between these two types of correspondence is that the congruence theory demands structurally identical accordance between elements of facts and statements while for the correlation theory it is sufficient if the facts and statements correspond as whole units. In fact, that is one of the reasons the correlation correspondence theory of truth was built on the language convention. The criterion of identical congruence seems to be improper in case of complicated statements which could be difficult to separate into individual elements without the partial loss of objectivity of comparison.

To be thorough, Austin's theory counts on the possibility of congruence, i.e. "mirroring" of elements of statements (convictions) in outside events (reality). However, if it happens, it is a result of linguistic efficiency.[18] The reason for truthfulness is not structural accordance between individual elements, but, the accordance between the descriptive and demonstrative language convention.[19]

Austin's construction of truthfulness consists of four elements. To understand his theory, it is necessary to realize the definition of demonstrative and descriptive convention and not to see them misleadingly (regarding the general meaning of those words). Unlike Russell's theory, statements as testimonies (not convictions) play the key role. To continue, descriptive conventions correlate words (sentences) with events or situations of the same kind. Demonstrative conventions correlate testimonies with particular situations in the outside world. Hence, a statement is true, when a specific situation (correlating with the statement/testimony) is a type of typical situation, which is linked to the linguistic expression of that very statement.[20] However, do not forget that the linking bridge of this correlation is a matter of language convention, not structural accordance.

Consider the sentence "I forgot my bag" as an example. This sentence is true if I do not have my bag in a particular situation (and I wanted to have it with me). That means I also forgot the items I packed into it, and this situation is a type of a unit of

---

[16]Kolář (2002), p. 71.

[17]Kirkham (1995), p. 119.

[18]Ibid., p. 124.

[19]Austin (Urmson, Warnock eds) (1979), p. 125.

[20]Ibid., p. 122.

events, in which somebody does not have the things they wanted to have with them as a result of forgetting a bag (because we do not usually forget just an empty bag).

2.2 Coherence Theory

The coherence theory of truth is partly a reaction to the correspondence theory. While the correspondence theory focuses on outside reality as a referential criterion of truthfulness, according to the coherence theory, a statement is true when it fits into a unit of known true convictions. If a considered statement makes a group of coherent, harmonic convictions with other true statements in the mind of a thinking person, then the considered statement is true.[21] It means it is not the compliance with the outside world that this theory wants to determine, but a coherent group consisting of our gained conviction thus far (considered true). A considered statement must fill in this coherent complex to be proved. A testimony is true if it is not in any contradiction with other convictions as elements of a relevant complex. Such a referential complex has to consist of convictions that are logically non-contradictory, harmonic, and fully filled.

Looking out of an outside reality and focusing on our mind instead is a result of a hypothesis that if the knowledge is part of our mind then the truth must be as well. It does not mean a statement cannot originate in outside reality. According to Brand Blanshard, it is important to assume that any item, event, etc. taking place in an objective reality represents a subject to our internal thoughts, which is relevant for determining truthfulness.[22] Blanshard claims that thinking is searching for understanding.[23] Such a process is different from any external activity. That is why Kirkham stresses that this kind of truthfulness needs to be gained by these processes of mind.[24]

It may seem that the biggest weakness of the coherence theory is how to determine the truthfulness of the original convictions. Such convictions are considered true before a particular statement is regarded by them as a criterion of truth. At this point, we still do not know, why these previous convictions are true as they were part of the mind before the whole process started. I will try to explain the key arguments for a defense of this theory.

At first, we need to realize which questions the coherence theory aims to answer. This also means that we need to determine what it means that a complex of internal convictions is non-contradictory, harmonic, and fully filled.

[21] Kolář (2002), p. 81.

[22] Blanshard (1955), p. 261.

[23] Ibid.

[24] Kirkham (1995), p. 105.

Not all protagonists of this theory want to clarify the concept of truth itself. Rather, they focus on a justification of a statement that is considered true.[25] Although some of the representatives of the coherence theory aim to determine the term of truth,[26] hereafter I will focus on the procedural part of the conception being in question. Hence, in the connection with the theme of this contribution, I will concentrate on coherence as a way of justifying truth.

The key meaning of non-contradictory, harmonic, and fully filled complex rests on the idea that each of its parts is consistent with any other part of the same complex of convictions. It also means that each part is supposed to be implied by other parts; altogether and also individually.[27] Petr Kolář sees the harmony and satiety of a complex together as completeness.[28]

According to Kirkham, Blanshard left out the possibility that just coherence of a testimony with other convictions does not necessarily mean it is true.[29] Blanshard does not consider the intensity of a connection of a testimony with convictions, hence, coherence does not need to mean proof of truth but only a level of probability that particular statement is true. Kirkham simply concludes that the only thing coherence proves is that a considered statement is coherent with others.[30]

In a process of judicial decision making it is important to admit that cognition of absolute truth is often impossible and, what is more, we cannot leave out the role of probability when evaluating evidence.

I see the weaknesses of the coherence theory arise from its non-intuitive conception compared to the theory of correspondence. We commonly use the external reality as an empirical criterion of proof. That is probably why Kirkham reminds us that the deficiency of the coherence theory is an unwillingness of evaluating the testimony in relation to external reality.[31]

However, the theory in question has also its strengths. Consider a situation when a court does not have enough evidence to (dis)prove a claimed fact on the basis of correspondence. It is not difficult to imagine such a situation that a judge could find herself in,[32] especially in this age with an enormous amount of information. Depending on a nature of a particular fact, we cannot exclude a possibility that "true" convictions in the mind of a judge could make a criterion of truth. These convictions work in the mind as an experience with a similar situation in the past. Thus, we need to state a question, whether it is more intuitive to compare such a claim with "true" convictions gained in the past in a case when it is not possible to compare the claimed fact with the reality. It will be shown that sometimes it seems

[25] Ibid., p. 104.

[26] Blanshard (1955), p. 260.

[27] Ibid., p. 264; see also Kirkham (1995), p. 104.

[28] Kolář (2002), p. 86.

[29] Kirkham (1995), p. 106.

[30] Ibid.

[31] Ibid., p. 111.

[32] Dworkin (1991), p. 373.

too strict of a demand to achieve the correspondence relationship as a proof of a fact. That is why Blanshard thought that demanding correspondence as a criterion of truth every single time excludes the knowledge of the truth when the possibility of direct verification of a testimony is missing.[33]

3 Fundamental Approaches to Legal Fact-Finding

In this chapter, I would like to describe two fundamental approaches to the process of legal fact-finding concerning the truthfulness of claimed facts. These approaches are mostly known as the so-called principle of formal truth and the principle of substantive (or material) truth. These principles were abundantly used by the Soviet legal science[34] but mostly under a bit of a different meaning than today.

3.1 Historical Context

Searching for material truth was a leading procedural principle in Soviet countries in the second half of the twentieth century. It was claimed that only this material approach to legal fact-finding can find the *real* truth in a judicial process.[35]

The original idea of this concept is that a liberal concept of justice in western countries uses "formal" truth as a decisive factor between the subjective truths of parties.[36] While the material truth principle was supposed to ensure looking for objective truth to guarantee a just verdict, the opposite approach to legal fact-finding could make the justice of a court's decision a matter of coincidence.[37]

Searching for the real/objective truth is a problematic aim since we know the human ability to acquire knowledge is naturally limited. Representatives of this historical concept of material truth acknowledge the existence of absolute and objective truth, which is supposed to be realized as a product of thinking about mankind not just as an individual.[38] A true understanding of a fact by an individual is a relative truth by which the absolute truth is supposed to be consisted of.[39] This relative truth is partial knowledge of the "whole" truth, not just a subjective perception of the truth.

[33] Cited by Kirkham (1995), p. 111.

[34] As an exception to the rule see Summers (2000), p. 285.

[35] Rubeš (1970), p. 46.

[36] Vyšinskij (1950), p. 238.

[37] Rubeš (1970), p. 46.

[38] Boura (1954), p. 79.

[39] Idid.

Modern thinking is either skeptical to use these principles[40] or understands them differently than before. Nowadays, the conception of material (substantive) truth is not strictly linked to absolute knowledge as an actual aim; it could be better described as a requirement for a thorough process of court's finding of facts. This conception is constructed as an opposite position to the formal truth, which is understood as a fact-finding process based on strictly followed procedural rules.[41] In this conception, the formal truth is not meant as the subjective truth of parties but as a result of a detailed legal structure of judicial finding of facts. Hence, substantive truth is also described as a fact-finding process without formal limitations.[42]

3.2 *Objectivity of Finding the Facts of a Case*

The key reason for the claimed importance of finding the real truth as a factual basis for a judicial decision is a distrust of the subjective truth of an individual.[43] But, the material truth meant as an objective truth was rather a political principle[44] than an actual approach to determine the facts of a case. It is not necessary to analyze the ideological background of those times; let us focus directly on the possibility of making objective factual conclusions when applying the law. It may seem obvious that the court tries to get as close as possible to true knowledge about the facts. But what does it really mean?

We know that acquiring factual "material" of a case is enabled by empirical recognition. Through the sensorial mechanisms and intellectual processes of the mind, we try to learn the things and events which took place in the past. That means learning experience from judicial evidence is mostly an indirect process with unsure outcomes. Of course, the probability of proving facts will differ. But the probability may never be a hundred percent since a judge tries to recognize something which had happened before the trial began. To be precise, an individual judge perceives evidence directly, but the evidence shall hold information about something which is not present. To be complete, direct perception of evidence is possible, but not so common, for example during an examination (site inspection, etc.).

In the judgement from 14 January 1885, the German Imperial Court of Justice noted that "*as a result of limited means of human understanding, nobody can (except for cases of direct observation of a particular action) come to absolutely sure knowledge of existence or non-existence of a fact; there are always conceivable options that key facts did not happened.*"[45]

[40] Zoulík In: Frischmann et al. (1996), p. 38.
[41] Winterová and Macková (2018), p. 80.
[42] Ibid.; Knapp (1995), p. 217.
[43] Štajgr (1954), p. 107.
[44] Boura (1954), p. 75.
[45] Cited by Macur (2001), p. 127.

Once we admit limitations to human understanding and idealistic nature of acquiring an absolute truth, we must also refuse the idea of the so-called material truth as it was designed during the Soviet era. Which means, we should either fulfill the material principle with different content or abandon it. That is why modern authors think that the material truth today means the subjective conviction of a judge as an opposite position to the formalistic following of procedural rules. Of course, such a distinction is not enough. We must add that such a subjective conviction of truth needs to be supported by a sufficient quantum of proof and also a solution of situations when a judge is not convinced about either the truth or the falsity; thus, to think about the rules of a burden of proof as well.

4 Truthfulness in Legal Fact-Finding

4.1 Material "Correspondence" Approach

A few basic features of the correspondence theory of truth were presented in Sect. 2.1. This theory is built on the existence of internal, perhaps hidden, truth and its recognition through the elements of the correspondence relation.

As it was said above, according to the correspondence theory of truth, a statement is true when it corresponds with facts. Its essence is the reflection of external reality and exploring its concordance with examined statements.

From such a conception arises a possible influence on a modern nature of the so-called material truth principle.[46] Let us think of the material truth principle in its "soft" version as a fact-finding process not bounded by formal limitations. This means a process not formally determined by its details but where the subjective conviction of a judge is crucial for deciding the state of facts. To some extent, a potential judge compares a concordance—correspondence—of stated facts with the reality of external world acquired by evidence. If a judge concludes the ascertained facts match the "reality", the claimed facts are recognized as true. According to ascertaining a correspondence, a judge gains true "factual substrate" for decisions followed by the application of legal rules on such a "real" material.

Two basic ways to ascertain the factual material for judicial decisions are perception and evidence. Thus, the purpose of evidence is to prove the key facts of a case. Unlike evidence, perception helps a court to ascertain facts directly, followed by deliberating as a non-experience-based process.

Direct judicial fact-finding is only possible by site inspection. We then speak about a minor way of fact-finding—about perceiving. Other facts, which had not happened before a judge or jury, that are not accessible by the direct perception by senses, are ascertained by evidence indirectly.

---

[46] See Holländer (2012), p. 269.

Let us get back to theories of truth and the material truth principle. If a court's decision is based on directly perceived facts, then it would be easy to state that the correspondence theory of truth is applied. There are usually correspondence requirements for deciding on the truthfulness of claimed facts.[47] However, using the correspondence theory for evidence is more complicated since the mostly indirect nature of it. Knowledge gained by evidence is followed by a judge's thinking and these factual inferences are a kind of information about the facts of external world. This information also represents a criterion of truth in the sense of the correspondence theory.

According to the congruence correspondence theory, a statement is true when its individual elements structurally fit elements of a relevant part of external reality. It might be right to consider potential facts true using the congruence correspondence when we think of things or events (or evidence) that happened in the judge's presence. For example, a plaintiff claims her house is seven meters high but during the court's site inspection it is found to be just six meters high, then her testimony was false. This conclusion is based on a simple observation—perceived by senses, so there is no other evidence needed to prove the height of the building.

Well, as I said before, most of the factual claims need to be proved by indirect evidence. For instance, the plaintiff claimed that the defendant paid the agreed amount of money after the agreed maturity date, so she asks for late charges. Think of a situation when the defendant claims he returned the money to the plaintiff during a personal meeting. It is obvious that the judge cannot directly observe such an event.

The correlation correspondence theory considers a statement true when its demonstrative correlation is a type of descriptive correlation. When the testimony about a claimed fact meets the typical range of this type of fact, then it is true, because the language convention says that the mutual correspondence of those two conventions means truthfulness of the testimony. The court would consider if (when) the personal meeting of a plaintiff and a defendant happened and if a defendant gave the agreed amount of money to a plaintiff. Judge's subjective conviction of the existence of such a meeting cannot be considered a fact of external world. This conviction was based on evidence, and both logic and experience-based processes of the mind, so its truthfulness is never a matter of certainty but always a level of probability.

The descriptive convention in such an example consists of an experience that a meeting of the contractual parties shortly before the maturity date is usually purposed to pay the debt. In the case of a judge's subjective conviction of the existence of all relevant elements of the descriptive and demonstrative convention, there is nothing that keeps her from concluding the statement is true (on a basis of the correlation correspondence theory of truth). Let us consider the testimony of a meeting of those two parties correlates with a proven meeting of a plaintiff and a defendant (demonstrative convention). Let us also imagine such a fact corresponds

[47] Macur (2001), p. 11.

with reliable testimonies about the meeting of the contractual parties while these statements would correlate with a typical real state of a meeting (descriptive convention). When a judge's conviction of relevant elements of searched correspondence meets these conditions, then the two examined sets could be considered mutually corresponding and the examined statement true.

Besides the correspondence theory, there are two basic types of material truth as well, as they were outlined above. The correspondence theory was so far analyzed for a type of procedural principle which does not necessarily aim to find the real objective truth. I outlined the basics of congruence (especially when site inspection is ordered) and correlation correspondence (in cases more often aimed at proving past events). The latter indirect evidence is used by a court in the process of examining events or states that happened before the judicial proceedings.[48] Typically, we could see the elements of correlation during the examinations of witnesses. So, it remains to explore a more ambitious type of material truth principle, aiming to find the *real/objective* truth.

Concerning the second type, we do need to realize its nature as an ideological proclamation. It is useless to search for correspondence in real truth because the real truth in its common meaning would always bear correspondence elements.

While thinking about a real truth we do not explore the real truth because its finding is the actual and ideal goal of the finding of facts. Finding the real truth would actually mean finding an absolute correspondence. But, in the context of what was said before, such an aim faces significant epistemic difficulties. Indirect probation cannot detect congruence correspondence between a claimed fact and a past event as a structural accordance of a statement and reality. That accordance could only be found in the correlation correspondence.

When the procedural aim of a finding of facts means finding the real truth, then it is the ideological proclamation of the absolute objectivity of fact-findings, and the congruence correspondence is a proclamation as well. A claimed search and finding the real truth would mean a permeation of correspondence through the process of finding of facts. Due to the fact the correspondence theory is not a theory of absolute truth, then has its part—the correlation—always been relatively probabilistic in nature. We could also find elements of correlation when considering the material or substantive truth search for the real truth. That's because an individual judge has to aim to ascertain facts, which does not mean finding the real truth every time; finding the real truth is an ideal goal of such a process. Actually, a judge ascertained more or less probable knowledge she considered "true".

Trying to detect what it means for a finding of facts that the facts are true in the terms of the correspondence theory, we mainly need to think about the correlation version of correspondence. This type especially enables a determination of a "truthful" basic in fact-finding concerning the procedural approach, which takes the fundamental epistemic difficulties into account. In different words, it is not often possible to determine the one absolute truth, it is obviously not possible to think

[48] Risinger (2013), p. 808.

about the philosophical truth[49] used in a judicial process as a mirror image of external reality in claimed facts. As it was mentioned, such a simple comparison would not work in most cases. Considering that kind of option is a result of an epistemic "trap". It arises from an idea that where there are objective facts, there is also an objective truth.[50] But, the key epistemic goal is not the concept of such truth but how to find it. Since the process of finding of facts is a practical legal process, this kind of criterion—one objective truth—seems too idealistic and hardly achievable.

But the judicial decision is, of course, not a resignation on being based on true facts. Knowing such natural difficulties is mirrored in a justification of factual conclusions. The justification process is independent of the truthfulness of a judge's belief.[51] Which does not mean some factual claims would be absolutely relevant and some others not at all.[52] It also does not mean that all factual statements are equal because, of course, some of them are more significant to resolve a case than others. That means the process of finding of facts should lead to conclusions that are based on as many "strong" facts and arguments as possible, which, however, do not necessarily aspire to find the absolute truth. Instead of finding the real truth, it should aim to acquire as probable factual conclusion as possible, which is supposed to be justified as good as it could be.

Though, fact-findings shall be acquired plausibly and properly, the process of finding of facts is not the same as searching for the truth. In other words, a judge cannot be sure of objectively true facts which would have been independent of her mind. What is important is that regarding this metaphysical barrier, it is not the goal of a court to determine metaphysically objective knowledge but more of a socially determined state of facts.[53] What a court tries to find is, as well as its own job, part of social reality. However, during a finding of facts, a court needs to find answers to factual questions determined by past events.[54] We talk about objective fact-finding because we want to know the facts that objectively happened before in external, objective reality. However, strictly speaking, it is not the same as absolutely objective knowledge we could talk about—for example in natural sciences. A court does not explore natural laws entirely independent of the mind of a judge.

Facts that need to be found during a course of a proceedings are determined by past events as an objective state of things. But, in a judicial process, those facts almost always partly have a subjective nature. John Searle noticed that ontologically subjective matter could be epistemically objective.[55] I suppose that knowledge considered subjective from the perspective of natural sciences might in a sense

[49]Meant as truth in a strictly philosophical sense.

[50]Nicolson (1994), p. 737.

[51]Coleman (1997), p. 183; Ho (2008), p. 116.

[52]Nicolson (1994), p. 732.

[53]See Damaška (1998), p. 291.

[54]See Šámal (2008), p. 349.

[55]Searle (1995), pp. 200, 203.

sometimes be objectively used in social sciences. That is because, unlike natural science during a lawsuit, a judge subjectively interprets and completes indirectly perceived reality because she is a human being with a partly "subjective" mind.

Think about months of a year. Twelve months of a year and a year itself, counted from the 1st January until the 31st December, are human "products". Strictly speaking, there are no January, February, etc. that we discovered. These intervals exist only as parts of the social reality determined by human activities and human laws. Objective facts, in this case, are only the Earth circulation around the Sun and the time passing. Nevertheless, for the purposes of adjudication, these "products" are objective facts, which even cannot be a subject of evidence.

Summarized, searching for truth ought to be the key aspect in finding the facts of a case. The need for justification requires external, epistemic conditions for searching. Try to issue a just decision should include an attempt to search for truth, i.e. also with just process of justification of court's factual conclusions.[56]

4.2 Formal "Coherence" Approach

In Sect. 2.2 of this chapter, it was said that the coherence theory of truth kind of reacts to the correspondence theory; the essence of truth is found in the coherence between statements and a complex of internal convictions considered to be true.

Once we think of the formal approach to finding of facts of a case as structured procedures determining this process, it occurs to compare this legal principle with the coherence philosophical theory. What these two conceptions have in common, is looking out of external reality as a criterion of truth.

Exploring the factual basics of a case at least partly using the formal approach is based on following formal procedural rules, by which the factual claims are examined. Of course, that does not mean the whole process of finding the facts is determined by procedural rules. But it also means that when a particular procedural institute is built and applied on such an intellectual construction, then the facts of a case are at least partly dependent on following such norms. We basically compare claimed facts with an already known complex of "true" convictions delivered by the strict following of procedural rules. That is why we call it "formal" truth.

That leads me to the idea of mirroring the elements of the coherence theory of truth in a formal procedural approach as it was outlined above. A factual finding acquired by a court by abiding by a formal procedure is a continuation of "evidence coherence" of the procedural norm. This norm represents the basic precondition of the finding of the facts of a case; hence a result of the application of such a norm is represented by fact-finding.[57] The fact founded by such a formal procedure is dependent on the applied legal norm, thus, they need to be coherent. The mutual

[56] See Dennis (2007), p. 49.

[57] See Amaya (2013), p. 6.

relationship between a procedural norm and dependent factual findings acts as a cause and a consequence.

It is not surprising that a cause and a consequence are coherent in general. However, not each coherence must be true. In other words, not all coherent facts gained by the formal process of finding the facts need to be true under the coherence theory of truth. If not, such a conception would lead to absurd conclusions; every result of an application of a legal norm would be true because their coherence is a consequence of the realization of required behavior being contained in the applied norm. Such an outlined consistency is not a result of the truth, but of the fulfillment of the factual essence of a norm in its hypothesis, according to which the actual rule is realized.[58]

The criterion for a coherence truth is a complex of internal convictions which are considered true for a particular reason. Well, this complex is a part of mental consciousness of an exploring subject. We could speak about coherence truth only if the procedural rule refers (indirectly) to the judge's convictions about truth.

As for a coherence conception of a court's finding of the facts not to be just a relation of a cause and a consequence (which is tautological concerning the value of truth), the criterion of truth must originate outside the legal rule. I.e. outside a procedural rule resulting from the formal approach and such a criterion needs to have "truthful potential". By this potential I understand a certain factual extent of a procedural rule, which regulates the quality of factual findings. Or at least part of the quality is an indirect result of an application of such a rule. When we consider for example procedural norms regulating conditions for abatement, they affect the extent of findings of the facts (because they actually prevent the court from acquiring the factual findings). Nevertheless, they have no influence on their quality. *Vice versa*, even the rules regulating the issuance of a decision based on fact-findings without evidence, influence the quality of factual conclusions a lot. We could see such rules concerning a judgement to reject an 'out-of-time' claim or a recognition judgement.

During the regular application of a legal norm without "truthful potential", it is the relation between a statement and a piece of knowledge we talk about Paul Thagard describes that as coherence between a piece of knowledge and a hypothesis of such knowledge.[59] When a hypothesis explains particular knowledge they are mutually coherent. This relation being some kind of coherence does not mean this coherence is relevant from the view of the coherence theory of truth. The difference is that the legal coherence does not always need to be the result of using the formal procedural approach to legal finding the facts of a case. Formal truth could mirror certain elements of coherence theory but is not a result of searching for philosophical truth, but more of a procedural formalism or pragmatism, affecting the extent and quality of fact-findings.[60]

---

[58] Gerlich (1934), p. 15; Lavický (2017), pp. 93–94.

[59] Thagard (1989), p. 459; Thagard (2002), p. 43.

[60] In this case, I do not mean formalism as a formalistic application of law but only an approach to determine certain kinds of procedural rules.

The same problem could be detected in proving the truth concerning the philosophical theory of coherence, as we could see in this formal approach. I mean proving why the internal convictions shall be true in the first place. When a complex of proven facts does not show any contradiction—is internally consistent and harmonic, this does not guarantee such a complex was acquired by the usage of rules established to accomplish true fact-findings. Therefore, this does not mean that a factual conclusion must correspond with external reality.

Doubting this type of factual conclusion being true comes from the absence of correspondence intuition in the coherence theory, as it was outlined in Sect. 2.2. These conclusions could be doubted as well because the making of procedural rules being in question is also influenced by others, shall we say pragmatic motives, which does not aim to find the "correspondence" truth, i.e. truth in its basic sense (see Sect. 2.1).

It should be noted that the absence of empirical verifying of a statement is partly compensated by the nature of the complex of internal true conviction. These convictions must also originate from external experiences. The criterion of truth being part of an exploring mind does not mean its content is arbitrary. The difference is that concerning the coherence theory we think about external facts as facts mirroring in our mind.[61] If a judge does not acquire facts through evidence, but still thinks these facts are true, then such truthfulness must be arising from the coherence of a statement with previous experience with a similar statement. The coherence theory does not try to define the truth but more to justify a process leading to the conviction that the statement is true.[62]

The formal truth approach contains elements of the coherence theory of truth and has a similar weakness as the coherence theory. This weakness is a result of mutual measuring of the correspondence and the coherence truth. That problem arises from formal truth looking away from external reality and lacking a sufficient level of correspondence intuition. Such a lack of intuition might be at least partly compensated by the judge's experience which was originally considered true on a ground of correspondence.

I consider the correspondence intuition a natural phenomenon, which strictly speaking (on its own) does not say anything important about the truth. Claims tried to be proven in court refer to facts being regulated by substantive law, while concerning the formal truth approach we explore their coherence with "true" experience due to procedural law (certain procedural rules). However, substantive rules do not become a part of procedural rules. Procedural rules aim to protect rights arising from relations based on substantive law.[63]

---

[61] Blanshard (1955), p. 261.

[62] Kirkham, (1995), p. 105.

[63] Macur (2001), p. 59.

5 Conclusion

In this contribution, two key philosophical conceptions of truth and two main ideological approaches to the process of finding the facts of a case were outlined. After analyzing their nature, I designed a few ideas about what they have in common, which led me to conclusions about what they are like.

We could say that mainly used and perhaps the most "natural" philosophical way to explain what the truth is, is the correspondence theory. Not surprisingly, the key idea of a statement being true when it corresponds with the facts is mostly used in the application of the law. Carrying on, the first type of the correspondence theory—the congruence correspondence theory could be used only when we observe evidence directly or when we generally think about fact-findings supposed to be objectively true. Once it is established, we can hardly imagine finding the objective truth by standard evidence, we must focus on the correlation correspondence theory as a fundamental approach to determine the truth. However, that also forces us to admit the truth in adjudication has predominantly subjective and probabilistic nature.

On the other hand, the signs of the coherence theory of truth could be also found in judicial decision-making. Mostly, when legal rules bind the court to decide on the factual ground which was not proven true before. This does not happen very often but is still important; especially in the case of a judgement to reject an 'out-of-time' claim or a recognition judgement. The moment of coherence rests on the judge's experience that a particular factual claim is true because similar claims in similar procedural situations (when some kind of formal norms must be applied) are usually true. The lack of the correspondence intuition and verifying by evidence are partly compensated by the external origin of such experience and could be explained as a result of simple practical issues that need to be solved by some kind of procedural pragmatism.

To conclude, it shall be noted, that using the idea of the correspondence and the material truth is not meant as searching for objective truth. It is more of a focusing on realistic aim concerning the results of an analysis of what the truth means. We can hardly fully understand what it is. However, we shall try to at least approach this goal as close as possible. Even though we could detect some elements of truth in finding the facts of a case, this legal process and philosophical conceptions exploring the truth are not the same. Despite the fact they do have something in common, the process of finding the facts cannot be fully divided into searching for the truth by simply using different theories of truth. The legally binding process aiming to deliver a right and just verdict needs to meet various practical conditions and cannot be confused with logical and philosophical approaches to searching for truth.

References

Acquinas T (Štěpinová M ed) (2003) About truth. About mind. Krystal OP, Prague
Amaya A (2013) Coherence, evidence, and legal proof. Legal Theory 1:1–13
Aristotle (2003) Metaphysics. Petr Rezek, Prague
Austin JL, (Urmson JO, Warnock GJ eds) (1979) Philosophical papers. Oxford University Press, Oxford.
Blanshard B (1955) The nature of thought. Allen & Unwin, London
Boura F (1954) Evidence according to the civil procedure code: on the theory of evidence in civil procedure. Orbis, Prague
Coleman J (1997) Rational choice and rational cognition. Legal Theory 2:183–203
Crivelli P (2006) Aristotle on truth. Cambridge University Press, Cambridge
Damaška M (1998) Truth in adjudication. Hast Law J 2:289–308
David M (2016) The correspondence theory of truth. The Stanford Encyclopedia of Philosophy. Available via http://www.plato.stanford.edu/archives/fall2016/entries/truth-correspondence/. Accessed 23 June 2018
Dennis I (2007) The law of evidence. Sweet & Maxwell, London
Dworkin R (1991) Pragmatism, right answers, and true banality. In: Brint M, Weaver W (eds) Pragmatism in law and society. Routledge, New York
Frischmann P, Mikeš J, Hlavsa P, Zoulík F, Macková A, Salač J, Winterová A (eds) (1996) The law of civil procedure: textbook. Institute of Social Relations, Prague
Gerlich K (1934) Fact-finding and legal assessment in judicial process. Orbis, Prague
Habermas J (2003) Truth and justification. MIT Press, Cambridge
Ho HL (2008) A philosophy of evidence law: justice in the search for truth. Oxford University Press, Oxford
Holländer P (2012) Philosophy of law. Aleš Čeněk, Pilsen (Czech Republic)
James W (1927) The meaning of truth: a sequel to pragmatism. Longmans, London
Kirkham RL (1995) Theories of truth: a critical introduction. MIT Press, Cambridge
Knapp V (1995) Legal theory. C. H. Beck, Prague
Kolář P (2002) Truth and fact. Filosofia, Prague
Lavický P (2017) Burden of proof in civil procedure. Leges, Prague
Macur J (2001) Postmodernism and fact-finding in civil procedure. Masaryk University, Brno
Nicolson D (1994) Truth, reason and justice: epistemology and politics in evidence discourse. Mod Law Rev 5:726–744
Risinger DM (2013) Searching for truth in the American law of evidence and proof. Georgia Law Rev 3:801–835
Rubeš J (ed) (1970) Czech Civil Procedure Code: Commentary, vol. 1. Orbis, Prague
Russell B (1991) The problems of philosophy. Oxford University Press, Oxford
Russell B (2009) Philosophical essays. Routledge, London
Šámal P (2008) Executing the evidence during the trial and absolute and relative inefficacy of the evidence in the intention of the czech criminal procedure code. Crim Law Revue 12:349–357
Searle JR (1995) The construction of social reality. Simon and Schuster, New York
Štajgr F (1954) The material truth in civil procedure. Orbis, Prague
Summers RS (2000) Formal legal truth and substantive legal truth in judicial fact-finding. In: Summers RS, Laporta F, Peczenik A, Schauer F (eds) Essays in legal theory. Kluwer Academic Publishers, Dordrecht
Tarski A (1956) Logic, semantics, metamathematics: papers from 1923 to 1938. Clarendon Press, Oxford
Thagard P (1989) Explanatory coherence. Behav Brain Sci 12:435–467
Thagard P (2002) Coherence in thought and action. MIT Press, Cambridge
Vyšinskij AJ (1950) Theory of judicial evidence in the soviet law. Mír, Prague
Winterová A, Macková A (eds) (2018) The law of civil procedure, vol 1. Leges, Prague

Part III
Legal Evidence Put in Practice

Expert's (Meta)Testimony: An Epistemological Perspective

Adam Dyrda and Maciej Próchnicki

Abstract Expert witnesses play an important role in a legal process. Courts often appoint up to several experts to help resolve a specific factual case at hand. The mere fact that a judge decides to appoint experts to provide special information suggests that from the judicial perspective, such experts are (1) epistemically superior to a judge and (2) equals, i.e. epistemic peers with respect to each other. The problem arises when the opinions provided by two or more experts differ substantially. In our paper, we would like to address how such disagreements can be resolved by means of the institutional structure of the judicial process. For example, a judge may be allowed to evaluate the opinions herself to appoint another expert witness, or to ask for a meta-testimony (meta-opinion). The following issues arise: How can a judge, lacking of special knowledge, assess the correctness of expert opinions (as inferior on the epistemic level)? A judge has no grounds to provide a reliable argument as to which opinion is more plausible. An appointment of another expert may be an instance of "cherry-picking". As we will argue, in cases where experts are not able to discuss their differences (conciliate) in order to reach a joint opinion, it might be best to appoint a meta-expert who will assess the reliability and correctness of disagreeing opinions. At the end of the paper, we provide certain normative, *de lege ferenda* suggestions as how to shape the institution of a meta-expert in legal proceedings.

Adam Dyrda was supported by National Science Centre, Poland (Grant no. 2020/37/B/HS5/00272). Maciej Próchnicki was supported by National Science Centre, Poland (Grant no. 2017/27/B/HS5/01407).

A. Dyrda (✉) · M. Próchnicki
Jagiellonian University, Kraków, Poland
e-mail: adam.dyrda@uj.edu.pl; maciej.prochnicki@uj.edu.pl

V. Klappstein, M. Dybowski (eds.), *Theory of Legal Evidence - Evidence in Legal Theory*, Law and Philosophy Library 138,
https://doi.org/10.1007/978-3-030-83841-6_8

1 Introduction

The field of legal evidence is troubled by a plethora of different types of problems. A particular sort of problem arises in regard to so-called scientific evidence, i.e., the type of evidence that makes use of the newest developments in applied sciences, or otherwise requires special knowledge.[1] This particular body of knowledge is usually incorporated into legal proceedings through the opinions of expert witnesses. Due to dynamic progress in forensics, expert knowledge is nowadays fairly common in legal proceedings, mostly in criminal cases, but not only. Legal evaluation of expert witnesses' opinions is exceptionally troublesome for a few reasons. Firstly, as noted by Paul Roberts,[2] forensic science is complex: although it stems from the specific goal of providing methods for proving facts, the problems related to applying science to legal proceedings are in fact a set of intertwined technological, institutional, and regulatory issues. Forensic science is also continually changing, which means that we cannot generally establish rules of conduct regarding particular methods, other than a few methodological principles. As a result, examining expert evidence in court settings is an overwhelming epistemic challenge.

In the following article, we will focus on one particular type of problem related to expert evidence, namely, the epistemological questions of disagreement between the expert witnesses, putting a lot of other questions on the margin. Firstly, we are setting aside the general problems related to the legal version of the demarcation problem, i.e., distinguishing science from non-science and pseudo-science, and whether to accept methods that are on the margins between sound science and so-called junk science[3] in the courtroom. Thus, we assume that in the case of genuine expert witness disagreement (GEWD), all competing parties are using sound methods and fulfil all other assumed criteria that qualify them as being experts. The criteria for qualification as an expert in a discourse will be briefly discussed further in the next section (both from the juridical as well as more general epistemological points of view). Moreover, we exclude cases in which disagreement is only apparent, but due to the specific procedural settings, the discrepancies between the two opinions are highlighted.[4] We will also not be addressing problems related to the disproportionate approval or scepticism shown by judges or juries.

Our main problem to tackle is rather to analyse (*in abstracto*) the situation in which the court has to assess and resolve a disagreement between two or more experts who are initially taken as equals (i.e., epistemic peers with respect to the factual matter described by the court). The court that appoints experts takes them to be epistemic authorities—and the essence of the problem is that the court is generally epistemically inferior. In other words, it is unable to solve genuine scientific

[1] This means that for the sake of expert opinion, scientific evidence will be understood broadly, not being limited to 'science' in the strict sense. See Sect. 2.

[2] Roberts (2018), p. 30.

[3] See, for example, Kaplan and Puracal (2017).

[4] Roberts (2018), p. 34.

disagreements.[5] Nonetheless, the problem must be solved somehow to establish a factual basis for the ruling and fulfil the goals of the legal procedure. We see clearly that there are two types of authorities involved: the epistemic authority possessed by experts and the normative authority possessed by courts.

We adopt an institutional perspective on the proceedings and distinguish three possible solutions to the problem.[6] The first is to allow the judges to decide themselves. This decision could go in a number of ways: accepting the opinion of only one of the experts (for example, perceiving one of them as a better qualified expert, or assessing the credibility of methodology), trying to propose one's own view by drawing on conflicting opinions, or refraining from taking a stand in the epistemic conflict (and resolving the issue by using extra-epistemic legal principles, such as presumption of innocence). The major problem related to this strategy is that any action taken by a judge in this respect demands further solid justification which s/he, as epistemically inferior, simply cannot provide.[7]

The second solution would be to appeal to a higher normative authority, i.e., a higher-instance court. While freeing first-instance judges as triers of fact from the burden of deciding, it seems to not provide any solution other than passing on the "hot potato".

The third option would be to appeal to a higher epistemic authority, i.e., another expert. As it may seem the best fitting alternative, two main questions arise. Should the third expert offer another opinion regarding the issue, or maybe prepare a "meta-opinion" (testimony) in which s/he evaluates two (or more) conflicting ones? Apart from these, should a mere number of opinions—a purely quantitative factor—be a decisive factor in answering this question? Our main frame of reference will be epistemology, leaving a number of practical problems related to the efficiency of the proceedings as secondary issues.

These and similar problems have been thoroughly discussed by epistemologists in the context of the wider problem of the "epistemology of peer disagreement". It seems that at least some of the general solutions developed within epistemological debates may be applied here.

In the article, we also take an initial civil law view on the procedure, which means two things. Firstly, we will address judges as the main decision-making body in the

[5] Roberts (2018), p. 35.

[6] Cf. Roberts (2018), p. 48 onwards, where a slightly different framework is adopted.

[7] Deirdre Dwyer, an author of a comprehensive epistemological inquiry on expert evidence, argues for the limited competence of triers in assessing expert evidence: '[T]he non-expert tribunal of fact is epistemically competent to make some assessment of the reasoning of experts, since the way in which experts perform inferential reasoning is fundamentally the same as the approach of non-experts (. . .). This epistemic competence is, however, limited. The limitations are imposed for a number of reasons, but in particular because syntactical similarities between expert and nonexpert reasoning do not allow us to extend the competence to differences in the semantic content of the knowledge applied by experts and nonexperts, and because cognitive psychology shows us that we often do not, in practice, reason as rationally as we would like to think that we do'. See Dwyer (2008), p. 131.

court, competent both in decisions regarding the admissibility of evidence as well as evaluating it. Most of our remarks, however, seem to also be applicable to the jury system (which is especially visible in the context of the discussion of the relevance of Daubert requirements). Secondly, it is sometimes pointed out that the problem that we are discussing—conflicting expert witnesses' opinions—may be more typical for adversarial systems rather than inquisitorial systems because in the former, both parties call their own experts, whereas in the latter expert witnesses are generally appointed by the court. Nonetheless, our considerations apply *mutatis mutandis* to inquisitorial systems as well, in part because expert witnesses' opinions can be freely challenged by all parties, and this situation is not infrequent even in the inquisitorial types of proceedings.

2 Expert Witnesses

The idea of the admission of expert testimony within the legal process is widespread and thus explicitly stated in various codes of procedure across jurisdictions. For example, article 193. § 1 of the Polish Code of Criminal Procedure states: "If the determination of material facts having an essential bearing upon the resolution of the case requires some special knowledge, the court shall consult an expert or experts". Similarly, rule 702 of the Federal Rules of Evidence states: "... witness who is qualified as an expert by knowledge, skill, experience, training, or education may testify in the form of an opinion or otherwise if: (a) the expert's scientific, technical, or other specialized knowledge will help the trier of fact to understand the evidence or to determine a fact in issue; (b) the testimony is based on sufficient facts or data; (c) the testimony is the product of reliable principles and methods; and (d) the expert has reliably applied the principles and methods to the facts of the case".[8]

The general requirement of "an essential bearing" of the "special[ized] knowledge" upon the resolution of a case was traditionally understood as a requirement of "true necessity" where the subject of opinion (inference) "must [have] be[en] so distinctively related to a science, profession, business, or occupation as to be beyond the ken of lay persons".[9] This traditional view seemed, however, to put in jeopardy the substantial element of the free evaluation of evidence principle at least in two ways. Firstly, what is visible in the US context, the 'specialization' issue has been relaxed since there has been an argument for a certain scope of discretion in administering Rule 702. As a result, an expert opinion can be invited on matters about which jurors (triers of fact) may have general knowledge if it would refine their

[8]This example shows that despite differences between civil and common law systems, the legal institution of expert witness is generally very similar. In our text, we will focus mostly on the US rulings as they are a benchmark for other judicatures with regard to the problems of expert witness opinions, adding some examples from the Polish legal system—as it is the most familiar to both authors. Nonetheless, the aim of our analysis is universal.

[9]Broun et al. (2014), p. 35.

understanding of the issue. Sometimes it is even claimed that it can be invited even if the "specialized" knowledge appears simply to be "helpful" in any way.[10] Thus, the general requirement here seems to be the following: the expert's testimony shall make some epistemological difference in judicial minds (either with respect to *knowledge* or to their *understanding* of relevant problems). A few remarks on the range of topics and content of expert witnesses' opinions are in order here. Special knowledge is not limited to "science" in the strict sense because it also includes technical knowledge, or other types of practical or theoretical knowledge that cannot be specified *a priori.* In the famous case of Kumho Tire Co. v. Carmichael, expertise in tire manufacturing served as a body of knowledge that is non-scientific *per se*; nonetheless, it should be assessed with the scrutiny typical of scientific expert witness opinion. This is a matter of many controversies. Firstly, we need to distinguish the types of knowledge that are sound. This leads to the aforementioned "legal demarcation problem", i.e., distinguishing the bodies of knowledge that are reliable enough to enter the courtroom as base for establishing the facts. It should be remembered that not every scientific enterprise is applicable to the forensic context and *vice versa* because of the different norms and goals pursued in law and science.[11] To solve this problem, courts established various standards that a method applied by an expert witness should reveal. The first notable standard came from the case Frye v. United States, 293 F. 1013 (D.C. Cir. 1923). The Frye standard states that in order to be admissible, the technique employed by an expert must be generally accepted within the relevant scientific community (the general acceptance standard). It was followed and superseded[12] by a more complex Daubert standard[13] that requires not only the criterion of acceptability in the scientific community but also introduces the requirements of falsifiability, peer review, and publication, known or potential rate of error, as well as the existence of standards allowing the control of the method. Yet, there are many methods that are debatable in the context of the Daubert standard. As mentioned above assessing these standards lies far beyond the scope of this article. Nonetheless, even if we assume that we can establish solid methods of distinguishing types of knowledge that are sound enough to enter the courtroom, more problems arise. Due to the heterogeneity of various scientific disciplines and other relevant bodies of knowledge, it may be difficult to establish generalized

[10] Broun et al. (2014), p. 36.

[11] See Schauer (2010).

[12] Some states are still adhering to Frye or have adopted some slightly different standards. For an overview see e.g. a report by Matthiesen et al. (2019).

[13] *Daubert v. Merrell Dow Pharmaceuticals, Inc.*, 509 U.S. 579 (1993): 'The specific factors explicated by the *Daubert* Court are (1) whether the expert's technique or theory can be or has been tested—that is, whether the expert's theory can be challenged in some objective sense, or whether it is instead simply a subjective, conclusory approach that cannot reasonably be assessed for reliability; (2) whether the technique or theory has been subject to peer review and publication; (3) the known or potential rate of error of the technique or theory when applied; (4) the existence and maintenance of standards and controls; and (5) whether the technique or theory has been generally accepted in the scientific community'.

criteria for assessing the quality of an expert witness' opinion. For example, a sociological opinion may not be strictly assessed through Daubert criteria, as noted in Tyus v. Urban Search Management 102 F. 3d 256 (7th Cir. 1996). In another ruling, Kannankeril v. Terminix International Inc., the court loosened the review and publication criterion in light of the support of "widely accepted scientific knowledge". However, a set of general criteria proposed by Douglas Walton[14] may be very helpful in virtually every case. To evaluate expert witness (E) opinion supporting a given claim (A), we need to ask ourselves the following questions:

1. Expertise Question: How credible is E as an expert source?
2. Field Question: Is E an expert in the field that A is in?
3. Opinion Question: What did E assert that implies A?
4. Trustworthiness Question: Is E personally reliable as a source?
5. Consistency Question: Is A consistent with what other experts assert?
6. Backup Evidence Question: Is E's assertion based on evidence?

However important these criteria are, in situations of GEWD, both conflicting experts may fulfil all above with the obvious exception of consistency as the claims will be contradicting each other. Nonetheless, we may assume that these criteria are fulfilled when both opinions in question find significant support in relevant fields.

Secondly, it became obvious that an expert opinion is not supposed to simply supersede judges' deliberation and evaluation, even if in practice it sometimes seems to be so.[15] Surely, a judge who sees an appointment of an expert witness inevitably has to evaluate whether a given expert witness meets certain requirements (e.g., the expert witness must be capable of performing the "task at hand" in the sense of being more qualified than laypeople and the judge), but this is not to say that an expert witness who passes even the highest possible requirements for appointment becomes *ipso facto* a full, delegated "authority" on the issue.[16] The Daubert standard treats a judge as a "gatekeeper" who must exclude unreliable experts' testimony (as the jury is the trier of fact). Thus, a judge is obliged to establish whether expert witnesses are "proposing to testify about matters growing naturally and directly out of research they have conducted independent of the litigation, or whether they have developed their opinions expressly for purposes of testifying";[17] "whether the expert has unjustifiably extrapolated from an accepted premise to an unfounded conclusion"; "whether the expert has adequately accounted for obvious alternative explanations"; whether the expert "is being as careful as he would be in his regular professional work outside his paid litigation consulting"; and "whether the field of expertise

[14] Walton (1997), p. 223.

[15] See, e.g., Zienkiewicz and Leśniak (2002). This is a problem often pointed out by practitioners in the Polish legal system, which even resulted in Polish ombudsman interventions. See Bodnar (2018) and the reports of the government and non-government organizations cited therein.

[16] In Polish legal doctrine, there is a common saying that 'the court is the supreme expert witness'. See, e.g., Żołna (2008), p. 47.

[17] *Daubert v. Merrell Dow Pharmaceuticals, Inc.*, 43 F.3d 1311, 1317 (9th Cir. 1995).

claimed by the expert is known to reach reliable results for the type of opinion the expert would give".[18] It is the judge's task to evaluate whether the given expert's opinion is reliable and thus admissible.

Therefore, every expert witness in legal proceedings is in fact assessed twice. Firstly, at a gatekeeping stage[19] where their reliability is assessed. Here, the law may propose some *a priori* criteria to assess the initial credibility of the expert (e.g., the law may prohibit people without a given amount of experience from giving their expert testimony) and his or her methods (e.g., according to the Daubert standard). Then, after the opinion is presented, it must be assessed again *post hoc*. In the first stage, the expert opinion has only the claim to reliability, whereas in the second it has the claim to correctness. In the case of reliability, the most notable ruling is from the case of General Electric Co. v. Joiner (1997).[20] The Supreme Court stated that when the conclusions presented by an expert witness are not properly inferred from the evidence and theory behind the opinion, such an opinion may be excluded. We can see that in the first assessment of experts' reliability, only the first Waltonian criterion can be applied, and only after the opinion has been presented (i.e., we can see the methodology proposed by the expert "in action") may the rest be assessed. Let us look at the correctness claim.

It must be recognized that the reliability standard differs from a correctness standard. For one thing, just because an expert's testimony is reliable, one should not infer that contradictory expert testimony is unreliable. In the same vein, just because the expert testimony is reliable does not mean that one should infer that it is correct. In *Heller v. Shaw Industries*, it was explicitly stated that "expert testimony cannot be excluded simply because the expert uses one test rather than another, when both tests are accepted in the field and both reach *reliable* results";[21] and in *Ruiz-Troche v. Pepsi Cola*, it was stated that "Daubert neither requires nor empowers trial courts to determine which of several *competing* scientific theories has the best provenance"[22] (italics ours). Hence, to put it briefly, there may be many equally reliable, but substantially different, expert witnesses' opinions having essential bearing upon the resolution of the case. These would be the situations of genuine expert witness disagreement, as described below.

The general problem here, as we see it, is twofold. First is the problem of reliability. In judicial opinions and relevant literature this has been thoroughly discussed, although sometimes it seems that the factors relevant for evaluating the reliability of an expert witness are mixed with the factors for evaluating the reliability, so to say, of the very opinion (testimony) such an expert prepared. The established reliability of the expert, resulting in his/her appointment, does not

[18] Legal Information Institute (2019).

[19] On the problems of gatekeeping in the proceedings in the US, see, e.g. Cecil (2005).

[20] General Electric Co. v. Joiner, 522 U.S. 136 (1997). The case is included, along with Kumho Tire Co., in the so-called Daubert trilogy. See also, e.g., Grudzinskas and Appelbaum (1998).

[21] Heller v. Shaw Industries, Inc., 167 F.3d 146, 160 (3d Cir. 1999).

[22] Ruiz-Troche v. Pepsi Cola, 161 F.3d 77, 85 (1st Cir. 1998).

automatically allow us to infer that the provided testimony is reliable. At most, we can say that it is *prima facie* reliable, but this issue is to be settled eventually by the court itself. Some of the abovementioned Daubert requirements oblige the judge to check the general reliability requirement (and to see whether an expert witness is in fact a recognized expert in the field), whereas some others focus on whether the expert "has unjustifiably extrapolated from an accepted premise to an unfounded conclusion" (the Joiner criterion) or "whether the expert has adequately accounted for obvious alternative explanations". These requirements refer to the opinion and its justificatory force.

The second problem is the criteria of the final selection between such equally reliable but contrary opinions. Post-Daubert standards seem to suggest that the judge should focus "solely on principles and methodology, not on the conclusions they generate",[23] but the only given criterion for evaluating these elements is the "experience in the expert's field".[24] Actually, the suggestion provided by these uncodified standards is a negative one: "When an expert who purports to apply professionally recognized methods reaches a conclusion that other experts in the field deny, the judge shall suspect that the methods have not been faithfully applied".[25] This strategy of further elimination refers to something we might call "a common opinion" of the scientific community, reminding us of the Frye standard. However, even this criterion is dubious epistemically—how can a judge adequately refer to such an opinion without asking for a further "meta-expert witness" testimony? What if the community is divided in half in its evaluation of the results?

Thus, the judge (as the trier of fact) has to evaluate three things: the expert's personal reliability (*a priori* basis for an appointment), the reliability of the expert's testimony, and, eventually, the correctness of the expert's testimony (the latter two are *a posteriori* as they deal with the provided expertise). In the first case, the verdict can rely on the general communal recognition of an expert witness as an expert in the field.

The traditional requirement that expert witnesses should be competent—i.e., have sufficient skills or knowledge related to the pertinent field and the ability to draw "helpful" inferences for a trier—is by no means idealistic.[26] To achieve that, from the epistemological perspective, the trier (judge) and a proposed expert have to positively answer the twofold "better position question":[27] the judge must agree that there is someone who is in an epistemically superior position than him/her in the relevant field; on the other hand, the expert has to admit that s/he is in a better

[23] Legal Information Institute (2019).

[24] In a commentary on Rule 702, we read: 'The trial judge in all cases of proffered expert testimony must find that it is properly grounded, well-reasoned, and not speculative before it can be admitted. The expert's testimony must be grounded in an accepted body of learning or experience in the expert's field, and the expert must explain how the conclusion is so grounded' See Legal Information Institute (2019).

[25] Legal Information Institute (2019).

[26] Broun et al. (2014), p. 35.

[27] Frances (2014), p. 28.

position to answer that question. Both answers require justification pertaining to the *person* and his/her purported *ability* to produce a relevant opinion. However, usually this problem is institutionally resolved by the introduction of certification and official lists of expert witnesses established by independent expertise bodies/institutions.[28] In some jurisdictions, experts are included on the list of expert witnesses for a given scientific discipline if they are positively reviewed by other experts (this is a kind of *a priori* review). Moreover, usually further expert witnesses' activities at court are peer-reviewed (a kind of *a posteriori* evaluation). Such a solution provides a judge with a *prima facie* ready-made answer with respect to the "better position question". The answer is, however, not definite. After appointing an expert, all Daubert and similar considerations related to the admissibility of an expert and her opinion still apply.

The above presented institutional solution does not apply to *ad hoc* expert witnesses: in this case, judges have to fully determine on their own whether a particular person possesses special knowledge and abilities relevant to solving an issue in court.

Once again, the problem of *a priori* assessment of experts returns. How can an epistemically inferior person (such as a judge) assess the quality of claims made by an epistemic superior? How can a judge responsibly apply Daubert standards?[29] The requirement of an opinion based on reliable methodology may exclude more obvious instances of pseudoscience, but it tells us nothing about the borderline cases and cannot address the problems of opinions in well-established bodies of knowledge that nonetheless are open to interpretation (which of course still needs to be properly grounded). We may employ some additional requirements of people who want to testify as experts. One of the proposed criteria may be experience (or a record of the expert). While reasonable at first, it is still a fallible heuristic—there may be a lot of experts who were trained some time ago and continue to use outdated methodology despite the progress in sciences, so a rule "the more experienced the expert, the better" may be misleading. Another criterion that may be used is education. It is as fallible as the former one—there is no guarantee that an expert witness who is a successful academic will also be a skilful practitioner. Therefore, full reliance on such criteria is not a satisfactory way out.

The institutional forms of expert witness selection rely heavily on the (presumably correct) assumption that science (or any other specialization field that cannot be

[28] Expert-institutions like the Polish 'Instytut Ekspertyz Sądowych' ('Institute of Forensic Research').

[29] Dwyer discusses this problem at length. She notices that 'the [. . .] problem for Daubert is that it requires judges to second-judge experts on whether the methods that they are employing are properly 'scientific', and as such reliable. The relevant factors here are: testability; peer review or publication; the known or potential rate of error; widespread acceptance. On a practical level, this requires a degree of scientific literacy on the part of judges that it is unreasonable to expect. On a philosophical level, it is unclear that the four Daubert factors would actually be accepted by all (or sufficient) scientists as indicating reliable scientific method' Dwyer (2008) p. 343.

considered "scientific" in a robust sense) is a collective enterprise.[30] However, the idea of "expertise" along with the requirement of its intersubjectivity (or even objectivity) also seems to suggest that even an expert *ad hoc* must be one who is a member of a possible community of "experts" on the given matter.

Peerhood and peer review are essential features of such an enterprise. The issue of peerhood has been thoroughly determined in the recent philosophical literature on the epistemology of disagreement. Here, we would like only to draw some conclusions from the epistemological disputes that may be relevant for the expert witness role in any legal proceedings. We will focus on the consequence of "there are many possible experts" for a trier of fact. This fact becomes especially relevant in cases where either (1) the judge is not entirely convinced by the first and the only provided expert's opinion or (2) where two or more expert opinions are inconsistent or even contradict each other. However, as we shall suggest, the fact that science is a communal enterprise justifies not only the requirement—which we want to argue for—that in any case a trier of fact (the judge) shall refer to more than one opinion, but also explains the natural possibility of experts' disagreement on the matter. In the latter case, the relevant question is the question of normative epistemology of disagreement: what should a judge do in the case of peer disagreement between expert witnesses? Note that the kinds of requirements that one may frame in answer to these questions seem to narrow down the judicial leeway provided by the general principle of free evaluation of evidence.[31]

3 Peer Expert Witnesses' Disagreement

GEWD would be a type of reasonable and resolvable "mature peer disagreement".[32] This means that it cannot be an instance of a "bedrock dispute",[33] which refers to fundamentally conflicting assumptions. Examples of such a discussion can be found within philosophy, religion, politics, etc., and mostly refer to normative aspects, values, etc. In this case, referring to an expert witness is in some ways futile because these kinds of disputes are inconclusive at best, or are not at all even a domain of knowledge from which an expert argument could be reasonably invoked. Note that the "conclusiveness" requirement is strictly related to the so-called "uniqueness

[30] Dwyer rightly notices that this poses another problem for Daubert standards: 'that Daubert presents a mixture of epistemology and politics. By this I mean that Daubert's criteria for establishing justified belief relate to the extent to which that belief is accepted by a community, rather than whether the belief is true' Dwyer (2008), p. 345.

[31] This is the problem that lies beyond the scope of this paper. For a discussion of the 'free evaluation of evidence' principle see e.g. Sladič and Uzelac (2016).

[32] The criteria for defining 'mature disputes among mutually recognized expert epistemic peers' are provided by Earl Conee (2009), p. 314.

[33] See Chalmers (2011).

view", according to which "a particular body of evidence justifies at most one attitude towards any particular proposition" (belief, suspension or disbelief).[34]

Let us now look at how the situation of GEWD can arise in the courtroom. As we suggested above, there are naturally many available expert witnesses in any domain of expertise. Hence, apart from easy cases where no expert witnesses are needed, or cases where only one expert witness is appointed and his/her opinion is finally acceptable to the court and all parties, there are at least two scenarios in which more than one expert witness testifies before the court. In any of these situations, reasonable disagreement between experts, usually founded in the difference with respect to the merit of opinions, can arise.

The first type of scenario is characteristic of "inquisitorial" proceedings. After appointing the first expert witness, the trier may feel dissatisfied with his/her opinion. There may be many types of dissatisfaction. For instance, the opinion may not be helpful at all, so the trier would still lack information relevant for the resolution of the case. The judge may then ask the expert to provide an additional, supplementary opinion to explain and fix the shortcomings of the original opinion. If such additional measures prove unsuccessful and the opinion is eventually reckless, the right thing to do would presumably be to demote an expert and dismiss his opinion as unauthoritative. In such circumstances, it would be necessary to call for a second expert. There may also be a situation in which the first expert's opinion is reliable but inconclusive. Then calling for another expert would also be a must, but after providing an opinion, the amount of evidence to be considered by a judge would be greater (however, we cannot automatically say that the "conclusive" opinion should prevail over the "inconclusive" one; thus, the peer disagreement arises).

Another possibility is that the first provided opinion would be unsatisfactory for a judge in the "realist" sense that it contradicts his intuitions about the way a case should be resolved. In such cases, judges may naturally try to confirm their intuitions by referring to another expertise. In Poland, this problem has been expressed by appellate courts that introduced a principle that in order to dismiss an already provided expert witness' testimony, a judge cannot refer simply to his/her intuition, or even his/her own argument, but has to ask for another expert witness' testimony—the principle was then confirmed by Supreme Court.[35] This principle seems to correctly reflect the assumption that a judge is not "a peer" for an expert and thus can never epistemically prevail. On the other hand, this kind of rule may be—and probably is—instrumentally used by judges who would appoint new experts as long as any of them would confirm their (mostly intuitive) judgement.

The second scenario is characteristic of "adversarial" proceedings where all parties "come" to court with contradicting experts' opinions. In this kind of

[34] Feldman (2007), p. 205. Note that this assumption conforms to the rationalist meta-justification of legal fact-finding in western legal systems. See Dwyer (2008), pp. 43, 45; Twining (1985), pp. 1–18.

[35] The relevant rulings are as follows: I ACa 1140/12, V CSK 125/13, IV CSK 197/17, III CSK 109/18.

proceedings, both sides usually have relevant expert opinions at hand. These opinions reflect a kind of "isolated" judgment: they were prepared before the full disclosure of higher-order evidence to the expert witnesses. By higher-order evidence we mean "evidence that there is evidence".[36] Naturally, in cases in which an expert witness has unlimited access to the case file, every expert witness opinion in the proceedings would be such a higher-order evidence for his/her peer expert witness. In scenario one, where the unsatisfied trier appoints ("cherry-picks") new expert witnesses, it is highly probable that an expert would know at least the conclusion provided by another expert. As indicated before, with regard to Daubert standards, even though an "expert has to adequately account for obvious alternative explanations", such an account would be performed differently in isolation, i.e., without any knowledge about *really disagreeing peers*, unlike situations of partial or full disclosure of (higher-order) evidence (knowledge of the whole opinion, or at least its conclusions).[37]

The considerations above become relevant in the face of the epistemological definition of the peer. Epistemic peers are usually defined in the following way: S_1 and S_2 are epistemic peers if and only if they are equal in reasoning ability, intelligence, intellectual virtues, all available evidence, background information, as well as with respect to the concepts they possess.[38] Both peers are capable of "getting it right" and are equally justified in believing their arguments to be true after full disclosure of all available evidence, or at least after the disclosure of *the same* (or—in some cases, less relevant in court—*equally good*) evidence. If the scope of evidence differs for them, then—*ceteris paribus*—the main peerage condition is impaired.[39] In that case, the second expert in the first scenario is automatically in a better epistemic position than the first one in the sense that he has additional higher-order evidence at his disposal (because there already exists a first opinion and the expert knows about its conclusions). Some epistemologists argue that this additional point of (higher-order) evidence may bring more problems for a second expert. Everything depends on the normative theory of the role that such evidence ought to play for an epistemic peer adopted, at least implicitly, by an expert

---

[36] 'Intuitively, first-order evidence *E* is evidence that bears directly on some target proposition or hypothesis *H*. Higher-order evidence is evidence about the character of *E* itself, or about subjects' capacities and dispositions for responding rationally to *E*'. See Kelly (2016). For a detailed discussion of the concept of 'higher-order evidence', see also Feldman (2005); Kelly (2005); Kelly (2010); Matheson (2009); Christensen (2010).

[37] We do not want to discuss the role of higher-order evidence here. However, the idea of higher-order evidence must be invoked in the context of evaluation of experts' opinions.

[38] Matheson (2009), p. 270. Adam Elga argues, however, that if supposed peers disagree on a host of related issues, they do not share enough to be genuine epistemic peers. See Elga (2007).

[39] The peerage (peer disagreement) factors are: data, evidence, time, ability, background knowledge, circumstances of investigation, Frances (2014). Obviously expert witnesses should have access to the same data, be given the same amount of time. With respect to other factors we have to realistically suppose that they are roughly equal for all experts. The inquiry whether these are equal whenever there are many expert witnesses appointed in the process should be one of the first obligations of a 'gatekeeper' (a judge) and/or an appointed meta-expert.

witness. (These kinds of problems do not arise in isolation; that is why we further argue for inviting *a priori* several expert witnesses and never choosing them one by one).

Usually peers would disagree about the truth value of a proposition P, where P is some fairly narrow claim.[40] The recognition of an epistemic peer who disagrees with one's claims has an immediate "epistemic impact" on one's attitude towards the matter. One may feel that there is something wrong either with one's peer and/or his/her claim, or with one's claim. The main task of normative theories of peer disagreement is to answer the following questions: What is the *rational* thing to do in such a situation? Can (or should) one still rationally disagree?[41] What *pro tanto* reason (if any) is given to anyone disagreeing with his/her epistemic peer?[42]

One answer is to claim that the recognition of a disagreeing peer naturally diminishes the degree of belief one is justified in adopting towards a disputed proposition (this is an immediate *negative* epistemic impact of the peer's disagreement).[43] The other way is a sceptical reaction directed not towards one's claims but rather towards one's peer's general reliability. These positions are discussed usually from the first person peer perspective: a peer seeing another peer disagreeing can either stay steadfast or try to conciliate. Although these considerations apply to peer expert witnesses who are aware of other peers' positions, they may also apply by means of a certain analogy to a trier as well. However, let us first focus on the peer-level perspective.

Firstly, it seems that in the face of disagreement between peers S_1 and S_2, a type of doxastic conciliation is required on the condition that one of them does not possess any higher-order reason (that is, evidence) to discount the other peer's conclusion. S/he may have good reason to think that, *on this particular occasion,* the other peer is less likely than usual to get it right. This may be due to unusual transient cognitive problems (e.g., S_2's drunkenness, mental disorder, or insomnia) or to the content of the disputed proposition (e.g., regarding some evaluative factors). Possession of such an *undefeated* reason allows S_1 to assume that peer S_2 has clearly failed to get it right, leading to a normative conclusion that, regarding the rightness of S_1's own arguments, he or she should stay put or at least make more modest concessions.[44] Note that these are basically the same criteria a trier should consider when accounting for the reliability of a given expert. All these considerations should be well justified, just as the rest of the opinion should be.

If there is an undefeated reason concerning S_2's capacity, and S_1 has an equivalent undefeated reason with respect to his or her own capacity, the problem resurfaces. If both peers possess equal evidence (this is a meta-claim), the situation is a stalemate. It is most interesting from our perspective since the question is what a

[40] Bergman (2009), p. 339.

[41] Bergman (2009), p. 337.

[42] Enoch (2010), p. 957.

[43] Enoch (2010), p. 957.

[44] Matheson (2009), p. 270.

trier should decide in the case of such a stalemate between experts in court proceedings.

In cases where the best evidence is actually available to all peers, the rational procedure of conciliation would involve the delivery and accurate presentation of the overall evidence. Genuine conciliation would require also a very disagreement to be mutually recognized by both peers, providing either a basis for *shared* scepticism about a peer's competence to resolve the matter or an additional reason to suspend judgment. The acceptance of such a conclusion is not a matter of *propositional justification* of the conclusion (as supported only by all available evidence) but rather involves so-called *doxastic justification*, in which recognition of peer disagreement affects the groundedness of opposing conclusions.[45] The meta-claim cannot simply be ignored and the situation is not a standoff. However, the problem here is related to the peers' convictions about grounding their beliefs correctly in the available evidence.[46] The new independent reason for sustaining or doubting their position depends on whether or not they find themselves *more trustworthy* than their peers. This type of insight is not a theoretical insight about what propositions we find to be true (in fact) but rather a practical insight about how justified we are to use these propositions in public (as an argument).

In such circumstances, peers might either suspend their judgment on the matter or try further to conciliate. This conciliatory contention is based primarily on the presumption that it must be theoretically *irrational* to disagree in an "equal weight" situation (after full disclosure of evidence).[47] In any case, suspension of judgment or conciliation would be a pragmatic solution to the problem. Note, however, that peer expert witnesses in the proceedings cannot suspend judgement. They are appointed as expert witnesses to provide an opinion (and suspending judgment is rather a form of withdrawal of an opinion) and this procedural fact is of utmost importance. Hence, eventually the only action they can take in the case of a stalemate where they find their competing positions equally *trustworthy* is to conciliate regarding the matter *together and reach a concurrent* opinion. This includes the possibility of them eventually claiming *together* that there is no *one* truth on the matter, which in consequence means that there was never any space for appointing expert witnesses in the first place (for the disagreement is not GEWD).

[45] van Wietmarschen (2013). According to Richard Feldman: 'S's belief that *p* at time *t* is [*doxastically*] justified (well-founded) if (i) believing *p* is justified for S at *t*; (ii) S believes *p* on the basis of evidence that supports *p*'. Thus, the doxastic justification refers to right sorts of reasons we have to believe p, Feldman (2002), p. 46. A true belief that p is supported by wrong, non-evidential reasons (e.g., psychological reasons: private inclinations, attitudes, supposed strengths of arguments, denials and suspensions of judgments) is not 'justified' but only 'justifiable'.

[46] It is not 'evidential' in common terms, but for conciliationists like Feldman, such an expressed doxastic attitude affecting opponents' trustworthiness in a particular proposition would stand as evidence, since 'evidence of evidence is evidence'.

[47] Elga (2007), p. 490.

From the point of view of the alternative normative strategy, peers shall not conciliate in the situation of the epistemic stalemate. Rather, they may remain "steadfast". David Enoch suggests that from the perspective of the person who claims to be right, the mere fact of disagreement shall be counted as a perfectly legitimate piece of evidence against peers' reliability and as a good enough reason to demote them from the status of peer.[48] Enoch claims that it is a perfectly legitimate piece of evidence on par with every other piece of evidence.

In the context of the discussion above, we would like to suggest that a legal proceeding itself may provide a certain framework influencing peers' attitudes (with respect to trustworthiness) as well as point to certain ways of dealing with disagreements of peer expert witnesses. The idea of such a framework should endorse the two basic principles of proceedings to the least extent: the principle of free evaluation of evidence (by the trier) and the principle of substantial (material) truth.

For example, a judge (or even the lawgiver through specific regulation of the proceedings) could adopt a position that would confront experts in disagreement and encourage them to make a common position in a conciliatory way. That would solve the problem of disagreement, but this solution would probably be achievable in a limited number of cases. Moreover, it would be time-consuming. On the other hand, by adopting a position that favours steadfastness, we need a person who would pick one of the conflicting opinions and point to it as correct—the meta-expert. This issue is not limited to judicial considerations related to the appointment and assessment of experts' testimonies. These epistemic considerations may also stand as a backbone for the introduction of certain general procedures for examining expert witnesses in the proceedings. The conciliatory theory would require experts to discuss and exchange opinions before the court (trier) during the trial. The steadfastness theory, on the contrary, would suggest that experts should not conciliate, or eventually should conciliate only in a limited way. After conciliation, such a 'steadfast' procedure would require the appointment of a meta-expert.

4 Meta-Experts and Meta-Opinions

As mentioned above, propositional justification pertains to sufficient reasons to believe a given proposition, whereas doxastic justification concerns whether a given belief is held appropriately (e.g., well grounded, inferential[49]). Both jurisprudential materials cited in the first and the second sections, as well as epistemological remarks in the third section suggest that the justification required from expert witnesses is rather the justification of the second kind. It is impossible for a trier (a judge), being inferior to an expert, to see whether there are (objective) reasons supporting a given expert's opinion. However, even if the required justification is

---

[48] Enoch (2010), p. 981.

[49] Cf. Ichikawa and Steup (2018).

doxastic, since the core issue is whether the beliefs of an expert are held in an *epistemically* appropriate way, the judge cannot assess thoroughly an expert's opinion from this perspective unless he/she is an expert in the field. Daubert standards seem to confirm that. Therefore, the first strategy—solving the GEWD by the judges themselves—seems to be epistemically ungrounded, despite the normative acceptability at first glance.[50] The second strategy—referring to a higher-instance court, however pragmatic, since it takes off the burden of assessment of the experts from the first-instance judges, does not provide any solution. The higher-instance court is also epistemically inferior to experts. One could argue that judges sitting in higher-instance courts may possess more experience, which grants them better competence to evaluate experts. However, in many jurisdictions, higher-instance courts are focused on assessing strictly legal, not factual, issues, whereas first-instance courts deal with factual issues daily and are more apt to deal with the newest forensic techniques and methods.

This consideration suggests that it would be best if in any proceedings with more than one expert witness, there is another expert appointed post hoc who would serve as a meta-expert, the "reviewer", who would be responsible for assessing the "justifiability" of provided expert opinions.

Meta-opinions seem to differ significantly from the traditional expert witness testimony. Their specific function is to evaluate the credibility, reliability, and finally the correctness, of the opinion already presented during the proceedings. Rather than providing answers to the specific questions asked by the trier of fact, the topic of the meta-opinion is universal and uniform—it concerns the assessment of the opinion in light of the aforementioned criteria. Analogically, the conclusions are different as well. Rather than adding another piece to the facts of the case, they are aimed at eliminating the misleading elements from the trial. Introducing the meta-opinion to the proceedings eliminates the problem of epistemic inferiority of the judge. Moreover, the meta-expert should be able to tell whether the issue is resolvable by an expert opinion at all, i.e., whether the aforementioned condition of uniqueness is fulfilled. A negative answer to that question is a sign to the court that such an opinion could not be delivered effectively.

A typical argument formed against meta-opinions concerns the problem of their topic. A meta-opinion does not explicitly refer to the evidence providing a tool to establish the facts of the case but instead assesses the reliability and correctness of conflicting opinions. It may be pointed out that the function of evaluating evidence is the prerogative of the court and not anyone else.[51] This argument is based on confounding two types of authority: epistemic and normative. The court does not possess the epistemic authority to assess experts; this is definitely a matter that requires special knowledge. On the other hand, the court still possesses normative

[50] This theoretical claim also finds some empirical support. As shown by studies conducted by Sophia Gatowski and her colleagues, Gatowski et al. (2001), the understanding of science and methodology behind Daubert criteria by state court judges was far from perfect.

[51] Widła (2007).

authority and can evaluate the meta-opinion as well. Another concern is the topic of the meta-opinion: by assessing the experts, we do not refer to a piece of reality that should be assessed to decide a case.[52] An obvious counterclaim to this type of criticism would be to acknowledge that assessing two (or more) conflicting experts and choosing one correct opinion does contribute to the determination of the set of facts by eliminating alternatives accessible to the decision-maker, from which s/he does not have the epistemic competence to choose. Of course, one can argue that the meta-expert can also potentially get into the situation of GEWD after s/he makes a decision, when s/he adheres to one of the conflicting positions (hence the problem of multiplying the opinions *ad infinitum*)—but rather than making an opinion which regards the factual issue, they evaluate the opinion itself. That assessment should inform the normative authority which expert may be more reliable. Therefore, we can say that thanks to the meta-expert, the judge is granted some epistemic grounds to relate to for problems such as peer-review criteria. Moreover, to avoid cherry-picking on the meta-level, the judges in their decision to appoint a meta-expert could be assisted by a special institution (such as forensic institutes, scientific associations, etc.). The institution could advise a judge in nominating a meta-expert, or could even serve as a meta-expert itself (institutional experts are present in some jurisdictions/ types of proceedings, see, e.g., Article 193. § 2 of the Polish Code of Criminal Procedure).

As pointed out by Józef Wójcikiewicz,[53] meta-opinions, however useful in the case of many instances of epistemic trouble in the courtroom, such as the assessment of the newest forensic methods, should not be abused to assess single opinions that are clearly incomplete or vague. These situations require a supplementary opinion from the same expert, or appointing another one (since the meta-expert should not perform new studies but rather assess the quality of the first-level experts).

5 Conclusions

In this section, we would make some normative (*de lege ferenda*, but nonetheless rather abstract) suggestions and propose a general model of expert witness appointment which may be adopted by a judge. Of course, the following considerations should be treated as non-binding guidelines rather than a strict algorithm.

In simpler cases, we should start by appointing one expert. If any justified[54] concerns about their methodology arise (they may be raised both by the disputing parties and by the judges themselves), the judge should appoint another expert. At

---

[52] Tomaszewski (2000), p. 31.

[53] Wójcikiewicz (2009).

[54] Because it may be difficult to assess whether the concerns raised against the expert are sound, we would rather favour appointing another expert. One could call that an '*in dubio pro perito*' principle.

this stage, the additional expertise should be aimed at the merits of the case rather than being a meta-opinion. The second opinion may concur with the first, which in most cases should be enough to provide solid evidence. However, the dissent in the second opinion leads to GEWD. In that case, i.e., when individually appointed expert witnesses present opinions that are not consistent, there should be a space for conciliation (discussion of experts). Each expert should be able to assess the reliability of others as peers and explain his possible "steadfast" position. The will to conciliate means that all experts agree that they are peers. If such conciliatory measures prove unsuccessful, a meta-opinion is required. Ideally, the decision to introduce conciliatory measures or, on the other hand, appoint a meta-expert should be justified and acknowledge the epistemological limitations of disagreement.

In more complicated[55] cases, a pair of independent experts may be appointed immediately, *simultaneously,* and *in isolation* to inquire into the issue. This postulate relates to the very fact that there are many possible expert witnesses who may naturally disagree on the issue at hand. Appointing expert witnesses at different times and at different stages of the proceedings may result in those experts who were appointed later embracing the role of both an expert and a meta-expert. This is a dangerous and unreliable result because expert witnesses who were appointed earlier might have decided differently if they knew that other peer experts disagree with them. Despite the fact that such a solution may generate costs, it is not absent from binding statutory regulations in some jurisdictions (e.g., Article 202 of the Polish Code of Criminal Procedure requires at least two expert psychiatrists to evaluate the mental health of the defendant; moreover, it points out that the experts should be independent of themselves). Then, the discussed situation is analogical—either we get a concurrence of opinions or a disagreement. Disagreement may be solved by conciliation or, eventually, by a meta-opinion.

How should we effectively introduce meta-opinions and expert witnesses' evaluation in the proceedings? As we mentioned before, some help from professional institutions could be crucial. In some jurisdictions, there is both *a priori* and *a posteriori* review of experts. Experts are included on the list of expert witnesses for a given scientific discipline (*a priori* review), but expert witnesses' activity at court is peer-reviewed (*a posteriori* review). Since the second form of review is external to a given proceeding in the sense that it is not revealed to a trier, we recommend introducing another form of *a posteriori* review: *internal* a posteriori *review,* which would amount to a super-review within the given proceedings of all previously provided expert opinions. This kind of solution is typical for various peer-review processes (such as scientific research grant competitions or journal peer reviews) where super-reviewers, being also experts in the field, evaluate the discussion between applicant-experts (those who apply for a grant or journal publication)

[55] It is difficult to provide a full list of such instances, but we consider a case complicated when, e.g., the method that has to be used by an expert is novel, the body of evidence presented before a court seems to be self-contradictory, the defendant is facing a potentially harsh punishment (in criminal cases) or the value of the matter at issue (in civil cases) exceeds some extraordinary limit.

and peer-reviewers (with respect to whether: suggestions of reviewers were substantial and the response of applicants/authors adequate). The super-reviewer role would be to provide a trier with the methodological strengths and weaknesses of all expert witnesses' opinions. Such an expert would also serve as a "gatekeeper". The reason why we urge introducing this kind of institution is that a trier is almost never an expert in the field.

A separate issue is whether the review provided by a meta-expert should be in any sense binding for a trier. We would suggest that the aforementioned principle—that in order to dismiss an already provided expert witness' testimony, a judge has to ask for another expert witness' testimony—should apply to the opinion of a meta-expert rather than to the opinion of an expert. In case the disagreement is "levelled up" to disagreement between meta-experts, the judge should have full discretion. Otherwise, the judge should follow the instructions provided by a meta-expert. This principle shall not pertain to regular expert witnesses because it allows for "cherry-picking" and thus manipulating the proceedings. A judge's inferior intuition is not enough for supervision here. We should, however, remember that some institutional reviews, made outside of particular proceedings, may be binding for the court (i.e., lists of expert witnesses that would be approved by professional associations). What is interesting is that within some particular types of proceedings in which the expert also serves as the legal decision-maker, the need for invoking such a separate meta-expert diminishes. An example would be the disciplinary type of proceedings where both expert witnesses and triers of facts (disciplinary judges) belong to the same profession.[56]

References

Bergman M (2009) Rational disagreement after full disclosure. Episteme 6(3):336–353

Bodnar A (2018) Wystąpienie RPO do Ministra Sprawiedliwości w sprawie projektu ustawy o biegłych sądowych [An Address of the Ombudsman to the Minister of Justice With Regard to the Project of the Expert Witness Act]. https://www.rpo.gov.pl/sites/default/files/Wyst%C4%85pienie%20RPO%20do%20Ministra%20Sprawiedliwo%C5%9Bci%20w%20sprawie%20ustawy%20o%20bieg%C5%82ych%20s%C4%85dowych.pdf. Accessed 18 Oct 2019

Broun K, Dix G, Imwinkelried E et al (eds) (2014) MacCormick on evidence, 7th edn. West Academic Publishing

Cecil JS (2005) Ten years of judicial gatekeeping under Daubert. Am J Public Health 95(S1):S74–S80

Chalmers D (2011) Verbal disputes. Philos Rev 120(4):515–566

Christensen D (2010) Higher-order evidence. Philos Phenomenol Res 81(1):185–215

[56] There are situations where disciplinary courts disagree with the claims established during the preceding criminal proceedings on the basis that the criminal court, notwithstanding the fact it relied on evidence provided by appointed expert witnesses, misunderstood the nature of such evidence. As far as judges in medical disciplinary courts, e.g., are medical professionals, they seem to be more qualified to assess the value of the expert testimonies provided by other medical professionals before the criminal court than the criminal court (made up of non-medical professionals) itself.

Conee E (2009) Peerage. Episteme 6(3):313–323
Dwyer D (2008) The judicial assessment of expert evidence. Cambridge University Press
Elga A (2007) Reflection on disagreement. Nous 41(3):478–502
Enoch D (2010) Not just a truthometer: taking oneself seriously (but not too seriously) in case of peer disagreement. Mind 119(476):953–997
Feldman R (2002) Epistemology. Prentice Hall, Upper Saddle River
Feldman R (2005) Reasonable religious disagreements. In: Antony L (ed) Philosophers without gods: meditations on atheism and the secular. Oxford University Press, Life
Frances B (2014) Disagreement. Polity Press, Cambridge
Gatowski SI, Dobbin SA, Richardson JT et al (2001) Asking the gatekeepers: a national survey of judges on judging expert evidence in a post-Daubert world. Law Hum Behav 25(5):433–458
Grudzinskas JA, Appelbaum KL (1998) General Electric Co. v. Joiner: lighting up the post-Daubert landscape? J Am Acad Psychiatry Law 26(3):497–503
Ichikawa JJ, Steup M (2018) The analysis of knowledge. In: Zalta E (ed) The Stanford Encyclopedia of Philosophy (Summer 2018 Edition) https://plato.stanford.edu/entries/knowledge-analysis/. Accessed 18 Oct 2019
Kaplan AB, Puracal JC (2017) It's not a match: why the law can't let go of junk science. Albany Law Rev 81:895–939
Kelly T (2005) The epistemic significance of disagreement. Oxford Stud Epistemol 1:167–196
Kelly T (2010) Peer disagreement and higher order evidence. In: Feldman R, Warfield TA (eds) Disagreement. Oxford University Press, Oxford, pp 111–174
Kelly T (2016) Evidence. In: Zalta E (ed) The Stanford Encyclopedia of Philosophy (Winter 2016 Edition) https://plato.stanford.edu/entries/evidence/. Accessed 18 Oct 2019
Legal Information Institute (2019) Rule 702. Testimony by Expert Witnesses https://www.law.cornell.edu/rules/fre/rule_702. Accessed 18 Oct 2019
Matheson J (2009) Conciliatory views of disagreement and higher-order evidence. Episteme 6 (3):269–279
Matthiesen BW, Wickert GL, Lehrer WL (2019) Admissibility of Expert Testimony in All 50 States. https://www.mwl-law.com/wp-content/uploads/2018/02/ADMISSIBILITY-OF-EXPERT-TESTIMONY.pdf. Accessed 18 Oct 2019
Roberts P (2018) Making sense of forensic science evidence. In: Roberts P, Stockdale M (eds) Forensic science evidence and expert witness testimony. Edward Elgar Publishing, pp 27–70
Schauer F (2010) Can bad science be good evidence: Lie detection, neuroscience, and the mistaken conflation of legal and scientific norms. Cornell Law Rev 95:1191–1219
Sladič J, Uzelac A (2016) Assessment of evidence In: Rijavec V, Keresteš T, Ivanc T (eds) Dimensions of evidence in European civil procedure. Kluwer Law International, pp 107–132
Tomaszewski T (2000) Dowód z opinii biegłego w procesie karnym. Wydawnictwo IES, Kraków
Twining, W (1985) Theories of evidence: Bentham and Wigmore. Stanford University Press
van Wietmarschen H (2013) Peer disagreement, evidence, and well-groundedness. Philosophical Rev 122(3):395–425
Walton D (1997) Appeal to expert opinion. Arguments from authority. Penn State University Press
Widła T (2007) Ekspertyzy irrelewantne. Prokuratura i Prawo 10:5–16
Wójcikiewicz J (2009) Temida nad mikroskopem. Dom Organizatora, Toruń
Zienkiewicz D, Leśniak M (2002) Wpływ opinii pismoznawczej na kształtowanie się przekonania sędziowskiego. In: Kegel Z (ed) Problematyka dowodu z ekspertyzy dokumentów. Katedra Kryminalistyki Wydziału Prawa, Administracji i Ekonomii Uniwersytetu Wrocławskiego, Wrocław, pp 959–964
Żołna MM (2008) Kryteria oceny opinii biegłych. Problemy Kryminalistyki 259:44–48

Rethinking Expert Opinion Evidence as an Argument from Epistemic Authority

Bohdan Pretkiel

Abstract In the modern age dominated by technical thinking and overabundance of information, judges, as never before, have become dependent on expert witness opinions without having necessary assessment tools at their disposal. Legal dogmatics, especially that of civil law procedure and penal law procedure, needs data feedback from argumentation theory to be used to augment and change the existing legal order concerning court expert institution, and to provide basis for developing techniques that could help lay people in the court environment in evaluation of experts and their opinions in a way inaccessible for legal dogmatics alone. On the other hand, it should be stressed that every theory of legal argumentation always has to take into consideration a given legal culture with its traditions, values, rules and legal science. The tools that are used to accomplish this are based on Douglas Walton's logical argumentation, Bayesian probability and Bayesian belief networks. The author's own way of combining Bayesian network with Walton's critical questions method is viewed as a new tool that employs a questionnaire to gather data to be subsequently used in Bayes theorem calculations. The degree to which the argumentation theory tools prove to be useful depends on the amount of data gathered during the argumentation evaluation and the number of opportunities when dialectical critical testing can be performed.

1 Introduction

An argument from the expert's authority can be used to analyse the institution of an expert witness in its dialectical aspect as an element of persuasion in judicial proceedings. Given the vital time limit for court proceedings and the importance of the institution of an expert witness, it is critical that there are systemic solutions

B. Pretkiel (✉)
Faculty of Law and Administration, Warsaw University, Warszawa, Poland
e-mail: b.pretkiel@wpia.uw.edu.pl

V. Klappstein, M. Dybowski (eds.), *Theory of Legal Evidence - Evidence in Legal Theory*, Law and Philosophy Library 138,
https://doi.org/10.1007/978-3-030-83841-6_9

enabling the judge to decide on the acceptance of the premises of an argument from authority.

The use of argumentation theory, informal logic in particular, to describe and analyse the functioning of the institution of procedural law such as expert witness allows to clearly see deficiencies in particular legal systems that can significantly hinder the court's assessment of the evidence in the form of an expert opinion, such as lack of centralised expert witness database or absence of even basic institutionalised scientific methodology training of legal professionals.[1] Legal dogmatics, especially that of civil law procedure and penal law procedure, needs data feedback from argumentation theory to be used to augment and change the existing legal order concerning court expert institution, and to provide basis for developing techniques that could help lay people in the court environment in evaluation of experts and their opinions in a way inaccessible for legal dogmatics alone. On the other hand, it should be stressed that every theory of legal argumentation always has to take into consideration a given legal culture with its traditions, values, rules and legal science.[2]

If the judges are not able to familiarize themselves with the court expert's previous work as an expert, they are not able to check the quality of opinions they had previously prepared or their timeliness. The judges do not always have instruments or knowledge allowing for substantive assessment of the expert opinion, and it is naïve to say that they should undergo training in the methodology of individual scientific disciplines.[3] Much depends on procedural law in a specific country and its legal culture. Legal norms determine the scope of a possible application of informal logic instruments, while the application of argumentation theory to a specific legal order allows deducing proposals to change the existing regulations necessary to increase the usefulness of these instruments.

2 Expert Opinion Evidence as an Argument from Epistemic Authority

As the basis of this paper, Bochenski's distinction between deontic and epistemic authority will be used although it should be mentioned that by no means is this distinction dichotomic or complete despite what Bochenski wrote.[4]

[1] See Walton and Zhang (2013, 2016).

[2] To compare with relation between legal discourse and culture See Zeidler (2011) pp. 156–157 and Zeidler (2020), pp. 135–148.

[3] Walton and Zhang (2013).

[4] Bocheński (1993); There is authority from fame (celebrity authority) or from reverence (like in Theodor's Mommsen definition—less than an order more than a suggestion [Mommsen 1867]) among others.

Deontic authority's domain is made of orders. Deontic authority is someone that has right to determine others' future actions e.g. a manager for their employees. Declarative sentences make up the domain of epistemic authority.[5] This is an argument from the "knowing" authority, meaning someone who knows more than us, has a greater amount of data in the area of interest and the ability to communicate them. Bochenski points to the need to fulfil several conditions for someone to be considered an epistemic authority: the subject of the authority must be convinced that the authority knows more than them in a given field and that they really know the field, are competent and truthful.[6] Recognition of greater competence and truthfulness of the subject in a given field is a necessary condition for the recognition of epistemic authority. There are two types of argument from epistemic authority: an argument from authority of someone who knows more (for example a witness of a murder) and an argument from an expert opinion.[7] The most commonly used formalization of an argument from an expert opinion is that used by Douglas Walton:

E [for expert] is a genuine expert in S [the subject under discussion].

E asserts that A.

A is within S.

A is consistent with what other experts say.

A is consistent with available objective evidence (if any is known).

Therefore, A can be accepted as a plausible presumption.[8]

2.1 *Douglas Walton's Critical Questions*

With the help of critical questions, we examine whether the given argument from authority was used correctly logically, and thus, whether the presumption of the truth of the thesis, resulting from the authority supporting the expert thesis, is justified, not whether the thesis is true.[9] Critical questions are a tool to verify that a given argument scheme has been used correctly. If the answer to a given question is negative (it questions the way the pattern is used), the argument is challenged. In all other cases (if the answer is positive or it is impossible to give it), the argument remains valid. A specific argument used in the discussion, which is an instance of a certain argumentation scheme, does not need to contain all the premises listed in the scheme explicitly. Such an argument with hidden premises is called an enthymeme.

[5] Bocheński (1993).

[6] Ibidem, p. 243.

[7] Cf. Walton (1997), pp. 82–83: "being in a position to know".

[8] Ibidem, p. 102.

[9] Walton (2013).

Critical questions are also used to detect enthymemes in arguments (e.g. to show that a hidden premise is false). Lists of critical questions, such as the one by Walton that is presented below, can never be considered exhaustive, but they are sufficient to detect most of the misuse of a given argument scheme.

CQ1: Expertise Question. How Credible is E as an Expert Source?

1.1. What is E's name, job or official capacity, location and employer?
1.2. What degrees, professional qualifications, or certification by licensing agencies does E hold?
1.3. Can testimony of peer experts in the same field be given to support E's competence?
1.4. What is E's record of experience, or other indications of practiced skill in S?
1.5. What is E's record of peer-reviewed publications or contributions to knowledge in S?

CQ2: Field Question. Is E an Expert in the Field that A is in?

2.1. Is the field of expertise cited in the appeal a genuine area of knowledge, or an area of technical skill that supports a claim to knowledge?
2.2. If E is an expert in a field closely related to the field cited in the appeal, how close is the relationship between the expertise in the two fields?
2.3. Is the issue one, where expert knowledge in *any* field is directly relevant to deciding the issue?
2.4. Is the field of expertise cited an area in which there are changes in techniques or rapid developments in new knowledge, and, if so, is the expert up to date in these developments?

CQ3: Opinion Question. What Did E Assert that Implies A?

3.1. Was E quoted as asserting A? Was a reference to the source of the quote given, and can it be verified that E actually said A?
3.2. If E did not say A exactly, then what did E assert, and how was A inferred?
3.3. If the inference to A was based on more than one premise, could one premise have come from E and the other from a different expert? If so, is there evidence of disagreement between the two experts (separately) asserted?
3.4. Is what E asserted clear? If not, was the process of interpretation of what E said by the respondent who used E's opinion justified? Are other interpretations plausible? Could important qualifications have been left out?

CQ4: Trustworthiness Question. Is E Personally Reliable as a Source?

4.1. Is E biased?
4.2. Is E honest?
4.3. Is E conscientious?

CQ5: Consistency Question. Is A Consistent with What Other Experts Assert?

5.1. Does A have general acceptance in S?
5.2. If not, can E explain why not, and give reasons why there is good evidence for A?

CQ6: Backup Evidence Question. Is E's Assertion Based on Evidence?

6.1. What is the internal evidence the expert themselves used to arrive at this opinion as their conclusion?
6.2. If there is external evidence—for example, physical evidence reported independently of the expert—can the expert deal with this adequately?
6.3. Can it be shown that the opinion given is not one that is scientifically unverifiable?[10]

2.2 *Combining Walton's Logical Arguments and Bayesian Networks: Current Research*

The starting point of the research on the use of Bayesian probability was the thesis that methods based on subjective probability can solve problems occurring in the methods of argumentation theory used so far. Douglas Walton points out that the normative status of critical questions is not established, which is a fundamental issue.[11] Answers to critical questions can be formulated in an evasive or inadequate way to be considered correct, and critical questions, for example regarding the argument from the expert's authority, can be divided into more detailed ones ad infinitum. There were no clear criteria for recognizing the answer as correct, nor was there a closed catalogue of critical questions.

Walton also admits that the problem arises when we get satisfactory answers to some of the questions during the discussion, but not all of them, or we get answers to, for example, six questions, but during the discussion it turns out that there is yet another relevant question, which we have not asked or have not received an answer to.[12] The formal criterion of having to answer all critical questions as a condition for considering an argument to be correct must be objectionable.[13] For each of the critical questions described, you can get answers with varying degrees of compliance with expectations, for example, other experts may agree with the expert, but not with all relevant elements of the opinion. The lack of a comprehensive answer to even one of the main six critical questions should not automatically result in the argument

[10] Most commonly used critical questions by Douglas Walton, e.g. Walton (1997, 2013, 2016).

[11] Walton (2016).

[12] Hahn and Hornikx (2016), p. 1837.

[13] Goodwin (2011); Ciurria and Altamimi (2014).

being recognized as a fallacy, given their difference in terms of quality and the lack of clarity of the criteria for considering a given answer to be correct.[14]

Proponents of combining Bayesian methods with the methods of evaluating Walton's arguments believe that the abovementioned problems make it necessary to combine argumentation schemes and critical questions with another normatively grounded method. According to them, integration with the Bayesian probability instruments is beneficial in the form of combining a solid normative source and clear criteria with the possibility of evaluating the arguments present in everyday life.[15]

On a Bayesian perspective, probabilities represent degrees of belief. The probability *P(h)* represents a degree of belief in the hypothesis *h* being true. Crucially, the framework offers a means for relating beliefs to other beliefs. Central here is the notion of conditional probability: *P(a|b)* is the probability of event *a* conditional on *b*, that is, its probability given that *b* is true. The importance of the notion of conditional probability to evidential contexts rests on the fact that it allows one to calculate a degree of belief in a claim, such as hypothesis *h*, given evidence, *e*, for that hypothesis. Probabilities as degrees of belief reflect the degree of certainty one might have concerning a proposition, ranging from $P = 0$ for a claim that is necessarily false (such as a logical contradiction) to $P = 1$ for claims that are definitely true. Applications to argumentation derive from the fact that *e* may readily be viewed as a reason for believing *h*: in evaluating the quality of an argument from *e* to *h*, we consider to what extent it rationally increases one's belief in conclusion h. From a Bayesian perspective, any kind of reason offered to support a conclusion can broadly be regarded as evidence for a hypothesis.[16]

Bayesian probabilities—as degrees of belief—are subjective, and the probability calculus is about coherence, just as classical logic is about the relationships between statements, not their truth or falsity per se.

Since Bayes' theorem can be used to calculate hypothesis (A), provided that certain evidence (B) is available, then if the evidence is the opinion of an expert, the argument from the authority will be evaluated.[17] Bayes' theorem allows us to show a change in the measure of the probability of a hypothesis under the influence of an expert's opinion, however, provided that the quality of their opinion is precisely quantified. The difference between a priori conditional probability and a posteriori probability can be used to determine the strength of an argument.[18] The following example is intended to show the difficulty of using the Bayes' formula to evaluate an authority argument:

P (A) is the probability of event A, i.e., in this example the probability that the image purchased in the gallery is the original image of a recognized artist – 60%, from which, based on the negation rule, we can calculate the value of P (~ A) as 100%–60% = 40%;

[14] See Walton (1997) p. 258.

[15] Hahn and Hornikx (2016), p. 1837; Bustamante and Dahlman (2015).

[16] Harris et al. (2016), p. 1502.

[17] Godden and Zenker (2016).

[18] Dalhman et al. (2015).

P (B | A) is the conditional probability of event B from A, i.e., the probability that the expert will report the image as true if it is true. For example, let's determine the value, e.g. theoretically, we can imagine a situation where we have statistical data covering the last × assessments of the veracity of images and the expert stated that it was true in 60% of cases, of which in 20% he considered a true image that was later identified as false, and in 10% of cases he considered a false picture that was true as 100%–10% = 90%.

P (B | ~ A) is the conditional probability of event B from ~ A, the probability that the expert will define the image as true even though it is false. In our example, it will be 20%.

Only with the above information can we calculate P (B):

$$\mathrm{P}(B) = P(B|A)X\ P(A) + P\big(B|\tilde{A}\big)XP(\sim\mathrm{A})$$

Which in turn will allow us to use Bayes' theorem:

$$\mathrm{P}(A|B) = \frac{\mathrm{P}(B|A)X\ \mathrm{P}(A)}{\mathrm{P}(B)}$$

$$\mathrm{P}(A|B) = \frac{\mathrm{P}(B|A)X\ \mathrm{P}(A)}{\mathrm{P}(B) = P(B|A)XP(A) + P\big(B|\tilde{A}\big)XP(\sim A)}$$

$$\mathrm{P}(A|B) = \frac{0,9X\ 0,6}{0,9X0,6 + 0,2X0,4} = 0,54 : 0,62 = 0.870967$$

P (A | B) conditional probability of event A from B, i.e. the probability that the image is true, taking into account the expert opinion, which in the example given will be 87.0967%—about 87%, so there was a significant increase from 60% of the initial probability.

2.2.1 Bayesian Networks

Bayesian networks (belief networks, Bayesian belief networks) are sometimes called belief or causal networks and are based on Bayes' theorem. In the literature[19] combining Bayesian networks and Douglas Walton's 6 main critical questions were grouped into 3 categories: trust in the expert, proficiency of the expert (expertise) and the initial probability of the hypothesis. In a simplified view, the evidence and opinions of other experts are included in the probability of a priori hypothesis.[20]

---

[19] See below.

[20] This is a radical simplification of the Bayesian network topic in context of expert opinion, for topic expansion and proper definition of Bayesian networks cf.: Hahn and Oaksford (2006); Hahn et al. (2013); Hahn and Hornikx (2016); Harris et al. (2016); Jaynes (1986).

1.Trust in the expert (Trustworthiness)

2.Proficiency of the expert (Expertise) → Expert Report

3.Initial probability of the hypothesis

based on all prior evidence and experts

Because this method is based on assigning a numerical value to terms such as "trust in an expert" or "expert proficiency" that do not have legal definitions contained in the law,[21] there existsalso no one right method to measure them, and thus the basic problem is to assign them values in a non-arbitrary way. Assuming that the evaluation of the argument from authority is to serve primarily the parties of discourse, they should assign a numerical value to these concepts. Previous attempts to use the Bayesian network in the evaluation of arguments encountered a number of problems, the most serious of which is the lack of a non-controversial method for determining the values of variables found in the Bayesian network, both the probability of factors conditioning the a priori probability and the relationship between these factors.[22]

2.3 New Approach

The questionnaire, completed by the participants of the court procedure, together with the relevant Bayesian network and with a thoroughly justified assessment of the expert opinion itself—assessed in terms of formality and its completeness, logic and certainty—would constitute a clear map showing the reasoning of the court. The most important proponent of the argument of expert authority is the court; therefore, in the following example, a hypothetical evaluation by a judge filling in a questionnaire will be presented. As the factors correspond to Walton's critical questions, the numerical value they get will depend on the answers to these questions. In order to obtain more reliable results, the largest number of detailed critical questions should be used, many examples of which are listed by Walton. Each of the answers received is rated on a scale from 0 to 5, with 0 being no answer, 1 a completely unsatisfying answer, and 5 a fully satisfactory answer. The answer here should be understood not only as given by an expert or a party, but also evidence, case files, expert data or the content of court databases. To this end, to additionally take into account that the list of specific critical questions is an open list depending on a specific case and that critical questions have different weight (also in the subjective sense of the addressee

[21] At least in the Polish law. See Dzierżanowska and Studzińska (2019).

[22] Ibidem, Zenker (2012); Olson (2002); Bench-Capon (2002); Fenton et al. (2013); Fenton and Neil (2000).

of the argument—for example, for one recipient practical experience of the expert will be more important, and for another, a title/degree), each value is assigned a multiplier (assigned by the addressee of the argument), and the sum of multipliers cannot be greater than twice the number of questions. For example, with three questions, the recipient can assign multipliers, the sum of which is 6, to the value of the answer, depending on the weight they have for them, e.g. 1, 1 and 4. Later the obtained number is divided by the sum of the "used" multipliers (questions weight).

Therefore, we can calculate the value of trust in an expert, for example based on the answers to the following questions:

(1) Question regarding the credibility of the expert: Is E reliable as a source of information (expert knowledge)?
For example, let us assume that the expert has already issued opinions on several occasions, the person is known to the court as a reliable source of expert knowledge, but the expert has only worked for the justice system for several years and the court assigned 4. The importance of this question: 2.

(2) Is E prejudiced/biased?
In the previously conducted proceedings, there was no expert's bias, none of the parties even tried to prove that the expert was biased or had reason to be biased: 4.5. The importance of this question: 2.

(3) Is E truthful?
The expert has not convicted by a final and binding sentence for a crime that would indicate his lack of truthfulness, the expert enjoys a good reputation in his environment, and none of the parties in the trial revealed the expert's lie: 4.5. The weight of the question: 2.

(4) Is E Diligent/Ethical? (Conscientious)
The expert enjoys an unblemished reputation in his environment, no disciplinary proceedings have been brought against them at the workplace/professional corporation, all opinions prepared so far have been made within a reasonable time without undue delay: 4.5. The weight of the question: 2.

Calculation: $(4 \times 2 + 4.5 \times 2 + 4.5 \times 2 + 4.5 \times 2)$: $8 = 4.375$ out of 5 points and if we want to include the value in percent, we will get 87.5%—trust.

Now we can calculate the expert proficiency (expertise) value by assigning a numerical value, depending on the quality of the answers to subsequent critical questions:

(1) Question regarding the expert: How reliable is E as a source of expert knowledge?
This question concerns the knowledge that the presumed expert has.

He has been registered on the court list of experts for 2 years, meets all the criteria for listing, is an expert in the field of knowledge, in which it is necessary to have special messages to refer to the facts of the case: 4. Weight of the question: 3.

(2) What are the data of E, such as name, occupation, position, location of the business and current and previous employers/associates?
He is an engineer by profession, in addition to being a court expert, he has been working on construction sites for 10 years, he has been the construction manager for 8 years, the current and previous employers are not bound in any way with the involved parties : 4. Question's weight: 3.

(3) What titles, degrees, professional qualifications and certifications, issued by recognized institutions, does E have?
E is an engineer, he graduated from Warsaw Polytechnic, he has no academic title, he has qualifications of a construction manager: 3.5. The weight of the question: 1.

(4) Do the statements/testimonies of other experts confirm the competence of E?
Neither party has made a statement challenging the competence of E: 3. The importance of the question: 1.

(5) Does E have documents or other certificate indicating the practice/experience in S?
E has a full package of documents confirming a 10-year practice in the field of building construction.

and documents confirming the qualifications of a construction manager: 4. Weight of the question: 2.

(6) Does E have a certificate of his contribution to the development of the S field of knowledge or academic articles (preferably peer-reviewed)?
An expert is not an academic, an irrelevant question.

(7) Question regarding the field: Is E an expert in the field of S in which A is located?
Yes: 5. Weight of question: 2.

(8) Is the field of knowledge in the field of which reference to authority is a real field of knowledge or the area of technical skills that support the aspirations to possess knowledge?
Irrelevant question—the area of technical skills (some of the critical questions are irrelevant).

(9) Is E an expert in a field similar to the field in respect of which there is a reference to authority, and if so, how close is the relationship between these domains?
Due to the affirmative answer to question 7, question 9 becomes irrelevant.

(10) Is Expert Knowledge really necessary to establish factual circumstances?
Yes, irrelevant to the abovementioned range.

(11) Are there significant changes in methodology/technology/knowledge in the field of knowledge in respect of which there is an appeal to authority, and if so, is the expert familiar with these changes?
On the basis of previous statements of the expert and his previous opinions, it can be concluded that the expert was familiar with the changes: 4. The importance of the question: 2.

Relevant questions (7): 4 × 3 + 4 × 3 + 3.5 × 1 + 3 × 1 + 4 × 2 + 5 × 2 + 4 × 2): 14 = (12 + 12 + 3.5 + 3 + 8 + 10 + 8): 14 = 4.0357 out of 5 possible points, and the percentage can be presented as: 80.7%—proficiency/expertise.

Using the same algorithm, we can perform an example evaluation of a weak argument from an expert's authority. For example, we can calculate the value of trust in an expert based on the answers to the following questions:

(1) Question regarding the credibility of the expert: Is E reliable as a source of information (expert knowledge)?
The expert has been appointed ad hoc; the person is not on the list of court experts. The expert has not provided any evidence of his previous expert activities.

The court acknowledged 3. The weight of this question: 1.

(2) Is E prejudiced/biased?
One of the parties showed that the expert worked for many years for the defendant as an external consultant (e.g. art historian, advising on the creation of a private collection): 1. The importance of this question: 4.

(3) Is E truthful?
The expert has not yet been convicted for giving false testimony, however, he lied, claiming that he has no relationship with the parties that could affect his impartiality—1. Weighting of the question: 2.

(4) Is E diligent/ethical? (Conscientious)
The concealment of information about receiving remuneration from the defendant for many years and the subsequent lie cast a shadow over the assessment of the expert's professional ethics: 2. Weighting of the question: 1.

Calculation: (3 × 1 + 1 × 4 + 1 × 2 + 2 × 1): 8 = (3 + 4 + 2 + 2): 8 = 1.375 and as it is 1.375 out of 5 possible points, we can express this percentage as 27.5%—trust.

Now we can calculate the expert proficiency (expertise) value by assigning a numerical value, depending on the quality of the answers to subsequent critical questions:

(1) Question regarding the expert: How reliable is E as a source of expert knowledge?
This question concerns the knowledge that the presumed expert has. The expert is not on the list of court experts. The expert is an expert in the field of knowledge in the field of which it is necessary to have special knowledge to refer to the facts of the case, but is not a specialist in the knowledge required for the case, e.g. is an art

historian, but he specializes in sculpture, not painting and the matter concerns the authenticity of a painting—2. Weight of the question: 3.

(2) What are the personal details of E, such as name, occupation, position, location of the business and current and previous employers/associates?

(3) What titles, degrees, professional qualifications and certifications issued by recognized institutions, does E have?
The expert has a professional title of Master of Arts in History, he graduated 5 years ago in History of Art from the University of X. The expert has no additional certificates or documented qualifications—3. Weight of the question: 1.

(4) Do the statements/testimonies of other experts confirm the competence of E?
The plaintiff provided a private opinion, constituting the position of a party, undermining the competence of an expert, a private opinion was prepared by an acknowledged art historian—2. Weight of the question: 1.

(5) Does E have documents or other certificate indicating the practice/experience in S?
E has few references confirming his 5-year practice as an art advisor, however, he indicates that he specializes mainly in sculpture—2. Weight of the question: 2.

(6) Does E have a certificate of his/her contribution to the development of the S field of knowledge or scientific articles (preferably peer-reviewed)?
Expert does not have such certificates nor contribution to history of art—1. Question weight: 1.

(7) Question regarding the field: Is E an expert in the field of S in which A is located?
The expert refused to answer the question asked, arguing that the fact of his academic degree and his name being on the list of experts means that the above question is considered offensive and purely rhetorical. (the expert used the argument ad verecundiam to evade the question)—0. Question weight: 4.

(8) Is the field of knowledge in the field of which reference to authority is a real field of knowledge or the area of technical skills that support the aspirations to possess knowledge?
Irrelevant question.

(9) Is E an expert in a field similar to the field in respect of which there is a reference to authority, and if so, how close is the relationship between these domains?
Yes, E is an expert in a field similar to the field in which there is a reference to authority, both fall in the field of art history—4. Weight of the question: 1.

(10) Is Expert Knowledge really necessary to establish factual circumstances?
Yes, irrelevant to the abovementioned range.

(11) Are there significant changes in methodology/technology/knowledge in the field of knowledge in respect of which there is an appeal to authority, and if so, is the expert familiar with these changes? In recent years, when it comes to the painting of the painter, there were no significant changes in knowledge—Questions 4. Weight: 2.

Relevant questions (9 questions): $(2 \times 3 + 2 \times 3 + 3 \times 1 + 2 \times 1 + 2 \times 2 + 1 \times 1 + 0 \times 4 + 4 \times 1 + 4 \times 2): 18 = (6 + 6 + 3 + 2 + 4 + 1 + 0 + 4 + 8): 18 = 32: 18 = 1.888$ out of 5 points possible, and 37.76% in percentage—expertise.

To use Bayesian network framework for full probabilistic analysis of the appeal to the expert opinion, initial hypothesis probability is still needed together with conditional probability tables. The problems concerning those variables do not fall within the limited scope of this publication, but it can be pointed out that there are examples of conditional probability tables in the literature mentioned before,[23] and initial hypothesis probability can be in many instances assessed by prudent analysis of other evidence or in worst case scenario randomized, in either case, it could be assessed (in this new approach) based on the justified belief of the proponent of the argument.[24] The author's method of using responses to critical questions in the form of a survey to obtain feed data (allowing to determine initial probability values) of the Bayesian network does not allow to refute Walton's allegation that it is impossible to view other people's internal reasoning processes directly.[25] However, also an indirect insight into the reasoning process of participants based on self-reflection and internal dialogue can be a source of information enabling the assessment of a participant's coherence of reasoning concerning the argument from an expert authority based on their own, and therefore subjective reflection. According to its definition, the subjective probability is after all nothing more than an interpretation of the probability, according to which the probability can be determined on the basis of the subjective belief of a person, (alas! it should be a reasonable expectation) depending on the data currently available to him.

According to the commitment rule, in Walton logical argumentation, if the participant of the trial considered an expert witness competent and credible (through external manifestations, e.g., an order to appoint an expert), they should maintain their position until they receive new data,[26] e.g., information about successful bribing of the expert witness or their removal from the list of persons authorized to practice the profession. For example, in the Polish legal system, relying on the weak argument from the authority of the expert in trial practice would translate into the violation of the principles of free assessment of the evidence in connection with the violation of the principles of logical reasoning, including lack of consistency in

[23] Harris et al. (2016), p. 1504.

[24] Cf. Walton and Zhang (2013), pp. 1–2.

[25] Walton and Zhang (2016), pp. 64–68.

[26] Walton (2013); Walton and Zhang (2016), pp. 66–68; Walton Zhang (2013).

the reasoning of adjudicators.[27] The application of the instrument presented in the paper will often help to avoid weak arguments from epistemic authority already at the stage of selecting an expert. Nonetheless its should be taken into consideration that the degree to which the argumentation theory tools prove to be useful depends on the amount of data gathered during the argumentation evaluation and the number of opportunities when dialectical critical testing can be performed. Especially the use of big data and data mining tools would be an essential step, preceded by digitalization of judicial documents.

3 Conclusions

An indirect insight into the reasoning of participants of the process resting on self-reflection and internal dialogue is a source of information enabling the assessment of the participants' reasoning in relation to the argument of the expert's authority based on their own and therefore subjective reflection. In accordance with the principle of commitment, in logical argumentation, if the participant in the process has recognized the expert as competent and credible, (through external manifestations, e.g. the decision to appoint them as an expert), they should uphold their position. In practice, this translates into a much wider possibility of proving a violation of the principles of free evaluation of evidence in connection with violation of the principles of logical reasoning showing the lack of consistency in the course of reasoning.[28]

Persistent use of *ad verecundiam*[29] in a way that makes evaluation impossible should automatically lead to the rejection of the argument from authority (even if the opinion proved very valuable—the lack of the possibility of its evaluation as part of rational discourse should be a sufficient reason to reject it).[30] The requirements arising from law, doctrine and judicature are also not examined here. Failure to meet these requirements, e.g. the inconsistency of the opinion, its incompleteness, can be verified by a layman and such verification should be a separate part of the procedure for the final assessment of evidence from an expert opinion.

The argument against the introduction of such an application of the theory of argumentation is the potential abuse of criticism of the subjective assessments contained in such a provision in order to form appeal allegations. The remedy could be to fill in an identical questionnaire with the application of the algorithm presented by the parties at the stage of selecting the expert and issuing the decision on his appointment. In this way, the court would be able to understand the parties' position as to the credibility and the assessment of the expert's alleged competence

[27] See Dzierżanowska and Studzińska (2019).

[28] In Polish legal system See Dzierżanowska and Studzińska (2019).

[29] Understood in this instance as a fallacious use of an argument form expert authority based on abuse of authority to deflect critical questioning.

[30] Cf. Walton (1997), pp. 259–261.

even before the opinion was prepared, the substantive value of which (tested during the proceedings) could possibly verify the said credibility and competence The result would be greater transparency in the assessment of this part of the evidence, in the form of an expert opinion, which in turn could translate into a greater acceptance of the judgment by the involved parties.

References

Bench-Capon T (2002) Agreeing to differ: modelling persuasive dialogue between parties without a consensus about values. Inf Logic 22(3):231–245

Bocheński JM (1993) Co to jest autorytet? In: Logika i filozofia. Wybór pism. Warszawa

Bustamante T, Dahlman Ch (eds) (2015) Argument types and fallacies in legal argumentation. Springer, pp 3–19

Ciurria M, Altamimi K (2014) Argumentum ad verecundiam: new gender-based criteria for appeals to authority. Argumentation 28(4):437–452

Dalhman C, Wahlberg L, Sarwar F (2015) Robust trust in expert testimony. Humana Mente J Philosophical Stud 28:17–37

Dzierżanowska J, Studzińska J (2019) Biegli w postępowaniu sądowym cywilnym i karnym. Warszawa

Fenton NE, Neil M (2000) The Jury observation fallacy and the use of Bayesian networks to present probabilistic legal arguments. Math Today 6(36):180–187

Fenton NE, Neil M, Lagnado DA (2013) A general structure for legal arguments about evidence using Bayesian networks. Cogn Sci 37:61–102

Godden D, Zenker F (2016) A probabilistic analysis of argument cogency. Synthese Library 195:1715–1740

Goodwin J (2011) Accounting for the appeal to the authority of experts. Argumentation 25 (3):285–296

Hahn U, Hornikx J (2016) A normative framework for argument quality: argumentation schemes with a Bayesian foundation. Synthese Library 193(6):1833–1873

Hahn U, Oaksford M (2006) A Bayesian approach to informal argument fallacies. Synthese Library 152:207–236

Hahn U, Harris A, Oaksford M (2013) Rational argument, rational inference. Argument Comput 4 (1):21–35

Harris AJL, Hahn U, Madsen JK, Hsu AS (2016) The appeal to expert opinion: quantitative support for a Bayesian network approach. Cogn Sci 40:1499–1533

Jaynes ET (1986) Bayesian methods. General background. In: Maximum entropy and Bayesian Methods in Applied Statistics Proceedings of the Fourth Maximum Entropy Workshop University of Calgary. Cambridge University Press, Cambridge

Mommsen T (1867) Historia Rzymska vol. 1–4. Warszawa

Olson EJ (2002) What is the problem of coherence and truth. J Philos 94:246–272

Walton D (1997) Appeal to expert opinion. Arguments from authority. Pennsylvania

Walton D (2013) Methods of argumentation. New York

Walton D (2016) Some artificial intelligence tools for argument evaluation: an introduction. Argumentation 30(3):317–340

Walton D, Zhang N (2013) The epistemology of scientific evidence. Artif Intell Law 21:173–219

Walton D, Zhang N (2016) Ratio. Juris 29(1):59–82

Zeidler K, (2011) Restytucja dóbr kultury ze stanowiska filozofii prawa. O trudnych przypadkach na granicy kultury i prawa, Warszawa

Zeidler K (2020) Aesthetics of law. Gdańsk University Press - Wolters Kluwer

Zenker F, (ed) (2012) Bayesian argumentation: the practical side of probability. Synthese Library

Testimony and Hearsay

Giovanni Tuzet

> *There is no opinion, however absurd, which men will not readily embrace as soon as they can be brought to the conviction that it is generally adopted. (Schopenhauer,* The Art of Being Right, *30)*

Abstract While many epistemologists stress the importance of testimony, psychologists warn us about its dangers. In the legal domain testimony is usually accepted as evidence, with some restrictions compared to acceptance in everyday contexts. Additional restrictions apply to hearsay, and the traditional ban on hearsay in legal factfinding seems to support a reductionist view of testimony: testimony is valuable insofar as it is based on first-hand knowledge, that is, on perception reported as such, with no inference nor assessment by the declarant. However, contemporary legal systems are more liberal in the admission of hearsay, and this may count as an argument in favor of anti-reductionism.

The paper claims that the practical stakes explain the different attitudes towards testimony and hearsay, and that a dichotomy between reductionism and anti-reductionism is unsatisfying in that we need an account that makes sense both of the social importance of testimony and of our preference for the information sources that are closer to the relevant facts.

A first version of this work was presented in the "Atelier Témoignage et Expertise" (with J. Lackey and R. McKenna) organized by P. Engel at EHESS in Paris, March 2018. Some of its topics were also discussed in the special workshop "Theory of Legal Evidence" organized by M. Dybowski and V. Klappstein at the IVR congress in Lucerne, July 2019. I thank the organizers and the audiences of those events for valuable insights and helpful comments.

G. Tuzet (✉)
Bocconi University, Bocconi, Italy
e-mail: giovanni.tuzet@unibocconi.it

V. Klappstein, M. Dybowski (eds.), *Theory of Legal Evidence - Evidence in Legal Theory*, Law and Philosophy Library 138,
https://doi.org/10.1007/978-3-030-83841-6_10

1 Introduction

There is an interesting mismatch in contemporary work on testimony. On the one hand, according to social epistemology, testimony is an exceptionally important source of knowledge. This is so because it is the only source that requires a social interaction to operate.[1] We know many things we have no direct experience of, and we know them since others informed us about them. I know there are kangaroos in Australia, though I have never been there. I know that World War I ended in 1918, though I was yet to be born. Examples can easily multiply. On the other hand, according to the psychology of testimony, we must be very cautious about it.[2] Perception generally works well, but sometimes deludes us. Introspection is generally fine, but not always so. Memory works less well than perception. Our inferential capacities are remarkable, but we sometimes incur in fallacies and errors of various sorts. So, when we report something to someone else it is not guaranteed that what we report is correct. We might have been wrong in our perceptual judgments; our memories might be wrong, or might have been distorted; and our inferences might be fallacious. In addition, the way we express our beliefs can be misleading regardless of our intentions. People can misunderstand what we report, because they do not hear it properly, or because they misinterpret it. Then their memories might delude them too. And so on, for any and every link in a testimonial chain.

The resulting picture is somewhat paradoxical. Many epistemologists stress the value of testimony, while psychologists warn us about it. Those epistemologists seem to uphold what we may call a *principle of trust*: believe what you are told, unless you have a reason to doubt it. Psychologists seem to recommend a different thing, namely what I would call a *principle of distrust*: do not believe what you are told, unless you have a reason to accept it.

The law is an interesting field in this respect. Testimony is generally accepted as evidence. Both in civil and criminal proceedings, though to a different extent, witnesses are heard for the purpose of reconstructing the relevant facts. All legal systems, as far as I know, have rules concerning some aspect of testimony, be it admission, presentation, evaluation, or else. At the same time many legal systems seem to be quite suspicious about some uses of testimony and hearsay. It is one thing to declare I saw Thomas punch David; it is quite another to declare I was told that Thomas punched David.

Common law systems are traditionally skeptical about hearsay. Traditionally, they ban it. If we consider this in a philosophical perspective, the traditional ban on hearsay seems to support a reductionist view of testimony: testimony is valuable insofar as it is based on first-hand knowledge, that is, on perception reported as such,

[1] See among others Lackey (2008), Haddock et al. (2010), and Zagzebski (2012). Cf. Vassallo (2003, pp. 24–32).

[2] See e.g. Loftus (1979) and Wells and Olson (2003). Cf. Jackson and Summers (2012, pp. 325, 329, 364). Some issues were already discussed at length in the first decades of the twentieth century; see e.g. Münsterberg (1908), Altavilla (1925), and Musatti (1931).

with no inference nor assessment by the declarant. However, as I will point out, contemporary legal systems are more liberal in the admission of hearsay, and this counts as an argument in favor of anti-reductionism about testimony. All things considered, it is sensible to find an intermediate position between reductionism and anti-reductionism, making sense of the social role of testimony and of the concerns about it that motivate the preference for the information sources that are closer to the relevant facts.

This paper proceeds as follows. Section 2 clarifies some points about testimony and hearsay, remarking that hearsay rules concern lay testimony (not expert testimony) and that hearsay in a broad sense encompasses both reporting what people say (hearsay in a strict sense) and reporting what some specified source said to the witness (indirect testimony). Section 3 explores some philosophical motives of suspicion and hope about hearsay, namely some considerations of Locke, Hume, Reid, Mill and Peirce. Section 4 is about the ways the law generally deals with testimony and hearsay. I claim that the practical stakes explain the different attitudes we have with respect to testimony and hearsay in different contexts. I also claim that what I call *principle of maximal proximity* (Tuzet 2021) explains why we generally prefer sources of information that are closer to the relevant facts. For instance, pictures over testimonies, and direct testimonies over indirect ones. It is a version of the *best evidence principle* (Nance 1988), a version which disambiguates the best evidence idea by focusing on the proximity condition. Section 5 concludes by claiming that the dichotomy between reductionism and anti-reductionism with respect to testimony is somewhat exaggerated and misleading. Legal practice shows that second-hand knowledge cannot be reduced to first-hand one, as testimonial knowledge cannot be reduced to perceptual one; however, first-hand knowledge and direct testimony are preferred as far as possible.

2 Kinds of Testimony and Hearsay

Some clarification points are needed before we go into the argument. First, Anglo-American legal systems generally distinguish *lay* from *expert testimony*. The former is given by lay people, witnesses with no specific competences related to the subject the testimony is about. The latter is given by expert witnesses, in virtue of the competences which qualify them as experts with respect to a debated issue.

Second, expert testimony is peculiar in some respects. For one thing, it is often the case that the non-expert receivers experience difficulty in understanding it. If they were at ease with it, why would they need expert witnesses? The need to call an expert witness depends upon the fact that non-expert people (including judges and jurors) are at pains to make up their mind about some cognitive issue they face. Then some expert is needed. But frequently experts do not illuminate the factfinders, as they use a toolkit of categories and devices that non-experts can hardly handle. In addition, expert testimony is not mere transmission of information, as lay testimony is supposed to be, but *production* of information. Think of blood or tissue analysis.

The expert is supposed to deliver the information that the analysis produced. Reporting that the defendant was sweating, say, is different from reporting that the biological traces found at the crime scene point at the defendant.

Third, hearsay troubles concern lay testimony. Experts ordinarily rely on what others have said: on the studies of their fellows, on techniques developed by others, on experiments run by others, or more generally speaking on the literature about the issue they deal with. Ideally speaking, the expert's voice is the voice of the scientific community. Hearsay is different. It is just the fact that I was told something and I report it. With expert testimony, and scientific testimony in particular, there is some reliability assumption at work: we assume that what the expert is going to say is reliable to some extent; the more it is so the more the testimony relies on sources that can be checked. Which is not the case with hearsay.

Fourth, also hearsay needs disambiguation. One thing is information from unspecified sources ("People say that Timothy and Anastasia have an affair"), either because unspecifiable or because the witness doesn't want to specify them. A different thing is information from specified sources ("Basil said that Timothy and Anastasia have an affair"), available or unavailable. The difference is obviously important. Hearsay from unspecified sources is less reliable than hearsay from specified sources. And it is important to understand why a source is unspecified, and if, when specified, the source is available or not for direct examination. Fine-grained rules provide for these various possibilities. However, in the following "hearsay" will be generally used in the broad sense encompassing the strict sense of the term (reporting what people say) and the circumstances of indirect testimony (reporting what some specified source said to the witness).

Fifth, some legal systems (like the U.S.) have rules that define "hearsay" as out-of-court statements offered to prove the truth of the matter asserted. This encompasses both oral and written statements, both reported and recorded utterances—something bizarre for the systems which establish more rigid barriers between documentary and testimonial evidence. In the following, "hearsay" will be generally understood in terms of a testimonial oral chain.

3 Sources of Suspicion and Hope

Common law countries are traditionally skeptical about the value of hearsay and follow some exclusion rules, that is, some rules that exclude hearsay from admissible evidence.

It is fascinating to reconstruct the philosophical debate that accompanies the settling of those rules. Due to space and competence constraints I will only deal with some episodes of that complex plot.[3]

[3]For a more detailed and extended discussion see Coady (1992). Cf. Lipton (1998) and Pouivet (2005).

In his *Essay Concerning Human Understanding*, originally published in 1690, John Locke says that "any Testimony, the farther off it is from the original Truth, the less force and proof it has." (Bk. IV, Ch. XVI, § 10; in Locke 1975, pp. 663–664) The "original Truth" is the one about the facts, in the traditional sense of correspondence to them. If Thomas punched David, the "original Truth" is that Thomas punched David. Locke's point about testimony is that, *the farther it is from the facts, the less probative value it has.*

Suppose that someone sees Thomas punch David. This person can be a witness; call this person W_1. Then W_1 reports to another person that he saw Thomas punch David. Call this second person W_2. W_2 can tell W_3 that he was told that Thomas punched David; and so on up to W_N. Now, as you move from the testimony of W_1 to the testimony of W_N you decrease the probability of an accurate account of what happened.[4]

Locke supports this view with a reference to English law. He observes that there is a "Rule observed in the Law of England; which is, That though the attested Copy of a Record be good Proof, yet the Copy of a Copy never so well attested, and by never so credible Witnesses, will not be admitted as a proof in Judicature." (Bk. IV, Ch. XVI, 10; in Locke 1975, p. 663) Call it, in a nutshell, Locke's "copy principle": the copy of a copy has lower probative value. So for witnesses: the testimony of a testimony has lower probative value.

> The Being and Existence of the thing it self, is what I call the original Truth. A credible Man vouching his Knowledge of it, is a good proof: But if another equally credible, do witness it from his Report, the Testimony is weaker; and a third that attests the Hear-say of an Hearsay, is yet less considerable. So that *in traditional Truths, each remove weakens the force of the proof*: And the more hands the Tradition has successively passed through, the less strength and evidence does it receive from them. This I thought necessary to be taken notice of: Because I find amongst some Men, the quite contrary commonly practised, who look on Opinions to gain force by growing older; and what a thousand years since would not, to a rational Man, contemporary with the first Voucher, have appeared at all probable, is now urged as certain beyond all question, only because several have since, from him, said it one after another. (Bk. IV, Ch. XVI, § 10; in Locke 1975, p. 664)

That explains and justifies, according to Locke and his followers, the traditional ban on hearsay in English law.

On the other hand, Locke acknowledges that history is of great use (Bk. IV, Ch. XVI, §11; in Locke 1975, pp. 664–665). This claim is in tension with the "copy principle", since our account of historical facts is nothing but the upshot of a testimonial chain. When we assert that Brutus stabbed Cesar we rely on a chain that goes from W_1 to W_N, where W_1 is some person who was presumably present at the time and place of the stabbing and saw Brutus stab Cesar, while W_N is the person

---

[4]For Locke, the grounds of probability are conformity with our own *experience* and the *testimony* of others' experience. "In the Testimony of others, is to be considered, 1. The Number. 2. The Integrity. 3. The Skill of the Witnesses. 4. The Design of the Author, where it is a Testimony out of a Book cited. 5. The Consistency of the Parts, and Circumstances of the Relation. 6. Contrary Testimonies." (Bk. IV, Ch. XV, § 4; in Locke 1975, p. 656) Notice the adversary insight of considering "contrary testimonies".

who has reported it to us, say a schoolteacher. Why rely on these chains if the testimony of a testimony has lower probative value? What is the epistemic value of historical reports?

In one passage of the *Essay*, Locke articulates a view which is slightly but significantly different from the preceding one. He says that "no *Probability* can arise higher than its first Original. What has no other Evidence than the single Testimony of one only Witness, must stand or fall by his only Testimony, whether good, bad, or indifferent; and though cited afterwards by hundreds of others, one after another, is so far from receiving any strength thereby, that it is only the weaker." (Bk. IV, Ch. XVI, § 11; in Locke 1975, p. 664) This passage is ambiguous in that it contains two claims. The first is that no probability can be higher than it was, as we move along the testimonial chain. If for instance the testimony of W_1 is attributed probability 0.8 of being correct, the testimony of W_N can't be given a higher probability value. This is compatible with the testimony of W_N being attributed the same value, i.e. 0.8. The second claim is that probability values necessarily decrease as we move along the testimonial chain. They will be "only the weaker". If W_1 is attributed probability 0.8 of being correct, the testimony of W_N will necessarily have a value <0.8. This is incompatible with W_N being attributed the same value. The first view can make sense of history, for historical reports can have the same value of direct testimonies; the second view seems to condemn history as a practice that necessarily ends in poor epistemic value.[5]

In his *Enquiry Concerning Human Understanding*, originally published in 1748, David Hume launches a well-known attack on the belief in miracles. This topic is not directly relevant to the one of the present paper, but the way Hume deals with it is interesting for our purposes. In Sec. 10 (*On Miracles*) of that work he says that experience is our "only guide" in matters of fact, but it's fallible.[6] "A wise man, therefore, proportions his belief to the evidence." (Hume 2007, p. 97) This evidence can be testimonial in kind. Hume does not want to deny the value of testimony, for "there is no species of reasoning more common, more useful, and even necessary to human life, than that which is derived from the testimony of men, and the reports of eye-witnesses and spectators"; but the assurance we have in it as a source of knowledge derives from observation: "our assurance in any argument of this kind is derived from no other principle than our observation of the veracity of human testimony, and of the usual conformity of facts to the reports of witnesses." (Hume 2007, p. 98) The justification of testimony is *a posteriori*, for "the ultimate standard,

[5] A way-out is probability updating given multiple independent sources, documents, etc. The probability value of a certain report can be higher once those sources and documents are taken into account. If the report of one historian is confirmed by those of others historians who independently worked on the issue, the report will have in the end a higher probability value. That would explain why history matters to knowledge. But that updating process applies to any testimony and evidentiary item; there is nothing special about history in this respect.

[6] "Though experience be our only guide in reasoning concerning matters of fact; it must be acknowledged, that this guide is not altogether infallible, but in some cases is apt to lead us into errors." (Hume 2007, p. 97)

by which we determine all disputes ..., is always derived from experience and observation." (Hume 2007, p. 98)

> The reason why we place any credit in witnesses and historians, is not derived from any *connexion*, which we perceive *a priori*, between testimony and reality, but because we are accustomed to find a conformity between them. (Hume 2007, p. 99)

We are entitled to trust witnesses and testimonies only insofar as experience confirms their sayings.[7] Then comes the argument against miracles, which is in fact twofold. The first claim is that miracles are *violations of natural laws*. If a witness testifies to the happening of a miraculous event we are not entitled to believe it, because experience tells us there are no violations of the laws of nature.

> A miracle is a violation of the laws of nature; and as a firm and unalterable experience has established these laws, the proof against a miracle, from the very nature of the fact, is as entire as any argument from experience can possibly be imagined. (Hume 2007, p. 100)

Hume gives a telling example of this:

> It is no miracle that a man, seemingly in good health, should die on a sudden; because such a kind of death, though more unusual than any other, has yet been frequently observed to happen. But it is a miracle, that a dead man should come to life; because that has never been observed in any age or country. (Hume 2007, p. 101)

The second critical claim is that, on the principle that experience is our guide, we should reject the greater miracle: "no testimony is sufficient to establish a miracle, unless the testimony be of such a kind, that its falsehood would be more miraculous, than the fact, which it endeavours to establish." (Hume 2007, p. 101) If the falsehood of a testimony on an alleged miracle would require a greater miracle, then we would be entitled to accept the miraculous testimony. The irony in the claim is apparent, for that situation seems to be purely counterfactual.[8]

> Upon the whole, then, it appears, that no testimony for any kind of miracle has ever amounted to a probability, much less to a proof; and that, even supposing it amounted to a proof, it would be opposed by another proof; derived from the very nature of the fact, which it would endeavour to establish. It is experience only, which gives authority to human testimony; and it is the same experience, which assures us of the laws of nature. (Hume 2007, p. 112)

Locke had a nice example worth discussing with Hume's position in mind. It is the case of the Dutch Ambassador, "who entertaining the King of *Siam* with the particularities of *Holland*, which he was inquisitive after, amongst other things told him, that the water in his Country, would sometimes, in cold weather, be so hard, that Men walked upon it, and that it would bear an Elephant, if he were there. To

[7] As an interesting reconstruction of Hume's reductive argument, see Kusch (2002, p. 31): distinguish first-hand knowledge and testimonial reports; then distinguish these three groups: (a) reports confirmed by first-hand knowledge; (b) reports in conflict with it; (c) reports for which you have no first-hand check; then, given that (a) vastly outnumbers (b), assume that this will hold also for (c).

[8] Cf. Hume (2007, p. 102ff). It is the *passion of surprise and wonder* that fosters the belief in miracles, given the "strong propensity of mankind to the extraordinary and the marvellous" (103).

which the King replied, *Hitherto I have believed the strange Things you have told me, because I look upon you as a sober fair man, but now I am sure you lye.*" (Bk. IV, Ch. XV, § 5; in Locke 1975, p. 657) The King of Siam cannot believe the Dutch Ambassador, despite the fact that he took him to be "a sober fair man". He cannot believe his report that water in Holland can be so hard in wintertime that men can walk upon it and that it would bear even an elephant.

Notice that the King of Siam is right in one respect and wrong in another. He is wrong because the Dutch Ambassador is telling the truth. He is right because, based on his experience of the world, water cannot be like that. His experience prevents him from accepting the Ambassador's statement. This example is somewhat embarrassing for the Humean view. Because the appeal to experience is precisely what deceives the King. On the other hand the Humean can point out that the Ambassador was not reporting a miracle, precisely because the laws of nature explain that phenomenon. The problem with the King was that, on his experience of the world, he took what he was told as a miracle and, as a good Humean, he refused to believe it.

The moral of the story goes like this: it is good to check testimonies against the laws of nature, but one should remember that our beliefs about such laws are not necessarily correct. Our experience of the world might be incomplete, or misleading in some respects. We should not forget that we are fallible. Locke's reaction to the case of the Dutch Ambassador and the King of Siam is in line with the spirit of Peirce's fallibilism: never block the way of inquiry, never take your beliefs for absolutely granted. In a perplexing case like that we need to exert our cognitive powers and virtues to our best.[9] Or at least we can suspend judgment, remembering that not believing that *p* is different from disbelieving that *p*.[10]

John Stuart Mill observed (in his *System of Logic*, 1843) that what surprises us and even appears to be unbelievable can be the result of an unknown natural cause,[11] and that we should not overlook the distinction between improbability before the fact

[9] "The difficulty is, when Testimonies contradict common Experience, and the reports of History and Witnesses clash with the ordinary course of Nature, or with one another; there it is, where Diligence, Attention, and Exactness is required, to form a right Judgment, and to proportion the *Assent* to the different Evidence and Probability of the thing; which rises and falls, according as those two foundations of Credibility, *viz.* Common Observation in like cases, and particular Testimonies in that particular instance, favour or contradict it." (Bk. IV, Ch. XVI, § 9; in Locke 1975, p. 663) On Peirce's fallibilism see Haack (2014b).

[10] This was a point made by Mill in his *System of Logic* before discussing Hume's "doctrine of miracles" and the case of the Dutch Ambassador (see Mill 1973, p. 622; cf. Hume 2007, p. 100).

[11] "If we do not already believe in supernatural agencies, no miracle can prove to us their existence. The miracle itself, considered merely as an extraordinary fact, may be satisfactorily certified by our senses or by testimony; but nothing can ever prove that it is a miracle: there is still another possible hypothesis, that of its being the result of some unknown natural cause: and this possibility cannot be so completely shut out, as to leave no alternative but that of admitting the existence and intervention of a being superior to nature." (Mill 1973, pp. 625–626)

and improbability after it.[12] Charles Sanders Peirce, in a paper entitled *Hume on Miracles* (c. 1901), contended that all our knowledge "may be said to rest upon *observed facts*" (CP 6.522), but judgment makes it possible that we exert some control over the process and content of it, so that knowledge extends beyond what is observed, since it involves additions to it. "The making of those additions is an operation which we can control; and it is evidently a process during which error is liable to creep in." (CP 6.523) We are fallible, and error can creep in in our mental processes as it can at any link of a testimonial chain. Still, we are able to perform various mental operations and inferences that, especially in combination with one another, give us knowledge.

The operation of mind that makes observed facts applicable to other circumstances is *hypothesis* (CP 6.524), and Peirce stresses the importance of *testable* hypotheses.[13]

> The first starting of a hypothesis and the entertaining of it, whether as a simple interrogation or with any degree of confidence, is an inferential step which I propose to call *abduction*. This will include a preference for any one hypothesis over others which would equally explain the facts, so long as this preference is not based upon any previous knowledge bearing upon the truth of the hypothesis, nor on any testing of any of the hypotheses, after having admitted them on probation. (CP 6.525)

The operation of testing a hypothesis is what he calls instead *induction*.

> The operation of testing a hypothesis by experiment, which consists in remarking that, if it is true, observations made under certain conditions ought to have certain results, and then causing those conditions to be fulfilled, and noting the results, and, if they are favorable, extending a certain confidence to the hypothesis, I call *induction*. (CP 6.526)

While *deduction* is the inference of facts that "necessitate the truth, or the falsity, or the probability in some definite degree, of the hypothesis." (CP 6.527) Now the point about miracles is that Hume's argument is based upon subjective likelihoods, not objective probabilities.

> Hume's argument against miracles is substantially based upon the assumption that we ought to judge of testimony by balancing the likelihood that the witnesses tell the truth against the likelihood that no such event as that to which they testify ever took place. (CP 6.537)

---

[12] "If we disbelieved all facts which had the chances against them beforehand, we should believe hardly anything. We are told that A.B. died yesterday: the moment before we were so told, the chances against his having died on that day may have been ten thousand to one; but since he was certain to die at some time or other, and when he died must necessarily die on some particular day, while the preponderance of chances is very great against every day in particular, experience affords no ground for discrediting any testimony which may be produced to the event's having taken place on a given day." (Mill 1973, p. 631; note that the example is again a case of *testimony*)

[13] "There are, moreover, many hypotheses in regard to which knowledge already in our possession may, at once, quite justifiably either raise them to the rank of opinions, or even positive beliefs, or cause their immediate rejection." (CP 6.524)

No abduction, no explanation of a surprising fact is possible if we stick to such likelihoods as those of our preconceived ideas.[14] However the force of Hume's argument was in the requirement of a balance of likelihoods. "The truth is that, as soon as it is granted that it is proper to judge of testimony by the balance of likelihoods and unlikelihoods, Hume's reasoning about miracles has been substantially admitted." (CP 6.542)

Another line of reasoning against Hume's view can be traced back to Thomas Reid. In his *Inquiry into the Human Mind*, originally published in 1764, he establishes an analogy between perception and the credit we give to human testimony. Reflect on a phrase like "the testimony of the senses"; for Reid we must take it seriously.[15]

> In the testimony of Nature given by the senses, as well as in human testimony given by language, things are signified to us by signs; and in one as well as in the other, the mind, either by original principles or by custom, passes from the sign to the conception and belief of the things signified. (Reid 1975, p. 90)

Both processes, perception and human testimony, work with signs. As we naturally trust the sensations we have, we naturally believe the words we are told. Reid summarizes his view into two principles,[16] which he calls *principle of veracity* and *principle of credulity*.

> The first of these principles is, a propensity to speak the truth, and to use the signs of language so as to convey our real sentiments. This principle has a powerful operation, even in the greatest liars; for where they lie once, they speak the truth a hundred times. Truth is always uppermost, and is the natural issue of the mind. It requires no art or training, no

[14]That doesn't mean that the testimonial evidence we have of his miracles is sufficient to prove the divinity of Jesus (CP 6.538). What is interesting about Hume, for Peirce, is that he "defined a miracle as a violation of a law of nature, and that the great bulk of his contemporaries were not sufficiently at home in philosophy to see that he was giving the definition a metaphysical turn that was quite uncalled for." (CP 6.539) Until the scholastic doctors, "a miracle was nothing more than a great wonder." (CP 6.540) It was Aquinas who said that "a miracle was an interruption of the order of nature" (CP 6.541) and when Hume took up the subject of miracles he conformed to that definition because he needed to claim that a miracle should be something completely at variance with our experience. Hume also changed the phrase, from "an interruption of the order of nature" to "a violation of a law of nature", which was at the time a more familiar way to put it (CP 6.541). "If there was any difference, it lay in this, that to the majority of scholastics, the order of nature was something absolutely real, having a being in or behind the very essence of nature; while for the majority of modern thinkers a law of nature is relative to the human understanding." (CP 6.542) On Peirce's metaphysics, see Tiercelin (2011, p. 203ff).

[15]For others it is just a metaphor; see e.g. Austin (1962, p. 11): "our senses are dumb – though Descartes and others speak of the 'testimony of the senses', our senses do not *tell* us anything, true or false." To make sense of both positions one may distinguish *percepts* (neither true nor false) and *perceptual judgments* (true or false); perceiving red is not the same as judging "This is red", even though the latter builds on the former.

[16]"The wise and beneficent Author of Nature, who intended that we should be social creatures, and that we should receive the greatest and most important part of our knowledge by the information of others, hath, for these purposes, implanted in our natures two principles that tally with each other." (Reid 1975, p. 93)

> inducement or temptation, but only that we yield to a natural impulse. Lying, on the contrary, is doing violence to our nature; and is never practised, even by the worst men, without some temptation. (Reid 1975, p. 94)

We naturally speak the truth, according to Reid. Lying is a more demanding operation, a kind of artificial behavior, which does "violence to our nature". "I find that truth is always at the door of my lips, and goes forth spontaneously, if not held back. It requires neither good nor bad intention to bring it forth, but only that I be artless and undesigning." (Reid 1975, p. 94)[17] At the same time, as we naturally tell the truth, we naturally believe what we are told.

> Another original principle implanted in us by the Supreme Being, is a disposition to confide in the veracity of others, and to believe what they tell us. This is the counterpart to the former; and, as that may be called *the principle of veracity*, we shall, for want of a more proper name, call this *the principle of credulity*. It is unlimited in children, until they meet with instances of deceit and falsehood; and it retains a very considerable degree of strength through life. (Reid 1975, p. 95)

As a consequence, testimony is naturally accepted. "It is evident that, in the matter of testimony, the balance of human judgment is by nature inclined to the side of belief; and turns to that side of itself, when there is nothing put into the opposite scale." (Reid 1975, p. 95) In other words, testimony is believed by default, and rightly so.[18] Hume is wrong in claiming that the justification of testimony is only *a posteriori*.[19]

To assess whether it is true that men naturally believe what they are told, or believe it by default, we would need empirical data. I don't have them. To form a view about that, try to figure out the extent to which you believe what you are told in a day, and the extent to which you don't believe it (either because you suspend judgment or because you disbelieve it). It is an empirical question. A different question is the normative one about the *reasons* to believe, or the extent to which we are justified in believing (or not) what we are told.

A further line of argument against the Humean view focuses on the implicit testimonial premises of Hume's account (see Coady 1992, pp. 8–11, 80ff). Consider again some of Hume's passages quoted above: it is experience that "assures us of the laws of nature"; "we place any credit in witnesses and historians ... because we are

[17] "There may indeed be temptations to falsehood, which would be too strong for the natural principle of veracity, unaided by principles of honour and virtue but where there is no such temptation, we speak truth by instinct" (Reid 1975, p. 94).

[18] "Reid argued that the evidence of testimony should be trusted unless there is reason to think it untrustworthy and by analogy, that the evidence of the senses should be trusted unless there is reason to think it untrustworthy." (Lehrer and Smith 1985, p. 21)

[19] Hume is right in denying that it is reason that gives us the belief in the continuance of nature's laws: it is instinct that inclines us to believe so, as it is instinct that makes us rely upon testimony (Reid 1975, p. 100). But in this sense the principle of credulity is *a priori*. However, *nature never lies, men do*. "Men sometimes lead us into mistakes, when we perfectly understand their language, by speaking lies. But Nature never misleads us in this way: her language is always true; and it is only by misinterpreting it that we fall into error." (102)

accustomed to find a conformity" between testimonies and reality; "that a dead man should come to life ... has never been observed in any age or country". To whom such words as "we" and "us" refer to? What is the kind of experience that Hume takes as a basis entitling him to such claims? His own individual experience? The experience of the community he belongs to? The experience of mankind? When he says that it has never been observed "in any age or country" that a dead man comes to life, he relies upon the experience of mankind. When he says that experience "assures us of the laws of nature" he relies upon a mass of observations and reports that go well beyond his individual experience and cognitive powers. It is the experience of mankind, passed down through generations, transmitted and refined, from individual experience to common sense and to science.[20] Science in particular is built upon testimony, upon the reports of those who collect data, run experiments, observe results, etc. Even the most fierce empiricist cannot deny this and pretend to have a picture of the world strictly limited to first-hand knowledge.

Bearing all this in mind we can return to the issue of testimony and hearsay in law.

4 Testimony and Hearsay in Law

Let us grant, for the sake of argument, that Reid was descriptively right about testimony. We generally believe what we are told, or believe it by default and depart from this habit only when we have some reason to doubt. This would apply to testimony in everyday contexts, such as ordinary conversations with friends and relatives, telephone calls, exchanges with passersby, etc. Would it also apply to particular contexts such as legal disputes? Is it the case that factfinders naturally believe what they are told and with good reason?

Let us also suppose that in everyday contexts we frequently accept hearsay. What about legal contexts? Do factfinders believe indirect testimony and hearsay?

Legal systems usually regulate the admission and taking of testimony in some respects. Some systems are more liberal than others. It also depends on the kind of case. For instance, some systems restrict the use of testimony in civil cases when it would be about a contract and the value of the contract exceeds a given amount of money.[21] The greater the economic interests, the stronger the temptation to lie. So a ban on testimony works as an incentive to arrange more secure evidence from the beginning, for instance documentary evidence in case a contractual issue arises.

Special restrictions, or exclusion rules, usually apply to hearsay in criminal contexts. And, in case it is legally admitted, hearsay is treated with caution. Why is that? We need an explanation of the different attitudes we have towards it. My simple intuition is that we treat it differently depending on the practical stakes. When

---

[20] In Tuzet (2018) I explored the differences and relations of the singular and general varieties of experience.

[21] Consider, for instance, Art. 2721 of the Italian Civil Code and Art. 1359 of the French Civil Code.

the stakes are high, we are more cautious. When the stakes are low, we are more liberal. This applies to both testimony and hearsay. If you ask a passerby where is the closest tobacconist you are normally inclined to take the answer as true and follow the directions you are given. It would be odd to disbelieve or doubt what you are told, unless you have a definite reason. If the passerby answers in a strange tone of voice or looks like possessed you might have a good reason not to believe what you are told. *Mutatis mutandis* the point applies to hearsay too, in my understanding. Suppose the passerby answers that he is not from the place either but he heard there is a tobacconist around the corner. It would be odd not to go there and look for it. The stakes are low. Now suppose that the consequences of accepting the testimony or hearsay are quite serious. In that situation you would be more cautious and rightly so, for the stakes are different.

A legal dispute is a context where the stakes are usually high. These may be economic or personal values. For instance the property rights over a significant asset, or a compensation claim following an accident, or the value of personal freedom—or even life—when one is charged with a serious criminal offense. Then testimony cannot be taken as we take it in everyday contexts with low stakes. *A fortiori* hearsay should be handled with care. Factfinders are not supposed to believe witnesses just because they talk before them. To my impression, if it is true that in everyday contexts we follow some principle of trust or credulity, it is also true that in special contexts like legal proceedings we follow some principle of distrust. Here we don't believe by default, also because we know that the interests in play can induce witnesses to lie or misreport the facts in some respects.

In addition, it is usually the case that the litigating parties provide different items and sources of evidence to support their different accounts of the matter. If just for the fact that they are told so the factfinders would believe the prosecution's witness declaring that he saw Thomas punch David, and would believe the defendant's witness declaring that he saw that things went differently, factfinders would wind up in a state of inconsistent beliefs. Of course that doesn't happen. For some principle of distrust is operative and factfinders assess the different accounts before they decide what to accept and how to proceed. The legal rules that put some limits on the admission of testimony and hearsay articulate the same logic at a different level.

The traditional ban on hearsay can be well understood along those lines. First, as Locke put it, the farther a testimony is from the "original Truth", the less probative value it has. Second, the possibility of cross-examination is very limited with respect to hearsay. It is traditional wisdom of the common law world, adopting the adversary model of factfinding, that cross-examination plays a crucial role. It is not only a question of fairness or procedural correctness. It is also a question of knowledge. Or, to give a comprehensive account, it is a question of fairness intrinsic to the inferential process of factfinding (see Ho 1999). Cross-examination, the arguments goes, is the best device we have to extract information from the witnesses. Basically it works like this: the party calling a witness examines the witness first (direct examination); then it is the business of the adverse party with a right to cross-examine the witness.[22] In the end the same witness is examined from two perspectives, and the process is supposed to reveal (much) more than a single examination. To use a metaphor, one can think of that in particular and of the adversary model in general as the operation of a double beam, a double way of illuminating the same thing, from different perspectives in order to see more and see better. It works on the assumption that one party has an interest to uncover what the other has an interest to cover, and vice versa. John Henry Wigmore put it quite emphatically when he claimed, famously, that cross-examination is "the greatest legal engine ever invented for the discovery of truth" (Wigmore 1904, p. 1697; see also Wigmore 1913, p. 659). Nowadays it is not unlikely to find critical voices according to which cross-examination works in a perverse way, permitting various kinds of abuse on witnesses by unscrupulous lawyers.[23] Such lawyers, the arguments goes, try to demolish the credibility of the adverse party's witnesses by resorting to fallacies, tricks and attacks of various sorts, including *ad hominem* fallacious attacks, with no genuine interest in the discovery of truth, and the only purpose of prevailing in the case. However, abuses apart (which judges should sanction), the bad intentions of the lawyers should not matter too much because the system is precisely designed to neutralize them, or even to exploit them. What one party is unwilling to ask, or is willing to ask in a misleading way, the other party is willing to ask and to ask properly. The things that both don't ask are likely to be irrelevant.

Now, what matters for our purposes is the fact that cross-examination is possible to a very limited extent in cases of indirect testimony and hearsay. If W_1 declares he saw Thomas punch David, both parties can ask him various things about the relevant circumstances. If W_2 declares he was told by W_1 that Thomas punched David, it is possible to ask him about the circumstances in which W_1 reported that, but it won't be possible to ask him about the circumstances of the criminal act. Supposedly, what W_2 can report is just what W_1 told him. This motivates the traditional exclusion of hearsay.

Philosophically speaking, the traditional ban on hearsay supports a reductionist view of testimony: testimony is valuable insofar as it is based on first-hand knowledge (or information), that is, on perception reported as such, for witnesses are required to abstain from inference and assessment. It is a reductionist view in that testimony is valuable and justified as it can be reduced to perception. (But notice again the difference with expert testimony, where inference and assessment are required).

[22]See for instance Rule 611 of the U.S. Federal Rules of Evidence. Cf. Art. 498 of the Italian criminal procedure code.

[23]Cf. e.g. Langbein (1985, pp. 833–834); Haack (2004); Hunter (2007, p. 262ff); Taruffo (2009, p. 156ff).

Yet tradition is not immutable. According to some scholars[24] contemporary legal systems are more liberal in the admission of hearsay, and the American hearsay rule of exclusion is almost dead, for it has become in fact a rule of admission. The evolution of the American hearsay rule has transformed "the British fetishism with first-hand knowledge into a general rule of admission" (Allen 2016, p. 1398) Those who examine Art. VIII of the U.S. Federal Rules of Evidence are understandably puzzled by its "weird structure".[25] It is in principle a rule of exclusion (Rule 802). But there are 23 exceptions regardless of whether the declarant is available as a witness (Rule 803). Then there are 5 exceptions when the declarant is unavailable as a witness (Rule 804). And there is a final residual exception that may capture situations not covered by the rules above (Rule 807). The exceptions seem to be more lively and significant than the pale rule posited at the beginning.[26]

To give an example of how it operates in practice, consider in short *U.S. v. Boyce* (an appellate case of 2014).[27] Boyce's girlfriend made a 911 call saying that Boyce had just hit her, was going crazy and had a gun. He was charged with unlawful possession of a firearm among other things. But neither party called his girlfriend to testify at trial, presumably because the prosecutor feared she would recant what she said before and the defendant feared that her young age (when their sexual relationship began she was only 15) would bias the jury against him.[28] Then her 911 call was admitted as hearsay. Under what exception to the pale rule of exclusion? Rule 803 (1), on "Present sense impression". And Rule 803(2), on "Excited utterance". What Boyce's girlfriend said in the 911 call was considered to be uttered under "present sense impression" and to be an instance of "excited utterance", which made it unlikely that it was a conscious fabrication. Her statement was therefore admitted into evidence, trumping the pale rule of exclusion. Boyce was convicted given that hearsay and further evidence.

The present is not a work in comparative scholarship and I don't plan to run a survey of legal systems with respect to the ways they deal with hearsay. But another example may be useful to supplement the philosophical reflection on the matter. Let me take the Italian legal system in its present state. According to Art. 257, § 1 of the

[24]See in particular Allen (1992) and Pardo (2007, p. 148ff). Cf. Jackson and Summers (2012, p. 328ff).

[25]I borrow the phrase from Allen (2016, p. 1400).

[26]See also the safety valve provision (especially in favor of defendants) in the English Criminal Justice Act (2003), where it is said that, among other conditions, hearsay can be admitted "in the interests of justice" (s. 114(1)(d)).

[27]See in particular Posner's concurring opinion on the outcome of the case; he claims that it would be good to have a simpler rule making hearsay generally admissible (in line with Federal Rule of Evidence 807) and giving wider discretion to judges. Allen (2016) replies that reform proposals should be checked against the objectives of the field of evidence, the objectives of the Federal Rules of Evidence, and how well the hearsay rule advances, or retards, those objectives.

[28]By the way, this is an interesting example of a shortcoming of the adversary system unmitigated by judicial intervention. In a Continental system the judge would most likely summon Boyce's girlfriend.

Italian *civil* procedure code if a witness refers to other persons who allegedly know the facts, the judge *can* call those persons to testify. There is wide judicial discretion and very limited control of the parties over this. According to Art. 194, § 3 of the Italian *criminal* procedure code the witness shall be examined on specific facts; he shall not testify on public rumors nor give his personal opinions, unless they are an inseparable part of the testimony. By forbidding reports on rumors the rule addresses hearsay in its strict sense (e.g. "People say that that person is a sexual harasser"), but the system does not exclude indirect testimony (e.g. "She told me he is a sexual harasser"). Art. 195 of the criminal procedure code provides as follows:

> 1. If a witness reports information on facts he has been told of by other persons, upon request of a party, the judge shall order to summon these persons to testify.
>
> 2. The judge may order, also ex officio, the examination of the persons referred to in paragraph 1.
>
> 3. Failure to comply with the provisions of paragraph 1 results in the exclusion from the proceedings of the statements related to the facts of which the witness has been informed by other persons, unless the examination of these persons is impossible because they are dead, ill or untraceable.
>
> ...
>
> 7. The testimony of persons who refuse or are not able to indicate the person or source that informed them of the facts under examination shall not be used.

The rule imposes a duty on the judge if a party makes a request to call W_1 when W_2 refers to W_1. If the judge doesn't comply with this duty the indirect testimony shall be excluded (this is a reason to appeal a conviction) unless W_1 is unavailable. If parties don't make any request, it is up to the judge to decide whether to call W_1. This means that the judge has discretion on this point and may be satisfied with indirect testimony. Finally, if W_2 does not specify the source of information then the testimony shall not the used.

Just to give an example, in a case decided in 2005 the defendant was the former human resources director of a private clinic, charged with sexual assault.[29] Two women who worked in the clinic (two alleged victims) testified against him. Others persons working there stated that in the clinic the director had a bad reputation in that respect. People in the clinic said he was a sexual harasser, with an inclination to harass the women working there. Was the latter evidence admissible? If it fell under Art. 194, § 3 it was a case of hearsay in the strict sense of the word ("People say etc."). Therefore it was to be excluded. But the court argued that the people involved belonged to the same context, as they all worked in the same clinic. The information they reported originated there. They had some knowledge of the context that people outside couldn't have. It was possible to specify their identity. Therefore their testimony was not inadmissible. The director was eventually convicted.

On philosophical reflection the admission of hearsay along those lines appears to be a deviation from the principle of maximal proximity, which recommends the use

[29] Cass. pen. Sez. III, n. 14501/2005.

of the information source closest to the relevant facts. However, hearsay can be used to corroborate or supplement direct testimony. This is perfectly fine in a rather holistic model of evidence assessment (Haack 2014a, p. 208ff). And in some cases, when there is no direct testimony, hearsay can be the best evidence we have.

5 Conclusion

As scholars have observed, the exclusion of testimony and hearsay can be justified on the best evidence principle, namely the principle that promotes the use of the best available evidence.[30] When relevant documents are available, there is no point in hearing witnesses; when first-hand knowledge can be transmitted, there is no point in listening to second-hand reports or hearsay. The principle of maximal proximity focuses on this dimension of the best evidence idea, namely the proximity condition. We must go as close as we can to the "original Truth". But the same principles can justify some exceptions to the exclusionary rules, as is the case with the "excited utterance" of the dying victim: "there is no point in using the exclusionary rule to provide incentives to litigants to produce the best evidence when that evidence is unavailable." (Redmayne 2006, pp. 818–819) To speculate on possible situations that require sensible determinations, consider also the case of the eyewitness who at a later date gives a weak testimony (e.g. because of memory failure), whereas the hearsay of his original report is strong (Coady 1992, p. 217; Ho 1999, p. 418).

The exceptions to the traditional exclusion of hearsay count in favor of an anti-reductionist position on testimony. There are different stripes of reductionism and anti-reductionism about testimony. For present purposes, take the reductionists as claiming that the value of testimony is nothing but the value of first-hand knowledge (acquired by perception). Against this, anti-reductionists contend that perception too is fallible, that perceptual judgments depend on conceptual frameworks or even on theories, and that these require a language and a social environment; so they argue against the reducibility of one source of knowledge to another, as beliefs come in systems the sources of which include testimony (Strawson 1993). In this spirit one is invited to see the interplay of such sources as perception, memory, testimony, and inference.

> Simplifying somewhat, we could say that memory as an information source makes past perceptions of the individual available in the present, testimony makes the past and relatively present perceptions of others available to those who did not perceive for themselves, and inference takes information from all these sources and yields unsuspected information latent in them, new possibilities and prospects in the direction of future perception. (Coady 1992, p. 146)

---

[30]This is how Redmayne (2006, p. 806) put it: "second hand evidence may be excluded in order to encourage the parties to seek out and present first hand evidence (this might provide a justification for the hearsay rule)."

Still, first-hand knowledge is preferred when available. The principle of maximal proximity is no surprise in this sense. And the traditional suspicion about hearsay was not the attitude of a biased and underdeveloped civilization. The fact that now legal systems are more liberal towards hearsay counts in favor of anti-reductionism but the principle of maximal proximity pulls in another direction.

All of that tells against a dichotomy between reductionism and anti-reductionism concerning testimony, for things are more complex and nuanced. Recent work in epistemology testifies that we need an intermediate position which accommodates the social role of testimony and the importance of being epistemically vigilant by having epistemic filters and avoiding blind trust.[31] Consider in this respect the amazing and alarming dynamics of contemporary media and social networks (with fake news and so on). As legal wisdom and legal practices show, second-hand knowledge cannot be reduced to first-hand one, and testimonial knowledge cannot be reduced to perceptual one. However, first-hand knowledge and direct testimony are preferred as far as possible, since they are generally closer to the truth.

References

Allen RJ (1992) The evolution of the hearsay rule to a rule of admission. Minn Law Rev 76:797–812

Allen RJ (2016) The hearsay rule as a rule of admission revisited. Fordham Law Rev 84:1395–1405

Altavilla E (1925) La psicologia giudiziaria. Utet, Torino

Audi R (1997) The place of testimony in the fabric of knowledge and justification. Am Philos Q 34:405–422

Austin JL (1962) Sense and Sensibilia. Oxford University Press, Oxford

Burge T (1993) Content preservation. Philos Rev 102:457–488

Coady CAJ (1992) Testimony. A philosophical study. Clarendon Press, Oxford

CP. In: Hartshorne C, Weiss P (vols 1–6) and Burks A (vols 7–8) (eds) Collected papers of C.S. Peirce. Harvard University Press, Cambridge, 1931–1958. (References by volume and paragraph number)

Engel P (2005) Faut-il croire ce qu'on nous dit? Philosophie 88:58–71

Haack S (2004) Truth and justice, inquiry and advocacy, science and law. Ratio Juris 17:15–26

Haack S (2014a) Evidence matters. science, proof, and truth in the law. Cambridge University Press, Cambridge

Haack S (2014b) Do not block the way of inquiry. Trans Charles S. Peirce Soc 50:319–339

Haddock A, Millar A, Pritchard D (eds) (2010) Social epistemology. Oxford University Press, Oxford

Ho HL (1999) A theory of hearsay. Oxf J Leg Stud 19:403–419

Hume D (2007) In: Buckle S (ed) An enquiry concerning human understanding. And other writings. Cambridge University Press, Cambridge (1st ed. 1748)

Hunter J (2007) Battling a good story: cross-examining the failure of the law of evidence. In: Roberts P, Redmayne M (eds) Innovations in evidence and proof. Integrating theory, research and teaching. Hart, Oxford, pp 261–289

[31] See Engel (2005), Lackey (2008), and Sperber et al. (2010). Cf. among others Burge (1993), McDowell (1993), and Audi (1997).

Jackson JD, Summers SJ (2012) The internationalisation of criminal evidence. Beyond the common law and civil law traditions. Cambridge University Press, Cambridge

Kusch M (2002) Knowledge by agreement: the programme of communitarian epistemology. Clarendon Press, Oxford

Lackey J (2008) Learning from words. Testimony as a source of knowledge. Oxford University Press, Oxford

Langbein JH (1985) The German advantage in civil procedure. Univ Chic Law Rev 52:823–866

Lehrer K, Smith J-C (1985) Reid on testimony and perception. Can J Philos Suppl 11:21–38

Lipton P (1998) The epistemology of testimony. Stud Hist Philos Sci 29:1–31

Locke J (1975) In: Nidditch PH (ed) An essay concerning human understanding. Oxford University Press, Oxford (1st ed. 1690)

Loftus EF (1979) Eyewitness testimony. Harvard University Press, Cambridge

McDowell J (1993) Knowledge by hearsay. In: Matilal BK, Chakrabarti A (eds) Knowing from words. Kluwer Academic Publishers, Dordrecth, pp 195–224 (also Ch. 19 of his "Meaning, Knowledge, and Reality", Cambridge and London, Harvard University Press, 1998)

Mill JS (1973) A system of logic ratiocinative and inductive. In: Collected works of John Stuart Mill, vol VII. University of Toronto Press-Routledge & Kegan Paul, Toronto (1st ed. 1843)

Münsterberg H (1908) On the witness stand. Essays on psychology and crime. McClure Company, New York

Musatti CL (1931) Elementi di psicologia della testimonianza. Cedam, Padova

Nance DA (1988) The best evidence principle. Iowa Law Rev 73:227–297

Pardo MS (2007) Testimony. Tulane Law Rev 82:119–190

Pouivet R (2005) L'épistémologie du témoignage et les vertus. Philosophie 88:11–27

Redmayne M (2006) The structure of evidence law. Oxf J Leg Stud 26:805–822

Reid T (1975) An inquiry into the human mind. In: Beanblossom RE, Lehrer K (eds) Inquiry and essays. Bobbs-Merrill, Indianapolis, pp 1–121 (1st ed. 1764)

Sperber D et al (2010) Epistemic vigilance. Mind Lang 25:359–393

Strawson PF (1993) Knowing from words. In: Matilal BK, Chakrabarti A (eds) Knowing from words. Kluwer Academic Publishers, Dordrecth, pp 23–27

Taruffo M (2009) La semplice verità. Il giudice e la costruzione dei fatti. Laterza, Roma-Bari

Tiercelin C (2011) Le Ciment des choses. Petit traité de métaphysique scientifique réaliste. Ithaque, Paris

Tuzet G (2018) Two concepts of experience: singular and general. Pragmatism Today 9:132–144

Tuzet G (2021) On probatory ostension and inference. In: Ferrer J, Vázquez C (eds) Evidential legal reasoning: crossing civil law and common law traditions. Cambridge University Press, Cambridge, forthcoming

Vassallo N (2003) Teoria della conoscenza. Laterza, Roma-Bari

Wells GL, Olson EA (2003) Eyewitness testimony. Annu Rev Psychol 54:277–295

Wigmore JH (1904) A treatise on the system of evidence in trials at common law, vol II. Little, Brown & Company, Boston

Wigmore JH (1913) The principles of judicial proof. Little, Brown & Company, Boston

Zagzebski LT (2012) Epistemic authority: a theory of trust, authority, and autonomy in belief. Oxford University Press, Oxford

Neuroscientific Evidence in Courtroom: Clash of Two Anthropological Paradigms

Marcin Romanowicz

Abstract The emergence of forensic neuropsychology—an empirical science assuming on the philosophical level a causal vision of the world and humans in particular—coincided with the change in the paradigm of criminal policies: in connection to increasing security concerns in many European societies, legislators have introduced new legal regulations targeting the elimination, or at least a reduction of (the) risk of specific types of crime (mainly sexual and violent crime). The contemporary criminal policy, based on fear and on the will to eliminate future threats, creates a singular frame for the interpretation of neuroevidences. Such an evidence most probably be evaluated as a source of indicators or even and instrument for assessment of the offender's future dangerousness. Within forensic neuropsychology the problem of whether a psychopath can be held responsible for the crimes of rape and murder with extreme cruelty has also emerged. This dilemma was brought to the fore by the case of Brian Dugan. This case is an example of the entering new qualitative evidence into practical legal discourse. Evidence that brings with it scientific assumptions that the human behavior is determined by its neurobiological constitution. Such an assumption cannot be adapted to legal anthropology, but at the same time neuroscientific evidence cannot be ignored in cases with "neuro-element" (e.g. psychopathy)—such evidence must be critically assessed by legal decision-makers (judges). Therefore, it is necessary to develop and discuss in the field of the theory of evidence the directives for assessing such "anthropological intrusions" in practical legal discourse.

M. Romanowicz (✉)
Faculty of Law and Administration, University of Warsaw, Warsaw, Poland
e-mail: m.romanowicz@wpia.uw.edu.pl

V. Klappstein, M. Dybowski (eds.), *Theory of Legal Evidence - Evidence in Legal Theory*, Law and Philosophy Library 138,
https://doi.org/10.1007/978-3-030-83841-6_11

1 Opening Remarks: Forensic Neuropsychology and Its Offer

Doors to the contemporary courtrooms have been opened wide to neuroevidence. The road leading from neuroscience to the temples of Themis is called forensic neuropsychology. It is a dynamically developing sub-discipline of clinical neuropsychology dealing with the knowledge about the relation between the brain and behaviour when applied to making legal decisions. In other words, forensic neuropsychology is a branch of knowledge, where people expert in this discipline are called upon, within court proceedings, to provide a scientifically substantiated opinion to the judge or the members of the jury, allowing them to formulate a legal decision.[1] Forensic neuropsychology applies theories, research methods, and principles of clinical neuropsychology in formulating answers to legally relevant questions pertaining to the state of someone's brain, cognitive functions, and behavior.[2] If during the court proceedings (whether civil or criminal) issues concerning connections "brain-mind-behavior" emerge, this is where forensic neuropsychology may be applied.

In the case of the US legal system, historically, the discipline of forensic science began in 1974, with the ruling in *Indianapolis Union Railway v. Walker*. In this case, the plaintiff Ronald Walker was seeking damages for personal injuries resulting from a collision between a locomotive of the defendant Indianapolis Union Railway Company and an automobile in which the plaintiff was a passenger. At the stage of findings of fact, the neuropsychological assessment of brain impairments suffered by the plaintiff as a result of the collision was crucial. Neuropsychologist Ralph M. Reitan provided testimony about localization, causes, and stability of these brain impairments; his testimony was questioned by the defendant during the appeal. The neuropsychologist's expert opinion was contested because it was not based on proven medical knowledge, and the testifying individual, not a licensed medical doctor, could not be considered an expert. As a consequence—in the appellant's opinion—he had no qualifications to testify about the neurological state of the plaintiff. The Court of Appeals of Indiana (First District) rejected Indianapolis Union Railway Company's allegations and stated that Dr. Reitan's education, training, and professional position (he was a consultant to neurosurgeons)

[1] See: MacNeill Horton Jr. (2010), pp. 3–5.

[2] In this sense, forensic neuropsychology is *de facto* the same as forensic neuropsychiatry, which centers on formulating a legal assessment of somebody's behaviour based on the knowledge of relations between the state of the brain and mental disorders. In this chapter, I do not include in the discussion the ongoing dispute about the demarcation between neuropsychology and neuropsychiatry. The only difference I highlight here is the difference in their origins: neuropsychology stems from psychology, neuropsychiatry from medicine, in the area where psychiatry integrates with neurology. The consequence of this difference in genealogy is the currently perceived institutional difference between the positioning of professions of neuropsychologist and neuropsychiatrist (the former does not belong to medical professions), but the area of interest is in principle the same for both and focuses on relations between the brain and behaviours.

demonstrated his expertise. What's even more important, the Court also expressed its approval of the examination procedure used by Dr. Reitan, which consisted of monitoring by laboratory employees of the neuropsychological tests which were used to assess the patient and of the final formulation of the interpretation of the obtained results.[3]

Today, neuropsychological and neuroscientific data are increasingly used in court proceedings. The scope of this phenomenon in legal practice in the US may be reflected in the number of court cases where the expression "neuropsychology" has been quoted: in 1994, there were approx. 400 such cases before federal and state tribunals, in 2004, the number grew to 1200, and in 2009, it reached 2200[4] cases. Gradually, the courts have been admitting further research methods used in the neurosciences (including neuropsychology). Examples of rulings which have shaped the role of neuroevidence and brain data in contemporary legal practice in the US are shown in Table 1.

What can contemporary forensic neuropsychology offer to the legal profession? In the arsenal of research methodologies describing the relations between the brain, the mind, and behaviour, currently figure:

- neuropsychological tests (e.g., Wisconsin Card Sorting Test—WCST),
- batteries of neuropsychological tests (e.g., the Halstead-Reitan Neuropsychological Test Battery),
- psychological tests (e.g., Minnesota Multiphasic Personality Inventories—MMPI/MMPI-2, Hare Psychopathy Checklist-Revised—PCL-R, Violence Risk Appraisal Guide—VRAG, and Sex Offender Risk Appraisal Guide—SORAG),
- eye-tracking,
- brain imaging techniques—neuroimaging (e.g., MRI, PET, SPECT).

These research and diagnostic methods may be used to determine the degree of cognitive deficits caused by brain impairments, hence determining the scope of damage suffered by the victim as a consequence of someone else's action or inaction. Forensic neuropsychology may offer an expert assessment of the brain (mind) which can be translated into a legal ruling about the scope of civil responsibility and guide the court concerning the amount of damages to be awarded. In civil and criminal cases, forensic neuropsychology and neuroevidence could be used to determine the scope of civil responsibility of the perpetrator of damage or criminal

[3]Indianapolis Union Railway v. Walker, 318 N.E.2d 578 (1974), no. 1-573A88. https://law.justia.com/. Accessed Nov 20, 2019. The case which made possible the quoted ruling was the case *Jenkins vs. United States*, which states that "psychologists may qualify as experts on the question of mental disease or defect under the standards set forth." These standards consist of two requirements: (1) "the subject of an inference must be so distinctively related to some science, profession, business, or occupation as to be beyond the ken of the average layman," (2) "the witness must have such skill, knowledge, or experience in that field or calling as to make it appear that his opinion or inference will probably aid the trier in his search for truth"—see: Vincent E. Jenkins, Appellant, v. United States of America, Appellee, 307 F.2d 637 (D.C. Cir. 1962), no. 16306. https://law.justia.com. Accessed 20 Nov 2019.

[4]For more detailed data, see: Kaufman (2012), p. 73.

Table 1 An overview of examples of rulings by US courts on admissibility of neuroevidence

No.	Case	Legal assessment of neuroevidence
1.	*Grenitz v. Tomlian* (2003)[a]	In this ruling, Florida Supreme Court defined the boundaries for neuropsychological testimony, separating the issue of the brain impairment impact on behaviour from inquiring about the reasons for the impairment itself. The Court concluded that: "...the neuropsychologist was permitted to testify with regard to the etiology (brain damage) of the behavior he evaluated. He should not have been permitted to testify as to the medical causation of the organic brain damage itself." This ruling could be interpreted as meaning that in the Court opinion, a neuropsychologist should not substitute for a neurologist: the distinction between neuropsychology and medicine should be maintained. The ruling was not unanimous. The dissenting opinion stated that, "the field of neuropsychology has evolved significantly in the past decades (...) Further, neuropsychologists are an integral part of the study, diagnosis, and treatment of brain damage, often working side-by-side with the medical profession (...) In fact, diagnosing the existence of brain damage depends many times on the results of a battery of standard neuropsychological tests, a highly accurate and specialized method of determining the existence, location, and cause of brain damage."
2.	*State v. Kuehn* (2007)[b]	The Nebraska Supreme Court ruled that the testimony of an expert based on **magnetic resonance imaging** (MRI) and **computed tomography** (CT) is admissible and satisfies requirements of reliability defined by the so-called Daubert standard.[c]
3.	*Baxter v. Temple* (2008)[d]	The New Hampshire Supreme Court ruled in abundant detail on the admissibility of neuroevidence based on the administration of **battery of neuropsychological tests** and concluded that the so-called fixed battery approach, like in the Halstead-Reitan Neuropsychological Test Battery or the Luria-Nebraska Neuropsychological Test Battery, does not raise concerns but tests based on the flexible battery approach, e.g., the Boston Process Approach, may not meet the Daubert standard, because they have no known or potential error rate.
3.	*Allen v. Bloomfield Hills School District* (2008)[e]	The Michigan Court of Appeals took into account in its ruling an opinion claiming "decreases in frontal and subcortical activity consistent with depression and post traumatic stress disorder" based on brain scans performed by **positron emission tomography** (PET).
4.	*Simmons v. State* (2012)[f]	This case generated a question fundamental to legal use of neuroevidence, i.e., who can function as expert giving neuropsychological testimony? The Florida Supreme Court rejected Dr. Larry Holder's opinion concerning PET scans. It seems that the negative assessment of this opinion was mainly due to the fact that Dr. Holder was neither a

(continued)

Table 1 (continued)

No.	Case	Legal assessment of neuroevidence
		neurologist, nor a neuropsychologist but a diagnostic radiologist and professor of radiology. This ruling may serve as an example of a serious lack of understanding of the use of PET[g] technology and of the need to educate judges about neuroevidence.
5.	*Forrest v. Steele* (2012)[h]	United States District Court criticized PET technology highlighting the limitation of this method and ruled that: "Generally speaking, a PET scan can reveal diminished energy usage in particular areas of the brain, thereby signifying damage. However, it cannot show the cause of damage, nor can it demonstrate the existence of diminished capacity, predict future behavior, or establish a person's state of mind."

[a]Grenitz v. Tomlian, 858 So.2d 999 (Fla. 2003). https://cases.justia.com. Accessed Nov 21, 2019
[b]State v. Kuehn, 728 N.W.2d 589 (2007), 273 Neb. 219, no. S-05-888. https://law.justia.com. Accessed Nov 20, 2019
[c]Daubert v. Merrell Dow Pharmaceuticals Inc., 509 U.S. 579 (1993). https://supreme.justia.com. Accessed Nov 20, 2019
[d]Baxter v. Temple , 949 A.2d 167, (N.H. 2008). https://cases.justia.com. Accessed Nov 20, 2019
[e]Allen v. Bloomfield Hills School District, 760 N.W.2d 811 (Mich. App. 2008). https://law.justia.com. Accessed 20 Nov 2019
[f]Simmons v. State, 105 So.3d 475 (Fla. 2012). https://cases.justia.com. Accessed Nov 21, 2019
[g]See: Hardcastle (2015), p. 59
[h]Forrest v. Steele, WL 1668358 (2012). https://law.justia.com. Accessed Nov 20, 2019

responsibility of the accused, because an empirical analysis of the link between the state of the brain (mind) and the behaviour of the perpetrator facilitates an attempt to determine (*resp.* reduce) the scope of his fault. This was the original basic task given to forensic neuropsychology: to perform an assessment of the mental-neurological state of the perpetrator from the point of view of his or her responsibility for the acts committed or for failing to act. Recent changes in criminal policies have given forensic neuropsychology a new task which should give cause to intellectual concerns of these representatives of the legal science who conceptualize ideological foundations of law, i.e., legal philosophers. This controversy will be presented in the next section.

2 Forensic Neuropsychology, Criminal Policies and Social Fear

We are currently witnessing a change in the paradigm of criminal policies: in connection to increasing security concerns in many European societies, legislators have introduced new legal regulations targeting the elimination, or at least a reduction of the risk of specific types of crime (mainly sexual and violent crime). An example of this new approach to the goals of criminal law is provided by the Swiss referendum of 2004, which concerned lifelong detention for extremely dangerous and untreatable sexual and violent offenders. As a consequence of this referendum, the following article 123a was added to the Constitution of the Swiss Confederation:

1. If a sex offender or violent offender is regarded in the reports required for sentencing as being extremely dangerous and his or her condition assessed as untreatable, he or she must be incarcerated until the end of his or her life due to the high risk of reoffending. Early release and release on temporary licence are not permitted.
2. Only if new scientific findings prove that the offender can be cured and thus no longer represents a danger to the public can new reports be drawn up. If the offender is released on the basis of these new reports, the authorities granting his or her release must accept liability if he reoffends.
3. All reports assessing sex offenders or violent offenders must be drawn up by at least two experienced specialists who are independent of each other. The reports must take account of all the principles that are important for the assessment.[5]

The quoted regulation of the Swiss Constitution, in section 1 expresses most clearly the change of the paradigm of criminal law: the basis of even a life detention could not only be the responsibility for committed crimes but rather “a high risk of reoffending.” Elimination of recidivism constitutes *ratio legis* of this new regulation of the Swiss law which highlights the essence of the current reorientation of criminal policy. Criminal law is no longer based exclusively on the principle of retributive justice which requires punishment for committed crimes (bad deeds), but—looking into the future—seeks the prevention of crimes through forced treatment,[6] and also the isolation of perpetrators from society. Fear of crime fosters change in criminal policy which has impacted criminal law in France, Germany, Italy, Belgium, the UK[7] and Poland.[8]

The case of this 2004 amendment of the Swiss highest law reveals another aspect of the paradigmatic change discussed here: paragraphs 2 and 3 of the article 123a of the Swiss Constitution indicate that *science* should decide the fate of the perpetrator. The opinion of an expert scientist is supposed to decide on isolation dictated by the high risk of re-offending, as well as on the rationale for release based on medical

[5]Adopted by the popular vote on February 8, 2004, in force since February, 8 2004 (FedD of June 20, 2003, FCD of April 21, 2004)—see: Federal Constitution of the Swiss Confederation of April 18, 1999. https://www.parlament.ch/en/%C3%BCber-das-parlament/how-does-the-swiss-parliament-work/Rules-governing-parliamentary-procedures/federal-constitution. Accessed Nov 21, 2019.

[6]See: Rose (2010) and Looney (2009).

[7]See: Gkotsi and Gasser (2016), pp. 59–60.

[8]In case of Poland, a change of criminal law was introduced: (1) by the law of November 22, 2013 on proceedings involving people with mental disorders threatening life, health, or sexual freedom of other (Dziennik Ustaw 2014, posting 24 with later changes) and (2) by the law od February 20, 2015 on the change to the Criminal Code and some other laws (Dziennik Ustawa 2016, posting 396). The first of the two laws, called *lex Trynkiewicz* (from the name of the sex offender Mariusz Trynkiewicz), was deemed to be in accordance with the Constitution of the Republic of Poland by the Polish Constitutional Tribunal (ruling dated November 23, 2016, K 6/14).

advances (the "new scientific findings") making possible a successful treatment of the mental disorder which is clearly assumed to be the reason for criminal behaviours and a factor of recidivism. Scientification of law in this case leads towards neuropsychology and other neurosciences. Empirical disciplines studying relations between the human interior—his psychological side—and the behaviour are expected to answer the needs of the new criminal policy. The ability of prediction, understood as forecasting of future events or states, is part of the aspirations of every empirical science, including also neuropsychology. Its goals align with the new functions of the criminal law which should not remain only as an instrument of just retribution but also of prevention of recidivism. The contemporary criminal policy, based on fear and on the will to eliminate future threats, creates a singular frame for the interpretation of expert-neuropsychologist's opinion in criminal trials; his or her testimony will most probably be evaluated as a source of indicators or even an instrument for assessment of the offender's future dangerousness. Within such an interpretative frame, the judge, acting under pressure of the societal need for security, may understand neuropsychological data being introduced in a criminal trial as an objective assessment of the risk of reoffending.[9]

The half-centennial history of forensic neuropsychology reached another milestone in the form of a paradigmatic change of criminal policy. In view of the observed changes, considering the traditional functions of this discipline of criminology, we can conclude that forensic neuropsychology is perceived from the inside of the practical legal discourse, as an empirical science able to provide answer to three types of questions:

- the question of cognitive (mental) deficits of the injured person, resulting from the brain impairment—the answer will be of interest to judges in civil cases,
- the question of the scope of awareness of the perpetrator of a given act or of a person who failed to act; the answer will serve to determine the degree of guilt, or the scope of civil or criminal responsibility—the answer will be of interest to judges in civil, as well as criminal cases,
- the question of the risk of reoffending by committing the same type of crime (the risk of recidivism)—the answer will be of interest to judges in criminal cases.

Are expectations of such answers justified? In the case of the first type of question, history of forensic neuropsychology points to a positive answer—such possibility exists and its realization depends on the proper use of an adequate neuropsychological instrument by the expert. In the case of the other two types, the matter is not as obvious and requires further thorough investigation.

[9] See: Gkotsi and Gasser (2016), pp. 58–59.

3 Neuroevidences and Crime: Neuroimaging as Example of Expectations

Neuroimaging, a neuropsychological method, has become today a symbol, and even an icon of neuroevidence. Technologies, such as MRI, PET, or SPECT, allow a view of structures and processes which constitute the material basis for human mind and subjectivity the brain. Neuroimaging allows the generation of empirical data in a form exceptionally accessible for eyesight driven species of *Homo sapiens sapiens*, i.e., colourful plates which serve to visualize brain structures or processes occurring there (e.g., by capturing local magnetic fields surrounding atomic nuclei in the spectroscopy of the nuclear magnetic resonance, which allows the monitoring of the blood flow and changes in oxygenation in areas of the brain in *functional magnetic resonance imaging*). An example of such informational stimulus is shown in Fig. 2.

During recent years, we have observed an increase in the number of studies and scientific projects which use neuroimaging to identify biological causes of mental disorders. The thrust of interdisciplinary research connected to cognitive neuropsychology, psychology of emotions, philosophy of mind, and other neurosciences is directed towards an empirical exploration of relations between the state of the brain and violent behaviour, moral decisions, and emotional reactions based on empathy.[10] Neuropathology of violence provides many observations of the relations between violent behaviour and dysfunctions of neurotransmitters, brain abnormalities, or traumatic brain injury.[11] The use of positron emission tomography and functional magnetic resonance allows for discovery of reduced brain function in the prefrontal cortex in murderers[12] (Fig. 1).

The correlations occurring between aggressive behaviour and frontal lobe disorder and damage to the neural circuit connecting the amygdala (Fig. 2) to the prefrontal cortex have been identified in neuropsychological literature as factors predicting future aggressive behaviour.[13] Particularly abundant empirical studies of psychopathy resulted in highlighting a connection between this mental disorder and structural and functional abnormalities in ventromedial prefrontal cortex and anterior cingulate cortex (Fig. 2).[14] Frontal and temporal abnormalities and smaller amygdala volume are associated with psychopathy, and also with pedophilia.[15] Neuropathological imaging of psychopathy, constructed using fMRI, allows for the capturing of the brain dynamics of this mental disorder: psychopaths in comparison with healthy people show a lower activity of the brain areas constituting the so-called moral

[10] See: Gkotsi and Gasser (2016), p. 61.

[11] See e.g., Volavka (2008) and Hardcastle (2015).

[12] See: Raine et al. (1994, 1998) and Frierson and Finkenbine (2004).

[13] See: Brower and Price (2001), Raine (2001) and Fabian (2010).

[14] See: Kiehl (2006) and Koenigs (2012).

[15] See: Mohnke et al. (2014) and Müller and Walter (2014).

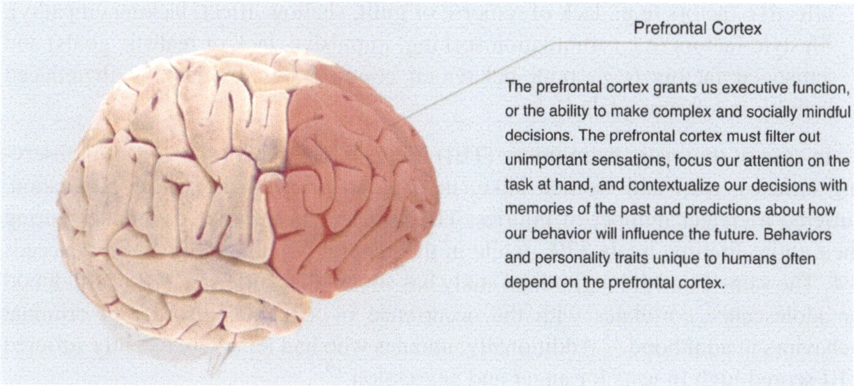

Fig. 1 Prefrontal cortex—source: https://www.brainfacts.org/, Nov 29, 2019 (© Society for Neuroscience 2017)

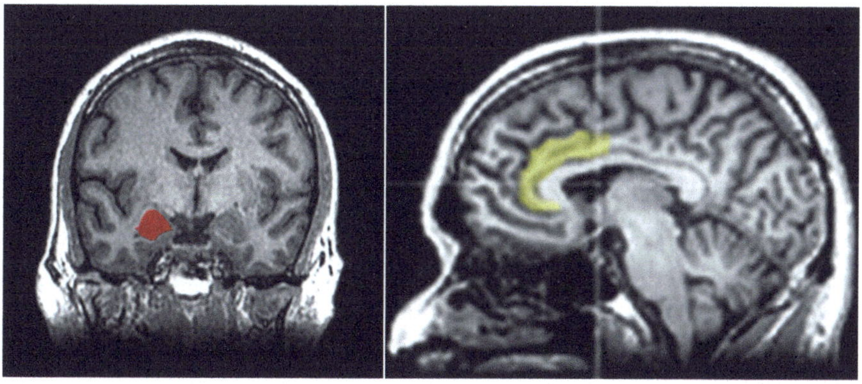

Fig. 2 Sagittal MRI slice with highlighting indicating location of the amygdala (red) and the anterior cingulate cortex (yellow)—source: Wikimedia Commons (Creative Commons CC0 1.0 Universal Public Domain Dedication)

neural circuit.[16] It is composed of functionally integrative connections: (a) amygdala, (b) posterior cingulate, (c) medial prefrontal cortex, (d) angular gyrus. The circuits become active when people make decisions entangled in moral dilemma and they are responsible for experiencing empathy. Various dimensions of psychopathy, analyzed according to the multiple regression model, prove to be correlated with the level of activity in the components of the neural moral circuit, i.e.:

- interpersonal factors (glib, superficially charming, manipulative, pathological lying, grandiose sense of self-worth) are associated with reduced activity in left amygdala, posterior cingulate, medial prefrontal cortex and angular gyrus,

[16]Cf. Glenn et al. (2009), pp. 5–6.

- affective factors (e.g., lack of remorse or guilt, shallow affect, lacking empathy), lifestyle factors (e.g., stimulation seeking, impulsive, lack of realistic goals) and antisocial factors (e.g., poor behavioral control) are associated with reduced activity in left amygdala.[17]

In case of traumatic brain injury (TBI), Finnish researchers succeeded in observing inmates, men and women alike, in comparison with the whole population, suffered a greater number of injuries: TBI indicator in the case of inmates during their entire lifetime totals 87%, while in the general population, it slightly exceeds 8%. The same Finnish longitudinal study has shown that suffering TBI in childhood or adolescence correlates with the occurrence of a mental disorder or criminal behaviors in adulthood.[18] Additionally, inmates who had relatively recently suffered TBI scored high in tests for anger and aggression.[19]

There are abundant examples in neuropsychological literature of observed connections between the offenders' brain state and their criminal behavior. The vast mosaic of these empirical discoveries defines the area where forensic neuropsychology is expected to contribute. A common characteristic of empirical discoveries aggregated by neuropsychology of crime appears to be the fact that they display certain connections "brain/mind-behaviour" repeatedly occurring in various individuals cases. Re-occurrences of these relations is statistically significant and should be considered a scientific discovery, i.e., a contribution to knowledge, and added to the human sciences which have been developed and maintained for centuries. Discoveries of clinical neuropsychology, including those signalled above as examples of scientific determination relevant in the area of criminology and policy towards criminality, belong to **the nomothetic approach**. The essence of this knowledge is captured through simple and experimental observation of a repeated occurrence of two types of variables: (1) specific states of the brain (anatomical, physiological, functional) and (2) human behaviour which either presents cognitive deficits (e.g., amnesia, inability of planning actions), or has a criminal character (e.g., use of violence). Neuropsychological theories describe in nomological fashion the regularities which can be observed using research methods such as neuroimaging; these are purposefully expressed as general "laws" of this area of nature to which the human brain and human behaviour belongs (the Greek word "*nomothetikós*" means "legislative"). For that reason, we cannot be surprised by the expectations resulting from a superficial review of neuropsychology, namely, that it will provide explanations and predictions of human behaviour. This expectation is well aligned with the aspirations of the new, preventive criminal policy.

Yet, when clinical neuropsychology enters the courtroom and becomes forensic neuropsychology, its "methodological configurations" are also transformed. This metamorphosis is best observed in criminal cases: humanity as such, with its

[17] See: Glenn et al. (2009).

[18] See: Timonen et al. (2002); Luukkainen et al. (2012); Hardcastle (2015), p. 56.

[19] See: Slaughter et al. (2003).

statistically significant regularities occurring between the biological side and activities in the world, cannot become the accused, such role falls to an individual, or a group of individuals. Neuropsychology can be expected to produce *cases,* i.e., descriptions and explanations of the perpetrator's behaviour based on an empirical examination of their brain/mind. In the course of court trials, **idiographic expectations** are revealed (the Greek word "idios" means "belonging to someone," "private," "specific," and the word "gráphō" means "I write"), because a forensic neuropsychologist's task is to produce a scientific opinion which will make an understanding and assessment of the accused's deeds possible. The subject of the court discovery which will be facilitated by the presence of the forensic neuropsychologist, is the individual and not general laws of nature.

However, idiographic function of forensic neuropsychology can cross with the nomothetic approach, which is very well illustrated by the case of Brian Dugan, who was sentenced for committing two murders.[20] In 1983, Brian Dugan kidnapped, raped, and beat to death a ten-year old girl. The following year, a twenty-seven year old nurse became his next victim, he raped her and drowned her in a quarry. In 1985, he kidnapped a seven-year old girl when she was riding a bike, he raped her, murdered, and abandoned her body in an irrigation canal. Dugan was accused of the third murder three weeks after he committed it. He was also suspected of killing the nurse. During plea bargain, he offered to the prosecution a confession to all three murders, but under the condition that the prosecution would not ask for the death penalty. Because Dugan's testimony in case of the ten-year old girl seemed inconsistent and not credible to the investigating officers, and also because two men had already been condemned to death for this crime, the offer of plea bargain was declined. Finally, Dugan was judged guilty of two murders and condemned to a double life sentence.

His case was reactivated after a decade: both men sentenced for murder of the ten-year old were cleared of wrong doing, and the investigating officers pursuing the lead of DNA connected Dugan with this crime in 2002. In 2009, Dugan confessed to the murder of 1983, but his lawyers tried to argue for leniency enlisting the help of forensic neuropsychology. They requested a medical examination of their client, as well as an opinion from an outstanding criminal neuropsychologist, Kent Kiehl, who at the time was practicing neuroscience at the University of New Mexico in Albuquerque. Application of *Hare Psychopathy Checklist*[21] allowed for the diagnoses of Brian Dugan with psychopathy—he obtained 38 out of 40 points possible. This result placed Dugan in the 99.5 percentile of all inmates. Dugan's brain was then examined using fMRI, which revealed temporal lobe abnormalities, i.e., a brain pathology described earlier by K. Kiehl and his collaborators as neuronal indicator of psychopathy.[22] Kent Kiehl's idiographic determinations were considered by

---

[20] My description of this case is based on: Hughes (2010).

[21] This diagnostic instrument assesses 20 aspects of personality and behaviour using a partly structured interview.

[22] See: Kiehl et al. (2004).

B. Dugan's lawyers a promising source of mitigating circumstances for their client. The court proceedings were launched.

During a court session in October 2009, the issue of admissibility of neuroevidence in the form of fMRI scans, according to Frye[23] standard, was supposed to be decided. It would have been a "debut" of this neuroscientific method in a courtroom. However, the prosecution brought up an intriguing argument—namely, that neuroscientific explanations can be particularly seductive to the layman, which may preclude making a balanced decision by the jury. The judge announced a truly Salomonic solution, ordering the jury not to view fMRI scans of B. Dugan's brain but allowing them to listen to the neuropsychologist's (K. Kiehl) testimony describing the results of neuroimaging and presenting his interpretation. On November 5, 2009, K. Kiehl testified for six hours presenting B. Dugan's *Hare Psychopathy Checklist's* results, and—using a PowerPont presentation—explained his fMRI results. The neuropsychologist's expert testimony allowed B. Dugan's lawyers to formulate a legal argument that their client as a person suffering from a mental disorder and experiencing negative effects of his own brain's dysfunction, could not control his murderous impulses. While in the case of B. Dugan, his defense did not formulate the argument that their client's psychopathy "forced" him to kill people, but it could be presented as a mitigating circumstance in charging him with the responsibility for the high degree of cruelty towards the victims.

In response to K. Kiehl's testimony, the prosecution called their own expert—Jonathan Brodie, a psychiatrist at New York University—who questioned the relevance of neuroimaging also using the argument of timing: B. Dugan's fMRI scan was performed twenty-six years after he had committed the murder and because of that could not be the source of knowledge about the state of the murderer's brain during the crime. Jonathan Brodie also noted that K. Kiehl's testimony was based on his knowledge of psychopaths gained from averaged results of multiple neuropsychological exams. Brian Dugan's individual difference does not necessarily fall within the conclusions of these exams—speaking metaphorically, the prosecution's expert said that from the fact that the average height of basketball players is high, it is wrong to conclude that all tall people are basketball players.

In the instance of that concrete forensic discourse, it was revealed that idiographic and nomological aspects of neuropsychology intersect: neuropathological theory of psychopathy constructed according to the nomothetical approach was used to explain and assess behaviour of an individual, i.e., with an idiographic purpose. Was this reasoning valid and did it follow the logic and the method of the submitted neuroevidence? This question will be explored in the next stage of our critical journey in the land of forensic neuropsychology. However, before we deal with that, we should present the finale of B. Dugan's case. The jury reached a verdict after less than an hour: ten votes for the death penalty, two for life imprisonment. A death sentence requires unanimity of the jurors. Still, one of the jurors asked the judge

[23]Frye v. United States, 293 F. 1013 (D.C. Cir. 1923). https://cases.justia.com. Accessed 30 Nov 2019.

grant more time for deliberation, the judge agreed. During the continued deliberation, the jurors also asked for a transcript of K. Kiehl's testimony. The next day, all twelve jurors were unanimous—death penalty. The hopes B. Dugan's lawyers had placed in neuroevidence failed them. The appeal did not have an outcome positive for the accused, but in 2011, the Governor of the State of Illinois, Patrick Quinn, abolished the death penalty, and B. Dugan's sentence was commuted to (another) life sentence.

4 The Problem with Forensic Neuropsychology: Two Conflicting Anthropological Models Clash in Courts

The case of Brian Dugan revealed a certain disturbing expectation facing forensic neuropsychology. The defense wanted to use the results of idiographic examinations (fMRI and *Hare Psychopathy Checklist*) of their client. These, presented against the background of a nascent nomothetical theory of psychopathy, were supposed to not only explain the client's actions but also to partly *justify* them. How? By presenting Brian Dugan as a person determined by the state of his own brain to act in a specific manner, i.e. with surpassing cruelty for which his emotional disorder and dysfunction of empathy, factors of his mental disorder, were supposedly *responsible*. Forensic neuropsychology created the expectation that it would reveal a *causal relationship* between the biological state of the perpetrator (the condition of his brain) and the manner of his actions. This **claim of causality** seems to be embedded in deeper layers of the phenomenon of forensic neuropsychology.

In his paper, suggestively entitled, *Forensic Neuropsychology: are we there yet?* Jim Hom defined the essence of forensic neuropsychology from the teleological point of view, i.e., he assumed that its goal is to provide an answer to the *Forensic Question* (FQ). This objective determines the task, role, and responsibility of a clinical neuropsychologist, who "becomes" a source of evidence in the court proceedings.

> [T]he primary responsibility of the clinical neuropsychologist participating in forensic work is to provide information based on scientifically-validated neuropsychological principles and clinical methodology that is pertinent to the Forensic Question at hand (. . .).[24]

As examples of Forensic Questions, J. Hom suggests two questions, the first of which appears to be representative for civil cases, the second for criminal cases, i.e.:

1) Does the plaintiff suffer from significant cognitive deficit as a result of the mild head injury sustained in a motor vehicle accident?
2) Can the defendant's criminal behaviors be explained by brain damage he sustained as a teenager?[25]

---

[24] Hom (2003), p. 831.

[25] *Ibidem.* Classification of question (1) as relating to civil law and question (2) as relating to criminal law has neither logical nor normative character, i.e., neither the (logical) nature of civil and

An analysis of both questions leads to the conclusion that they include a claim of revealing causality, i.e., the "civil" question (1) demands to reveal and describe the causal relationship potentially occurring between damages to the brain (suffered during a "motor vehicle accident") and cognitive dysfunctions present in the victim, while the "criminal" question (2) demands a discovery and description of the causal relationship potentially existing between the brain impairments of the accused (suffered during puberty) and his criminal behaviour. Jim Hom, motivated precisely by the need to determine a causative relation, explains the meaning of the Forensic Question and of the task of an expert in court proceedings:

> The forensic neuropsychologist must be able to demonstrate a causative link between the cognitive impairments and the event at hand. (...) What is required is a methodology that can independently predict the cause of any deficit found.[26]

Still, J. Hom's interpretation, as well as both analyzed by him cases (patient CL and patient CR[27]), which are intended to clarify the meaning of the Forensic Question and of the role of clinical neuropsychology in answering it, are limited to the "civil" type of the Forensic Question. Thus, they may only reflect the requirement for discovering a causality between brain impairments and cognitive deficits. No surprise there—when we study the beginnings of forensic neuropsychology uncovering its genealogy, it becomes clear that its application was limited to the "civil" question about the cause of injury which may be called *cognitive injury* (the term covers impairments of cognitive functions). Only after a Forensic Question of the "criminal" type appeared, a faulty application of the forensic neuropsychology and neuroevidence in court proceedings became a serious risk. Forensic Questions of this type are based on the requirement for revealing causality between the state of the perpetrator's brain and the perpetrator's behaviour. Causality here undergoes an *ontological displacement*, i.e., it ceases to be a relation between the brain (a tissue of the human body) and mind (human cognitive functioning), but becomes a relation between the brain and human behaviour—significantly—for past or future behaviour. I posit that through the appearance of the Forensic Question of the "criminal" type, the original requirement for revealing causality which belonged and still belongs to the Forensic Question of the "civil" type, was extrapolated as shown on Fig. 3. Neuropsychology is clearly a discipline which deals with organic (brain)

criminal cases, nor the current law predetermine that the question (1) may appear only in civil cases, and the question (2) only in criminal cases. Quite the opposite: the question about the mental condition of the perpetrator may surface also in a civil case (in which assigning responsibility may be based on the determination of guilt of the perpetrator of harm), and the question about the scope of harm suffered by the victim of the crime may be crucial in a civil case. The classification is realistic, i.e. is based on the observation that the question about cognitive impairments occurs more often in cases seeking compensation (in other words, in civil cases), and the question about the mental state of a perpetrator of a deed, negatively viewed by law, occurs more often in criminal cases. This is the reason why I refer to two types of Forensic Questions, and use adjectives "civil" and "criminal" in quotation marks, as metaphor-labels.

[26] *Ibidem*, p. 833.

[27] See: *ibidem*, pp. 833–842.

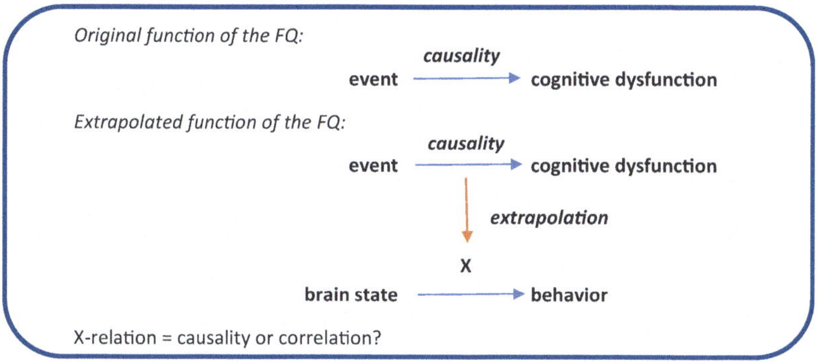

Fig. 3 Extrapolation of the requirement for revealing causality included in the original Forensic Question (of the "civil" type)

foundations of various functions of the human mind and because of that, we can expect from it an answer to the question, whether the change A on the level of the brain could be accompanied by the change B on the level of the mind. The issue of relations between the brain and behaviour is something entirely different.

What is *de facto* the subject of research in neuropsychology as a human science and what it can determine with validity? Neuropsychology describes empirically relations between the brain, on the one hand, and the mind and behavioral control, on the other.[28] An analysis of the research method of neuropsychology, i.e., observation and experiment, as well as of the applied statistical instruments confirms that the relations described by neuropsychology can be identified and recognized as **correlated relations**. A neuropsychologist is able to establish a co-existence of specific states of the brain (first ontological domain) and sets of behaviour (second ontological domain). On this basis, it is possible to predict the degree of probability of a co-existence of behaviour X after confirming a brain state Y. The correlation between the ontological domain of the brain and the ontological domain of behaviour can be captured in neuropsychological tests, but causality cannot be directly observed, and at best, only assumed. Asking forensic neuropsychology to reveal a causality between the state of the perpetrator's brain and his behaviour is pointless because it targets the area of philosophical assumptions, not the area of exploratory activities of neuropsychology, where gradually, with the use of empirical methods, a fragment of the world surrounding us is being gradually uncovered and described. Clinical neuropsychology, like any natural science, relies on certain ontological assumptions which are beyond scientific verification, and for the reason of its position in the methodological structure of a given science, they are perceived as requiring no proof.

The vision of the underlying world of (forensic) neuropsychology includes a concept of a human being as part of a mechanically organized whole, dynamically

[28] See: Berlucchi (2009), p. 1001.

governed by causality. Based on this "axiome," the stimulation of a given area of the brain, associated with specific emotional states, may be *interpreted* as cause of aggressive behaviour. On the level of informational data, neuropsychology may confirm with certainty only that these two phenomena coexist, but an ontological assumption about a deterministic organization of the world, only allows us to formulate an interpretation saying that the first phenomenon is the cause of the second. Interpretative frames for combining data about the state of the brain with data about the behaviour of an individual is provided by a specific kind of anthropology which explains human behaviour as a deterministic product of processes taking place in the human brain. If this behaviour is understood, in general, as a consequence of the decision making process, such a decision is not voluntary, but is determined by physiological factors (e.g., the state of neurotransmitters), electrical stimulation of specific neuronal paths, anatomy of the brain (including all traumas and anomalies), which induct specific emotions and cognitive associations—the causes of making decisions about specific behaviours.[29] According to this anthropological paradigm, the state of the brain becomes an explanation and a cause of an observed human behaviour, the mind is reduced to the role of a middle link in a causal chain. An immoral behaviour or crime are not perpetrated by the mind where the decision is made by the actor, but they are treated as mechanical reactions to the processes occurring on a level of the material, organic brain. These actions (neuronal processes) may be interpreted in turn as mechanical answers to the stimuli coming from the environment. As a result of such interpretation of human behaviour, we arrive at reductionism or elimination of the element of free will:

> The cause of moral violation and crime is no longer an abnormal mind making aberrant decision and moral judgment. Instead, the cause of moral violation and crime is traced back to a dysfunctional brain–environment relationship manifested both in abnormal brain-based neuropsychological processes and in aberrant norms and values. Accordingly, the nature of explanation shifts from an abnormal mind to a dysfunctional brain–environment relationship.[30]

This is the crucial moment when the greatest danger of the entrance of neuropsychology—accompanied by neuroscientific anthropology—to the practical legal discourse is revealed. **Anthropology, upon which (forensic) neuropsychology is based, collides with anthropology serving as basis for law, and the resulting clashes occur in the arena provided by today's courtrooms.**

If in the court proceedings, the objective is to assess whether charging someone with legal responsibility for that person's actions and behaviours, the issue of legal responsibility should be recognized as one of the central legal concepts to which belongs the essence (*eidos*) of the phenomenon of law. A phenomenological analysis of legal responsibility in its two varieties: civil and criminal, leads to the conclusion that is a voluntarist category, i.e., based on an anthropological assumption that a human being has free will and because of that is a relatively autonomous maker of

[29] See: Witzel et al. (2008), pp. 120–125.

[30] *Ibidem*, p. 124.

his behaviours.[31] The attempt to introduce to the court's legal discourse a different anthropology through presenting neuroevidence—determinist instead of voluntarist—threatens the concept of legal responsibility established based on philosophical and legal bases. If human behaviour is the only mechanical reaction to the cause of the anatomical and physiological state of the brain, it becomes impossible to blame an agent for an act or a lack of action, and in consequence, to attribute responsibility: what happened had to happen, because it was predetermined by biological brain factors. Activation of this course of argument is noticeable in the case of B. Dugan: in the opinion of the defense, the perpetrator of these unusually cruel murders was not responsible for his cruelty because his behaviour was not a consequence of an intentional decision but a mechanical reaction to emotional dysfunctions generated by a faulty brain, which was to be demonstrated in the court proceedings by neuroevidence in the form of fMRI scans and testimony of an expert neuroscientist.

The usage of neuroevidence which allegedly demonstrates a determinist necessity of specific behaviour by the accused, or the defendant, and at the same time questions the possibility of attributing legal responsibility may be considered an attempt at breaching the "hard core" of the philosophical structure of contemporary law. This risk was discerned in a critical reflection on the role of forensic neuropsychology. Georgia Martha Gkotsi and Jacques Gasser, among others, commented as follows:

> [A]ccording to some authors, recent neuroscientific research has been able to put into question the existence of free will and responsibility and reveal another kind of determinism and show that responsibility is a vague and imprecise concept which should be abolished. (...) From this perspective, punishment is irrational. If agents are unable to control their conduct because of the determined nature of their brains, then it makes little sense to punish people for their conduct. For these authors, our criminal justice system should change radically in the light of new neuroscience as it is imprudently concerned with an agent's intention (...); instead of punishment, the criminal justice system should focus on therapeutic interventions aimed at ameliorating future harm.[32]

The pressure exercised by neuroscientific anthropology seems to enforce a change in the paradigm of law which is not supposed, any more, to base itself on the concept of responsibility and on assessing the degree of guilt of the perpetrator of a given deed or of not acting. Instead, a "new law" should reject the retributive theory of punishment and satisfy utilitarian demands to apply legal punishments in order to eliminate future crime, i.e., the risk of recidivism.[33]

> [W]hen responsibility and blame are defined by determined neuropsychological processes, being sentenced to prison will be of no remarkable effect, as can be seen in worldwide available statistics referring to the risk of redelinquency of prisoners.[34]

---

[31] See: a phenomenological analysis of legal responsibility in: Romanowicz (2013).

[32] Gkotsi and Gasser (2016), p. 63. See also: Greene and Cohen (2004) and Erickson (2010).

[33] See: Gkotsi and Gasser (2016), p. 63.

[34] Witzel et al. (2008), p. 122. See also: Nunes et al. (2007).

In such a new paradigm of law, tort or crime become a therapeutic challenge and legal sanctions transform into methods of medical treatment or preventive measures against future undesirable behaviours, which may now be perceived as symptoms of a disease diagnosed by a neuropsychologist. The novelisation of the Swiss Constitution presented in part 2 of this chapter, seems to display this train of thought. At the same time, such a paradigm of law fully corresponds with the contemporary criminal policies.

The introduction of neuropsychology to courtrooms and the creation of the category of neuroevidence has clearly weighty consequences which appear in practical as well as theoretical legal discourse. In the former, there is pressure exercised on judges or jurors to assess the behaviour of the accused or defendant as mechanically determined by the state of his brain, or unintentional, which should lead to the conclusion that it would be impossible to attribute legal responsibility, hence also to apply a legal sanction (e.g., punishment). In the case of the latter, the pressure of neuroscientific anthropology is designed to change the paradigm of the law and reformulate or even abandon certain central legal concepts, such as guilt, responsibility, retributive justice, or the function of legal sanctions. Is this persuasive impact of the neuroevidence justified? If the measure for answering this question lies in the accumulation of data empirically gathered by neuropsychology resulting in knowledge about the relations between the brain, the mind and human behaviour, we should reply: "no." The pressure of neuroscientific anthropology which appears at times to replace legal anthropology, is not based on a superior value of the scientific vision of the human beings, inherent in (forensic) neuropsychology. These two anthropological models belong to the level of philosophical assumptions, hence, it cannot be said that one of them has been scientifically validated (in the sense of empirical verification), and the other has not. A perceived methodological equivalence of both polarized anthropologies appears to be the key to a critical theory of neuroevidence which today becomes an urgent need for the practical legal discourse (legal practice, particularly in court).

5 Closing Remarks: The Need for a Theory of Neuroevidence

Neuroevidence may be perceived by judges and jurors as "hard" evidence, i.e., based on empirical research methods and meeting the ideal scientific standards. It is difficult to question scientific evidence, it is difficult as well to evaluate it without being an expert. The evidence based on neuroimaging, or on another neuroscientific methods, introduced to court proceedings, may produce a certain "Christmas tree effect."[35] On the surface, such data are easy to understand, are legitimized by their scientific character, and to some extent, checking their accuracy and integrity seems

[35] See: Nugent (2012), p. 259.

superfluous, yet, at the same time, they may be presented in an attractive format, e.g., fMRI scans. "Charmed" by the accessibility and colours of neuroevidence, the judge, or a member of the jury, may not apply the necessary critical reflection to thoughtfully assess whether a given neuroevidence provides indeed the conclusions claimed by one of the parties of court proceedings. This is noticeable for example in B. Dugan's case. Neuroevidence submitted in the course of his trial was intended to reveal mitigating circumstances, i.e., a mental disorder (psychopathy) which captured at the organic level, i.e., as a functional anomaly of the brain, was supposed to justify cruelty in the perpetrator's behaviour. However, the neuroevidence itself did not empirically prove a causality between B. Dugan's brain dysfunction and his behaviour, such causative relation was "added" to the interpretation of the fMRI results, which was formulated in a certain intellectual framework typical for sciences and assuming materialism and determinism of the world at the level of ontological "axioms." In this way, the neuroevidence admitted in the court proceedings opened the court discourse to the neuroscientific anthropology, which remains in contradiction with legal anthropology perceiving a human being as an autonomous entity, equipped with free will. In B. Dugan's trial, the jury distinguished itself finally by a critical assessment of the neuropsychologist's testimony, even though after their first deliberation, it seemed that the trial would end according to B. Dugan's defense lawyers' expectations.

Determinist anthropology, taking away free will eliminates the central legal concepts of responsibility, guilt, and retributive justice. In combination with predictive and preventive goals of the new criminal policy, it may cause certain dangerous effects, as noted by G.M. Gkotsi and J. Gasser:

> If neuroscientific data are interpreted as evidence of dangerousness, rather than responsibility, it is highly likely that the judge will impose heavier sentences and/or – in European continental systems – security or therapeutic measures, which can be indeterminate in length.[36]

Neuroevidence may prove a "double-edged sword": instead of leading to a non-attribution of guilt (and by the same token lack of responsibility) through fostering in the minds of those who make legal decisions an image of the perpetrator according to categories of determinist (neuroscientific) anthropology, neuroevidence may produce an assertion that criminal behaviour of the perpetrator (the sick patient) is inevitable, which in turn, would justify his forced treatment for an undetermined length of time.[37]

The persuasive power of the neuroevidence, which can be observed by those interested in the history and career of forensic neuropsychology, imposes the question about the risk of manipulation and deception, which appeared in the debate on the role of neuroimaging in court proceedings. The fear of the risk of using neuroevidence in courtrooms in a manipulative manner provokes a question about

---

[36] Gkotsi and Gasser (2016), p. 63.

[37] See: Barth (2007).

the scope of its admissibility and about the way it is presented during court proceedings:

> Simply by appearing colorful and simple, even though they are really statistically constructed maps with a host of assumptions built into them, a lay jury might take brain scans to be more reliable or relevant than they actually are. Should courts exclude brain scans for being more prejudicial than probative?[38]

The development of forensic neuropsychology and the increasing importance of evidence based on neurosciences simply forces the need to formulate a **theory of neuroevidence**. While in the debate about forensic neuropsychology (neuropsychiatry) the participants draw attention to fact that, the duty to indicate borders of the determinations, made by the expert using neuroscientific methods, accuracy and dependability of diagnostic instruments and limitations of conclusions which can be formulated from a given neuroevidence, belongs mainly to neuropsychologists and neuropsychiatrists.[39] The lacunas in the methodological awareness of neuroscientists[40] themselves, encourage demands for an adequate standard of critical assessment of neuroevidence submitted in court proceedings, according to legal theory and legal philosophy. Such a theory should formulate standards of assessment of neuroevidence including:

- a true subject of the neuropsychological description (states of the brain v. intentional states),
- the exploratory scope of the given research method (causality v. correlations), approach used to formulate conclusions from a given neuropsychological examination (idiographic v. nomothetical approach)
- and—possibly most of all—the logical form of the conclusions formulated by a neuropsychologist (descriptive v. normative). The contemporary forensic neuropsychology may provide an empirical description of a given clinical case but should not enter into the legal assessment of the behaviour of the accused or defendant, this task belongs to the judge or to the jury.

The debate focusing on neuroevidence abounds in critical observations about the limits of conclusions drawn from neuropsychological determinations. For instance, it is noted that neuroimaging (fMRI) as source of neuroevidence is not an adequate

---

[38] Hardcastle (2015), p. 60; see also: Langleben and Moriarty (2013).

[39] See: Aggarwal (2009), pp. 241–242.

[40] An example of insufficient methodological awareness of neuro-researchers consisting of a lack of recognition of direct exploratory possibilities of the neuropsychological methods and accepted in neurosciences ontological assumptions (among them, in the determinist anthropology), could be the following assertion: "*Recent advances in neuroscience show that decision-making is not merely a psychosocially determined mental process; instead, it is a bio-psychosocially determined neuropsychological process. As such, decision-making might not be as free and voluntary as presupposed in forensic psychiatry.*"—Witzel et al. (2008), p. 120. Did the discussed by these authors "*recent advances in neuroscience*" capture empirically the causative relations between states of the brain and human behaviour, or did they only describe occurrences of correllations?

instrument to examine the intentionality of the perpetrators.[41] Moreover, determinations concerning certain group regularities in relations between the states of the brain and behaviour or cognition, do not necessarily have to translated into the condition of a given individual.[42] For instance: lowered metabolism in a given area of the brain observed in PET scans of many TBI patients may vary in a statistically significant way from the results of the control group—healthy people. However within one statistical instrument average results of both groups are compared. A determination whether the results of a PET of a single individual allow diagnoses of TBI and define the risk of the occurrence of behavioral correlations of this disease is practically impossible without reaching for an additional diagnostic instrument.[43]

From a practical point of view, a legal theory of neuroevidence could resemble a developed Dubert standard to be used for critical assessment of a given neuroevidence submitted by the forensic neuropsychology. This way **Neuroevidence Assessment Questions** set could be formulated. Closing my reflection at this point, I propose the following list of questions:

1. Has the technique been tested?
2. Has the technique been subjected to peer review and publication?
3. What is the error rate in applying the technique?
4. To what extent has the technique received general acceptance in the relevant scientific community?
   (Daubert case standard)
5. Does the evidence contain descriptive conclusions or normative conclusions?
6. Does the technique allow to investigate regularities in human population (*nomothetic approach*) or the features of individual (*idiographic approach*)?
7. Does the technique allow to conclude about causality or correlation between brain state and behavior/cognition?

This is obviously an initial list of questions which could become a proposal of critically oriented legal theory and legal philosophy for legal practitioners who may in the future come in contact with neuroevidence. An assessment of accuracy and completeness of the proposed Neuroevidence Assessment Questions still require deeper reflection and the participation of a large group of theoretical legal discourse. The clash of two anthropological paradigms: neuroscientific and legal, seems to be a repeatable fact in the courtrooms. The task of the legal sciences is to equip the practical legal discourse with instruments that would help to deal with this conundrum.

[41] See: Aggarwal (2009), p. 240.

[42] See: Gkotsi and Gasser (2016), p. 64; also: Eastman and Campbell (2006).

[43] See: Hardcastle (2015), p. 60.

References

Aggarwal N (2009) Neuroimaging, culture, and forensic psychiatry. J Am Acad Psychiatry Law 37 (2):239–244
Allen v. Bloomfield Hills School District, 760 N.W.2d 811 (Mich. App. 2008). https://law.justia.com
Barth AS (2007) Double-edged sword: the role of neuroimaging in federal capital sentencing. Am J Law Med 33:501–522
Baxter v. Temple, 949 A.2d 167, (N.H. 2008). https://cases.justia.com
Berlucchi G (2009) Neuropsychology: theoretical basis. In: Squire LR (ed) Encyclopedia of neuroscience. Academic Press, pp 1001–1006. https://doi.org/10.1016/B978-008045046-9.00996-7
Brower MC, Price BH (2001) Neuropsychiatry of frontal lobe dysfunction in violent and criminal behaviour: a critical review. J Neurol Neurosurg Psychiatry 71(6):720–726
Daubert v.Merrell Dow Pharmaceuticals Inc., 509 U.S. 579 (1993). https://supreme.justia.com
Eastman N, Campbell C (2006) Neuroscience and legal determination of criminal responsibility. Nat Rev Neurosci 7(4):311–318
Erickson SK (2010) Blaming the brain. Minn J Law Sci Technol 11:27–77
Fabian JM (2010) Neuropsychological and neurological correlates in violent and homicidal offenders: a legal and neuroscience perspective. Aggress Violent Behav 15(3):209–223
Federal Constitution of the Swiss Confederation of 18 April 1999. https://www.parlament.ch/en/%C3%BCber-das-parlament/how-does-the-swiss-parliament-work/Rules-governing-parliamentary-procedures/federal-constitution
Forrest v. Steele, WL 1668358 (2012). https://law.justia.com
Frierson RL, Finkenbine RD (2004) Psychiatric and neurological characteristics of murder defendants referred for pretrial evaluation. J Forensic Sci 49(3):604–609
Frye v. United States, 293 F. 1013 (D.C. Cir. 1923). https://cases.justia.com
Gkotsi GM, Gasser J (2016) Neuroscience in forensic psychiatry: from responsibility to dangerousness. Ethical and legal implications of using neuroscience for dangerousness assessments. Int J Law Psychiatry 46:58–67
Glenn AL, Raine A, Schug RA (2009) The neural correlates of moral decision-making in psychopathy. Mol Psychiatry 14:5–6
Greene J, Cohen J (2004) For the law, neuroscience changes nothing and everything. Philos Trans R Soc B: Biol Sci 359(1451):1775–1785
Grenitz v. Tomlian, 858 So.2d 999 (Fla. 2003). https://cases.justia.com
Hardcastle VG (2015) Traumatic brain injury, neuroscience, and the legal system. Neuroethics 8:55–64. https://doi.org/10.1007/s12152-014-9221-4
Hom J (2003) Forensic neuropsychology: are we there yet? Arch Clin Neuropsychol 18:827–845
Hughes V (2010) Science in court: head case. Nature 464:340–342
Indianapolis Union Railway v. Walker, 318 N.E.2d 578 (1974), no. 1-573A88. https://law.justia.com
Kaufman PM (2012) Admissibility of expert opinions based on neuropsychological evidence. In: Larrabee GJ (ed) Forensic neuropsychology: a scientific approach, 2nd edn. Oxford University Press, New York
Kiehl KA (2006) A cognitive neuroscience perspective on psychopathy: evidence for paralimbic system dysfunction. Psychiatry Res 142(2):107–128
Kiehl KA, Smith MA, Mendrek A, Forster BB, Hare RD, Liddle PL (2004) Temporal lobe abnormalities in semantic processing by criminal psychopaths as revealed by functional magnetic resonance imaging. Psychiatry Res: Neuroimaging 130(1):27–42
Koenigs M (2012) The role of prefrontal cortex in psychopathy. Rev Neurosci 23(3):253–262
Langleben D, Moriarty J (2013) Using brain imaging for lie detection: where science, law, and policy collide. Psychol Public Policy Law 19:222–234

Looney JW (2009) Neuroscience's new techniques for evaluating future dangerousness: are we returning to Lombroso's biological criminality? Univ Ark Little Rock Law Rev 32:301–535
Luukkainen S, Riala K, Laukkanen M, Hakko H, Räsänen P (2012) The association of traumatic brain injury with criminality in adolescent psychiatric inpatients in Northern Finland. Psychiatric Res 200:767–772
MacNeill Horton A Jr (2010) Overview of forensic neuropsychology. In: MacNeill Horton A Jr, Hartlage LC (eds) Handbook of forensic neuropsychology, 2nd edn. Springer, New York
Mohnke S, Müller S, Amelung T, Krüger TH, Ponseti J, Schiffer B, Walter H (2014) Brain alterations in paedophilia: a critical review. Prog Neurobiol 122:1–23
Müller S, Walter H (2014) Neuroimaging can be useful in the hand of neutral experts ordered by the court. AJOB Neurosci 5(2):52–54
Nugent KM (2012) Practical legal concerns. In: Simpson JR (ed) Neuroimaging in forensic psychiatry: from the clinic to the courtroom. Wiley-Blackwell, Chichester, pp 255–274
Nunes KL, Firestone P, Wexler AF, Jensen TL, Bradford JM (2007) Incarceration and recidivism among sexual offenders. Law Hum Behav 31(3):305–318
Raine A (2001) Psychopathy, violence, and brain imaging. In: Raine A, Sanmartin J (eds) Violence and psychopathy. Academic Press, New York, pp 35–56
Raine A, Buchsbaum MS, Stanley J, Lottenberg S, Abel L, Stoddard J (1994) Selective reductions in prefrontal glucose metabolism in murderers. Biol Psychiatry 36(6):365–373
Raine A, Meloy JR, Bihrle S, Stoddard J, LaCasse L, Buchsbaum MS (1998) Reduced prefrontal and increased subcortical brain functioning assessed using positron emission tomography in predatory and affective murderers. Behav Sci Law 16:319–332
Romanowicz M (2013) Legal responsibility as a voluntaristic category. Philosophical-legal and neuropsychological remarks. In: Bokus B (ed) Responsibility. A cross-disciplinary perspective. Lexem, pp 201–228
Rose N (2010) 'Screen and intervene': governing risky brains. Hist Hum Sci 23(1):79–105
Simmons v. State, 105 So.3d 475 (Fla. 2012). https://cases.justia.com
Slaughter B, Fann JR, Ehde D (2003) Traumatic brain injury in a county jail population: prevalence, neuropsychological functioning, and psychiatric disorders. Brain Inj 17:731–741
State v. Kuehn, 728 N.W.2d 589 (2007), 273 Neb. 219, no. S-05-888. https://law.justia.com
Timonen M, Miettunen J, Hakko H, Veijola J, von Wendt L, Räsänen P (2002) The association of preceding traumatic brain injury with mental disorders, alcoholism, and criminality: the Northern Finland 1966 Birth cohort study. Psychiatric Res 113:217–226
Vincent E. Jenkins, Appellant, v. United States of America, Appellee, 307 F.2d 637 (D.C. Cir.1962), no. 16306. https://law.justia.com
Volavka J (2008) Neurobiology of violence. American Psychiatric Publishing, Washington
Witzel J, Walter M, Bogerts B, Northoff G (2008) Neurophilosophical perspectives of neuroimaging in forensic psychiatry - giving way to a paradigm shift? Behav Sci Law 26:113–130

An Epistemic Defense of Exclusionary Rules in the Criminal Justice System

John R. Harris

Abstract If we think that the point of a criminal trial is to arrive at the truth regarding the guilt of the accused, then exclusionary rules are curious. Exclusionary rules prevent the triers of fact from having access to all of the relevant information, and thus, one may worry, exclusionary rules make errors in criminal trials more likely. Thus, it is often thought, if we are to justify exclusionary rules, we must do so on moral grounds rather than for epistemic reasons. In this essay, I argue that we can justify exclusionary rules on epistemic grounds, and in fact, sound epistemic practices often require us to exclude relevant information from consideration both inside and outside the courtroom.

1 Introduction

On February 17th, 2004 the state of Texas executed Cameron Todd Willingham.[1] Though he maintained his innocence, Willingham was convicted of killing his three children by setting fire to the family home. The state's case against Willingham focused primarily on the testimony of arson experts who claimed that they found burn patters consistent with the use of an accelerant, they found traces of that accelerant by the entry to the home, and despite there being substantial damage to the home's floors, there were no burns on Willingham's feet who escaped the blaze bare footed. The state's arson investigator argued that there were over twenty indicators of arson found at the crime scene. The jury took less than hour to reach a guilty verdict. The problem, however, is that the evidence that the state relied upon to show that the fire was an act of arson was deeply flawed. According to a report submitted to the Texas Forensic Science Commission, the arson investigation in Willingham's case neither lived up to the current standard of care in such

[1] For an excellent summary of the case see Grann (2009).

J. R. Harris (✉)
Texas Christian University, Fort Worth, TX, USA
e-mail: j.r.harris@tcu.edu

V. Klappstein, M. Dybowski (eds.), *Theory of Legal Evidence - Evidence in Legal Theory*, Law and Philosophy Library 138,
https://doi.org/10.1007/978-3-030-83841-6_12

investigations at the time of the report (in 2009) nor did it live up to the standards of care at the time of the investigation (in 1991).[2] In short, Willingham's conviction relied on junk science.

The purpose of this essay is to offer a defense of exclusionary rules, and to argue in particular that we can justify exclusionary rules on epistemic grounds. I argue that the jury in the Willingham case would not have been rendered worse off had the testimony of state's arson investigators been withheld from them. As it turns out, this is a controversial position. Some of the most common defenses of exclusionary rules, grant the epistemic problems, but argue that there are other moral considerations that override those problems.[3] I will not pursue that strategy here. Rather, I will try to meet the skeptics on their own ground—I argue here that the epistemic challenges to exclusionary rules can be met.

This essay will proceed as follows: In the following section I will outline some basic contours of the debate. In Sect. 2, I will present the basic epistemic argument against exclusionary rules. The concern, in brief, is that exclusionary rules make error more likely rather than less. In Sects. 3 and 4, I will discuss two primary arguments offered in defense of the claim that exclusionary rules are truth thwarting: the claim that more evidence is always better and the claim that exclusionary rules rely on unproven psychological hypotheses. In Sects. 5 and 6 I seek to show those preceding claims are unwarranted. In Sect. 5, I argue that the empirical challenge can be met—we can show that some exclusionary rules are grounded on sound science. In Sect. 6, I argue that the claim that more evidence is always better is false. As we shall see, it is not always better to have more evidence.

2 Clearing the Ground

Exclusionary rules serve to prohibit certain information from being presented in trials. There are numerous exclusionary rules and they serve to exclude a wide variety of evidence. Consider some common exclusionary rules found in the U.S. legal system. In *Mapp v. Ohio* the US Supreme Court extended the Fourth Amendment protection against illegal search and seizure to state courts (previously the Court had ruled that the Fourth Amendment only applied to Federal Courts).[4] Effectively states are now prohibited from introducing evidence that was gathered illegally by police. This is but one example of the sorts of evidence that can be excluded from trials. Other examples include hearsay, spousal privilege, recanted confessions, key witnesses pleading the Fifth (i.e., refusing to testify on the grounds that they may incriminate themselves), evidence that is considered unfairly

---

[2]Beyler (2009), p. 51.

[3]See Ho (2019) "The Fair Trial Rationale for Excluding Wrongfully Obtained Evidence," and his essay, (2016) "The Criminal Trial, the Rule of Law, and the Exclusion of Wrongfully Obtained Evidence."

[4]Clark (1961).

prejudicial, and instructions that forbid jurors from taking the defendant's silence into consideration when considering their guilt—to name only a few. And, of course, one does not find exclusionary rules only within the United States.[5]

The problem, however, is that exclusionary rules appear to prevent juries and judges from considering *all* the relevant information that may speak to the guilt or innocence of the defendant(s). This practice seems at odds with the best practices employed by other enterprises that take their key function to be truth seeking. The scientific enterprise would be undermined, to say the least, if scientists ignored relevant information, were prevented from searching for further evidence, or were prevented from asking questions of those who provide key evidence, yet this is exactly what happens to jurors.

Objections to exclusionary rules along these lines are by no means new. Jeremy Bentham raised concerns with exclusionary rules in his essay "Rationale of Judicial Evidence, specifically applied to the English Practice." He writes, "...the practice of putting exclusion upon evidence, the effect is much more frequently to produce than to prevent injustice,—so much so, that it would be a prodigious benefit to justice, if exclusion of evidence were, in so far as it takes this for its ground, itself for ever, and in every instance, excluded...."[6] More recently Larry Laudan has picked up Bentham's torch and called into question the epistemic role of exclusionary rules in the US legal system, and he too worries that they do more harm, epistemically speaking, than good. It is to his arguments that I now turn.

3 The Case Against Exclusionary Rules

To begin, consider a basic argument against exclusionary rules:

P1. Truth is the principle aim of the criminal justice system
P2. If a practice or set of rules serves to interfere with or undermine the principle aim of an institution, then that aim should be altered or that practice or set of rules should be altered or abolished.
P3. Exclusionary rules interfere with or undermine the primary aim of the criminal justice system.
P4. The primary aim of the criminal justice system should be altered, or exclusionary rules should be altered or abolished
P5. We should not alter the primary aim (the truth seeking imperative) of the criminal justice system.
C. Exclusionary rules should be altered or abolished

The argument is valid, so we need to see if the premises are in fact true.

[5] See Ma (1999) See also, section 2 of Ho (2019).

[6] Bentham (1843) Vol 6, chapter 9.

Consider the case for premise 1—that truth is the primary goal of the criminal justice system. Jurists have long recognized that seeking the truth is a fundamental if not *the* fundamental aim of criminal legal proceedings.[7] But we need not rely on proclamations from jurists and scholars to make this case. There is a moral argument that supports premise 1. Given the profound harms that attach to criminal convictions we must do everything we can to ensure that the outcome of criminal proceedings is correct. Perhaps we are inclined to think that justice is an equally important value that the judiciary should be pursuing in conjunction with truth. This may be, but no doubt we want to be certain that when we punish someone, she is in fact guilty of the crime for which she has been convicted, and when we set someone free, she is in fact innocent.

Even if premise 1 is false, Laudan is interested in what implications accepting it would have on a legal system. That is to say, if we were generally focused on getting things right, how might a legal system be different than it is presently? So, for our purposes, even if premise 1 is untenable, let us grant it for the sake of argument to see where a focus on epistemology might take a legal system.

The case for premise 2 is fairly straightforward. Premise 2 tells us that if there are practices in place within an institution that undermine that institution's primary purpose, then we must either act to revise those practices, or should we feel particularly strong about those practices, then we should change the institution's primary purpose to reflect that. So, suppose a group takes the primary purpose of their religion that they go out and save lost souls by conversion to their religion. If this religious group also forbids proselytizing, then something here must give. They must decide if they are truly committed to converting the unsaved, and if so, they must abandon their prohibition on proselytizing. Alternatively, if upon reflection they find that the prohibition on proselytizing is more central to their fundamental values, then they must alter the primary purpose of their religion. Here we simply find a matter of consistency.

Consider how this applies to the present context. If it is true that exclusionary rules are at odds with the epistemic function of the legal system, then we find—given premise 2—that we must either abandon the epistemic imperative or we must get rid of exclusionary rules. Given what we have already said in defense of premise 1 it seems incredibly difficult to give up the epistemic imperative. What would it mean to abandon the truth-seeking imperative of the criminal justice system? Would we be prepared to accept false convictions now? It is something of truism within the legal system that it is better to let one hundred guilty people go free than to let one innocent individual go to jail. If we abandon our commitment to the truth will we also accept that innocent people must go to prison? Surely not. All of this would simply serve to corrupt a legal system. It seems best then, that if we are faced with a choice between keeping exclusionary rules and rejecting the epistemic imperative or keeping the epistemic imperative and rejecting exclusionary rules, the latter is the best option available to us. Premise 5 seems to stand on solid ground.

[7] See for example, Powell (1981)

But should we think that exclusionary rules interfere with the epistemic function of the criminal justice system? Premise 3 is the most contentious of the premises, and thus deserves more careful discussion than what has been said to this point. In the following two sections I consider two different lines of support for premise 3.

4 The General Epistemic Case Against Exclusionary Rules: More Evidence Is Better

Ideally, in a criminal case, jurors will be presented with all reliable, relevant, and comprehensive information necessary to reach a verdict. Efficiency demands that this process be streamlined to some extent. The analogy between a jury and a scientific inquiry is inexact.[8] Ideally, in a scientific inquiry, there will be no time limit in which the scientists must operate. They will be free to consider all relevant alternative explanations for a given phenomenon, and they can run tests to determine if those alternatives offer a more plausible explanation. Not so with criminal trials. Jurors' purposes are more narrowly focused. They are not charged with determining if a crime happened and if so, who did it. Rather, they are asked to determine if a crime happened and if so, is there sufficient evidence to conclude that the defendant did it. In effect, they are not asked to determine who really committed the crime. We could imagine a case in which there is strong evidence that Smith committed a crime. Suppose also that the evidence is strong enough that it satisfies the requirement that the defendant is guilty beyond a reasonable doubt, and the jury, as a result, convicts the defendant. All of this is consistent with the fact that there is other even stronger evidence that suggests that it was not Smith but Jones who committed the crime. If jurors did not consider the evidence in favor of Jones's guilt rather than Smith's, they have done nothing wrong. Their job is to evaluate the evidence in favor of Smith's guilt, not Jones's. If a scientific inquiry were conducted in the same way, we would think it had failed. We may think prosecutors and the police have failed in some way by not pressing the case against Jones, but that is beside the point. What we need to see here is that there are some significant ways in which the job of the juror is different from the job of the scientist.

Still, if we hope that such cases are anomalous, then we will want to ensure that jurors have access to all the reliable and relevant information. Even in this respect the juror's task is different from the scientist's. Consider how determinations of relevance are made in criminal justice cases. Whereas members of the scientific community are left to decide what information is relevant, this is not the case with jurors. Instead it is left up to the judge presiding over the case to determine if evidence is relevant. Laudan argues that a judge should consider the following hypothetical: *if the evidence were credible,* would it result in a change in probability that the crime occurred or that the defendant committed the crime? If so, then the evidence should

---

[8]For an interesting discussion of the differences here see Leiter (1997).

be presented to the jury.[9] The job of the judge is not to make an evaluation of the quality of the evidence. Rather the judge should simply determine if the evidence could have a bearing on the case. If so, the evidence should be heard. Of course, this may oversimplify. There may be cases in which IF some evidence were credible it would change the probability of the hypotheses that a crime occurred or that the defendant committed it, but we still think it should not be considered. So, more must be said about this. Laudan clarifies the idea at play here when he writes, "Any testimony or physical evidence that would make a *reasonable person* either more inclined or less inclined to accept these hypotheses is relevant. Everything else is irrelevant."[10] Suppose the prosecution wants to introduce evidence that the shape of the defendant's skull is such that she has a high propensity to commit the type of crime that she is accused of committing. Of course, phrenology is a pseudoscience and thus should not be considered. Rather, the hypothetical should be limited to what would lead a reasonable juror to alter her probabilities, and phrenology should not change a reasonable person's probabilities. Thus, phrenological data is irrelevant to the rational juror.

It is at this point that we can see why exclusionary rules might, as a general matter, thwart the epistemic goals of a jury trial. Exclusionary rules serve to preclude relevant information from being presented to the jury. So rather than having access to all the relevant information, jurors are given access to only some of it. Perhaps it is thought that a defendant's spouse witnessed the defendant commit the crime. However, because of spousal privilege, the spouse can refuse testify without having to risk perjuring himself. Further, if the judge deems some evidence unfairly prejudicial—evidence so sensational or inflammatory that ordinary jurors would be unduly swayed—then she can exclude that evidence. So, for example particularly gruesome crime scene photos may be excluded for this reason. The problem with exclusionary rules then, as a general matter, is that they serve to exclude relevant evidence. But, so the argument goes, if we are willing to trust juries with the lives of defendants—sometimes literally—then we must also trust them to properly weigh the evidence. In criminal cases jurors are the triers of fact, and exclusionary rules subvert that role by precluding them from considering all the potential facts.

So, we see the general case for premise 3 relies on what should strike as something of a truism: more evidence is always better. Indeed, Laudan offers a rule for determining what evidence should be admitted in criminal trials: "The triers of fact... should see all (and only) the reliable, nonredundant evidence that is relevant to the events associated with the alleged crime."[11] In fact, he goes on to note that the world 'reliable' should be struck from this rule. Jurors should be given all relevant, nonredundant evidence, and they should determine what is reliable and what is not. Presenting them with all the relevant evidence will leave them in a better position to do so.

[9]Laudan (2006), pp. 17–18.

[10]Laudan (2006), p. 18. My emphasis.

[11]Laudan (2006), p. 121.

5 The Empirical Case Against Exclusionary Rules: The Dangers of Folk Psychology

Laudan worries that many of our exclusionary rules are based upon unfounded assumptions about juror psychology. For fear that a crime scene photo will be too gruesome for the juror to rationally evaluate the defendant's guilt, the photo is excluded. But on what basis is it excluded? Rather than finding a basis in well-established empirical studies, judges are asked to prognosticate about the impact certain evidence will have on jurors and their deliberations. Such a basis for exclusion of evidence should strike us as wholly unreliable.

Consider recanted confessions. In some cases, defendants will confess to police, but later think better of it and they will seek to have those confessions excluded from the trial. Once a confession has been made it cannot simply be withdrawn. Here the burden shifts to the defendant to show that there is some reason to think the confession was improperly obtained.

In order for a judge to allow a recanted confession to reach the jury in the U.S., the confession must pass a three-part test. First, it must be the case that the confession was given voluntarily. The judge must deem that the defendant who now wishes to plead innocent gave the confession of her own free will. Next it must be determined that the confession was obtained legally. A familiar example where a confession would not pass the legality test is a case in which the defendant offered her confession without being read her Miranda rights. Of course, Miranda is not the sole consideration. The Supreme Court has ruled that confessions obtained from illegally detained individuals, even when they have been read their Miranda rights, should be excluded.[12] Finally, even when a judge is satisfied that the confession was given voluntarily and obtained legally, the confession must pass the test of corroboration. Here the judge must determine if some of the prosecution's other evidence supports some of the claims made by the defendant about the crime in the confession. If the confession passes these three tests, then it can be included in the trial. However, if the judge finds that the confession violates any of these three tests, then the confession may be excluded.

If juries are to be triers of fact, then suppression of evidence in such a case seems inexplicable. The problem with excluding confessions is that they are certainly relevant evidence worthy of consideration by the jury. This is not to doubt that there are false confessions, but again, this is something for the jury to sort out. If the defense believes that there are reasons to doubt the veracity of the confession, then this is the sort of thing that ought to be presented to jurors for consideration. What should not happen, according to Laudan, is that the confession should be suppressed.

It is worth focusing a moment on the intuitive case for including recanted confessions. We are inclined to think all confessions are relevant because it seems

[12] See *Brown v. Illinois*, 422 U.S. 590 (1975).

highly implausible that one would offer a confession for any other reason than that one is guilty. On this very point Laudan writes:

> Is it plausible that an innocent suspect, subjected to neither torture nor the threat of it, offered no particular incentives to confess, and treated reasonably humanely by arresting officers, is likely to tender a false confession simply to get himself out of the interrogation room and into a jail cell? The question answers itself. Innocent people, even when subjected to the humiliation of an arrest, do not routinely confess to crimes they did not commit, especially since they fear, understandably enough, that such confessions may mean several years in prison.[13]

It is this belief that innocent people do not confess that makes confessions such powerful testimony. We take it as given that with such high stakes almost no one would possibly admit to such a thing.

Without corroborating studies, judges find themselves in the unenviable position of trying to determine how jurors will respond to evidence. A situation in which judges, according to Laudan, must rely on data that does not rise above the level of folk psychology.[14] Rather than rely on such dubious claims, the much easier, and more epistemically principled move is to present the jurors with all the evidence and allow them to sort through it. We find then that dubious science also speaks to the strength of premise 3—exclusionary rules often rely on unreliable claims about juror psychology. Without better science on offer, Laudan is doubtful of the necessity of exclusionary rules.

6 The Epistemic Case for Excluding Recanted Confessions: Meeting the Empirical Challenge

Perhaps questioning the epistemic value of recanted confessions seems dubious. Indeed, if we agree that jurors should have access to all relevant information, then surely we must think that a confession, even if recanted, is relevant. Yet I will argue that we have very good epistemic reasons, at least in some cases, to exclude recanted confessions.

For example, Billy Gene Davis confessed to killing his girlfriend after failing two polygraph tests. His girlfriend was later found alive in Tucson, Arizona.[15] In another case, Daniel Williams, after 11 h of grueling interrogation, confessed to raping and murdering a neighbor, Michelle Bosko. The police soon discovered that Williams' account of the murder did not fit the details of the autopsy report. The police secured a new confession; one in which the details of the confession better fit the details of the crime. When DNA tests were returned from the autopsy it was discovered that

[13] Laudan (2006), p. 175.

[14] Laudan (2006), p. 122.

[15] Leo and Ofshe (1998), pp. 449–450.

the semen found in the victim was not Williams's. The police decided that Williams must have had an accomplice, so they secured a third confession in which Williams implicated his roommate, Joseph Dick (though no previous confession had mentioned anything about there being an accomplice). After a lengthy interrogation, Dick too confessed to the crime. Soon thereafter it was found that neither of the two men was the source of the semen. Deciding that there must have been even more accomplices—though none of the other evidence suggested that the attack involved so many individuals—the police secured yet another confession from Williams and Dick in which both implicated two more men. The two other men eventually confessed to the crime as well. Eventually another man came forward and confessed to the crime and told police he had acted alone, and in this case the DNA was a match. Three of the four men who confessed spent eleven years in prison and one spent eight.[16] In yet another case police were able to obtain confessions from Ruben Trujillo and Pedro Delvillar for a double murder and robbery. It was later determined that both were in police custody at the time that the crime occurred.[17]

While such stories are shocking one might point out that this is all anecdotal evidence. Yet, according the Innocence Project about 25% of DNA exonerations involve defendants who made incriminating statements or confessed to the crime.[18] District Judge Jed S. Rakoff conservatively estimates that as many as 20,000 people in prison today are there because they have pled guilty despite the fact that they are innocent.[19] It seems that false confessions are far more common than common-sense would have led us to believe.

Further, social scientists believe that confessions represent particularly powerful and compelling evidence at trial—even when that evidence is highly suspect. In one study 132 judges were presented with hypothetical cases in which there was weak evidence to support convictions, but in some of those cases there was no confession, in some there was a confession produced with little police pressure, and finally in some cases the confessions came as a result of high-pressure. In the high-pressure cases the defendants were questioned for 15 h, the defendants were threatened with the death penalty, a gun was waved, and the interrogators refused to consider the defendant's claims of innocence. 84% of the judges thought that the high-pressure confessions were not voluntary, but in spite of this and in spite of the fact that other evidence to support the charge was weak there was a 69% conviction rate among the judges in the high pressure/ weak evidence cases. Yet in the no confession/weak evidence cases there was only a 17% conviction rate among the same judges.[20] What we find is that even among professional jurists, and even when there is significant

---

[16] Warden and Drizin (2009), pp. 415–427.

[17] Leo and Ofshe (1998), p. 450.

[18] The Innocence Project (2019).

[19] Indeed, the number may be much higher. Social scientists argue that 2–8% of the 2.2 million people in prison have accepted plea bargains despite the fact that they are innocent. Rakoff's numbers are based on a more modest estimate of 1%. See Rakoff (2014).

[20] Kassin (2012), p. 434.

doubt about the voluntariness of the confession, the confession plays a substantial role in convictions. As it turns out, psychologists are gathering useful information about these things and the evidence supports the claim that people tend to overestimate the value of confessions. If Laudan's worries are that judges are relying on mere folk psychology when excluding evidence, then profession psychologists are helping allay that worry—just not in a way that supports Bentham or Laudan's thesis.

In part the impact of confessions is likely explained by the deep-seated belief, that many share with Laudan: innocent people do not confess to crimes that they did not commit. In one study 91.3% of the participants thought that they would not confess to a crime they did not commit when questioned by police. When the crime involved a serious offense like rape or murder the number rose to 93.3%.[21] So what can explain the fact that many do confess to crimes, serious crimes for that matter, they did not commit?

We may think that much of this is explained by acts or threats of violence, but the matter turns out to be much more complicated. Often investigators will attempt to convince the accused that claims of innocence are pointless—they will in effect ignore any claims of innocence. Police will often tell the accused that they possess some bit of incontrovertible evidence that proves that the accused is guilty, even if no such evidence exists. In some cases the accused are told that there is forensic evidence—such as DNA—that proves their guilt, that fingerprints or other evidence has been found, someone else has implicated them, or that a polygraph has shown their claims of innocence are false.[22] Police may say this even if none of it is true; the Supreme Court has ruled that police may mislead suspects during interrogations.[23] In conjunction with this there is also a two-part strategy of using maximization and minimization. In maximization the accused is told what severe consequences may follow if she continues to insist on her innocence. She may, should she fail to "come clean," face long sentences or even the death penalty. This strategy is combined with minimization where the interrogator offers a potential justification or mitigating circumstance to help justify why she may have reasonably committed the crime. Perhaps she was acting out of self-defense, the victim had it coming, or the accused was drunk or mentally impaired.[24] All of this produces a powerful incentive for the accused to confess, regardless of her guilt or innocence.

This is a rough outline of what is called the Reid Technique of interrogation, a method adopted by the police, the F.B.I., the C.I.A., and the Secret Service.[25] All of this then is consistent with standard practices. What is disconcerting about this is that despite Laudan's concerns that the three prong-test is needlessly restrictive, it appears it is not restrictive enough. That's because Reid Technique confessions are

[21] Costanzo et al. (2010), p. 238.

[22] Harris (2012), pp. 44–45.

[23] *Frazier v. Cupp*, 393 U.S. 732 (1969).

[24] Harris (2012), p. 45.

[25] Starr (2013).

thought to be susceptible to generating false confessions, yet this process is within bounds with respect to the three-prong test. That is to say, confessions produced by the Reid Technique are considered both voluntary and legal, despite the fact that social scientists worry about their propensity to garner false confessions.

Excluding a recanted confession, perhaps in cases in which there is fear that the confession was obtained using questionable means seems consistent with the best practices of an epistemic enterprise. Suppose you are conducting a very important experiment, one in which the stakes are quite high. Suppose also that I offer to give you a piece of evidence that would be relevant to your research. This evidence comes with a caveat. First, the evidence has been collected in a dubious manner that has a propensity to produce false positives. That's not to say all the results of this method are wrong, but that the propensity for false positives have led members of the scientific community to doubt that technique used to gather the evidence. Second, evidence of this sort tends to be extraordinarily compelling. That is, when people are provided with positive results from this test they are often treated as dispositive, even when people know that the information is error prone. If I were to ask you if you wanted this information, then I would think that the epistemically correct answer is no. Given that we do have information that suggests recanted confessions are highly influential, and given the serious doubts about how this information is collected, the epistemically correct thing to do is to exclude the evidence from consideration.

One may wonder if my skepticism runs so deep that I believe all confessions are epistemically worthless. This is not the case. As a matter of fact, many of the cases of genuine false confession that we know about came to light because the actual perpetrator came forward and confessed. Laudan himself argues that all confessions should be videotaped,[26] and indeed this tends to reduce false confessions, but this does not go far enough. The more serious concern here centers on the Reid Technique itself, and it is by no means clear that jurors would know that this method of interrogation has a propensity to produce false confessions. It would be much better if there were better standards used in interrogations themselves. Police need to be educated about the dangers of confirmation bias, and taught to test for indicators that the confession is false. For example, one very simple technique is to ask the confessor to detail the events of the crime in reverse order. Recounting the events of one's life in reverse order is often very easy to do if one is telling the truth, however when one is lying, and trying to keep manufactured details straight in one's mind, recounting them in reverse order proves extraordinarily difficult. The upshot of using such techniques is that it can also flag false declarations of innocence. Social scientists are producing very interesting information about these matters. They need to be incorporated into the best practices of more police agencies.

[26]Laudan (2006), p. 229.

7 The General Epistemic Case in Favor of Exclusionary Rules: More Isn't Always Better

I have argued that we have epistemic reasons to exclude some recanted confessions from consideration by jurors. This argument may not generalize. As a matter of fact, I think that in many instances Laudan is correct that exclusionary rules as they operate in the US legal system are confused and inexplicable. I do argue, however, that exclusionary rules can and should play an important epistemic function within the legal system. In some cases, like recanted confessions, I think the present practice works reasonably well or should be expanded to exclude more recanted confessions. In other cases, I think we should consider having more exclusionary rules. And, of course, in some cases, I think the exclusionary rules don't serve their epistemic ends.

Remember, that according to Laudan, jurors should be presented with all relevant and nonredundant evidence that speaks either for or against the defendant's guilt. Questions of reliability are to be left to the juror. According to Laudan, "physical evidence or testimony is relevant provided that, if true, it increases or decreases the likelihood of guilt or innocence of the accused."[27] A strong reading here invites us to think jurors will be presented with phrenological evidence, as discussed above, but the strong reading is not plausible. Rather, we must go with a weaker reading: Evidence or testimony is relevant provided that, if true, it increases or decreases the likelihood of guilt or innocence of the accused, for a reasonable person. Note, this is much more plausible since no reasonable person is moved by phrenological evidence. Also note, this is, in effect, an exclusionary rule. Even according to Laudan we are epistemically justified in excluding relevant but unreliable evidence.

Epistemically there is nothing curious about this at all. If a scientist ignores an improperly conducted study from consideration, she does not violate any epistemic norms, rather she satisfies them. So too with a judge who excludes epistemically dubious evidence from the jury. Thus, when a judge excludes an improperly obtained confession from consideration by the jury this does not undermine the epistemic purpose of the jury. Laudan may object that common law practices do not operate like this. Again, it has been traditionally the role of the jury to make determinations of fact.[28] But appeal to common practice does little work for Laudan—that this is the traditional role of the jury does not tell us it is the most epistemically defensible role for the jury. It is the latter claim Laudan must defend, yet he does not. While there is no doubt that this has been the traditionally conceived division of labor within the criminal justice system, what remains unclear is why this is epistemically justified.

---

[27] Laudan (2006), p. 120.

[28] This is not entirely correct. Judges are asked to make judgments about both the relevance and the reliability of expert witnesses. This is how it should be. We should work to ensure that judges consider excluding more forensic 'science' because of its unreliability. See *Daubert v. Merrell Dow Pharmaceuticals, Inc.* 509 U.S. 579 (1993).

Consider fingerprint analysis. The standard practice for analyzing fingerprints uses a process known as ACE-V: Analyze, Compare, Evaluate, Verify. What this means is that a fingerprint analyst is given a set of fingerprints and asked to evaluate if there is a match between the suspect and the prints found at the scene. In the analysis phase the analyst first examines the quality and quantity of loops and ridges to determine if there is enough evidence to make a match. If there is enough detail in the found print and the sample taken from the suspect, then a comparison is made. Here the analyst determines if there are sufficient similarities to determine whether the two sets of prints correspond to each other. If they do, then, in the evaluation phase, the analyst makes a determination that the points of correspondence are sufficiently similar to match the set of prints. At this point the analyst then renders a judgment: a match, an exclusion (there is substantial disagreement between the two sets of prints), or inconclusive. In the final stage, verification, another analyst repeats the process of analysis, comparison, and evaluation.[29]

Two problems stand out with this process. First, a declaration of a match is taken to be declaration that the unknown print has, with 100% degree certainty, come from accused. The problem however is that there are no established standards for declaring a match with such a high degree of certainty. The determination is a subjective judgment. As David Harris states in his book *Failed Evidence*, "This judgment comes not from comparisons of data that would ground the probabilistic judgment in statistics, as it should, but form the judgment of the human being making the comparison."[30] Thus, despite common belief that fingerprint analysis relies on hard science, in many cases it is much more subjective than that. Second, the verification process is often not blinded. The second analyst is often made aware of determination made by the first analyst. This, of course, subverts the scientific validity of the process. The problems with nonblind testing are well known, and thus we must fear that verification process is often biased by the initial findings. Similar problems arise with eyewitness testimony in which officers may often, even if unintentionally, provide cues to the witness about whom to select from a line-up or photo array.[31]

This only begins to scratch the surface of the problems that arise when looking at the relevance and reliability in forensic science. Serious questions surround bitemark analysis, blood spatter analysis, fiber analysis, even DNA analysis, and the list goes on.[32] It is in this way that I believe that Bentham and Laudan's efforts are misdirected. If our concerns are epistemic, then we should be worried that many forms of forensic 'science' are presented as being highly reliable forms of evidence, when in many cases they are not. Again, if we were to rely on the scientist as the paradigm of sound epistemic practices, we would have no problem if she ignored or excluded evidence that was not obtained using the best the practices of modern science. If we hope to improve the jury's ability to make epistemically reliable

[29] Harris (2012), pp. 24–26. See also Mnookin (2008), pp. 343–358.

[30] Harris (2012), p. 27.

[31] Harris (2012), pp. 47–55. See also Loftus (1996), pp. 178–203.

[32] Harris (2012), pp. 18–56; Murphy (2015), pp. 18–84.

judgments, we would do more to insist on improved forensic science than to demand that exclusionary rules be abolished or significantly limited. Excluding, relevant, but poorly obtained evidence is not, as a general matter, contrary to the epistemic goals of the legal system; it is entirely consistent with it—no *reasonable person* would include pseudo-science in her evaluations of what is true.

Laudan may consider this to be unacceptably paternalistic. Indeed, we may think that one of the primary reasons that judges should exclude unreliable evidence rather than juries is that we fear juries will likely fail to recognize unreliable evidence for what it is. But if we are willing to let jurors make weighty decisions about innocence and guilt in a criminal trial, then perhaps such fears are misplaced. But the more we learn about cognitive biases from social psychology, the more we know that we are subject to systematic errors of reasoning. Taking measures to address juror error may be paternalistic, but that does not mean doing so is unacceptable. Indeed, if our goal is epistemic, then taking measures to limit or avoid erroneous judgments is perfectly consistent with that goal. There is a growing amount of research on the juror's propensity to misunderstand jury instructions, to misinterpret data, and to engage in spurious reasoning. There is a role for epistemology to take measures to address this, and to lessen the impact of our cognitive biases on criminal trials.[33] While such measures may grate against our desire for full autonomy, they do not grate against our interest in getting things right, and that is our present concern.

8 Conclusion

There is much to be said for Laudan's objections to exclusionary rules, and indeed he makes a compelling case that many of the present exclusionary rules as they operate in the US legal system are questionable, at least on epistemic grounds. However, I have argued here that we can defend some of those rules as serving an important epistemic function. As we have seen confessions, even those given under questionable circumstances, can have a powerful impact on those rendering legal judgments. Given that many may be inclined to treat confessions as dispositive, there is a strong case to be made that in some cases excluding recanted confessions will allow the jury or judges to evaluate the evidence in light of the remaining, hopefully more reliable evidence. The empirical challenge can be met—we can see that some evidence has an outsized force on jurors' decision-making.

Further, I believe as a more practical matter exclusionary rules can play an important epistemic role in the legal process as a general matter. It is consistent with the best practices of science to exclude or ignore unreliably gathered evidence, and once we acknowledge that, we see there is an important role for exclusionary rules to play. Exclusionary rules do not always subvert epistemic processes; they can sometimes have an important role in ensuring we arrive at the truth. Thus, even if we

[33] Ahlstrom-Vij argues just such a thing, what he calls ameliorative epistemology, (2013), pp. 137–179.

find many of our current exclusionary rules to be suspect, that does not mean they should be done away with. Rather, we should consider revising the old, more dubious rules, and consider a new role that they may serve in improving the epistemic outcomes of trials. Thus, premise 3, the claim that exclusionary rules interfere with the primary role of the legal system, is false.

References

Ahlstrom-Vij K (2013) Epistemic paternalism: a defense. Palgrave Macmillan Press, New York

Bentham J (1843) The works of Jeremy Bentham: rationale of evidence, rationale of judicial evidence, vol 6. https://oll.libertyfund.org/titles/1923#Bentham_0872-06_284. Accessed 14 July 2018

Beyler CL (2009) Analysis of the fire investigation methods and procedures used in the criminal arson cases against Ernest Ray Willis and Cameron Todd Willingham. Submitted to the Texas Forensic Science Commission, Sam Houston State University, 17 August 2009

Blackmun HA (1975) *Brown v. Illinois*, 422 U.S. 590

Blackmun HA (1993) *Daubert v. Merrell Dow Pharmaceuticals, Inc*, 509 U.S. 579

Clark TC (1961) *Mapp v Ohio*, 376 U.S. 643

Costanzo M, Shaked-Schroer N, Visnon K (2010) Juror beliefs about police interrogations, false confessions and expert testimony. J Empir Leg Stud 7(2):231–247

Grann D (2009) Trial by fire. New Yorker, 31 Aug 2009

Harris D (2012) Failed evidence: why law enforcement resists science. New York University Press, New York

Ho HL (2016) The criminal trial, the rule of law, and the exclusion of wrongfully obtained evidence. Crim Law Philos 10(1):109–131

Ho HL (2019) The fair trial rationale for excluding wrongfully obtained evidence. In: Gless S, Richter T (eds) Do exclusionary rules ensure a fair trial? Springer, Cham, pp 283–305

Innocence Project (2019) Exoneration statistics and databases. https://www.innocenceproject.org/exoneration-statistics-and-databases/. Accessed 1 Oct 2019

Kassin SM (2012) Why confession trump innocence. Am Psychol 67(6):431–445

Laudan L (2006) Truth, error, and criminal law: an essay in legal epistemology. Cambridge, New York

Leiter B (1997) The epistemology of admissibility: why even good philosophy of science would not make for good philosophy of evidence. BYU Law Rev 1997(4):803–820

Leo RA, Ofshe RJ (1998) Consequence of false confessions: deprivations of liberty and miscarriages of justice in the age of psychological interrogation. J Crim Law Criminol 88 (2):429–496

Loftus E (1996) Eyewitness testimony. Harvard University Press, Cambridge

Ma Y (1999) Comparative analysis of exclusionary rules in the United States, England, France, Germany, and Italy. Policing: Int J 22(3):280–303

Marshall T (1969) *Frazier v. Cupp*, 393 U.S. 732

Mnookin JL (2008) Of black boxes, instruments, and experts: testing the validity of forensic science. Episteme 5(3):343–358

Murphy EE (2015) Inside the cell: the dark side of forensic DNA. Bold Type Books, New York

Powell L (1981) *Bullington v. Missouri* (dissent), 451 U.S. 430

Rakoff JS (2014) Why innocent people plead guilty. The New York Review of Books, 20 Nov, 2014

Starr D (2013) The interview: do police interrogation techniques produce false confessions? The New Yorker, 9 Dec 2013

Warden R, Drizin SA (2009) True stories of false confessions. Northwestern University Press, Evanston

Constitutional Evidence

Margarida Lacombe Camargo

Abstract This article aims to show how knowledge about facts is decisive in the judicial review. In order to do this, it uses the category of legislative facts as a more forward looking approach when compared to the traditional doctrine on evidence which privileges the areas of civil and common law by focusing on what happened in the past. It also works with the judicial review's premise that there must be a correspondence between the facts underlying the constitutional norm, the statutes and the precedents—derivative norms. There are two consequences to this: the proof of the facts serves as a justification for the restriction of freedom and as a limit to the legislator's will. Thus, it can be concluded that the standards of proof in constitutional law can guarantee legitimacy on judicial review.

1 Introduction

The purpose of this text is to draw attention to the importance of factual evidence to constitutional process, and to address some issues related to the notion of evidence that may provide high courts with reliable standards for the deployment of factual evidences in the constitutional process.

Evidence in the judicial review has not been receiving the attention it deserves by the doctrine, at least in the Roman-speaking world. In the United States, Henry Wolf Biklé (1924),[1] in the beginning of the twentieth century, highlighted that the facts underlying the laws condition their constitutionality. More recently, David Faigman (2008) revived the discussion regarding the interpretation of the constitution

[1] "[. . .] no court can undertake to decide upon the validity of legislation by a mere comparison of its provisions with those of the applicable constitution, but it must first be informed as to the truth of some question of fact which the statute postulates or with reference to which it is to be applied; and the validity of the legislation depends on the conclusions reached by the court with reference to this question of fact." Biklé (1924), p. 6.

M. L. Camargo (✉)
Federal University of Rio de Janeiro, Rio de Janeiro, Brazil

V. Klappstein, M. Dybowski (eds.), *Theory of Legal Evidence - Evidence in Legal Theory*, Law and Philosophy Library 138,
https://doi.org/10.1007/978-3-030-83841-6_13

connected to questions of facts. He examines the evolutionary features of facts and consequences as relevant standpoints for the maintenance of the constitutionality or unconstitutionality of a rule. Our knowledge about facts may evolve and the facts themselves may change to the point of altering the very understanding of the constitutional text. In Brazil, for instance, the exploitation and use of asbestos was permitted till it was found out that it poses high risks to those exposed to it. The Constitutional Court then held a public hearing about this issue, whereby experts were able to prove the severe damage that this substance causes. As a result of this, a process of *unconstitutionalization*[2] was initiated.

Faigman (2008) resorted to the significant distinction drawn in the 1940s by Kenneth Culp Davis between legislative facts and adjudicative facts: the latter are related to the adjudication of the law relying on finding out who did what, when, where, how and why—an action typically performed by law courts; the former concern the prospective aspects of the decision, which are characteristic of its normative dimension, which leads us to take into account the role of the judicial lawmaking (Davis 1942). The world in which the lawmakers live makes up the situations to which the enacted law will apply, helping the legislators (including judges acting as lawmakers) to determine the lawfulness or unlawfulness of human actions.

Four cases from the Brazilian Supreme Court may be advanced as examples: the use of products obtained from *cannabis sativa*; the exploration, industrialization and commercialization of asbestos; the termination of pregnancy (abortion) in cases of anencephalic fetuses; and the use of embryonic stem cells in scientific research. In these situations, among several others, facts are decisive in ascertaining the answers that the constitutional text offers. If the alleged damages cause by the consumption of *cannabis* are proved real, most probably the court will carry on sustaining its prohibition, while authorizing its use in exceptional cases in which the facts proved its medical value.

As the following schema illustrates, I assume that: (1) our knowledge of facts is related to our knowledge of rules, in the sense that norms are created out of facts; (2) no norm exists without previously proven and known factual relations that can be identified in the world; (3) consequently, the proof of the facts underling the creation of a norm will, ultimately, account for the restriction of freedom when it comes to the administration of a sanction in a specific case.

Thus, my aim here is to argue that the identification of those facts that underlie the creation of norms are essential to the justification of these very norms and that, if those facts cease to exist or are altered, this will affect the validity of the norms. Therefore, proving that those facts (still) exist or (still) have the same features they presumably had when the norm was created is of paramount importance to the

[2]The summary of the case reads as follows: "Process of *unconstitutionalization*. Change on the facts that underlies the rule. Carcinogenic nature of chrysotile asbestos and the unfeasibility of its use in an effective way. Existence of alternative raw materials.". ADI 3937/SP available on http://portal.stf.jus.br/processos/downloadPeca.asp?id=15339396406&ext=.pdf.

validity of the norms. These questions of fact, however, draw on personal skills of experts, not on legal expertise.

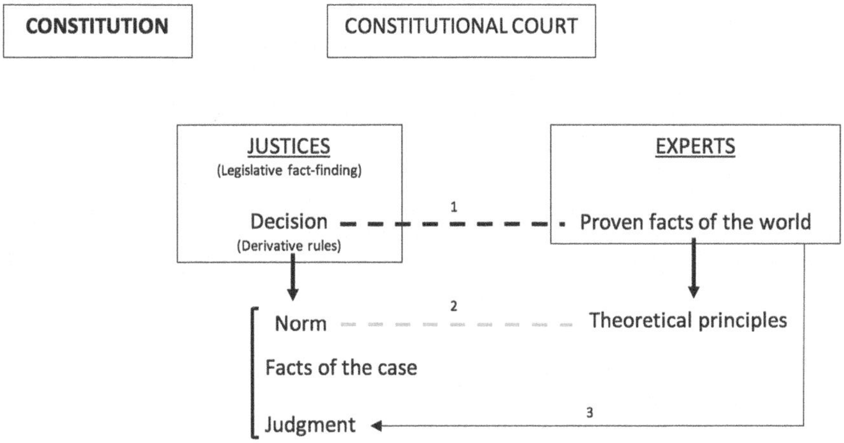

In what follows, I will first, in Sect. 2, approach the necessary existing relation between factual premises of statutes and lower judicial decisions as far as constitutional rights are concerned, with a view of addressing the topic of constitutional control of these decisions. This involves both direct and indirect (or incidental) forms of constitutional review, present both in civil and common law systems. Subsequently, in Sect. 3, I will show how the above-mentioned relation depends on the supply of evidence in courts, which is carried out by presenting the existence of certain facts to the judge, who, in this case, acts as a legislative factfinder. Finally, in Sect. 4, I suggest that the proportionality which includes formal principles (developed by Robert Alexy) may be used as a standard in the process of evaluating evidence in the constitutional scope.

2 The Adequacy of Factual Premises of the Constitution and Statutes

Judicial review examines the adequacy between the factual premises of the constitution and the law at issue, abiding in each case by the hierarchy of the legal system. The application of the constitution does not follow the logic of subsumption of legal facts under a general rule. It seeks rather to verify the consistency between a law and the constitution. In this sense, the dichotomy between questions of fact and questions of law does not arise because judicial review does not aim at proving the facts and assessing them according to a legal provision,[3] but at examining the consistence between what the norm predicts and what the constitution predicts.

A constitution is composed of rules and principles, and from the latter, derivative rules can be extracted as Robert Alexy (1993) shows in his theory.

Norms prescribe conducts based on a factual premise and a sanction. This is true both for constitutional rights, which result in derivative rules,[4] and for rules that are expressly created by federal and state powers (legislative, executive and judiciary), within their respective competences. A constitution consists of organizational rules (establishing the distribution of power among the branches of government) and of rules identifying a set of fundamental rights. Some of these rights may encroach on each other, which requires balancing them in the light of a specific case.[5] There must be, therefore, a correspondence between what the Constitution provides through its derivative rules, and what is established in the rules laid down by the legislature (statutes) or in the rules issued by courts, when they apply constitutional provisions directly to a concrete case.

The limitation of liberty, characterized by sanctions identified in the rules, must be based on the Constitution.[6] There must be an inquiry as to whether the facts, after their due verification, may be resorted to as a satisfactory justification for imposing a sanction that indicates the lawfulness or unlawfulness of the action. For instance, if it is shown that asbestos causes death, its exploration will be forbidden. If embryonic stem cells are indispensable to the advancement of science and they are taken from embryos with permission from their parents, the Constitution allows their use. If products derived from *cannabis sativa* are useful for the treatment of some illnesses and their use can be controlled, the Constitution also allows their use. And, lastly, if medical science proves that there is no possibility of extra-uterine life for anencephalic fetuses, the Constitution permits the termination of the pregnancy in these situations. Statements of facts, serving as evidence, can firmly tell us what the

---

[3]Here it is worth drawing on the assertion by Wróblewski (2008), p. 260, in the sense that "the legal rule is a rule that determines the consequences that must follow certain facts!" (free translation from: "la norma jurídica es una regla que determina las consecuencias que deben seguir a ciertos hechos.").

[4]In this paper we consider the existence of rules that derive from a Constitution, as explained by Robert Alexy. In cases of collision of principles, as occurs in the majority of the times in which fundamental rights are applied, balancing will show that in certain circumstances one principle will precede the other, generating a rule that functions as a base for deciding the specific case and for future cases. "Si el principio *P*1, bajo las circunstancias *C*, precede al principio *P*2: (*P*1 **P** *P*2) *C*, y si de *P*1 bajo las circunstancias *C* resulta la consecuencia *R*, entonces vale uma regla que contiene a C como supuesto de hecho y a *R* como consecuencia jurídica: *C* -> *R*.". Alexy (1993), p. 94.

[5]According to Robert Alexy's theory (1993), a constitution engenders derivative rules through a process of weighting principles that establish fundamental rights in the constitutional text. Drawing on arguments of fact in favor of the necessity and adequacy of a certain measure, and arguments of principles, of legal nature, that guarantee the proportionality *stricto sensu*, a norm can be extracted to justify a certain decision holding both for a current issue and for future cases.

[6]As per Kelsen (1967), sanctions, the feature of coercion of legal rules, are the distinctive element on these rules.

Constitution provides. As Robert Alexy argues, when there is no certainty about facts, the power to create rules is left to the discretion of the legislature and courts are not supposed to interfere in such cases.[7] Therefore, judicial review must not be applied to rules that are based on uncertain factual grounds.

However, we will see that every piece of evidence presented in court goes through a process of evaluation—which is also true for judicial review. The examples presented here do not apply retrospectively, as it happens in criminal and civil proceedings. The constitutional jurisdiction is mainly forward-looking. The application of the constitution implies a legal judgment with a potential or immediate effect for future cases. Instead of advancing hypotheses to explain what happened, the normative activity of constitutional courts creates hypotheses based on what happens.

A factual premise of a statute must correspond to a factual premise extracted from the interpretation of the constitutional text. This factual premise is linked to a sanction, which imparts normative force to the rules. The sanction, in turn, is justified by the theoretical principles established by the experts, through scientific investigation.

The legislature has the authority to make political choices and create laws but is limited by the constitutional text. The judiciary is the power in charge of determining the limits imposed by the Constitution. On the basis of solid arguments, the supreme court, enforcing fundamental rights, is vested with the power to establish boundaries on the legislature's decisions. Among the most compelling arguments are those advanced by science, especially when they are incontrovertible.

Therefore, the interpretation and application of the Constitution depends on the knowledge one has about the world of facts and about principles that explain events (observable phenomena). That is why, more weight will be given to proofs that are better suited to convince the judge who acts as a legislative factfinder. At issue here is a process of evaluation of proofs that demand that we focus our attention on the relation between facts and questions of law when it comes to the creation of norms by courts.

3 Proofs Relying on Facts as Justifications to Decide Over Questions of Law

According to Abbagnano (1999, pp. 429–431), an object is not a fact, but it is a fact that the object exists and has certain characteristics. The fact is not to be confused with the object. We refer to facts when we say something about an object or when we say that an object exists. Now, to say something about an object or to say that an

[7] Robert Alexy (2014), in Formal Principles, develops the principle of proportionality of second order, relating the distribution of legitimacy between legislative and judiciary branches to determine the validity of existing laws.

object exists is a sentence that may be confirmed or refuted when one puts forward certain proofs. That is why we can say that facts or, rather, sentences describing facts are related to reason as the faculty of justifying what one says. Fact, as it is understood by modern science, consists of an object's having a particular property. That objects in our world have certain properties can only be ascertained by observation and empirical verification. Moreover, the confirmation or, as the case may be, refutation of a sentence describing a fact is a matter of contingency, since it is limited to the verification tools presently available.

Factual evidence consists of hypotheses or assertions about the world of facts. The statement "it is proved that *p*" (where *p* describes a fact) expresses a hypotheses or assertion about the world of facts. Evidence, in this context, implies that no room is left for doubt, and is seen as a hallmark of truth, as a property of knowledge. In law, evidence works as a means to convince the factfinder that an event occurred (*factum probandum*), that is, an event constructed by a narrative corresponds to a hypothesis whose veracity is supported by evidence related to intermediary facts (*facta probantia*). It is in the construction of this narrative that different weights are attributed to the intermediary facts as a factor of evaluation.

In the constitutional sphere, the *factum probandum* is not past, but present. The purpose of the evidence provided by experts is to show to constitutional courts that the events at issue can be explained by science and by experience. Thanks to this scientific and empirical knowledge, judges can get to know the effects of the law they are interpreting and applying. In such cases, the factual world will point towards the decision. For example, the lethality of asbestos shows that its prohibition is legal, but its use may be allowed if protective measures prove themselves sufficient and reasonable. Consequently, what the Constitution asserts can only be determined by the facts it points to in present and future situations.

Evidence works as an input of elements of judgment[8] that are sufficient to justify a decision Beltrán (2005, p. 27). This reliance on assertions derived from factual knowledge by those who possess expertise to do so—technicians and experts—, is object of an inquiry as to whether the allegedly existing facts are sufficient to justify the enforcement of the State's police power, which is a question of law. If this investigation concludes that the factual knowledge at issue is sufficient to justify judicial decisions, questions of fact may be considered questions of law.

Questions of fact and questions of law are not to be confused, as they account for different narratives. Scientific discourse raises a claim of truth and abides by appropriate methods. It follows the truth-false logic. Questions of law observe rules of interpretation that are confined by the boundaries established by legal texts; by the hierarchical structure, coherence and consistency of a system; by procedural rules; and they aim to identify the command or action stipulated by the rule. They follow the simultaneous movement of creation and application of the law

[8]Beltrán (2005), footnote 24 and 35, defines elements of judgment as "any descriptive factual wording from which inferences for the corroboration or refutation of the main hypothesis of the fact may be direct or indirectly obtained".

as put forward by Kelsen.[9] We can agree with Scheppele (1990, p. 44) when she says that "judges usually learn the facts of cases in the same way that they learn the law". "The statements of the facts of cases in legal reasoning don't have a life of their own apart from legal interpretation, nor do legal texts have a meaning outside a context of facts. There are no 'pure' descriptions of the facts or 'abstract' descriptions of legal rules" (Scheppele 1990, p. 61). The description of facts interferes with the meaning of the law. The judicial categorization of events follows legal standards and, therefore, it is difficult to separate the legal description of facts from the application of the rule. To illustrate this, Scheppele resorts to the difference between the interpretation offered by a jury composed of laypeople (common citizens) and the one given by university-trained judges: The juries are tasked to figure out "what happened" relying on social skills ordinary folks possess whilst judges and other legally trained officials use their legal knowledge of the craft of fitting particularized descriptions into generalized legal categories. "The different background knowledges and conventions of description might produce quite different outcomes." (Scheppele 1990, pp. 62–63)

Nathan Isaacs argues that what the jury says are facts, whereas what the judges say is law. The jury interprets facts and judges interpret the law. Thus, "what was a question of fact becomes a question of law." (Isaacs 1922, pp. 4 and 12). To Joseph Wayne Smith (2009, p. 95), a question of law refers to "those questions which require essential reference to legal considerations and/or legal methods to be given an adequate answer." And "a question of fact is a question which can be resolved without recourse to expert legal knowledge, by observation, (primary facts), inferences from observations, or by scientific experimentation and theoretical explanation." (Smith 2009, p. 90)

David Faigman argues for a co-operation between law and science based on structural similarity shared by these two fields of knowledge. The interworking between law and science is made possible by the fact that both start from general principles to apply them to concrete situations. The laws of physics, broadly speaking, are principles that are capable of being confirmed by each situation that presents the predicted conditions. In the same manner, a legal norm conveys a general principle that is applied to each new situation that presents the same conditions, so that it will also cause a predicted result (Faigman et al. 2016).

Law and science interact when it comes to the normative activity performed by courts. Our thesis is that factual knowledge defines what the law prescribes. The generality of the laws of physics, for example, is similar to the generality of judicial norms. In both cases, there is a prevision about the occurrence of known phenomena construed as hypotheses subjected to future verification/application. As shown by Guastini and according to the subsumption logic used in law, questions of fact and questions of law are two distinct and indissoluble issues. Firstly, the judge must verify if the facts really occurred and, after that, if they can be qualified as legal

[9]The logic of creation and interpretation of the rule follows the leveled structure of the legal system presented by Hans Kelsen in chpt V (The Dynamic Aspect of Law) in *Pure Theory of Law*.

through an evaluation process. "The judge verifies facts [and] the decision around the 'legal value' of such facts is something completely different" (Guastini 2005, p. 71). In contrast, the correspondence between a hypothesis of a derivative rule from the constitution and a statute can draw on the same source to impose a penalty. The outcome is that, when applying the law to certain facts, these must be, by way of correspondence, authorized by what the Constitution prescribes.

For instance, if we know that a product derived from *cannabis sativa* is beneficial in some health treatments, its use will be permitted by the Constitution; if we know that there is no possibility of life for an anencephalic fetus, the Constitution will allow the termination of pregnancy in such cases. This is, obviously, not a simple determination. Legal theorists endeavor rationally to justify, resorting to legal arguments, decisions that entail legitimacy problems. However, factual knowledge—legislative fact-finding—is decisive for constitutional courts to ascertain what the Constitution permits, requires and prohibits, and what must be left to the legislature's discretion. In the same way as the factfinder considers the facts at issue to have been proven, and hence gives them enough weight to affect the verdict, the legislative factfinder does so to determine whether a rule is constitutional or not.

4 Evaluating Evidence in the Constitutional Sphere: The Standard of Proportionality

The issue of evaluating evidence leads us to pose questions as to the level of corroboration required by a factual hypothesis in different judicial proceedings (Beltrán 2007, p. 142); not only as a matter of justice, but also as a matter of rationality and transparency. This topic is well developed in the fields of civil procedure and criminal procedure, but it leaves much to be desired as far as constitutional matters are concerned. Maybe, that is due to the fact that, in theory, higher courts do not deal with questions of fact. Even when they are supposed to decide on issues related to a specific case, the relevant facts are to be proved in their generality, because it is the legal, rather than the factual aspects that matter for constitutional courts' decisions. The general principles that provide us with factual knowledge about the world will, in the long run, turn out to be precedents, guiding future conducts. As previously mentioned, we set up the hypothesis that technical and scientific knowledge directly account for the determination of the lawfulness or unlawfulness of an action. Factual connections identified by science show us what the Constitution prohibits, requires or permits, with implications for the separation of powers.

As already mentioned, we assume that law is reliant on facts. The major problem of constitutional jurisdiction is the identification of those who are to give the last word about the content of the Constitution: if the constitutional court or the legislature. The problem is political in nature, embedded in an institutional framework formally circumscribed to the certainty of the available empirical premises.

Therefore, there arises the need to create second-order standards, as Robert Alexy puts it (2014): in situations where one is certain about what the relevant empirical premises are, the constitutional court decides; in those marked by uncertainty as to what the relevant empirical premises are, the legislature will prevail.

The constitutional control system, in its strict sense, operates as follows: (a) through the application of the Constitution directly to a concrete case; (b) indirectly, when the constitutionality of a rule is verified; (c) when the interpretation of the rule according to the Constitution is established (Barroso 2019, p. 430). Constitutional decisions create precedents,[10] either when these decisions are made by the courts of appeals, or when they are taken following the concentrate model of judicial review of European tradition. Since a court's ruling will be used as a legal parameter for future decisions, the facts that were regarded as the facts that provide the basis for the decisions of the courts should be established. It is here that the legislative practice and solid knowledge of the facts presented as justification for the decision of a concrete case come into play. Facts that are classified in the same manner, fulfilling the same normative conditions, are supposed to be subjected to the same consequences of law. Be it for the sense of isonomy that is characteristic of justice, which requires the same treatment of essentially similar situations (Perelman 1963); or due to the universalizability characteristic of the law, as per MacCormick;[11] or to comply with the principle of legal certainty, as required by a more formalistic perspective.[12]

When a case is submitted to constitutional courts, evidence over what happened is already available in the proceedings conducted by lower courts, and no questions are accepted in this regard. The issue resides in knowing what answer the Constitution offers to what happened. If local courts rely on statutes to justify their decisions, the constitutionality of these statutes may be called into question and the *a quo* decision may be reviewed. This is the typical form of incidental judicial review. In countries where courts may exercise judicial review in its abstract form, the sanction predicted to a factual hypothesis must not go against the constitutional text. In these cases, we may inquire whether the rule established by the legislature, in its obligatory, optional or prohibitive character, is also commanded, permitted or prohibited by the Constitution. In order to answer such questions, it is necessary to possess sufficient knowledge of the facts to which the rule applies. This process is similar to what legislators do when they create abstract and general norms. However, the factfinder does not have the same level of discretion as the legislature. It is characteristic of the political activity to choose within what is permitted by the law, and in this case, the

[10] Precedent is here understood as a binding rule, and not as mere persuasion. Cf. Schauer (2009), chapter 3.

[11] The reasons that justify a particular case must be universalizable, that is, if in any specific case it is possible to assume, with good reasons, that X must take care of Y because X is the mother, then we can assume the same whenever the custody of a child is in question, although some exceptions may be considered, as long as they are also seen as universal. MacCormick (2005), pp. 88–89.

[12] This formalistic perspective favors the authoritative aspect for the benefit of the principle of legal certainty. Schauer (2009), chpt 3.

judge must only verify whether these choices abide by the limits established by the law or whether they do not violate the constitutional text.

Whenever one does not possess sufficient knowledge to determine what is commanded, prohibited or permitted by Constitution, one is faced with the phenomenon of epistemic discretion. Robert Alexy (2014) interprets epistemic discretion distinguishing different levels, in such a way that he at the same time connects it to the separation of powers. Fundamental rights interpreted by the Constitutional Court prevail if they are trustworthy, or if certain empirical premises are available. On the other hand, the will of the legislature shall prevail if the empirical premises are plausible, or at least not evidently false. Certainty about empirical premises, in turn, depends on what the experts bring to the proceeding, and this may be done in different ways: (i) by recourse to experts that testify in favor of parties; (ii) by assistance of *amici curiae*; (iii) by testimony borne by experts in public hearings; (iv) by research independently done by judges. Although all these methods are subjected to procedural rules that are specific to each country, especially if we consider the differences between the two main models, inquisitorial and adversarial, scholars have increasingly been defending the incorporation of the results of research into the proceedings, notably when they can be confronted with the legislature's assessment. It is here that the problem of deference shown by the courts to the facts that supported the legislature's activities arise. In North American legal doctrine, Laurens Walker and John Monahan argue that the order of the facts resulting from research made by judges in support to their decision should be part of the instructions given to the jury, who acts as a factfinder (Walker and Monahan 1987, p. 592). Kenneth Culp Davis (1964) might have been the first, in the United States, to argue for the possibility of legislative facts being admitted in proceedings as judicial notice. In spite of these views, one is still confronted with the difficulty that there is no legal provision admitting of the use of widely accessible knowledge of principles and knowledge provided by other areas (often used by judges as a parameter for the decision they make) as a kind of evidence admitted as judicial notice.

As to the question of fact that is submitted to courts, Caitlin E. Borgman (2009) emphatically argues that they should be able to confront the facts taken into consideration by the legislature as a result of the inquiries he/she carries out. Carl A. Auerbach (2008) believes that the facts that gave rise to a judicial precedent must be available for future revision and new justification. Orr Larsen (2014) has a more radical position, defending the thesis that it is the facts themselves that are binding—factual precedents—and not the legal prescription contained in the precedent. David Faigman (2008, chpt 6) sees it as fundamental to assess the weight of constitutional values implied in a concrete case in order to define the level of deference to be bestowed upon the legislature. The closer the case is to the Constitution, the greater the role played by courts.

But if we consider that the matters of fact prevail, insofar as it is the facts themselves that determine the creation of the norms, knowledge over it becomes indispensable. The judges of constitutional courts would have to set up hypotheses about the constitutionality of any act that is submitted to them, be it a law, a normative act or a judicial decision. They would have to decide on the basis of an assessment as to whether there is a conformity between the legal premises of both rules: statute vs. constitution or precedent vs. constitution. As far as evaluating evidence is concerned, general principles would be determinative or enough sound to convince the judge. These principles consist of explanations about events in the world that the specialist's expertise can offer. Nevertheless, general principles may be based upon the body of knowledge judges acquire. Thus, the greater the opportunity to acquire knowledge, the better; and we believe judges often make use of the several available sources, notably the internet. The problem, then, is to make this evidence available in the due process, so that also the parties are granted access to it.

This is to say that the more a decision about constitutional matter is based on attested scientific evidence, the more legitimate the validity claim raised by the courts will be when they decide on the constitutionality or, as the case may be, unconstitutionality of a law. Or, the other way around, the more dubious or tenuous the scientific knowledge, the more deferential the court must be to the legislature. This is the balancing analysis introduced by Robert Alexy which, in the wake of the principle of proportionality, may work as a proof standard in constitutional matters.

5 Conclusion

Pursuant to the old saying "Give me the fact, I will give you the law" (*Da mihi factum, dabo tibi ius*), the judge wants someone whom s/he can fully trust to give him/her the fact. Thus, once the obstacle which may prevent the acceptance of evidence in the constitutional jurisdiction has been overcome, we move on to the valuation phase, when the judge sets up a hypothesis based on what s/he considers as an accepted rule.

The legitimacy of the constitutional court to decide rests on formal principles of second order, supported by epistemological conditions. Legitimacy, in this case, derives from the degree of credibility of the available empirical assumptions.

In summary, the legitimacy claim to create laws becomes the legislature. Courts must hold sway over a great amount of accurate factual knowledge, if they are to draw upon themselves that competence that is originally held by the legislature. And they do so with the help of experts. The more thoroughly and accurately science and experience can prove general principles about facts, the more legitimately entitled a constitutional court will be to wield its counter-majoritarian power.

References

Abbagnano N (1999) Dicionário de Filosofia. Martins Fontes, São Paulo
Alexy R (1993) Teoria de los Derechos Fundamentales. Centro de Estudios Constitucionales, Madrid

Alexy R (2014) Formal principles. I•CON 12(3):511–524
Auerbach CA (2008) Legislative facts in Grutter v. Bollinger. San Diego Law Rev 45:33–46
Barroso LR (2019) Curso de Direito Constitucional Contemporâneo. Saraiva, São Paulo
Beltrán JF (2005) Prueba y Verdad en el Derecho. Marcial Pons, Madrid
Beltrán JF (2007) La valoración racional de la prueba. Marcial Pons, Madrid
Biklé HW (1924) Judicial determination of questions of fact affecting the constitutional validity of legislative action. Harv Law Rev 38(1):6–27
Borgman CE (2009) Rethinking judicial deference to legislative fact-finding. Indiana Law J 84:1–56
Davis KC (1942) An approach to problems of evidence in the administrative process. Harv Law Rev 55:364–425
Davis KC (1964) A system of judicial notice based on fairness and convenience. In: Pound R et al (eds) Perspectives of law. Little, Brown and Company, Boston, pp 69–95
Faigman DL (2008) Constitutional fictions. Oxford University Press
Faigman DL, Slobogin C, Monaham J (2016) Gatekeeping science: using the structure of scientific research to distinguish testimony. Northwest Univ Law Rev 110:859–904
Guastini R (2005) Das fontes às normas. Quartier Latin, São Paulo
Isaacs N (1922) The law and the facts. Colum Law Rev 22(1):1–13
Kelsen H (1967) Pure theory of law. University of California Press, Berkeley
Larsen AO (2014) Factual precedents. Univ Pa Law Rev 162:59–115
MacCormick N (2005) Rhetoric and the rule of law – a theory of legal reason. Oxford University Press
Perelman C (1963) The idea of justice and the problem of argument. Routledge & Kegan Paul Limited, London
Schauer F (2009) Thinking like a lawyer. Harvard University Press
Scheppele KL (1990) Facing facts in legal interpretation. Representations 30:42–77
Smith JW (2009) The analytic distinction between questions of fact and questions of law. Aust J Leg Philos 34:69–102
Walker L, Monahan J (1987) Social frameworks: a new use of social science in law. Va Law Rev 73:559–598
Wróblewski J (2008) Sentido y hecho en el derecho. Fontanara, Mexico

The manufacturer's authorised representative in the EU is Springer
Nature Customer Service Centre GmbH, Europaplatz 3, 69115 Heidelberg,
Germany. If you have any concerns regarding our products, please
contact ProductSafety@springernature.com

Printed and bound by CPI Group (UK) Ltd, Croydon, CR0 4YY
30/09/2026
02225687-0003